P9-BYC-474

Contents at a Glance

Beginning iOS Programming

FOR DUMMIES®

A Wiley Brand

by Rajiv Ramnath and
Cheyney Loffing

FOR DUMMIES®
A Wiley Brand

Beginning iOS Programming For Dummies®

Published by: **John Wiley & Sons, Inc.,** 111 River Street, Hoboken, NJ 07030-5774, www.wiley.com

Copyright © 2014 by John Wiley & Sons, Inc., Hoboken, New Jersey

Media and software compilation copyright © 2014 by John Wiley & Sons, Inc. All rights reserved.

Published simultaneously in Canada

No part of this publication may be reproduced, stored in a retrieval system or transmitted in any form or by any means, electronic, mechanical, photocopying, recording, scanning or otherwise, except as permitted under Sections 107 or 108 of the 1976 United States Copyright Act, without the prior written permission of the Publisher. Requests to the Publisher for permission should be addressed to the Permissions Department, John Wiley & Sons, Inc., 111 River Street, Hoboken, NJ 07030, (201) 748-6011, fax (201) 748-6008, or online at http://www.wiley.com/go/permissions.

Trademarks: Wiley, For Dummies, the Dummies Man logo, Dummies.com, Making Everything Easier, and related trade dress are trademarks or registered trademarks of John Wiley & Sons, Inc. and may not be used without written permission. All other trademarks are the property of their respective owners. John Wiley & Sons, Inc. is not associated with any product or vendor mentioned in this book.

LIMIT OF LIABILITY/DISCLAIMER OF WARRANTY: THE PUBLISHER AND THE AUTHOR MAKE NO REPRESENTATIONS OR WARRANTIES WITH RESPECT TO THE ACCURACY OR COMPLETENESS OF THE CONTENTS OF THIS WORK AND SPECIFICALLY DISCLAIM ALL WARRANTIES, INCLUDING WITHOUT LIMITATION WARRANTIES OF FITNESS FOR A PARTICULAR PURPOSE. NO WARRANTY MAY BE CREATED OR EXTENDED BY SALES OR PROMOTIONAL MATERIALS. THE ADVICE AND STRATEGIES CONTAINED HEREIN MAY NOT BE SUITABLE FOR EVERY SITUATION. THIS WORK IS SOLD WITH THE UNDERSTANDING THAT THE PUBLISHER IS NOT ENGAGED IN RENDERING LEGAL, ACCOUNTING, OR OTHER PROFESSIONAL SERVICES. IF PROFESSIONAL ASSISTANCE IS REQUIRED, THE SERVICES OF A COMPETENT PROFESSIONAL PERSON SHOULD BE SOUGHT. NEITHER THE PUBLISHER NOR THE AUTHOR SHALL BE LIABLE FOR DAMAGES ARISING HEREFROM. THE FACT THAT AN ORGANIZATION OR WEBSITE IS REFERRED TO IN THIS WORK AS A CITATION AND/OR A POTENTIAL SOURCE OF FURTHER INFORMATION DOES NOT MEAN THAT THE AUTHOR OR THE PUBLISHER ENDORSES THE INFORMATION THE ORGANIZATION OR WEBSITE MAY PROVIDE OR RECOMMENDATIONS IT MAY MAKE. FURTHER, READERS SHOULD BE AWARE THAT INTERNET WEBSITES LISTED IN THIS WORK MAY HAVE CHANGED OR DISAPPEARED BETWEEN WHEN THIS WORK WAS WRITTEN AND WHEN IT IS READ.

For general information on our other products and services, please contact our Customer Care Department within the U.S. at 877-762-2974, outside the U.S. at 317-572-3993, or fax 317-572-4002. For technical support, please visit www.wiley.com/techsupport.

Wiley publishes in a variety of print and electronic formats and by print-on-demand. Some material included with standard print versions of this book may not be included in e-books or in print-on-demand. If this book refers to media such as a CD or DVD that is not included in the version you purchased, you may download this material at http://booksupport.wiley.com. For more information about Wiley products, visit www.wiley.com.

Library of Congress Control Number: 2013954213

ISBN 978-1-118-79927–7 (pbk); ISBN 978-1-118-79931-4 (ebk); ISBN 978-1-118-79932-1 (ebk)

Manufactured in the United States of America

10 9 8 7 6 5 4 3 2 1

Table of Contents

Introduction

· ·

*A*lthough iOS powers only about 13 percent of the smartphones used by people in the U.S., its use increases to 55 percent when you consider traffic over the Internet — because iOS devices are bought by people who use their devices frequently. In addition to its loyal users, iOS comes with a well-designed Objective-C–based SDK with rich functionality that makes developing apps straightforward and fun. In other words, iOS is a perfect target market for an innovative app developer. With that, welcome to this book.

About This Book

This book guides you through the iOS SDK and how to build high-quality applications using it. It focuses on iOS 7 and Xcode version 5 and is of significant value to software developers, regardless of their level of experience.

- ✔ If you're a software developer and want to understand how to apply object-oriented concepts, techniques, and principles to iOS development, this book is for you.

- ✔ If you're a software developer and have developed other kinds applications but not those for mobile devices, don't worry. This book is a mobile applications primer that deals with resource conservation, network disconnection, change in location, hardware-software interaction, and more.

- ✔ If you're a software developer with experience in developing mobile applications and want to develop an equivalent iOS application (such as iPhone), you'll probably quickly understand the iOS programming model and then navigate on to the chapters you're most interested in.

Here are some of the conventions you will see in the book:

- ✔ **Code examples:** These appear in a fixed-width font so that they stand out, as illustrated here:

```
[self initializeGameSession];
```

- **Short URLs:** These appear in a monotype font as follows:

  `https://developer.apple.com`

- **Extras and updates:** For long URLs, I refer you to the book's website (for example: "To find out more about windows and views, go to `www.dummies.com/go/iosprogramminglinks` and check out the Windows and Views link in the web resources for this chapter." Also, I will continue to provide updates for the code and post other things you might find useful on the book's website.

- **Sidebars and technical information:** You'll find sidebars and technical information (the latter, flagged by a TechnicalStuff icon), which you can either read at your leisure or skip, though you may find them too interesting to skip.

- **Cheat Sheet:** An online resource that points you to facts, fast.

You can read this book one of three ways:

- You can read it from cover to cover. If this book is your first real exposure to iOS terminology, concepts, and technology, this method is probably the way to go.

- If you want to jump right into reading about object-oriented iOS app development and then come back to the actual how-to details, turn to Chapters 6 and 7; then read the other chapters as needed.

- Use this book as a reference. Read selected chapters or sections of particular interest to you in any order you choose. The chapters have been written to stand on their own as much as possible.

The chapters that delve into the capabilities of iOS are organized into two broad parts. The first part is a "how-to" section that describes various capabilities and provides lots of examples. The second part examines the capabilities from an object-oriented perspective.

When you finish this book, you'll know how to build appealing and engaging iOS apps. You'll know how to make high-quality apps fit for both enterprise and consumer markets. Your apps will be bug-free, and they'll perform well, even in stressful situations, such as during a network failure or when a device is running out of power.

Foolish Assumptions

The common denominator for those reading this book is an interest in developing high-quality apps for iOS. Also, because Objective-C is layered on C, I assume you're comfortable with C. (This book doesn't cover C; however, if you aren't familiar with it, I recommend a couple resources you can find on the web.)

I also assume that you've used at least one integrated development environment (IDE) to develop software so that Xcode isn't a complete surprise. That said, I cover Xcode in two chapters. Chapter 5 gets you started with Xcode, and Chapter 8 delves into more detail.

Icons Used in This Book

A few icons mark paragraphs that have special value.

The Remember icon identifies useful information that is worth remembering. (You have a copy of the book, so there's no special need to commit the whole book to memory. For most stuff, you can look it up when you need it.)

Some things are interesting, but not important for the sake of getting the job done. You can skip the Technical Stuff if you want.

A Tip can save you time or make your application better.

Watch out! You see a Warning when there's a pitfall ahead.

Beyond the Book

A lot of extra content that is not in this book is available at www.dummies.com. Go online to find the following:

- ✔ **Online articles covering additional topics at**

  www.dummies.com/extras/beginningiosprogramming

- ✔ **The Cheat Sheet for this book is at**

  www.dummies.com/cheatsheet/beginningiosprogramming

- ✔ **Updates to this book, if we have any, are also available at**

  www.dummies.com/extras/beginningiosprogramming

Part I
Getting Started with iOS Programming

getting started with iOS Programming

In this part . . .

- ✔ Essential application development guidelines
- ✔ The application model
- ✔ Basic design principles
- ✔ Advanced techniques
- ✔ Using classes, objects, methods, and variables
- ✔ Visit www.dummies.com for great Dummies content online.

Chapter 1

Entering Mobile Application Development

In This Chapter

▶ Identifying the market

▶ Following the design process

▶ Entering the world of object-oriented development

Mobile devices are everywhere. These smartphones and tablets run powerful applications and are making a difference in how people live, work, and play.

Many folks already use these devices as they do computers: to create and edit documents; to interact with others via e-mail, telephone, and chat; to play highly entertaining games; and to shop and manage money. Even schools, which used to ban cellphones in the classroom, are considering delivering educational materials to students via smartphones. Because they're common and robust, tablets and smartphones are now the primary computing and communication devices for many people.

A mobile device, in particular a smartphone, is more than a computing and communication device, however. Because it goes everywhere with you, you can be constantly connected to work and with other users. Also, because a smartphone can retain information about people you talk to, where you've been, and how much you spend, it in a sense "knows" you intimately. Mobile applications can take advantage of this device-user relationship to provide personalized and targeted services that users will depend upon and love.

Apps for a Mobile Platform

This book assumes that you've written applications for other platforms, such as desktop or laptop computers or the web. You can transfer a lot of this experience to writing applications for mobile devices like cellphones and tablets, including iOS devices.

However, when writing applications for iOS, you need to consider these differences:

✔ **Tiny keyboards:** iOS device keyboards make data entry *very* difficult. Data entry is no easy task to begin with, and *touchscreen* virtual keyboards, which you press with your thumbs, are prone to data-entry errors (for example, your app should provide smart spell-checking or allow the user to simply select from a set of options rather than making him type text).

Some applications are created primarily to enter data (think Twitter or e-mail apps). However, try to limit data entry by doing things such as prefilling commonly used default values and providing drop-down lists that users can select from.

✔ **Small display area:** Displays on iOS devices come in these three shapes and sizes (see Figure 1-1):

- 4-inch iPhone and iPod Touch
- 7.9-inch iPad mini
- 9.7-inch iPad

Figure 1-1:
Here are
the three
iOS device
sizes.

Compare these sizes to laptop screens, which are usually 15 inches or larger, and you'll see what I mean by limited screen space.

In order to be usable on small screens, an application must be designed so as to allow users to

- Move intuitively in the program (without getting confused by a maze of screens).

- Use controls (buttons, for example) that are large enough to press easily and place them in a way that helps to prevent click errors.

✔ **Universal applications needed:** In order for an iOS application to be popular, it must run on a range of devices with varied capabilities — that is, the iPhone, the iPad mini, and the 9.7-inch iPad (refer to Figure 1-1).

Applications need to function well on the smallest and largest iOS displays.

Note that previous generations of iOS devices had even smaller screens (iPhones prior to iOS 5 and iPod Touches prior to the 5th generation all had 3.5 inch displays). Also, Apple TV runs iOS. If Apple opens these platforms for app development with the latest iOS versions, the problem of creating universal apps will become even more complicated.

✔ **Limited storage:** iOS devices can store only about one-tenth of the information that PCs can, in both memory and persistent storage (flash or disk).

Don't store too many images, music, or (especially) video on the device because it can run out of space pretty darn quickly.

✔ **Unreliable networks:** It's a fact of life: Mobile devices periodically lose network connectivity. Even when a device has a stable connection, the amount of data that can be sent or received varies based on the strength of the connection. So make your app

- Buffer incoming data when the network connectivity is good.

- Save outgoing data locally.

- Receive and transmit data on a separate background thread.

✔ **Device unavailability:** A mobile device can be turned on and off depending on a user's situation (for example, when boarding a plane). A device can also be damaged (say, by being dropped), its computing speed can slowly degrade, and it can even shut down as its battery is consumed.

Your application must deal with all these situations. For example, it could periodically check-point its state and have low-power modes of operation (for instance, a video-playing app might switch to playing only audio when the battery is low).

✔ **A range of uses:** Mobile devices are used in a variety of locations: rooms with low ambient lighting or sports stadiums with high levels of background noise, for example.

Your applications must be able to adapt to these types of situations. For example, your app may lower the brightness of the screen when the ambient light is low or increase its audio volume when background noise is high.

✔ **Coding in Objective-C:** Apple made an early and highly innovative decision to base its development platform on Objective-C, well before standard object-oriented (sometimes referred to as OO) programming languages (such as Java, C++, and C#) came on the scene. Objective-C has an unusual syntax (as I explain in Chapter 3). It also has object-oriented semantics that are more like the early object-oriented languages like Smalltalk, but it's different from the later and now standard object-oriented languages like C++ and Java that most programmers are used to.

Apple has provided a robust, highly reliable framework and excellent documentation to help build up strong skills in iOS app development.

iOS Benefits

Although many types of smartphones and mobile devices are still on the market today, the battle for market share is now pretty much between iOS and Android.

The lure of Apple and its wonderful set of innovative devices are what make the iOS platform so popular, and developing on the iOS platform offers you several benefits:

✔ **Wide acceptance:** iOS has legs — it's inside millions of devices and is a major platform for application developers. So your app has a readymade market.

✔ **Powerful, built-in, reusable capabilities:** The iOS framework has lots of existing capabilities and services. It has built-in support for rich graphics, location finding, and data handling. In other words, you don't have to write all the code for your application from scratch.

✔ **Framework-based guidance for developers:** Because iOS is a framework — not just a toolkit composed of a set of libraries — it imposes a structure on applications by using an application model. In return for this imposition, you receive a lot of benefits. You get to follow a systematic path in designing a robust application, which frees you to focus on providing rich capability rather than on figuring out the application's structure and high-level design or on nonfunctional tasks, such as managing your application's lifecycle. (You know what I mean — the starting-it-up stuff and the restoring-its-state-after-shutdown stuff, for example.)

Doing the sample application thing

This book uses a simple Tic-Tac-Toe game as an example. Each player claims a symbol, usually an O or an X. Players alternately place their symbol in empty locations on a 3 x 3 grid, with the goal of placing the same symbol in three grid spaces in a straight line, either in a horizontal row, a vertical column, or on a diagonal. The figure shows a sample sequence of plays. This Tic-Tac-Toe application allows two players to play against each other or for one player to play against the device.

You want the application to offer the following game-related functionality (in these examples, a user is playing against a computer):

- Allow the user to create a profile, consisting of a playing name and who goes first in the game — the user or the computer (see Chapter 6).

- Allow the user to start and play the game (see Chapter 7).

- Allow the user to exit the game at any time (see Chapter 10).

- Identify when the game progresses to a draw, a victory for the user, or a victory for the computer, and show the results (see Chapter 7).

- Record and save the results of a completed game (see Chapter 6).

In addition to the basic gameplay features, an application intended for the Android market needs to be robust: *reliable and secure*. Here I show you how to give the app these additional benefits (for more on these topics, see Chapter 11):

- Make the user's game data private by creating player accounts.

- Keep a history of game play by having the program log to a file.

- Make the game crash-resistant so that it retains its preferences after a forced shutdown.

The Tic-Tac-Toe game also illustrates how to use iOS built-in capabilities with features such as these:

- Invoking external services — such as location services (see Chapter 12)

- Sending the results of a game by e-mail to an address book contact (see Chapter 13)

- Playing music from an audio file and recording music from the built-in microphone (see Chapter 13)

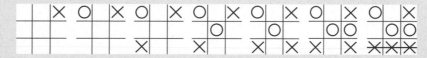

iOS App Development Essentials

Writing an application program would require a lot of work if you had only the device to work with. The good news is that the iOS framework uses a piece of software known as the *operating system (OS),* which provides device-independent interfaces to everything on the device (such as the file system, sensors, and so on). The OS also provides a standard interface to computing capabilities (such as for starting and stopping programs).

As a result, operating systems make writing and running applications easier, and they're especially helpful — in fact, essential — on mobile devices. Apple developed and owns iOS, the operating system for its mobile products. Originally called the iPhone OS, iOS was unveiled in 2007 for the iPhone and was later extended to support the other Apple devices, as well as the Apple TV device.

Unlike, say, Linux, which powers Android, iOS is a single-user operating system. That said, this and other limitations are artificial. At its core, iOS can do nearly everything that Apple's desktop operating system (OS X) can. For a variety of reasons, including secrecy and a genuine desire for tight quality control, Apple closely guards iOS, and only developers with special privileges are given access to its internals.

Devices

Every iOS device (like every mobile device) is a computer, composed of a set of hardware components: processor, memory, input/output (I/O) devices (such as a keyboard, touchpad, and screen), and storage (discs and flash, for example).

Unlike Android devices, the hardware configuration is controlled completely by Apple, so there are just four main variations of devices to consider when developing iOS apps:

- iPhone (of course)
- iPod Touch
- iPad
- iPad mini

Like other smart devices, iOS devices also come with several built-in hardware components, such as the following:

- Cameras (front and back facing)
- Audio inputs and outputs

> ✔ GPS
>
> ✔ Accelerometer
>
> ✔ Light sensor

Apple has yet to come out with a near-field communications-enabled device (or NFC-enabled device) but was recently awarded a patent for NFC-enabled data synching technology. For the inside story from Apple, check the link labeled NFC at www.dummies.com/go/iosprogramminglinks.

Unless you really and truly want to, you'll never see iOS, the operating system, nor will your program. However, you must recognize that it's there — the iOS framework does certain things in certain ways because it runs on iOS. For example, every running program is assigned a process. When an iOS app starts, an iOS process becomes active. This process takes over an area of the screen on the device and allows the user to interact with the application. If another application starts, it pushes the first application to the background. At this point, the process assigned to the first application may be (arbitrarily) terminated by the operating system to save device resources. Before this happens, the iOS runtime notifies the application to save its state.

This iOS operating system is the OS that manages the device *on which your apps run*. A different operating system manages the personal computer on which you develop apps (the Macintosh OS or OS X).

Application development technologies

Layered on the operating system are the iOS application development technologies. These are the technologies that you'll use to build iOS apps. These technologies are structured as a set of layers, as shown in Figure 1-2.

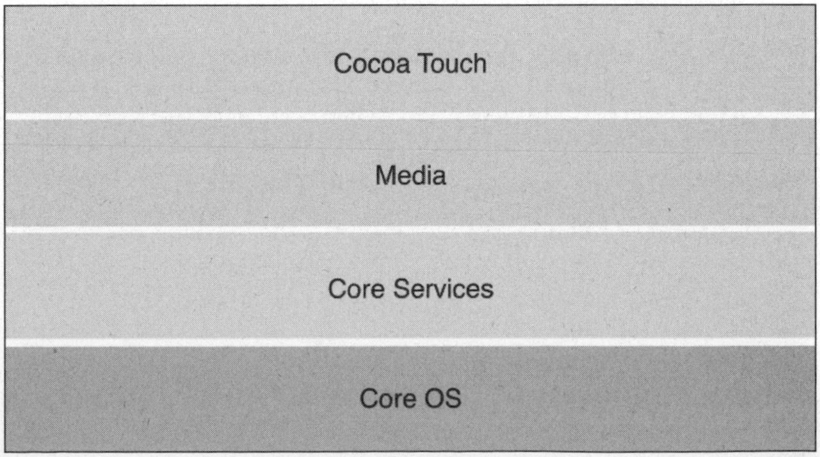

Figure 1-2:
Architecture
of the iOS
Technologies.

Cocoa Touch
Media
Core Services
Core OS

Unix ho!

If you're a Unix lover, you'll be pleased to see Core OS reveal its Unix roots.

For example, Core OS includes many of the typical libraries found on Unix systems (in the `/usr/lib` directory of the system, with header files in the `/usr/include` directory).

Dynamic shared libraries are identified by their `.dylib` extension.

I start with the bottom layer so that you see how the technologies are built from the hardware up.

Each layer exposes a set of components that Apple calls *frameworks*. As I describe each layer, I'll list and briefly describe each layer's capabilities. For Apple's introduction to these layers, check out the link labeled iOS Frameworks at www.dummies.com/go/iosprogramminglinks.

Core OS layer

The Core OS layer contains the operating system and the services upon which the other technologies are built. These services include the following:

- ✔ Image and digital signal processing
- ✔ Linear algebra (the math of matrix operations — primarily used for vector drawing)
- ✔ Bluetooth access
- ✔ Third-party device connections by serial port
- ✔ Generic security services
- ✔ System and networking services

You won't often use Core OS directly in your applications, except when you need to deal with communication or security capabilities at the operating system level or control an external hardware accessory (like a device connected to a serial port). However, you will use its functionality via the other layers.

For more information on Core OS, check the link labeled CoreOS Layer at www.dummies.com/go/iosprogramminglinks.

Core Services layer

The Core Services layer provides access to several more system services that most applications use. These services include

- ✔ **iCloud:** iCloud is a cloud-based storage service that gives you iOS devices to share documents and applications and to share small bits of data (such as preferences) across your multiple iOS devices.

- ✔ **Automatic reference counting (ARC):** ARC is the name of the new Objective-C compiler as well as a runtime feature that enables memory management within your program without you having to explicitly free memory. ARC automatically keeps track of all references to an object and then deletes the object when no references point to it. If you're a Java programmer, you'll recognize that ARC is essentially the iOS version of automatic memory management and garbage collections.

Apple's development environment (Xcode) provides tools that help you migrate from an older application that doesn't use ARC to one that does.

- ✔ **Block objects:** Block objects are inline code along with associated data that's treated as a function.

Block objects are particularly useful as callbacks — such as to user interface events or to thread events.

- ✔ **Data protection:** This is the capability to encrypt, lock, and unlock files that an application needs to keep secret.

- ✔ **File-sharing support:** This enables applications to share files via iTunes (version 9.0 and higher).

- ✔ **Grand Central Dispatch:** This is a concurrency-enabling mechanism that enables programmers to define concurrent tasks, rather than create threads directly, and then lets the system perform the tasks.

- ✔ **In-App Purchase:** This is the ability to purchase from vendors such as iTunes directly from an app. In-App Purchase is implemented by a framework known as the Store Kit.

- ✔ **Core Data:** Core Data is a framework for managing the lifecycle of persistent objects. Core Data works well with SQLite, which is probably the most widely used database on mobile devices. Core Data and its use of SQLite are discussed in Chapter 6..

- ✔ **JSON support:** This service provides support for parsing and creating JSON documents. You find more on this topic in Chapter 6.

The Core Services layer also provides a collection of frameworks for the following:

- Managing the address book
- Supporting ads
- Providing high-performance access to networks
- Manipulating strings, bundles, and raw blocks
- Making use of location, media, motion, and telephony
- Managing documents
- Downloading newsstand content
- Managing coupons and passes
- Presenting thumbnail views of files
- Accessing social media accounts
- Purchasing from the iTunes store
- Programmatically determining the network configuration and access of a device

The Core Services layer provides the object-oriented Foundation framework that does the following:

- Defines the basic behavior of object.
- Provides management mechanisms.
- Provides object-oriented ways of handling primitive data types, such as integers, strings and floating-point numbers, collections, and operating-system services.

The Cocoa Touch framework (see the section, "Cocoa Touch layer," later in this chapter) and the Foundation framework make up the two key iOS development components used by developers. Use all the other components on an as-needed basis.

For more information on Core Services, check the link labeled Core Services in www.dummies.com/go/iosprogramminglinks.

Media layer

The Media layer contains support for graphics, audio, and video technologies. This layer has the following components:

- **Core Graphics (also known as Quartz):** Natively handles 2D vector- and image-based rendering.
- **Core Animation:** Provides support for animating views and other content. This is also a part of Quartz.

✔ **Core Image:** Provides support for manipulating video and still images.

✔ **OpenGL ES and GLKit components:** Provide support for 2D and 3D rendering using hardware-accelerated interfaces.

✔ **Core Text:** Provides a text layout and rendering engine.

✔ **Image I/O:** Provides interfaces for reading and writing most image formats.

✔ **Assets Library:** Provides access to the photos and videos in the user's photo library.

This layer also allows you to manage images, audio, video, and audio and video assets (music and movie files, and so on), along with their metadata. A MIDI interface is provided for connection with musical instruments.

Integrated record and playback of audio is provided as follows:

✔ Through a media player that allows you to manipulate iTunes playlists

✔ Via lower-level components for

- Managing audio playback and recording
- Managing positional audio playback (such as surround sound)
- Playing system alert sounds
- Vibrating a device
- Buffering streamed audio content
- Airplay streaming

Video services provided include playing movie files from your application or streaming them from the network and capturing video and incorporating it into your application. Once again, this functionality is provided in several ways: from a high-level media player to lower-level components that give you fine-grained control.

Image handling operations include creation, display and storage of pictures, and filters and feature detection.

Also, this layer is the one that provides support for text and font handling — such as layout and rendering.

For more information on the Media layer, check the link labeled Media Layer at www.dummies.com/go/iosprogramminglinks.

Cocoa Touch layer

The Cocoa Touch layer contains most of the object-oriented developer-facing frameworks for building iOS applications. It's your single point of entry to app development.

The Apple guides encourage you to investigate the technologies in this layer to see whether they meet your needs, before looking at the other layers. In other words, Apple intends for Cocoa Touch to be your single point of entry into iOS app development.

Cocoa Touch is where you build your app's user interface, handle touch-based and gesture-based interactions, connect the user interface to the app's data, deal with multitasking, and integrate everything from state preservation to push notification to printing.

Cocoa Touch provides object-oriented access for managing your address book and events, building games, and dealing with ads, maps, messages, social media, and sensors. So, most of the time, you'll work through Cocoa Touch; it gives you access to the other layers of the technology. In particular, you'll work with the UIKit framework, which packages most of the functionality just described.

At times, you may need direct access to the lower layers. Although showing you how to achieve this kind of direct access isn't the focus of this book, I cover such access in the appropriate chapters in the book.

For a complete list of the iOS frameworks, check the link labeled iOS Frameworks at www.dummies.com/go/iosprogramminglinks.

Xcode

Xcode is two things. It's the kernel (the *engine* according to Apple) of Apple's integrated development environment (IDE) for OS X and iOS. It's also the name of the IDE application itself.

With Xcode, you can do the following:

- ✔ Create and manage projects.
- ✔ Manage project dependencies, such as specifying platforms, target requirements, dependencies, and building configurations.
- ✔ Build the app from the project.
- ✔ Write source code using intelligent editors that auto-check syntax and automatically format your code.
- ✔ Navigate and search through a project, program files, and developer documentation.
- ✔ Debug the app in an iOS Simulator, or on the device.
- ✔ Analyze the performance of your app.

Figure 1-3 shows the Xcode startup screen.

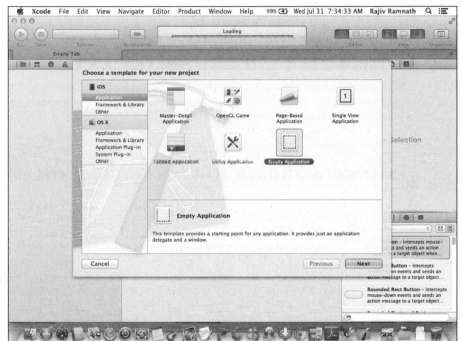

Figure 1-3:
The Xcode
IDE.

If you've used another IDE, such as Eclipse, NetBeans, or BlueJ, you'll find Xcode easy to use.

The Application Model

To begin with, note that the operating system on your iOS device starts a set of system programs when the device boots. This set of programs, which you can think of as the iOS runtime system, runs constantly in the background and manages every app that is run.

Technically, your app is nothing more than an executable program (like an `.exe` on Windows) that runs on the device and interacts with the iOS runtime system. The home screen on the iOS device simply shows icons for all such executable programs. When an icon is clicked, the operating system launches the executable corresponding to the icon and causes the program to run on the iOS device.

In other words, an iOS app is just a program that runs on the device — a pretty straightforward beast.

An Android app, on the other hand, consists of a set of Java classes that are loaded by and encapsulated inside the Android runtime system. This Android runtime system is a Java program that runs on the Java virtual machine.

When the app is built, it's linked with a standard main program along with an app-specific component generated by the Xcode IDE known as the *app delegate*. The main program and the app delegate together serve as the interface between your app and the iOS runtime. These components deal with user interface events, such as touches, and system events such when your app goes into the background — for example, because of a user's action or maybe an e-mail comes in (for more on this topic, see Chapter 6).

Understanding the lifecycle of an iOS app

An iOS app follows a typical lifecycle (see Figure 1-4). At the beginning, the app is simply an executable; it's not running, lying patiently in wait for a user to click its icon. When the app starts, it goes through numerous initialization steps. During this transitory period, the app is in the inactive state. The app *is* indeed running (and in the foreground) but will not receive events, so it can't interact with anything during this time. The app then transitions to the active state. Now, the app is making merry, and you and the app are making sweet music together. This active state is the app's useful state.

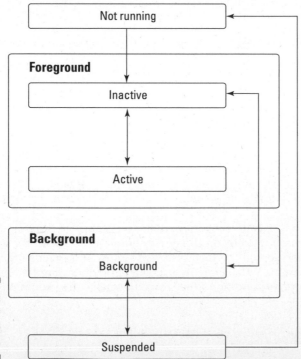

Figure 1-4:
The life-cycle of an
iOS app.

At some point — mostly when another app starts, say, a phone that's triggered by an incoming call — the iOS runtime will put your app in the background. At this point, the app is in the background state. Most apps stay in this state for a short time before being suspended. However, an app could request extra time to complete some processing (such as saving its state into a file for use the next time it starts). In addition, an app meant to run in the background will enter and stay in this state. Note that apps in the background can and do receive events, even though they don't have a visible user interface.

An app in the suspended state isn't running code; however, it is using power and the processor. The system moves an app to this state whenever it needs to further conserve resources, and does so without notifying the app. If memory runs low, the system may purge the app to create more space.

As the app transitions through its states, specific methods of the app (that is, code that you wrote) are invoked as explained here (and shown in Figure 1-5).

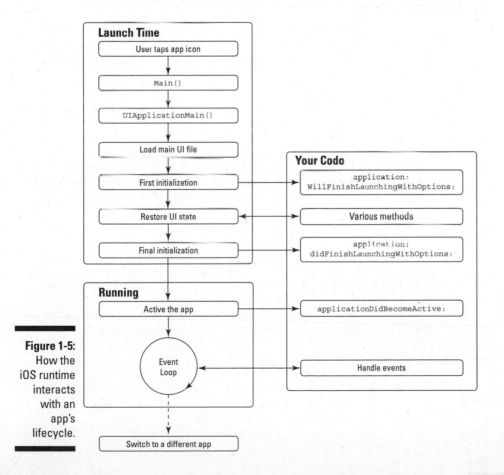

Figure 1-5: How the iOS runtime interacts with an app's lifecycle.

1. After the first initialization of the app, `appDidFinishLaunchingWith Options` is called, which in turn invokes the portion of the app's code that sets up its user interface.

   The user then sees the app. The app now sits in an event loop, where it waits for user interactions.

2. When a user interacts with the app, an event is triggered, and a callback method tied to the event is invoked. Most often, the callback method consists of code written by the app's developer, although it could be reusable code provided as part of the iOS framework.

3. Once the callback method is done, the app goes back to its event loop. This sequence of actions (of events triggering callback methods) proceeds until the app receives an event that causes it to either shut down or go into the background state.

Understanding the structure of an iOS app

Every iOS app follows a standard structure known as a Model-View-Controller (MVC) pattern. (I begin discussing patterns in Chapter 2 and expand on patterns in Chapter 4.) For now, it's enough to know that a pattern is a standard way of writing software for a particular goal.

Specifically, the Model-View-Controller pattern splits the code of an app into

✔ The data it manages (known as the Model)

✔ The user-interface elements (known as the View)

✔ The Controller, which is the component that sits in between the Model and the View (or views) and translates user actions into updates to the Model and the View

You can see this structure in Figure 1-6. The dashed lines indicate linkage. Therefore, the model is linked to the view, and the views are linked to the controller. The solid lines indicate actions. So, the view updates portions of the model while the controller updates the views (or more correctly, causes the views to update themselves). The controller also updates models as needed. iOS extends this pattern so that each app is really a hierarchy of controllers, each managing a set of views and potentially a model.

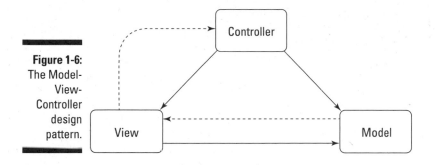

Figure 1-6:
The Model-
View-
Controller
design
pattern.

Object-Orientation Concepts

Object-orientation applies to iOS development a couple of ways:

- ✔ iOS apps are (mostly) written in Objective-C, an object-oriented programming language that implements object-oriented concepts.

- ✔ iOS apps are built around a core design pattern known as the *MVC design pattern* and follow several other design patterns as well.

  Design patterns are nothing more than standard templates for designing the classes and objects that make up your system. In other words, design patterns are higher-level concepts built on object-oriented building blocks.

This book guides you through iOS from an object-oriented perspective:

- ✔ Chapter 2 explains in depth what object-orientation means, its basic building blocks, and the higher-level concepts of patterns and frameworks.

- ✔ Chapter 3 introduces you to Objective-C.

- ✔ Chapter 6 takes you deep into object-oriented development using the patterns in the iOS framework. Chapter 6 also deconstructs the iOS framework in object-oriented terms.

- ✔ A complete example of object-oriented software development of an iOS app is worked out in Chapter 7.

- ✔ Other chapters, which focus on the extensive capabilities of iOS, are presented in object-oriented terms.

Chapter 2

Object-Oriented Design Principles

In This Chapter

▶ Common software development methods

▶ Essential object-oriented design concepts

▶ Transitioning to OO from basic procedural designs

*I*n its early days, computer programming was viewed as a tool for solving problems. You had a mathematical problem to solve? You wrote a program. You had another problem to solve? You just wrote another program. As software systems became more complex and longer lasting, developers needed better ways to develop software, including better ways to design software. That's where object-orientation came in. It provided a way to design and structure programs that were less complex and more amenable to growth and change.

This chapter explains object-orientation. It covers *what* it is, *why* it's considered a good thing to do, and *how* to apply it in practice.

Basic Object-Oriented Concepts

Object-oriented (or OO) design involves identifying and defining objects that represent information together with behavior, or how this information is manipulated, and designing the interactions (known as *collaborations*) among objects so that the application can do what it needs to do. What an object does is defined by a template called its *class*. How an object is used is described by its *type*.

If that sentence makes perfect sense, you're probably a veteran OO programmer in a language like Java or C++. You have my permission to skip to Chapter 3 and go directly to learning about Objective-C.

If you're coming to iOS without any programming experience, don't fret. This chapter is great for those starting to learn OO design concepts. Just read on, and I'll show you how.

Designing programs

To explain the difference between the old, or *procedural,* way of designing a program and the OO approach, allow me to compare it to the process for making a nice pot of tea.

Presenting procedural design — from goals to action

Procedural programming is the most straightforward way of programming. Each segment of code focuses on achieving a step toward a goal. In the case of making a pot tea, you can think of these steps as filling a vessel with water, boiling the water, and pouring the water.

This example began with a nice gift of fancy leaf tea, from India. Not having made tea from leaves before, I called my mom, and she gave me the following steps:

1. Turn on the faucet.

2. Put enough water in a kettle for the number of cups you want to make.

3. Put the kettle on the stove.

4. Turn on the stove.

5. For each cup, put a teaspoon of tea leaves in the teapot.

6. When the water boils, pour the water from the kettle into the teapot.

7. Let the tea steep for five minutes.

8. Pour the tea into each cup.

9. Enjoy!

And that's how a typical procedural program works, the kind people wrote before OO came into vogue. You had a problem to solve and a set of steps for solving the problem.

The recipe in Listing 2-1 is presented in *pseudo* (simulated) programming language. But it illustrates the concepts used in writing a real program.

Listing 2-1: Simple Tea Example

```
@implementation RecipeManager // Package named RecipeManager

- MakeTea:(int) NumberOfCups;
  { // the - prefix indicates a static method
      NSArray *Cups; // Declare an array of cups

      [Kitchen OpenFaucet];
      [Kitchen PourWaterInKettle:(NumberOfCups*CUPVOLUME)];
      [Kitchen PutKettleOnStove];
      [Kitchen TurnOnStove];
      For (i=1; i <= NumberOfCups; i++){
          [Kitchen PutOneSpoonTeaLeavesInTeaPot];
      }
      While(![Kitchen WaterBoils]); //keep looping till the water boils
      [Kitchen PourWaterFromKettleIntoTeapot];
      wait("5 minutes");
      For (i=1; i<= NumberOfCups; i++){
          [Kitchen PourTeaFromTeapotIntoCup:[Cups objectAtIndex:i]]; // Pour tea
              into the i<cup>th</cup> cup
      }
      NSLog("Enjoy Tea"); // Built in Objective-C function for debug messages
  } // End Recipe MakeTea
  ...
@end // of the Recipe class
```

The syntax of this pseudo-language is modeled after Objective-C (the language used to build native iOS applications). The comments are there for those of you who aren't familiar with Objective-C. Note that I left out things such as declarations of variables, and also certain steps.

With tea-making under your belt, the kitchen is a vista of grand opportunities. Perhaps you can bootstrap this new skill to making soup from bouillon cubes. So, building on your experience with tea making, take a look at the bouillon-making program shown in Listing 2-2.

Listing 2-2: Simple Bouillon Example

```
@implementation RecipeManager
...
- MakeTea:(int) NumberOfCups;{...}
...
- MakeBouillon:(int) NumberOfBowls;
  {
      NSArray *Bowls; // Declare an array of bowls

      [Kitchen OpenFaucet];
      [Kitchen PourWaterInKettle:(NumberOfBowls*BOWLVOLUME)];
```

(continued)

Listing 2-2 *(continued)*

```
    [Kitchen PutKettleOnStove];
    [Kitchen TurnOnStove];
    For (i=1; i <= NumberOfBowls; i++){
        [Kitchen AddOneBouillonCubeToTureen];
    }
    While(![Kitchen WaterBoils]); //keep looping till the water boils
    [Kitchen PourWaterFromKettleIntoTureen];
    wait("15 minutes");
    For (i=1; i<= NumberOfBowls; i++){
        [Kitchen PourSoupFromTureenIntoBowl:[Bowls objectAtIndex:i]]; // Pour
            soup into the i<sup>th</sup> bowl
    }
    NSLog("Enjoy Soup");

} // End Recipe MakeBouillon
...
@end
```

Did you notice that the two programs have similar steps (this was deliberate, by the way)? Given this similarity, chunks of code can be reused. For example, you could create a method to boil water in a kettle on a stove as follows:

```
- BoilWaterInKettleOnAStove:(int) Volume;
 {
    [Kitchen OpenFaucet];
    [Kitchen PourWaterInKettle:Volume];
    [Kitchen PutKettleOnStove];
    [Kitchen TurnOnStove];
    While(![Kitchen WaterBoils]); //keep looping till the water boils
} // Method BoilWaterInKettleOnAStove
```

Once this procedure is ready, you could use it in the two recipes. For example, the MakeTea recipe would look like Listing 2-3.

Listing 2-3:   Tea Example with Boiling Method

```
- MakeTea:(int) NumberOfCups;
 {
    NSArray *Cups; // Declare an array of cups

    [Kitchen BoilWaterInKettleOnAStove:(NumberOfCups * CUPVOLUME)];
    For (i=1; i <= NumberOfCups; i++){
        [Kitchen PutOneSpoonTeaLeavesInTeaPot];
    }
    [Kitchen PourWaterFromKettleIntoTeapot];
    wait(5 minutes);
    For (i=1; i<= NumberOfCups; i++){
        [Kitchen PourTeaFromTeapotIntoCup:[Cups objectAtIndex:i]]; // Pour tea
            into the i<sup>th</sup> cup
```

```
        }
        NSLog("Enjoy Tea");

} // End Recipe MakeTea
```

When the `MakeBouillon` recipe uses the boiling method, it looks like Listing 2-4.

Listing 2-4:   Bouillon Example with Boiling Method

```
- MakeBouillon:(int) NumberOfBowls;
{
        NSArray *Bowls; // Declare an array of bowls

        [Kitchen BoilWaterInKettleOnAStove:(NumberOfBowls*BOWLVOLUME)];
        For (i=1; i <= NumberOfBowls; i++){
            [Kitchen AddOneBouillonCubeToTureen];
        }
        [Kitchen PourWaterFromKettleIntoTureen];
        Wait("15 minutes");
        For (i=1; i<= NumberOfBowls; i++){
            [Kitchen PourSoupFromTureenIntoBowl:[Bowls objectAtIndex:i]]; // Pour
                soup into the i^th bowl
        }
        NSLog("Enjoy Soup");
} // End Recipe MakeBouillon
```

These two recipes (actually recipe programs) illustrate how procedural programming follows a very direct goal-to-solution paradigm and that common instructions can be reused. Only common actions (that is, *behaviors)* are reused.

This kind of reuse has some limitations. First, it's only effective with shareable behaviors. In particular, this kind of reuse is usually discovered over a period of time as shareable behavior is encountered. So, it's (mostly) ad hoc, and isn't done in a planned and systematic manner. Like most ad-hoc processes, procedural reuse doesn't capture all the possibilities for reuse; worse, the resulting software isn't optimally structured and is difficult to understand and maintain.

You may be wondering whether it's possible to achieve more systematic reuse and a better understanding of the domain as well (in this case, the kitchen and cooking) so that your next program is easier to write. If so, stay with me, because I explain those in the next section, where I illustrate OO thinking and design.

Thinking the OO way

Object-oriented design is a different way of designing programs, where the behavior is associated with objects. To illustrate, you once again make tea and soup. This time, you don't immediately leap into action. Instead, you act like a detective entering a crime scene. You step back, survey the domain (the kitchen), and try to understand what's in it. In other words, you think *objects first.*

> ✔ **You see a kettle.** You consider the kettle for a while and then say, "I can add water to it; I can pour water from it."
>
> ✔ **You look at a teapot.** As it looks back, you think, "I can add water to this, too, and pour water from it, as well, just like I can with a kettle."

Both the kettle and teapot appear to be able to take in and pour out water. They both also have state (the water being held). Therefore, you generalize that each of these objects is a vessel. You also think about the characteristics of these objects, that is, their attributes — such as their volume, color, and material.

You think about the other items in the kitchen, namely, the stove, the faucet, the cups and bowls, the various sorts of spoons, and the food items: soup, tea, and bouillon, even the kitchen clock. You think about their capabilities, as well. You try to generalize the kinds of objects into higher-level concepts, such as vessel.

Rather than thinking of a recipe only as a sequence of actions, you realize that a recipe is also an object. After all, you can create recipes, tear up recipes, and share recipes. A recipe is indeed something tangible; therefore, it's an object, an object with capabilities. When you follow a recipe, you can imagine that you're running it. So, you can make *run* a capability of a recipe. You can also make *setting up* and *cleaning up* responsibilities of a recipe object. Does a recipe have attributes? How about the level of difficulty of a recipe — easy or hard? What about its author (a *string*)? Or how many people it serves (an *integer*)? Finally, recipes clearly have a generalization hierarchy, with *Making Tea* and *Making Soup* being specializations of a generic *Recipe*.

Table 2-1 lists the various kinds of objects, their capabilities, their attributes, and their generalizations.

Table 2-1	Identifying Objects in the Kitchen		
Kind of Object	*Capabilities*	*Attributes*	*Generalizations*
Vessel	Add liquid; Pour out liquid	Volume, color, material	
Teapot	The capabilities of a Vessel (that is, Add and Pour)	The attributes of a Vessel	Vessel

Kind of Object	Capabilities	Attributes	Generalizations
Tureen	All the capabilities of a Vessel	The attributes of a Vessel	Vessel
Kettle	All the capabilities of a Vessel; Boil	The attributes of a Vessel	Vessel
Cup	All the capabilities of a Vessel; Drink from	The attributes of a Vessel	Vessel; I can drink from
Bowl	All the capabilities of a Vessel; Eat with spoon	The attributes of a Vessel	Vessel; I can consume liquids it holds, using a spoon
Stove	Put a Vessel on; Turn on; Turn off; Set level	Color	
Faucet	Open; Close	Color	
Tea	Steep	Type	Food item
Bouillon	Steep	Flavor	Food item
Clock	Wait		
Recipe	Set up; Run; Clean up	Level of difficulty; Creator; Number of people served	
Make Tea	Responsibilities of a Recipe	Attributes of a Recipe; Number of cups	Recipe
Make Soup	Responsibilities of a Recipe	Attributes of a Recipe; Number of bowls	Recipe

In Table 2-1, an entry like *All the capabilities* of a Vessel for the Cup object means that a Cup is understood to automatically have the Add liquid and Pour out capabilities because it is a Vessel. In addition, a Cup has the Drink from capability. In other words, you can do more with a Cup than you can with a plain old Vessel.

To put it in OO terminology, a Vessel is a generalization of a Cup, whereas a Cup is a specialization of a Vessel.

Listing 2-5 shows what the OO version of the `Make Tea` recipe could look like (note that I changed its name to `TeaRecipe` because a recipe is also an object.

Listing 2-5: The Object-Oriented MakeTea Recipe

```
@interface TeaRecipe : Recipe // Make Tea is a kind of Recipe
@implementation TeaRecipe

+ Setup; {...} // Sets up the recipe
+ Run:(int) NumberOfCups;
{ // this is an instance method
    NSArray *TeaCups; // Declare an array of cups

    [Faucet Open]
    [Kettle AddLiquid:(NumberOfCups * CUPVOLUME)];
    [Stove PutVesselOn:Kettle];
    [Stove TurnOn];
    For (i=1; i <= NumberOfCups; i++){
        [TeaPot Add:Tea Quantity:@"1 spoon"];
    }
    While(![Kettle IsBoiling]); //keep looping till the water boils
    [Kettle PourWaterFrom:Teapot];
    [Clock Wait:@"5 minutes"];
    For (i=1; i<= NumberOfCups; i++)[Kettle Pour:[TeaCups objectAtIndex:i]];
    NSLog("Enjoy Tea");
} // End MakeTea
+ Cleanup; {...} // cleans up after the recipe
@end
```

You make two cups of tea using this program:

```
MakeTea teaRecipeInstance = [[TeaRecipe alloc];
[teaRecipeInstance Setup];
[teaRecipeInstance Run:2];
[teaRecipeInstance Cleanup];
```

Once again, the syntax of the pseudo-language is based on Objective-C. If you aren't familiar with Objective-C, the comments should clarify the meaning of the program. Chapter 3 covers the basics of Objective-C.

This OO approach is different from the procedural approach in the following ways:

- Every action in the recipe is *explicitly* associated with a single object.
- These objects and their capabilities were identified before the recipe program was written, so writing the program essentially involved *composing interactions among objects*.

  Writing programs as interactions among objects is the key idea behind OO programming.

Listing 2-6 shows a similar OO recipe for bouillon.

Listing 2-6:   Object-Oriented Bouillon Recipe

```
@interface SoupRecipe : Recipe // Make Soup is a kind of Recipe
@implementation SoupRecipe

+ Setup; {...} // Sets up the recipe
+ Run:(int) NumberOfBowls; // this is an instance method
{
    NSArray *Bowls; // Declare an array of cups

    [Faucet Open];
    [Kettle AddLiquid:(NumberOfBowls*BOWLVOLUME)];
    [Stove PutVesselOn:Kettle];
    [Stove TurnOn];
    For (i=1; i <= NumberOfBowls; i++){
        [Tureen Add:Bouillon Quantity:@"1 spoon"];
    }
    While(![Kettle IsBoiling]); //keep looping till the water boils
    [Kettle PourWaterFrom:Tureen;
    [Clock Wait:@"5 minutes";
    For (i=1; i<= NumberOfBowls; i++) [Kettle Pour:[Bowls objectAtIndex:i]];
    NSLog("Enjoy Soup");
} // End SoupRecipe
+ Cleanup(){...} // cleans up after the recipe
@end
```

As you can see, this program is still quite similar to the `TeaRecipe` program
(and runs in the same way). You might consider trying the same kind of reuse
as in the procedural version of these programs by creating a `BoilWaterInK`
`ettleOnAStove(...)` program. You can certainly do that. In other words,
you don't *lose* anything in terms of reuse if you develop programs the OO
way. All the techniques of reuse that you had with procedural programming
are still here. However, there's a way to get greater reuse, specifically the joint
reuse of objects and their behavior. To do so, you make a generalized recipe
called `DrinkableFoodRecipe` that can be used to make either tea or soup,
as shown in Listing 2-7.

Listing 2-7:   MakeDrinkableFood

```
@interface DrinkableFoodRecipe : Recipe // Making Drinkable Food is a Recipe
@implementation MakeDrinkableFood
  Vessel *HeatingVessel, *ServingVessel;
  int NumberOfVessels;
  Class *EatingVesselType;
```

(continued)

Listing 2-7 *(continued)*

```
  Food *FoodItem;
  String *Dish;

+ Setup(HeatingVessel:(Vessel*) HeatingVessel
        ServingVessel:(Vessel *) ServingVessel_
        NumberOfVessels:(int) NumberOfVessels_,
        EatingVesselType:(Class *)EatingVesselType_,
        FoodItem:(Food *) FoodItem
        Dish:(NSString*) Dish_;
  {

      self.HeatingVessel = HeatingVessel_;
      self.ServingVessel = ServingVessel_;
      self.NumberOfVessels =  NumberOfVessels_;
      self.EatingVesselType = EatingVesselType_;
      self.FoodItem = FoodItem_;
      self.Dish = Dish_;

  } // Sets up the parameters of the recipe
+ Run;
{ // this is an instance method
      NSArray *EatingVessels; // Declare an array of eating vessels

      [Faucet Open];
      [HeatingVessel AddLiquid:(NumberOfVessels*VESSELVOLUME)];
      [Stove PutVesselOn:HeatingVessel];
      [Stove TurnOn];
      For (i=1; i <= NumberOfVessels; i++){
          [ServingVessel Add:Bouillon Quantity:@"1 spoon"];
      }
      While(![HeatingVessel IsBoiling]); //keep looping till the water boils
      [HeatingVessel PourWaterFrom:ServingVessel];
      [Clock Wait:@"5 minutes"];
      For (i=1; i<= NumberOfEatingVessel; i++)
          [HeatingVessel Pour:[EatingVessel objectAtIndex:i]];
      NSLog("Enjoy!");
} // End MakeDrinkableFood
+ Cleanup; {...} // Cleans up after the recipe
```

Making two cups of tea using this generalized class is a little bit more complicated than making tea with the TeaRecipe class, but it's pretty straightforward, as shown here:

```
DrinkableFoodRecipe teaRecipeInstance = [[DrinkableFoodRecipe alloc];
[teaRecipeInstance Setup:Kettle
    ServingVessel:TeaPot
    NumberOfVessels:2
    EatingVesselType:[TeaCup class]
    FoodItem:Tea
    Dish:@"Tea"
];
[teaRecipeInstance Run];
[teaRecipeInstance Cleanup];
```

What's interesting about this procedure is that you're generalizing at the *object* level, and not in terms of behavior alone. Here's how to use this procedure to make four bowls of soup:

```
DrinkableFoodRecipe soupRecipeInstance = [[DrinkableFoodRecipe alloc];
[soupRecipeInstance Setup:Kettle
    ServingVessel:Tureen
    NumberOfVessels:4
    EatingVesselType:[Bowl class]
    FoodItem:Bouillon
    Dish:@"Soup"
];
[soupRecipeInstance Run];
[soupRecipeInstance Cleanup];
```

More of the code ended up being reused. Could you achieve reuse with the procedural program? Sure. But the reuse will be at the level of actions and will be limited. Additional reuse will not happen as a natural outcome, as it did in the OO version.

Although using an OO language such as Objective-C naturally forces you to think in an object-oriented manner, you can use OO design thinking even when using a non-OO language. Start with objects first and then translate each object into a data structure. Next, translate methods to functions that operate on each data structure and declare these functions in the same file as you did the data structure. You'll be pretty close to an OO program.

Here's an overview of OO development:

- ✔ **Analyze:** Begin with analysis to identify the following:
    - • Objects
    - • Object capabilities (also known as its responsibilities, its behavior, its methods, or its functions)
    - • Object characteristics (also known as attributes or variables)
- ✔ **Consolidate:** Identify generalizations and specializations of objects (the Vessel object is a generalization of the Teacup object, which in turn, is a specialization of the Vessel).
- ✔ **Write program:** Write the actual program by composing interactions among the objects.
- ✔ **Reuse:** This happens with an entire object.

OO is a better way of thinking about and writing programs. The fact that it begins with an analysis means that you come away with a deeper understanding of the domain in which you're programming. This understanding will serve you in good stead as you write more programs in that domain, especially if you end up building large-scale software *systems* comprising many programs that share data and collaborate with each other. Basing your program on the objects in the domain (as opposed to the actions in the domain, that is, the behavior) makes your programs more stable because although many behaviors occur in a domain and behaviors also tend to evolve rapidly in the domain, the objects tend to be more constant. The fact that you think objects first and then write programs by composing interactions means that reuse is a focus from the start, rather than after the fact.

Structural and behavioral concepts in OO

Okay, time to get a little more formal about OO. In this section, I define and explain the core OO terminology while bringing in additional concepts that complete the building blocks of OO.

Object

An *object* is an individual, identifiable item, either real or abstract, that contains data about itself and descriptions of its manipulations of the data. In other words, an object might be either

- ✔ Something real and tangible, like the items in a kitchen
- ✔ A pure concept, such as a mathematical concept, like an integral

Identifying objects is the first step in analyzing a domain (as shown in the previous section by identifying Vessel, Teacup, Bowl, Stove, and so on).

Each object is considered an instance of a class.

Class

A *class* is a description of the organization and actions shared by one or more similar objects.

A *type* is a concept similar to that of class, and they're often used interchangeably. Within programming languages, a class also has a technical meaning. It is a *template* of an object, through which new objects can be created. However, the concept of a type separate from that of a class is captured in many programming languages (but not Objective-C) by a programming construct called an *interface*. Objective-C doesn't make a distinction between type and class, so this book doesn't use the term type.

In the earlier `DrinkableFoodRecipe` example, `Vessel` is a class. All the objects `Faucet`, `ServingVessel`, and `Stove` in `DrinkableFoodRecipe` are instances of classes.

Object-orientation also has the concept of a *metaclass,* whose instances are *classes.* There is one metaclass in Objective-C called `Class`. You see this metaclass used in the `EatingVesselType` member variable in the `DrinkableFoodRecipe` class.

Abstraction

When I identified the classes of objects and their capabilities in my example, I didn't consider those classes or capabilities that weren't relevant to the domain of cooking. For example, it's unlikely I would have brought in a class to represent the floor or the lighting in the kitchen. Nor would I bring in the capability of a teacup to be thrown.

This kind of modeling where I ignore what is irrelevant to focus on what is relevant for a particular domain is known as *abstraction*. Abstraction is the act of identifying the classes (and types) needed in order to pare down to those aspects that are relevant to the problem.

Generalization

The concept of *generalization* is exemplified in the relationship between the classes `Vessel` and `Teacup`. Generalization in a programming language is demonstrated through a mechanism known as *inheritance,* which allows the data and behavior of one class to be included in or used as the basis for another class.

Several programming languages have a root class from which all classes are inherited. In the Objective-C framework, the class is called `NSObject`. `NSObject` is equivalent to the class `Object` in Java.

A *subclass* is a class that inherits all the functionality from another class (known as the *superclass*). Furthermore, the subclass can override specific functionality by providing its own implementation of certain methods. The method of the superclass can still be called from the overriding method, if doing so makes sense. You can also extend the functionality of the superclass by providing additional methods, using additional member variables, and so on.

Similarly, a type (an *interface*) may also be extended using a subtype. Here, no functionality is overridden; it's just that the subtype has more methods that an object must implement.

An object typically stores data, also known as its *state*. This state is stored in holders of data known as *attributes*.

Objects (as defined by classes) also have capabilities. A *method* is a way to access that capability — in other words, to execute a set of instructions that set or manipulate an object's attributes.

Other objects cause these methods to be executed. They do so via *message passing,* which is the process by which an object sends data to another object or asks the other object to invoke a method. Message passing happens when another object calls the method of an object. Execution of a program typically begins with the calling of a function or method named *main* within a specific class.

The process of abstraction results in the creation of classes and types. Classes and types have one more characteristic: They constrain their use only through their methods and publicly accessible attributes. This is known as *encapsulation,* which can be defined as a technique for designing classes and objects that restricts access to the data and behavior by defining a limited set of messages that an object of that class can receive. Encapsulation prevents access to the internals of a class and prevents the details on how the class is implemented from being known. Encapsulation enforces *information hiding,* another key concept in object-orientation.

Abstract classes serve only as specifications to be reused by other classes. You can't create objects from abstract classes. Classes from which you can create objects are known as *concrete* classes. Of course, interfaces are always abstract.

An application consists of a collection of classes of various types. Objects of these classes interact with each other to implement the features of the application. The classes that a class interact with are known as its *collaborators*.

Polymorphism is the ability of different classes to respond to the same message, with each class implementing the method appropriately. The following line taken from `MakeDrinkableFood` illustrates this concept:

```
For (i=1; i<= NumberOfEatingVessels; i++)HeatingVessel.Pour(([EatingVessel
        objectAtIndex:i);
```

When tea is being made, `EatingVessel` is bound to a `Kettle` object. When soup is being made, `EatingVessel` is bound to a `Tureen` object.

It's useful to separate these concepts into structural concepts that tell you something about the composition of the program and behavioral concepts that tell you something about how the program works. The concepts of abstraction, encapsulation, metaclass, class, type, object, inheritance, and interface are all structural concepts. The concepts of a method, message passing, and polymorphism are behavioral concepts.

That's about it in terms of core OO concepts. The process of OO design involves identifying and defining appropriate classes and types and designing their methods and collaborations so that the application can do what it needs to do.

Principles of Object-Orientation

The concepts and core mechanisms of object-orientation are the building blocks of an OO app. In this section, you find out how to apply those concepts and techniques to create well-designed, easy-to-understand programs.

Separation of concerns is a design principle that calls for breaking your system (or program) into components, each of which either implements a certain piece of functionality, such as heating water (in the tea-making example) or encapsulates a nonfunctional quality such as performance.

Separation of concerns starts early in OO development, right at the time objects are identified and their classes are defined. Each class represents a concern, such as a Vessel, a Stove, or a Faucet. The domain naturally identifies these concerns for you.

The benefit of separating concerns is twofold:

✔ It reduces the complexity of developing the software by allowing development of the software in pieces.

✔ It allows *independent* evolution and maintenance of the system.

In order for independent evolution to happen, the system must be partitioned so that the components exhibit low coupling and high cohesion.

Coupling

Coupling is a measure of the dependency between two components. It's the degree to which one component relies upon the other component. In terms of software development, coupling is how much a "using" component needs to know about the *internals* of the used component and the *published interface* (the public methods and attributes) of the used component.

Here's an example of loose coupling versus tight coupling. In the Run method of the MakeTea class, I tested whether the kettle was boiling as follows:

```
While(![Kettle IsBoiling]);
```

In the above example, the recipe program doesn't know how the Kettle class implements IsBoiling (that is, this implementation is hidden). The Kettle class can change this implementation without the recipe program having to change. This is an example of *loose coupling* achieved by information hiding. The same test could have been written as follows:

```
While(![Kettle [Whistle IsSounding]]);
```

Here, the recipe program assumes that the kettle has a whistle. In other words, it's utilizing an internal secret of the kettle, and is therefore coupling itself to kettles that have whistles. If I were to use a kettle that has some other means of signaling that it's boiling (for example, by emitting steam), I would have to rewrite the recipe program. The fact that I have to rewrite the recipe program is a symptom of *tight coupling* between recipe program and the kettle.

Cohesion

Cohesion is a measure of how closely the functions within a single class are related to each other and to the responsibility of the class. Typical procedural programs (such as the kitchen example) are usually not very cohesive. As you can see, the initial `Kitchen` module turned on faucets and stoves, poured out kettles and so on, whereas the OO version of the program had a set of classes corresponding to objects in the kitchen and where each class (and object) managed its own responsibility in a cohesive manner.

A class with high cohesion is more easily understood and reused because it doesn't bring extra baggage with it. Also, making a class cohesive encapsulates related long-lived information (or state) in one class, so if a change needs to be made in a function, the change will be isolated to that one class.

In many cases, but by no means always, low cohesion within a class also results in high coupling to other classes — because if highly related methods are scattered across multiple classes (say, along with a bunch of other unrelated methods), the classes they're scattered across are likely to be coupled either through use or through shared data.

Designing an Object-Oriented Application

When identifying and defining appropriate classes and types and designing their methods so that the application can do what it needs to do, you simply begin with whatever is available. In many cases, like the example in this chapter, the natural environment is a great place to look. You can also use written documents or notes, such as concept or requirements documents and storyboards. If you don't have any of these, you can create them now.

 Trained software developers will go about this formally, through a process known as *requirements analysis.* But for small apps and simple systems, informal methods work quite well. Simply write up a page or two (or three) about your app, how it's supposed to work, and how its users are supposed to interact with it, and that's your documentation.

Follow these steps to analyze your material:

1. **Go through the material carefully and pull out**

   - *Nouns:* These become candidate (not final) *classes.*
   - *Verbs:* These become candidate *responsibilities.*

2. **Write the definition of each noun and verb.**

   If there are just a few nouns and verbs, you may even be able to keep track of the definitions in your head.

3. **Review your definitions, looking for similar items. If you find two nouns or two verbs that mean about the same thing, remove one of them.**

   If a noun or verb has more than one definition, see if splitting it into two nouns or verbs allows you to define each one specifically. Feel free to rename nouns and rewrite verbs so that they fit your definition better.

4. **Delete any nouns and verbs that are only physical objects in the environment in which your system operates. These physical objects are outside the context of your system.**

5. **Allocate the consolidated set of verbs (which are the responsibilities) among the nouns (the classes).**

   When you are done with this, each noun (that is, class) should have only those responsibilities that properly belong to that noun.

   Here's a quick test for proper allocation: The responsibilities should not cause the definition of the class to lose cohesiveness.

6. **Create a few detailed scenarios that capture the essential capabilities of your app. Use these scenarios to identify the collaborations by walking through the steps of the scenario in detail, identifying which class and which method enables that step.**

   You may also find *missing* classes and methods. If necessary, repeat Steps 2 through 6 to incorporate missing nouns and verbs in your classes and methods.

7. **For each class, run through this checklist for a good class:**

   • Does the class have a suitable name?

   • Does it have a cohesive description that says that it does just one thing?

   • Does it have responsibilities (methods)?

   • Does it have collaborators?

   • Does it — or its components — maintain state?

8. **Consolidate and clean up the class hierarchy.**

   Look for classes that have similar data and responsibilities to see if creating a superclass that holds common responsibilities (and having the original classes inherit from this superclass) will increase reuse.

   Before you do a consolidation, perform the "Is-A" test. Say (to yourself): "<Subclass> Is-A <Superclass>." If that sentence doesn't completely make sense, the creation of the superclass is incorrect. For example, say, "kettle Is-A vessel." This sounds correct. Now say, "Vessel Is-A stove." Doesn't sound so right, does it.

9. **Clearly specify (or at least understand) how each method functions:**

   - Actions that the method is supposed to perform

   - Inputs that it needs in order to do so

   Go class-by-class, method-by-method, and define its *signature,* that is, its input parameters and its output result.

Classes of naturally occurring objects (like in the team-making example) automatically tend to follow the preceding principles. This is one reason why extracting classes from your natural environment is a useful way to go about things. Chapter 7 has a detailed example of an application, where the preceding checklist has been applied to clean up a design.

Advanced OO Techniques

Built upon the concepts of object-orientation discussed in this chapter is a body of standard techniques for achieving more reusability.

Delayed binding

Delayed (or late) binding is a design principle that delays the selection of a component, object, or method to execute in response to a request until the latest possible moment, most often at the time the program is running (aka at runtime) and just before the functionality supported by this component is needed.

The delayed binding design principle is implemented by more than one technique, depending on what is being bound. Delayed binding for libraries became possible when most commercial operating systems started providing the capability to dynamically load and link shared libraries.

One common technique used to delay binding of objects in an OO program is *polymorphism* (which is the use of an object via its superclass). This is shown in the following line taken from DrinkableFoodRecipe:

```
For (i=1; i<= NumberOfEatingVessels; i++)HeatingVessel.Pour(([EatingVessel
     objectAtIndex:i);
```

When tea is being made, EatingVessel will be bound to a Kettle object. When soup is being made, EatingVessel will be bound to a Tureen object.

A second mechanism for late binding is *reflection*. You can see reflection in the MakeDrinkableFood example in the call to the Setup method of the class, as shown here:

```
MakeDrinkableFood teaRecipeInstance = [[MakeDrinkableFood alloc];
[teaRecipeInstance Setup:Kettle
    ServingVessel:TeaPot
    NumberOfVessels:2
    EatingVesselType:[TeaCup class]
    FoodItem:Tea
    Dish:@"Tea"
];
[teaRecipeInstance Run];
[teaRecipeInstance Cleanup];
```

Delegation

Delegation is a technique in OO programming where an object hands over a task to an associated helper object (or delegate), rather than implementing the task itself.

Here's an example of delegation from TeaRecipe. Say that the kettle being used to boil the water is a kettle with a whistle. Now consider the line

```
While(![Kettle IsBoiling]);
```

where the isBoiling() method is implemented as follows:

```
BOOL IsBoiling (
    Return [Self.Whistle IsSounding];
}
```

In this example, the Kettle object is delegating the test for isBoiling() to its Whistle component.

Because the handoff to the delegate is done at runtime, simply changing the delegate (at runtime) can change the implementation of the task (once again, at runtime). Therefore, delegation is often used for delayed binding of objects to service requests.

Design patterns

The book *Design Patterns: Elements of Reusable Object-Oriented Software* by the IBM Gang of Four (namely, Erich Gamma, Richard Helm, Ralph Johnson, and John M. Vlissides) was published in 1994. This book highly influenced the field of software design and became an important resource for learning OO design. This book provided common ways of designing classes and their interactions for solving common software design problems. Software developers were able to look up a catalog of designs and find patterns to solve problems like theirs. They could see whether the design pattern provided them with a template for beginning their design.

Design patterns are *not* canned solutions that you can simply take and plug into your code. They're simply a place to *start* your design.

The Model-View-Controller (MVC), shown in Figure 2-1, is a well-known design pattern in applications, especially web applications. This pattern isolates the application's domain logic from its user interface so that these two very important components of any application can be designed, implemented, and maintained separately. The logic of playing Tic-Tac-Toe based on the rules of Tic-Tac-Toe is the *domain logic* of the Tic-Tac-Toe application (the model). The Tic-Tac-Toe grid that's presented to users and with which they interact is the user interface (the view). The controller is a component interposed between the two that receives user actions (such as *The user clicked here*) and translates these commands to actions on the model and then takes the resulting model updates and notifies the user interface that it has to update itself.

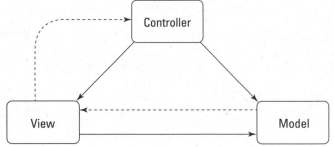

Figure 2-1:
The Model-
View-
Controller
design
pattern.

Inversion of control and software frameworks

A software framework is a set of components containing common code that provides generic functionality. This generic functionality can be selectively overridden or specialized by user code. In this manner, the framework can be customized (using OO techniques such as inheritance, polymorphism, late binding, and delegation) into providing specific functionality. This customization results in an app.

Frameworks also implement a technique known as *inversion of control.* Inversion of control means that the program's flow of control — how the program runs — isn't dictated by the user of the framework but by the framework itself, as default behavior. This default behavior is extended or modified by code that the user supplies in the form of classes that extend the base classes of the framework (which are usually abstract classes). These user-supplied classes either override certain methods or provide implementations of virtual methods. The user's classes may also implement specific interfaces that are then passed to and invoked by the framework.

Inversion of control distinguishes frameworks from software libraries that provide computational capabilities that your application can invoke, such as the string manipulation routines provided by the `java.lang` package.

iOS is, in fact, a framework. As I say in Chapter 1, it provides a set of base classes that you extend with your own classes and code and an overall sequence of computation in which you plug in these classes and your code.

So, what default functionality do frameworks provide? Among other things, they implement patterns (or variations of patterns). Therefore, a core component of the iOS framework implements the MVC pattern. A controller manages the interaction between its views and the application logic (that is, the domain logic) that is supposed to be done in that activity.

This domain logic can be implemented right in the activity. However, if it's complex, the design principle of separation of concerns says that this domain logic should be extracted into a separate class or set of classes. These classes make up the model.

Separating out the model, views, and controller results in components with higher cohesion, with each component responsible for a related set of responsibilities. Also, in order for inversion of control to work well, many different kinds of reusable components must be able to plug into the overall sequence of computation. The more these different components need to know about the framework, and vice versa, the harder it becomes to plug in a varied set of components. Consequently, loose coupling is also essential in frameworks.

The Application Development Lifecycle

In the previous sections, I explained the concepts and techniques behind OO design and programming. Keep in mind, though, that designing and programming are just about the *construction* of software. There are many aspects and steps before, after, and around designing and programming that you need to be aware of.

The OO construction of software is only its *how* aspect. There are the *why* and *who* aspects: What problem will the software solve or what benefit will it provide; Who will benefit. There is the *what* aspect: What features should the software provide and what should their qualities be (for example, speed and accuracy). There is the *where*, which can be thought of as the infrastructure on which the software will operate. Then, there is the *when*, which involves planning the order in which the various pieces of the software are built. All of these aspects help make up the context in which OO activities take place.

Software development lifecycle processes

Software development life cycle (SDLC) processes (also known as *methodologies*) are systematic ways of developing software systems (the how) while considering all the other relevant aspects (the why, what, when, who, and where) of these systems.

At this point, you may be tempted to ask, "Why can't I just write an app? Why do I need to consider these processes — processes that by themselves don't create value and, in fact, increase cost?" The answer is that software development is complex, and we need processes when doing anything complex in order to predictably meet expectations of functionality, capability, and time. Commercial software development is so complex that even following good processes doesn't guarantee success. They just reduce the risk of not meeting expectations.

A *process* is a systematically designed method of developing and maintaining a software system through its lifecycle. Essentially, a process serves as a structure for software development. It helps achieve

- ✔ **Repeatability:** A software process becomes a recipe you can repeat (well, kinda; see the following discussion on designing processes).

- ✔ **Prediction:** By repeating the same process, you get better at predicting how and when tasks will be completed.

- ✔ **Quality through standardization:** By standardizing the process, you can more likely ensure the quality of the product.

- ✔ **Continuous, targeted improvement:** You can identify components and improve them, and improve them, and improve them, and . . .

- ✔ **Training:** You can train new folks on a process if it's been well defined.

- ✔ **Traceability:** You know what a step in the process is responsible for. You also know the source of each software artifact. So by recording process steps, you achieve what's known as *traceability*.

Following a process results in psychological benefits as well, such as building confidence, in both individuals and teams.

With that said, note the emphasis on design in the preceding definition of a process. Rarely are the processes the same across companies or across different projects within the same company. Process must be customized to be effective.

Designing a software process for a project, product, or enterprise requires a fundamental understanding of what processes are made up of and best practices in processes. So you try to provide a framework consisting of principles and practices for processes and a set of design criteria.

Ugh. Another framework!

The phases and stages of a software development lifecycle (SDLC)

To understand how to design processes, you must understand process *phases,* which are a high-level categorization of process activities organized by common *intent.* Many of these activities involve object-orientation.

Here are the phases and their relationship to object-orientation:

- ✔ **Requirements identification:** This is the phase where you identify some of the *who* — the people affected by the software, such as users, the sponsor, and so on — some of the *why* — the problem to be solved and the business case — and the *what* — the features of the solution.

- ✔ **Analysis:** Analysis is all about understanding, as opposed to solving, aspects of the project and the software. This understanding needs to happen at multiple levels.

  - *Domain* analysis seeks to understand the environment in which the software will operate (such as your home, your kitchen, your likes and dislikes, and your needs in terms of food, and even potentially various kinds of cuisines).

  - *Problem* analysis tries to understand and characterize a specific problem in the domain (such as your difficulty in remembering and properly following recipes).

  - *Solution* analysis tries to understand how a proposed solution (such as a recipe program) might actually solve your problem.

  - *Object-oriented* analysis is the application of OO to analysis. In domain analysis, you might identify objects and their interactions in the domain; in problem analysis, you might identify objects and describe their interactions in the problem you're trying to understand; and in solution analysis, you might describe how the system works in terms of interactions between external objects (or actors) and the system.

✔ **Architecture and design:** Architecture and design taken together make up the phase where you determine the overall structure of the system and the design, which is what the individual components of the system are, all the way to the smallest granularity and how everything works together.

Architecture is also the description of the high-level components of the system and how they interact at a *component* level. Architecture rarely concerns itself with what is inside a high-level component.

It's hard to discern what is architecture and what is design. Think of architecture as consisting of those design elements that are hard to change once put in place, such as programming framework (iOS), choice of database, and the major components of the system and how they interact and fit together. Object-oriented design is the identification and definition of the classes that make up each component of the system, potentially all the way down to the smallest classes of a program, and a description of how these classes interact.

✔ **Implementation:** Implementation is the phase where the rubber meets the road, and you actually write and run the code that makes up the system. When you use OO languages in your implementation, the implementation is known as *object-oriented programming*.

✔ **Testing:** Testing is the phase where you check whether the system actually works. *Object-oriented testing* can take place at the level of individual classes, at which point it's called *unit* testing; after the classes and components are put together, where it's called *integration* testing; or at the level of the entire system or program, where it's called *system* testing. Developing production software involves all these levels of testing.

✔ **Deployment:** Deployment is the phase where you actually put the program to work. For commercially available iOS apps, deployment starts with putting the app on the Apple Store and continues to when a user installs and runs it on an iOS device.

✔ **Maintenance:** Maintenance is the phase where you keep the system working and useful as needs evolve by modifying the structure of the classes and the interactions between objects of these classes.

✔ **Project management:** This is the phase where you plan, organize, resource, lead, control, and coordinate. Project management consists of the steps needed in the overall monitoring and control of the process and project.

However, note that the preceding phases of the software lifecycle are groupings of activities clustered around a common *intent*. The phases are not steps done in a particular order.

If phases aren't ordered, what determines the process order? Software development steps are ordered in time by *stages,* starting from a stage of little understanding and moving to stages of progressively increased knowledge and predictability, with the activities starting with the sponsors or the visionaries and moving to the development team and then to the customer. There are four stages (see Figure 2-2):

- **Inception:** The inception stage is where things are being figured out — an approximate vision; a business case; scope; a high-level, potential architecture; and high-level estimates of efforts and cost. You might do some domain and problem analysis here.

- **Elaboration:** This is the stage where you refine the vision, validate the core architecture, and resolve risks. In fact, you might say that elaboration is all about the *resolution* of the risks. This is where most of the requirements identification is done and (with hope) realistic project management estimates are created. User demos intended to better understand requirements may also done here. The core architecture is designed here — that is, the elements that *have* to work. Design and implementation of the critical features are done here.

- **Construction:** The stage where you iteratively implement any remaining features and prepare for deployment. The construction stage is where the tasks are steadily adding more and more features. Plenty of detailed OO design, implementation, and testing takes place here.

  After elaboration is done, you have a good idea about how much the software will cost to build and how it will work. You can then proceed to more or less repeatable, cookie-cutter tasks that take place in the construction stage. Object-oriented activities take place in detailed problem and solution analysis and in the OO design and implementation of the core features.

- **Transition:** This is the stage where you deploy a finished released. Here, the software is turned over to users. Incidentally, you might also beta test a system in this stage. Activities from the deployment, testing, and maintenance phases take place here.

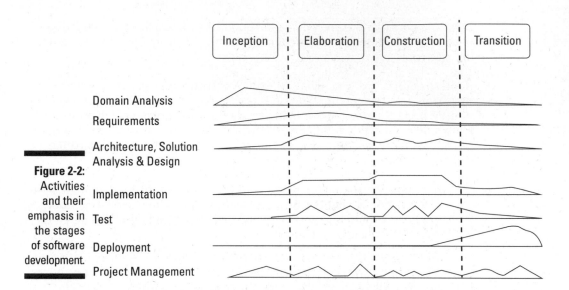

Figure 2-2:
Activities and their emphasis in the stages of software development.

Note that project management cuts across all the stages.

You might think that activities from most phases are done in most of the stages. You would be right; however, the degree or the proportion of time consumed in a stage by activities of a phase is different (also illustrated in Figure 2-2). Inception is heavy on analysis and somewhat on requirements, with only a little bit of prototype implementation thrown in. Elaboration is heavy on solution analysis, architecture, design, implementation, and testing. Construction is heavy on implementation and testing, whereas transition focuses on deployment and maintenance.

The guiding principles of SDLC methodologies

I suggest living by these guiding principles:

> ✓ **Commit to incremental, scenario-driven, and iterative development.**
>
> • Incremental simply means "to build in pieces."
>
> • Since most software systems are complex, you must try to reduce the complexity of development by attacking the system construction in chunks known as *iterations*. For each iteration, all the SDLC phases are revisited. You may take another look at the requirements and do some additional analysis, design, and most likely implementation and testing.

- Scenario-driven means that for each chunk make sure there's some user-visible functionality.

- Iterative development is a subclass or refinement of incremental, whereas scenario-driven development is a refinement of iterative development.

✔ **Apply separation of concerns.** In software processes, this means that you must be able to partition your software development process so as to address each aspect of the software system separately. For example, you must be able to capture requirements without worrying about or being constrained by technological capabilities, and you must separate the analysis activities of the system from the design and implementation activities. Larger teams also separate development from system testing because sometimes developers have a tendency to miss errors in their own code.

Customizing an SDLC methodology

All projects involving large or small systems, whether with big teams or small, go through the stages of inception, elaboration, construction, and transition. Software development projects involve activities from each of the phases, namely, requirements, analysis, architecture and design, implementation, testing, deployment, and maintenance. Here are the variations:

✔ How long each stage should last

✔ How detailed and well documented each activity must be

✔ What techniques and tools are available and should be used (for each activity)

✔ What the management philosophy for the project needs to be

So what determines the preceding aspects of a project? In their excellent book *Balancing Agility and Discipline: A Guide for the Perplexed*, Barry Boehm and Richard Turner identify five characteristics that I paraphrase as follows:

✔ **The mission criticality of the software:** Is the software a medical application responsible for keeping patients alive? Or is it a game whose primary purpose is entertainment? If lives depend on the software, a more predictive, structured approach with lots of documentation is needed. Lots of time will be spent in inception and elaboration.

✔ **The likely rate of change in software needs:** If the requirements of the software are well understood, the rate of change is likely to be low. On the other hand, if the sponsors of the software system need to *discover* what the software is supposed to do, it's quite likely that the rate of change will be high and the project will be very dynamic, oscillating among inception to elaboration to transition stages and not having a construction stage until deep into the project. Also, for such dynamic projects, it's counterproductive to create masses of detailed documentation because all that effort is likely to be wasted because of rework, or it may even be thrown away. For well-defined projects, though, less time is needed in inception and elaboration, with most of the effort going into construction and transition.

✔ **The skill level of the software developers:** If the software developers are skilled, they can be a bit less stringent in planning and executing the project than software developers who are inexperienced. The latter need to take a more measured, planned approach, once again spending lots of time in inception and elaboration.

Often, novice software developers aren't as careful in their approach to software development as they might be. However, ignorance isn't always bliss. If you're a novice developer, be sure to spend plenty of time planning and developing your project.

✔ **The anticipated size of the system and the number of people likely to be working on it:** For small systems and projects with just a few people, less structure is necessary and less time is needed in inception and elaboration, with most of the effort going into construction and transition.

✔ **How comfortable the team is with change:** A team of worrywarts will want to thoroughly structure and document its work, and knock itself out in the inception and elaboration stages.

Work products (documents), tools, and techniques are mostly organized by phases. Requirements are typically captured in use cases; object-oriented analyses and designs are captured in UML class and sequence diagrams. There are many tools for project management — for example, Gantt charts.

The iOS IDE provides a set of SDLC tools, as well. Xcode storyboards capture use cases of an app in terms of its screen flows. Xcode also provides a drag-and-drop user interface for building the core object model of an app.

Finally, you come to the fourth aspect of customization — the management philosophy behind the project. For large, mission-critical projects with big budgets and many personnel, the activities must be planned in detail so that project execution is highly predictable. For small, fun, or highly dynamic projects with small teams, the management philosophy doesn't need to be predictive. Instead, management efforts should be spent on close monitoring and adjusting as needed.

If you're reading this book, I bet you're either working alone or in a small team of peers on a small application. For this reason, I haven't gone into any more detail about software development methodologies and techniques in this or other chapters in this book. Generally, only big teams need to understand such details. However, incorporating the intent behind these methodologies is useful even for lone developers.

- Don't start by writing code. Think about, understand, and jot down just what you want your app to do. Write down — at a high level — the features you want and prioritize them.

- Sketch some rough user interfaces on whiteboard or paper to see what your app will look like. Understand who will use your app and tailor your UI to the intended users.

- You may need to do a little research into iOS so that you understand its capabilities and how you can use them.

- Identify the critical parts of your system. Understand what they should do and build them first. Make sure they work well. Don't forget to include requirements such as security, speed, and reliability.

- Test your app well.

- Release your app to your users in stages. With each release, find out what your users like and don't like.

You find out more about all these topics in subsequent chapters. For Apple's simple but insightful help on app development, see the link labeled App Design Basics at www.dummies.com/go/iosprogramminglinks.

Chapter 3

Effectively Using Objective-C

In This Chapter

▶ Examining a simple Objective-C program

▶ Learning the elements of an Objective-C program

▶ Analyzing how Objective-C implements OO

*O*bjective-C, the programming language used for iOS app development, bring the features of an iOS app to life. In this chapter, you use that programming language to apply the OO concepts, techniques, and principles set out in Chapter 2. By the end of this chapter, you'll understand the object-oriented features of Objective-C and be able to start writing Objective-C programs.

Note that this chapter isn't a comprehensive reference on Objective-C. You may want to check out the book *Objective-C (Developer Reference),* by Jiva DeVoe, which covers all of Objective-C. Also, for Apple's guide to Objective-C, check out the link labeled Apple Reference on Objective-C at `www.dummies.com/go/iosprogramminglinks`.

Thanks to the popularity of Apple's devices, and according to *Wired* magazine, Objective-C has become the world's third most widely adopted programming language (`www.wired.com/wiredenterprise/2012/07/apple-objective-c`). Not bad for what was once considered a quirky language with a cult following.

Examining an Objective-C Program

I start by showing you an example program for a postfix calculator that, although simple, illustrates Objective-C's elements and syntax.

In the beginning

Objective-C was developed in the early 1980s. Apple established it as the language for iOS development in 1996 when it acquired NeXT, Inc.

The early adoption of Objective-C as one of the first object-oriented languages for commercial application development reflected its structure. It's actually designed as a set of extensions to the C language (as opposed to being an entirely new language like, say, Java).

Because it's a set of extensions on C, it has a somewhat quirky syntax, mostly because it was based on Smalltalk, one of the earliest object-oriented programming languages. However, it has full object-oriented programming capabilities implemented in a simple and straightforward way (once you get used to the syntax, of course).

You can use C statements in your Objective-C program with ease. In fact, most of the statements in an Objective-C program are in C. The Objective-C extensions allow you to do the OO stuff — create classes and objects, invoke methods, and so on — but the control flow of the program, which is pretty much everything else, is all straight C.

If you don't know C or want to brush up on it, you can easily search for it on the web. Just use the keywords *the C-programming*. You'll find plenty of good material, including entire books you can download. You can also go to www.dummies.com/go/iosprogramminglinks and check out these two useful references: C Language Book and C Language Reference.

Using integer arithmetic, this program calculates the value of a postfix expression and prints it. In other words, the program acts as shown in Table 3-1.

Table 3-1	Illustrating Postfix Arithmetic
Input Postfix Expression	*Output Value*
5 4 +	9
5 4 + 3 /	3
5 4 /	1
4 5 /	0
44 55 +	99

Postfix expressions that can be calculated using the example program must follow these rules:

- The input postfix expression can consist of only integers.
- The terms in the expression must be separated by spaces.
- The only operators allowed are +, -, *, and / (add, subtract, multiply, and divide).

The sample program in this chapter is composed of three main components:

- ✔ **A** `PostfixCalculator` **class:** Objects of this class are initialized with a postfix expression upon creation (or *instantiation,* as object creation is formally termed).

  This class has the following methods:

  - `initWithExpression`: An initializer for the class. It's called when an instance of the `PostfixCalculator` class is created and is used to initialize the instance with a postfix expression string.

  - `getExpression`: Returns the postfix expression with which a `PostfixCalculator` object was instantiated.

  - `calculate`: Calculates the value of the postfix expression and returns the final value.

    In the example program, this method works only with correct postfix expressions and doesn't deal with incorrect postfix expressions. This method also prints a few debugging messages (that I deliberately left in).

- ✔ **A** `PostfixCalculator` **class:** Internally uses a stack of integers in order to calculate the postfix expression. This stack is an instance of a `StackOfInteger` class, which has three methods:

  - `IsEmpty`: Returns `YES` if the stack is empty, and `NO` otherwise.

  - `Push`: Accepts an integer value and pushes it on the stack. It has no return result.

  - `Pop`: Returns the integer at the top of the stack.

- ✔ **A** `main` **method:** This method instantiates a `PostfixCalculator` object with a suitable expression, calls the `calculate` method of this class, and then prints the integer result of this method. This main program also prints a slew of debugging messages.

The example program in this chapter illustrates the various elements of the Objective-C language. Given that the focus of this book is object-orientation (OO), I start with and focus mostly on the OO aspects of Objective-C.

You can find the program with all its source code in the file named `PostfixAll.m` on this book's companion website. To download it, go to `www.dummies.com/extras/beginningiosprogramming`. Feel free to bring up this code in an editor (or do the old-fashioned thing and print it) and follow along in the file as you read.

While I'm talking about the example program, let me also show you a quick way to build and run the test program — via the command line. Starting with Chapter 5, you will do most, if not all, your development in Xcode, but knowing how to compile and build code using the command line is useful, plus it takes some of the mystery out of the development environment.

Here's how you build the example program for this chapter:

1. **Copy the program** `PostfixAll.m` **to a suitable directory.**

2. **Open a new Terminal window on your Mac and navigate to the directory where you saved the** `PostfixAll.m` **file.**

3. **Type the command** gcc PostfixAll.m -o pfall -lobjc -framework Foundation.

   A compiler called GCC, which understands Objective-C (and C++ and C), is installed on every Mac. The command to run GCC is gcc.

4. **At the command prompt, enter** ./pfall.

5. **Watch the program run.**

Figure 3-1 shows a Terminal window and the commands used to run the program. For more information on the gcc command, type **man gcc** at the command prompt. For all kinds of useful information, including source code for the latest GCC compiler, go to the official GCC website at `http://gcc.gnu.org`.

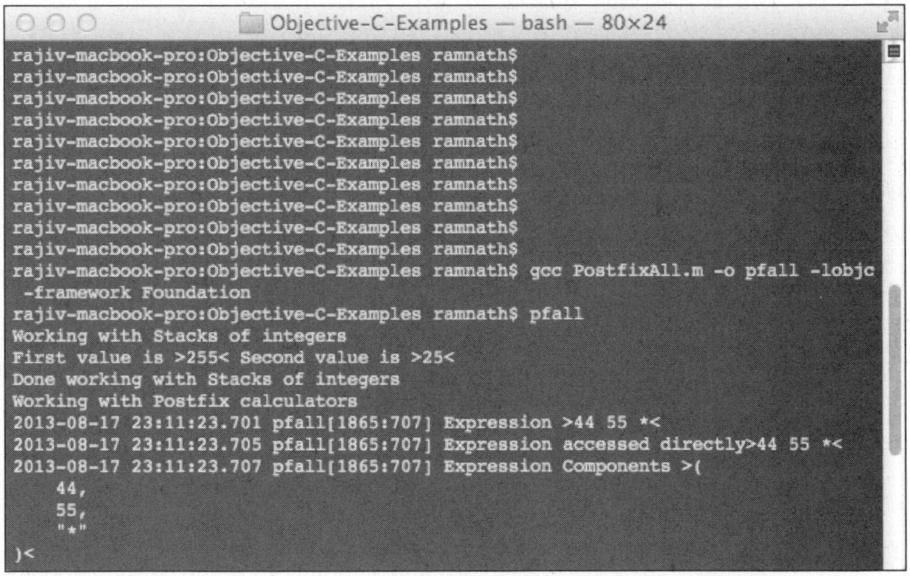

Figure 3-1:
Compiling the sample program from the command line.

```
○ ○ ○            Objective-C-Examples — bash — 80×24
rajiv-macbook-pro:Objective-C-Examples ramnath$
rajiv-macbook-pro:Objective-C-Examples ramnath$
rajiv-macbook-pro:Objective-C-Examples ramnath$
rajiv-macbook-pro:Objective-C-Examples ramnath$
rajiv-macbook-pro:Objective-C-Examples ramnath$
rajiv-macbook-pro:Objective-C-Examples ramnath$
rajiv-macbook-pro:Objective-C-Examples ramnath$
rajiv-macbook-pro:Objective-C-Examples ramnath$
rajiv-macbook-pro:Objective-C-Examples ramnath$
rajiv-macbook-pro:Objective-C-Examples ramnath$
rajiv-macbook-pro:Objective-C-Examples ramnath$ gcc PostfixAll.m -o pfall -lobjc
 -framework Foundation
rajiv-macbook-pro:Objective-C-Examples ramnath$ pfall
Working with Stacks of integers
First value is >255< Second value is >25<
Done working with Stacks of integers
Working with Postfix calculators
2013-08-17 23:11:23.701 pfall[1865:707] Expression >44 55 *<
2013-08-17 23:11:23.705 pfall[1865:707] Expression accessed directly>44 55 *<
2013-08-17 23:11:23.707 pfall[1865:707] Expression Components >(
    44,
    55,
    "*"
)<
```

Defining Classes

The core concept of object-orientation is a class. A class definition in Objective-C comprises two parts:

✔ Its *interface,* which simply describes its components (that is, its methods and attributes)

The interface file for Objective-C doesn't declare a Java or C# type interface. Instead, it lists the methods and member variables of an Objective-C class.

✔ Its *implementation,* which contains the actual code that makes up the class

For example, the interface for the `PostfixCalculator` class is

```
@interface PostfixCalculator:NSObject
{
    NSString* expression;
    StackOfInteger* calculatorStack;

}

-(id)    initWithExpression: (NSString *) postFixExpression;
-(int)    calculate;
-(NSString*) getExpression;

@end
```

Consistent with the definition of this class in the previous section, the interface for `PostfixCalculator` states that this class has the following:

✔ Three methods:
- `initWithExpression`
- `calculate`
- `getExpression`

✔ Two member variables:
- An expression that is an `NSString` object (or more correctly, a pointer to an `NSString` object)
- A `calculatorStack`, which is a `StackOfInteger` object

Here is the interface for `StackOfInteger`:

```
@interface StackOfInteger:NSObject
{
    NSMutableArray* elements;
    int last;

}
    -(BOOL) isEmpty;
    -(void) push: (int) n;
    -(int) pop;
@end
```

This class has two instance variables:

- ✔ An array named `elements` (that stores the elements of the stack)
- ✔ An integer named `last`

The class also has three methods: `isEmpty`, `push`, and `pop`.

As you can see, the interface directive is also where the name of the class is specified along with its superclass, if any. So, in abstract, an interface specification looks like this:

```
@interface <Class name> : <Superclass>
{
     Definitions of instance variables ...
}
     Methods declarations ...
@end
```

In the `StackOfInteger` example, the name of the class is `StackOfInteger`, and it inherits from a class called `NSObject` (which is now the standard root class in iOS).

As you can also see from the two examples and the abstract definition, the interface specification of a class has two parts:

- ✔ One where the instance variables are defined
- ✔ Another where the methods are declared, enclosed inside the `@interface` directive

You find more about directives in the next section.

The root class

The root is the class at the topmost level of an inheritance (or class) hierarchy. It doesn't inherit from any other class.

A root class provides a core set of functionality in all classes below it. For example, the most frequently used root class in the iOS framework is `NSObject`.

Through `NSObject`, objects inherit an interface to the iOS runtime system, which allows them to be managed by the runtime system — for example, for memory management.

Incidentally, Objective-C has a root class named `Object`. This root class is rarely (if ever) used in iOS app development because it doesn't provide any of the iOS-required capability needed by all classes in an iOS app.

Declaring instance variables

The instance variables are created for each instance (in other words, each instance gets a copy of these variables).

In the `PostfixCalculator` class, the instance variables are

- `expression`, which is (a pointer to) an `NSString` object
- `calculatorStack`, which is (also a pointer) to a `StackOfInteger` object

The *scope* of a variable defines where it can be used. There are four options:

- `protected`: Instance variables are visible and can be directly referred to (that is, used) in all instance methods of a class and any subclasses.

  `protected` is the default scope.

- `private`: These variables are used only in the class that defined them.

- `public`: These variables are visible to and can be used in any other class or method.

- `package`: These variables are accessible only within the library in which they're defined.

Take a look at an example from `PostfixCalculator`:

```
@interface PostfixCalculator:NSObject
{
    @public NSString* expression;
    @private StackOfInteger* calculatorStack;
}
    <Methods ...>
@end
```

Here, `expression` is declared as a `public` instance variable, whereas `calculatorStack` is declared as `private`.

Scopes other than `protected` aren't used very frequently in Objective-C programs, partly because most folks don't really understand them. I recommend consistently following one of two strategies:

- Leave every variable as `protected`, and write accessor methods for those variables you want to make visible outside the class hierarchy.

✔ To control access even more:

- Explicitly declare variables as `private`.

- Provide accessor methods for those variables you want to make accessible outside the class.

If at all possible, stay away from annotating variables as `public` and `package`.

Incidentally, to access an instance variable in `public` scope, you use the pointer to member operator (aka the arrow operator `->`). Say that the variable `expression` in the `PostfixCalculator` interface is declared as follows:

```
@public NSString* expression;
```

You access it like this:

```
myExpression = myCalculator->expression;
```

On the other hand, if the variable is declared as `private` (or the default of `protected`), you have to use an accessor method to get its value, as shown here:

```
NSString * myExpression = [myCalculator getExpression];
```

Some Objective-C compilers, such as the current gcc compiler on the Mac, don't yet enforce `private` scope. Instead, they only generate a warning if you use a variable declared as `private` outside the class in which it's declared. The warning is similar to the following:

```
warning: instance variable ... is @private; this will be a hard error in the
future.
```

On the other hand, the compiler inside Xcode does the right thing and says: `Instance variable ... is private.`

Declaring methods

All the *public* methods of the class are declared in the methods declaration section in the interface file, using the following format:

```
<-/+> <return type> <method name>: <list of parameters>
```

The initial – indicates that the method is an instance method. A + indicates that the method is a class method. Each parameter definition in the list of parameters looks like this:

```
<Parameter Label>:<Parameter Type> <Parameter Name>
```

Once again, look at the method in the interface specification for StackOfInteger:

```
@interface StackOfInteger:NSObject
{
    <Instance variables ...?
}
    -(BOOL) isEmpty;
    -(void) push :(int) n;
    -(void) push2 :(int) intValue1 another:(int) intValue2;
    -(int) pop;
@end
```

Note that for the first parameter — or if there's only one parameter — the label is *not* provided. This is an example of a method in StackOfInteger (with two parameters):

```
    -(void) push2: (int) intValue1 another:(int) intValue2;
```

This kind of declaration may look bizarre to anyone who is more familiar with other languages, such as Java or C++. However, there is a method (no pun intended) behind this madness. The labels make the method invocation more readable. For example, [anArray insertObject:anObject atIndex:5] is more readable than [myArray insertObject:anObject :5], where the meaning of the second parameter isn't readily clear. Therefore, in the postfixall program

```
push2 :5 another:6;
```

is a little more understandable than

```
push2 :5 :6;
```

although both mean exactly the same thing.

Only public methods need to be declared in the interface file. Your program can contain private methods and C functions, as well. These don't have to be declared in the interface file.

Note that the method CreateWithExpression is a class method that you can use in place of initWithExpression to create an instance of a PostfixCalculator already pre-initialized with a postfix expression.

Note that class methods aren't the same as static functions that you might declare within your file. Class methods can be inherited and overridden by subclasses. Static methods can't.

Interestingly, instance variables at the class level don't exist in Objective-C. However, they can be simulated. For an example of how to do so, go to www. dummies.com/go/iosprogramminglinks and check out the link labeled Instance Variables at a Class Level.

You can't have two methods with the same name but a different number, or even a different order of parameters. In other words, method overloading isn't possible, which isn't like most of the common OO languages such as C++ and Java.

Using forward references

At times, you may want to refer to a class (say A) in another class (say B) simply to declare an instance variable of the first class in the second class. One way to so is to include the interface file for A in the interface file for B. However, this may result in circular dependencies if A and B have member variables of each other's class. That is, an instance of A has a member variable that is an instance of B, and vice versa.

To get around these circular dependencies and also to simplify the use of one class in another, Objective-C provides what is known as a *forward* reference via a @class directive.

The @class directive sets up a forward reference to another class. Within the interface of PostfixCalculator (shown next), you see an example of a forward reference. The @class directive informs the compiler that the word StackOfInterface is the name of a class. So when the declaration of calculatorStack is compiled, the Objective-C compiler knows that this declaration is a valid declaration and also how to allocate memory for it.

This works because, when the compiler encounters a variable declaration, in order to allocate memory for an object-valued variable, it just needs to know that the variable is (a pointer to) an object of a class. The compiler doesn't need to know details such as how the class's methods are defined.

```
//------- @interface section -------

@class StackOfInteger; // forward declaration

@interface PostfixCalculator:NSObject
{
    @public NSString* expression;
    @protected StackOfInteger* calculatorStack;
}
    ... Methods ...
@end
```

Implementing classes

You implement the class by using an implementation specification bracketed by the @implementation directive, as shown here:

```
@implementation <Class Name>;
...
    <Implementation of methods and other code>
...
@end
```

This is the implementation for the StackOfInteger class:

```
@implementation StackOfInteger;

- (id) init{
    self = [super init];
    last = -1;
    elements = [[NSMutableArray alloc] init];
    return self;
}

- (BOOL) isEmpty{
    return (last == -1);
}

- (void) push: (int) intValue{
    NSNumber* intObject = [NSNumber numberWithInt:intValue];
    [elements addObject:intObject];
    last++;
}

- (void) push2: (int) intValue1 another:(int) intValue2 {
    NSNumber* intObject = [NSNumber numberWithInt:intValue1];
    [elements addObject:intObject];
    intObject = [NSNumber numberWithInt:intValue2];
    [elements addObject:intObject];
    last+=2;
}

- (int) pop{
    NSNumber* element = (NSNumber *) [elements objectAtIndex:last];
    last--;
    int intValue = [element intValue];
    [elements removeLastObject];
    return intValue;
}

@end
```

As you can see, the implementation of a class consists of the implementation of its methods. The preceding listing gives you a good idea about what a method implementation is and what a class's overall implementation specification looks like.

Using Classes, Objects, Methods, and Variables

Now that you know how to define classes, it's time to use them in a program to invoke methods on classes and objects and create objects from classes. I also show you how to take the other steps required to create a working program.

For this section, continue to follow the example in the file PostfixAll.m.

Invoking methods

Everything happens through method invocation, starting with creating instances of objects.

In the previous section, I said there are two kinds of methods: class methods and instance methods. In Objective-C, methods are invoked by sending a message to a receiver, where the receiver is a class for a class method and an object for an instance method.

Therefore, the general structure of a message for invoking a class method is

```
[<Name of class> <Name of class Method>:<List of actual parameter values>]
```

Now, look at the main function in the file PostfixAll.m. You see an assignment statement as follows:

```
PostfixCalculator* myCalculator =
    [PostfixCalculator CreateWithExpression:@"44 55 *"];
```

The right side of this statement sends the message, which invokes the CreateWithExpression method of the PostfixCalculator class, with a single parameter "44 55 *".

Note how this syntax for a message send is different from the equivalent Java or C++ syntax for a method call, which would look like this:

```
PostfixCalculator* myCalculator =
    PostfixCalculator->CreateWithExpression(@"44 55 *");
```

An invocation message of an instance method is similar:

```
[<Instance> <Name of instance Method>:<List of actual parameter values>]
```

Several invocations of instance methods are in the sample program. For example, the following message invokes the push method of the calculatorStack instance variable within the calculate method of a PostfixCalculator instance:

```
[calculatorStack push:result]
```

Sending a message with multiple parameters is also straightforward. Here is an example where two numbers are pushed on a StackOfInteger:

```
[myStack push2:25 another:255];
```

Creating objects

The next few sections describe how to instantiate objects and use them in various situations.

The alloc-init pattern

The act of creating an object from a class is known as *instantiation*. Usually, you create an instance by sending an alloc message to its class (which, as you've probably guessed, causes the alloc method of the class to be invoked). However, that isn't enough. Unlike other OO languages, Objective-C exposes memory allocation for objects and initialization as two separate steps, mainly so you can provide your own custom initializations. Consequently, you must also initialize the created instance by sending it an initialize method by doing something like this:

```
(SomeClass *) someObject = [[SomeClass alloc] <initialize method>];
```

Every class has a standard initialize method called init. In the main function of the sample program, you see a new instance of the StackOfInteger class being created as follows:

```
StackOfInteger *myStack = [[StackOfInteger alloc] init];
```

The init method is just the standard initialize method that exists for every class. A class can have additional initialize methods. For example, the PostfixCalculator class has a custom initializer called initWithExpression, which you can use as shown here (again, this statement is in the main function of the sample program):

```
PostfixCalculator *myCalculatorWithInit =
    [[PostfixCalculator alloc] initWithExpression:@"44 55 *"];
```

Here is the complete `initWithExpression` method of the
`PostfixCalculator` class:

```
- (id) initWithExpression: (NSString *) postFixExpression{
    calculatorStack = [[StackOfInteger alloc] init];
    expression = postFixExpression;
    return (id) self;
}
```

The id data type

The return type of the `initWithExpression` method is `id`. This type can
represent an object of *any* class. Every initialize method *must* return an object
of this type, as shown in the preceding method.

The `id` data type is already a pointer type. You don't have to make it a pointer
by adding a `*`, as you must do with other types such as `NSString`.

You may wonder why Objective-C provides an `id` data type rather than
return the root object (that is, `NSObject*`). It does so because `NSObject` is
actually not the base class for all Objective-C classes.

Class methods

You may also be required to instantiate an object via a class method. Such
methods are known as *factory* methods. Here is an example of a factory
method:

```
PostfixCalculator *myCalculator =
    [PostfixCalculator CreateWithExpression:@"44 55 *"];
```

Directives

Objective-C has implicit ways that certain standard objects are created. For
example, this statement creates an object of the class `NSString` from a C
string:

```
NSString* aStringObject = @"This is a C String";
```

The nil value

All Objective-C variables that hold objects are actually pointer variables.
They hold the *address* of an object in memory. If a variable doesn't point to
an object (that is, if the variable itself is uninitialized), the variable can be set
to a value called `nil`, which is a special object value signifying a nonexistent
object.

Using all the language features

Objective-C comes with all kinds of built-in, out-of-the-box capabilities. For example, you can freely use C within Objective-C and thereby use all the capabilities that C has. Methods can to refer to the object in which they exist. There are standard data structures for storing collections of objects. There are language extensions to language extensions that enforce OO concepts within your program. There are even to ways to introspect (that is, look inside) your classes and objects to find out useful things about them.

All of these built-in capabilities are there to make your OO programming life easier. But, more importantly, you need these capabilities to actually write a complete Objective-C program.

Using C in Objective C

As I mentioned earlier, Objective-C was designed as a set of object-oriented extensions to C, rather than as a completely new language. In fact, you must use C statements in your Objective-C program, particularly for the control flow of the program.

Although I don't cover all of C in this book, here are a few essential interactions between C and Objective-C:

✔ A few new scalar C data types were defined specifically for Objective-C. One is the BOOL, which is defined along with its legal values as shown here:

```
typedef signed char       BOOL;
#define YES              (BOOL)1
#define NO               (BOOL)0
```

✔ Control flow in Objective-C is also done via C. So, as with a C program, every Objective-C program has a main function that starts execution.

As with C, this main function must exist in one and only one place within the Objective-C program.

You can find an example of the main function in the sample program. Snippets are shown here, starting with the name and arguments:

```
int main (int argc, char *argv[])
{
    // Illustrating the implicit creation of an object using a
        directive

    NSString* aStringObject = @"This is a C String";
    NSLog(@"Printing aStringObject>%@<", aStringObject);
    ...
    /////////////// Working with StackOfInteger
        /////////////////////////////
```

```
    printf("Working with Stacks of integers\n");
        ...
    printf("Done working with Stacks of integers\n");

    ///////////// Working with Postfix calculators
            ////////////////////////

    printf("Working with Postfix calculators\n");

    // Creating a Postfix Calculator using the alloc and a custom init
        method
    ...
    return 0;
}
```

✔ `if` statements in Objective-C look just like they do in C, although you can embed Objective-C method calls in the condition, as shown here (taken from the calculate method of the class `PostfixCalculator`):

```
if([expressionElement isEqualToString:@ADD]){
    ...
}
```

✔ Loops are written in C. Here is a `while` loop in the `calculate` method:

```
while (done == NO){
    NSString* expressionElement = [expressionComponents
        objectAtIndex:k];
    NSLog(@"Expression Element >%@<", expressionElement);
    if([expressionElement isEqualToString:@ADD]){
        ...
    } else if([expressionElement isEqualToString:@SUB]){
        ...
    } else if([expressionElement isEqualToString:@DIV]){
        ...
    } else if([expressionElement isEqualToString:@MUL]){
        ...
    } else {
        ...
    }
    ...
    k++;
    if ( k == [expressionComponents count]) done = YES;
}
```

Here I restructured the same loop as a `do-while` loop to show how you can embed Objective-C method calls in the `loop` condition:

```
do{
    NSString* expressionElement = [expressionComponents
        objectAtIndex:k];
```

```
NSLog(@"Expression Element >%@<", expressionElement);
if([expressionElement isEqualToString:@ADD]){
    ...
} else if([expressionElement isEqualToString:@SUB]){
    ...
} else if([expressionElement isEqualToString:@DIV]){
    ...
} else if([expressionElement isEqualToString:@MUL]){
    ...
} else {
    ...
}
...
k++;
} while (k < [expressionComponents count])
```

✔ Most of the input and output capabilities (such as opening, reading, and writing files) in Objective-C come from C.

Objective-C, via the Foundation framework, does provide a useful function called NSLog that often is used for logging Objective-C objects as well as C data types, as shown here:

```
NSLog(@"Printing aStringObject>%@<", aStringObject);
```

And:

```
NSLog (@"%d", result);
```

✔ Because your code is a mix of Objective-C and C, often it will have to translate from Objective-C objects to C data structures, and vice versa. Objective-C classes give you convenient ways for doing so.

In particular, basic translation capabilities from scalar types such as strings and integers to and from objects exist in the Foundation framework, which I explain later in this chapter.

Most of an Objective-C program is indeed C. However, it's the Objective-C extensions to C that allow you to take advantage of object-orientation by creating classes, using objects, and invoking methods.

Object keywords

Objective-C provides several keywords for referring to certain key objects within your method code.

self

Within an instance method, often you must refer to the specific instance within whose context this method is being executed. You do so through the variable self, which is an implicit reference (you don't need to set it to a value because the Objective-C runtime does that for you) to this owning instance.

The following is from the example program that uses `self` from the `initWithExpression` initializer in the class `PostfixCalculator`:

```
- (id) initWithExpression: (NSString *) postFixExpression{
    calculatorStack = [[StackOfInteger alloc] init];
    expression = postFixExpression;
    return self;
}
```

Here `self` returns the newly initialized `PostfixCalculator` object.

A method can also use `self` to refer to an instance variable in a clear-cut way, as in the `pop` method of `StackOfInteger` shown here:

```
- (int) pop{
    NSNumber* element =
        (NSNumber *) [self->elements objectAtIndex:(self->last)];
    self->last--;
    int intValue = [element intValue];
    [self->elements removeLastObject];
    return intValue;
}
```

super

When a subclass is created, several of its methods are typically reimplemented in order to provide the subclass with specific functionality. These reimplemented methods override the methods provided by its superclass. However, a reimplemented method may still want to use the implementations of the overridden methods in its current class's superclass. Such a method can use an overridden method in the superclass using the variable `super`.

The `super` variable acts as a pointer to an implicit object whose type is the superclass of the current object's class. The following example uses `super` (from the `init` method of the `StackOfInteger` class):

```
- (id) init{
    self = [super init];
    last = -1;
    elements = [[NSMutableArray alloc] init];
    return self;
}
```

cmd

You can use the `_cmd` keyword to refer to the method being run from within the method itself.

Here is an example, from the same push method of StackOfInteger, where _cmd logs entries and exits from the method:

```
- (void) push: (int) intValue{
    NSLog(@"Entering method >%@<", NSStringFromSelector(_cmd));
    ...
    NSLog(@"Leaving method >%@<", NSStringFromSelector(_cmd));
}
```

Note the use of the NSStringFromSelector method to get the string name of a method.

Objective-C Foundation framework

An Objective-C installation comes with a standard library (or in Objective-C terminology, a *framework*) known as the Foundation framework. This library provides a grab bag of utility classes that round out Objective-C, which makes it useful as a general-purpose programming language. Apple then builds on this by providing additional frameworks, such as Cocoa Touch, to give you iOS–specific capability.

I describe a few of the important classes that are available through this framework below:

✔ You use NSArray and NSMutableArray to provide arrays, or ordered collections, of objects. You use NSArray to work with static arrays, and you use NSMutableArray when you need arrays that you can change.

The example in this chapter implements a stack using NSMutableArray, as you can see from the declaration of the instance variables in StackOfInteger shown here:

```
@interface StackOfInteger:NSObject
{
    ...
    NSMutableArray* elements;
    ...
}
```

This array is then manipulated inside the push and pop methods. The following code is taken from these methods. It shows how to add an object to the array by using the method addobject; how to get access to the object at a specific location in the array by using the method objectAtIndex; and how to remove the last object in the array by using removeLastObject.

```
- (void) push: (int) intValue{
    NSLog(@"Entering method >%@<", NSStringFromSelector(_cmd));
    NSNumber* intObject = [NSNumber numberWithInt:intValue];
    [elements addObject:intObject];
```

```
    self->last++;
    NSLog(@"Leaving method >%@<", NSStringFromSelector(_cmd));
}
- (int) pop{
    NSNumber* element = (NSNumber *) [self->elements
            objectAtIndex:(self->last)];
    self->last--;
    int intValue = [element intValue];
    [self->elements removeLastObject];
    return intValue;
}
```

✔ `NSString` and `NSMutableString` provide the interface for immutable strings (a string that's defined when it's created and which subsequently can't be changed) and mutable strings, respectively.

`NSString` is used in several places in the sample program. For example, see the following snippet in the `calculate` method of the `PostfixCalculator` class:

```
NSString* expressionElement = [expressionComponents objectAtIndex:k];
```

It's often necessary to convert C strings to `NSString` objects, as shown here:

```
NSString* aStringObject = @"This is a C String";
```

The `@` sign is known as a *directive*. In this case, the directive is short-hand for invoking a method that converts the literal string (enclosed in quotes) to the `NSString` object. I discuss directives in the section on compiler directives later in this chapter.

✔ You use `NSNumber` to represent object versions of scalar numeric types, such as `signed` or `unsigned char`, `short int`, `int`, `long int`, `long long int`, `float`, `double`, or as a `BOOL`; and to convert back and forth from C scalar types to Objective-C objects.

The following is from the `PostfixCalculator` example, from the `push` method of `StackOfInteger`:

```
NSNumber* intObject = [NSNumber numberWithInt:intValue];
```

The `NSNumber` class also defines a `compare` method to determine the ordering of two `NSNumber` objects.

✔ `NSLog` logs a message to the Apple System Log facility. `NSLog` isn't available within a class but as part of a set of directly callable functions provided as part of the Foundations library. See the link labeled Foundation Framework Reference in the web resources for this book (www.dummies.com/go/iosprogramminglinks) for more details about the Foundations framework.

For complete details from Apple on the functions in the Foundation framework, check the link labeled Foundations Framework Functions in the web resources for this book here (`www.dummies.com/go/iosprogramminglinks`). This page also shows a diagram with the complete class hierarchy within the Foundations framework.

Compiler directives

Within an Objective-C program, you find keywords and expressions that begin with @. These are compiler directives that are translated at compile time to executable code. You've already seen the `@interface` directive, which marks the beginning of the interface section of a class definition; the `@implementation` directive, which marks the start of the implementation of a class; and the `@end` directive, which you use to mark the ends of these sections.

Earlier in this chapter, you also saw the `@class` directive that allows the use of a class without knowing its complete interface. The `@private`, `@public`, `@package`, and `@protected` directives govern the visibility of instance variables. As I cover other capabilities of Objective-C, I'll show you additional directives that do other things, such as handle exceptions:

@autoreleasepool	@property
@catch()	@protected
@class	@protocol
@dynamic	@protocol()
@encode	@public
@end	@required
@finally	@selector()
@implementation	@"*string*"
@interface	@synchronized()
@optional	@synthesize
@package	@throw
@private	@try

Properties and property attributes

To make instance variables available outside their defining class in a controlled manner, the best practice is to write accessor methods (also called *getters* and *setters*). Properties provide a declarative way to do so through use of the property directives `@property` and `@synthesize`.

By declarative way, I mean a way to make your program do something without you writing any code. Code is written, but by the compiler (that automatically generates the accessor methods), not by you.

An example of a property from the StackOfInteger class follows next. The idea is to allow a user of this class to read the stack pointer without exposing the last variable and without writing any new methods.

To begin, the property must be declared in the interface of the StackOfInteger class. The following snippet shows how to do so using the @property compiler directive:

```
@interface StackOfInteger:NSObject
{
    @protected // This is the default
    NSMutableArray* elements;
    @private int last;
}
    @property (readonly, atomic) int stackPointer;
    ... other StackOfInteger methods
@end
```

Note that, even though the term *property* appears to be closer in meaning to a variable than to a method, the property definition goes in the section where methods are defined, not where the instance variables are defined. Note also that this property has two attributes: atomic and readonly. I discuss property attributes shortly, but for now, just know that atomic means that safe concurrent access is provided and readonly means that this property can be read but not modified.

Next, you need to synthesize the property using the @synthesize directive, which means that either a new instance variable must be generated for the property or an existing instance variable must be linked to it. Here's how you generate a new instance variable named the same as the stackPointer property:

```
@synthesize stackPointer;
```

In my example, I linked the stackPointer property to the instance variable last. The synthesize directive looks like this:

```
@synthesize stackPointer=last;
```

The property is now ready to use.

You can use the property two ways, as shown in the `main` function of the example:

- ✔ You can use an accessor method:

```
printf("Count of elements %d\n", [myStack stackPointer]);
```

- ✔ Or you can use dot notation to do the same thing, as shown here:

```
printf("Count of elements using dot notation %d\n",
    myStack.stackPointer);
```

The so-called dot notation is just shorthand for a method call. Rather than using the square braces, `[instance method]` for example, simply write `instance.method`. I don't like dot notation; to me it adds one more element to an already offbeat syntax, but it's your call (no pun intended).

Note that the names of the accessor (getters and setters) follow a naming convention. The getter method is the name of the property. So, for the property `stackPointer`, the getter method is also `stackPointer`. The setter method is the name of the property in camel case prefixed by the string `set` — the name of the setter method for `stackPointer` is `setStackPointer`.

Use *camel case spelling* (an uppercase letter in the middle of a term) when spelling these methods. Therefore, the *S* in the word stack is uppercase in the name of the setter method, even though it's not capitalized in the name of the property. Note that the setter method is not generated for this property because it is read-only.

It's time to move on to the attributes of properties. They're all in the following list along with what they do:

- ✔ `nonatomic`: By default, the accessor methods generated for properties include locking to make them safe for concurrent access by multi-threaded programs. Specifically, the default behavior is atomic. If you use the attribute `nonatomic`, no locking is used.

  There isn't an attribute named `atomic` (atomic operation is assumed by the lack of the `nonatomic` attribute).

- ✔ `readwrite`: If you use this property, it can be written to as well as read. Both a getter and a setter are made available upon synthesis.

- ✔ `readonly`: The compiler makes only a getter available.

Categories

Interestingly, Objective-C allows you to add your own methods to *existing* classes, even those classes that you have not written. Adding additional methods to a class is useful in a situation where the new behavior is used only in certain situations. As an example, you might find that a particular application (say, a palindrome checker) needs to reverse pretty much any string it is dealing with! It might make your program overly complicated to create your own subclass of NSString with the additional reverse method. Rather, you might find it much more convenient to add the new behavior to the original class. Wouldn't it be nice if you could add a reverse method to NSString itself!

Note you can't modify the original interface or implementation NSString because it is a framework class and you don't have the source code. However, you can extend the NSString class (or any other class) by defining a new category. In the file PostfixAll.m you will see that the NSString class has been extended with a method named reverse as follows:

```
@interface NSString (ReversibleString)
    - (NSString *)reverse;
@end
```

As you can see, defining a category is very similar to defining an interface for a class. In fact, providing an implementation for the methods of a category is also very similar to providing the implementation for a class in that the methods are enclosed in an @implementation block. You can see the implementation block for the category (that includes the code for the method reverse) below (in the file PostfixAll.m):

```
@implementation NSString (ReversibleString)

    - (NSString *)reverse {
        NSMutableString *reversedString = [[NSMutableString alloc] init];
        int stringLength = self.length;
        for (int i=stringLength-1; i >=0; i--){
            NSString *oneCharString =
                [self substringWithRange:NSMakeRange(i, 1)];
            [reversedString appendString:oneCharString];
        }
        return reversedString;
    }
@end
```

Finally, the *use* of a method defined in a category is no different from the use of any other method, as can be seen from the following code snippet taken from the main function of PostfixAll.m:

```
NSLog(@"Printing reversed string>%@<", [aStringObject reverse]);
```

For more information on categories, go to www.dummies.com/go/iosprogramminglinks, and in the web resources for this chapter, check out the Categories link.

Protocols

A protocol defines sets of methods that can be implemented by any class.

Think of protocols as defining interfaces that classes have to implement.

Protocols are often used to specify the interface for delegate objects. With the protocol feature, you can avoid having to force subclassing in order to create polymorphic classes. Objective-C (unlike C++) doesn't allow a class to have multiple superclasses. Protocols therefore are an essential feature in Objective-C because it doesn't allow multiple inheritance.

When a class implements the methods in a protocol, the class is said to *conform* to the protocol.

The definition of a protocol is similar to the definition of an interface for a class. However, a protocol doesn't have a parent class or instance variables. Here's an example of a protocol definition (`Printable`) from the postfix calculator program:

```
@protocol Printable
    -(void) printMe; // I can leave out @required, since it is the default
    @optional -(NSString*) printMeToString;
@end
```

With the arrival (and indeed with great fanfare) of Objective-C 2.0, protocol methods can be either required (the default) or optional. So I threw those compiler directives into the mix here, as well.

Here is the declaration of the `StackOfInteger` stating that it will implement the protocol:

```
@interface StackOfInteger:NSObject <Printable>
    ...
@end
```

Here is the implementation of the protocol in the `StackOfInteger` class:

```
@implementation StackOfInteger;
    ... Other StackOfInteger methods ...

/////////// Methods to implement the Printable protocol ////////////

- (void) printMe{
    int k, stackCount = [elements count];
    NSLog (@"Stack->Last >%d< \n", self->last);
    for(k=0; k<stackCount; k++) {
        NSLog (@"Element at [%d] = >%@<\n", k, [elements objectAtIndex:k]);
    }
}
@end
```

I didn't implement the `printMeToString` method because it's optional.

A program can test whether an object conforms to a protocol. The following code includes examples of this test (taken from the main program of the sample):

```
printf("Testing conformance to protocols\n");
if ([myStack conformsToProtocol:@protocol(Printable)]) {
    printf("Using protocol methods\n");
    [myStack printMe];
} else {
    NSLog(@"Object does not conform to protocol %@\n",
          @protocol(Printable));
}

id someObject = [[PostfixCalculator alloc] initWithExpression:@"44 55 *"];
if (![someObject conformsToProtocol:@protocol(Printable)]) {
    NSLog(@"Object does not conform to protocol");
}
```

Because the `myStack` object conforms to the protocol, its `printMe` and `printMeToString` methods are called. Since `someObject` (which is type `id` to make the example more meaningful) doesn't conform to the `Printable` protocol, the test for conformity fails.

You can also test for the existence of an optional method using the method `respondsToSelector`.

You can make a class adopt a protocol simply by implementing the methods defined by that protocol. That is, you don't have to declare the protocol in its interface. However, even though the class implements the protocols methods, it *will not* be conforming to the protocol and will fail the preceding conformance test.

Using introspection and dynamic invocation

Introspection refers to facilities in a programming language to examine the structure and other details of an object and its class at runtime. Such details can include

- ✔ An object's inheritance tree
- ✔ Whether it conforms to a specific protocol
- ✔ Whether it responds to a certain message

When you know what an object is made of, you can programmatically construct messages to send to it, which makes your program much more dynamic.

Getting the class of an object

You can get the class of an object at runtime. In fact, Objective-C treats classes as first-class objects. Every class object points to a data structure in memory, has a superclass (known as a *metaclass*), and can respond to messages that invoke methods.

 When you call a class method, you're really sending a message to the object of the class.

You can get a reference to the class object for the class by sending the class a `class` message (Boy! Was that confusing to write.), and you get the superclass of a class by sending the object a `superclass` message. For example, you can print the class and the superclass of an object, such as a `StackOfInteger` object, as follows:

```
StackOfInteger *aStack = [[StackOfInteger alloc] init];
NSLog(@"Class is %@, and super is %@.",[aStack class],[aStack superclass]);
```

Dynamically calling methods

You can then call a method on a class object like this:

```
Class postfixCalculatorClass = [someObject class];
[postfixCalculatorClass performSelector:@selector(printClassDescription)];
```

Two items need to be explained here. First, the `@selector` is a *compile*-time directive and returns a pointer to the method `printClass`. Second, you can then use `performSelector` to actually call that method.

In the previous example, the method name was translated to a pointer to the method at compile time. You can also call an instance method on an object by using the string name of a method, at runtime, as follows:

```
SEL printClassDescriptionSEL =
            NSSelectorFromString(@"printClassDescription");
[postfixCalculatorClass performSelector:printClassDescriptionSEL];
```

 In this example, you can use the SEL type (also known as a selector in Objective-C parlance, and so the SEL) to hold the internal representation of a method.

Checking the specification of an object

Once you have a handle to a class object, you can inspect it at runtime using the introspection functions provided in Objective-C. For example, you can test this object to see what kind it is. You can inspect it to see if it has a certain method or a certain attribute, and so on. Table 3-2 shows all the methods for testing the structure and capabilities of a class object and for performing actions on it.

Table 3-2	Introspection Methods for a Class
Method	*Question or Action*
`-(BOOL) isKindOf: class-object`	Is the object a member or descendant of a class?
`-(BOOL) isMemberOf: class-object`	Is the object a member of a class?
`-(BOOL) respondsTo: selector`	Can the object respond to a method?
`+(BOOL) instancesRespondTo: selector`	Can instances of the class respond to a message?
`-(id) perform: selector`	Apply the method specified by selector.
`+(BOOL) conformsToProtocol: (Protocol *) aProtocol`	YES if the receiver conforms to the protocol aProtocol; otherwise, NO.

For more details on introspection and how to use it, go to `www.dummies.com/go/iosprogramminglinks` and check out the Apple iOS Runtime Reference at the link labeled iOS Runtime Reference and the Apple Developer Objective-C Runtime Programming Guide at the link labeled Runtime Programming Guide.

Managing Memory

The easiest way to manage memory is to let the Objective-C runtime deal with it using a system called *automatic reference counting* (ARC) — please use it. (ARC has been available since 2011 in Xcode 4.2, or later.)

Internally, the ARC system uses the same reference counting system used for manual reference counting. However, to use ARC, you put your code in `@autoreleasepool` blocks like so:

```
@autoreleasepool{
... Your code ...
}
```

The *compiler* inserts appropriate memory-management method calls into the code so that anything created within this `@autoreleasepool` block is freed when the program exits from the block.

Manual memory management

When iOS was first introduced, you had to manually manage memory by keeping track of the lifecycle of the objects in your program. You did so by telling the Objective-C runtime system when to retain and when to release objects, using a scheme Apple called manual *retain-release,* which in turn used a technique known as *reference counting.* Although manually managing memory is certainly a nuisance, I explain it here because you'll see it in older iOS programs, so you may as well be prepared.

Here's what you do. First, you create a class that inherits from the root class `NSObject` in the Foundation framework. Your class then inherits three memory-management methods:

✔ `retain`

✔ `release`

✔ `autorelease`

These three methods all manipulate a *reference counter* in the object that essentially tells the runtime system how many places in your program (or other objects) want to maintain a reference to the object.

Here is how this reference count is managed by the iOS:

1. Every time `retain` is called on a target object, its reference count is increased by one.

   So, if five objects call `retain` on the target object, its reference count will be five (incidentally, when the object is allocated, `init` automatically increments the reference count).

2. As they stop needing the target object, the five objects will call `release` on the object. Each time `release` is called, the reference count of the target object is decremented (by one).

3. When the reference count becomes zero (that is, when the last object calls `release`), the object's memory is freed by the system.

The third method — `autorelease` — is called when an object you've created must be handed off to a thread and you want the thread to take care of freeing the object when the thread is done.

If you use ARC, you cannot use certain methods in your program, such as NSAllocateObject and NSDeallocateObject, which don't play well with ARC.

I chose not to include an example of using @autoreleasepool in this chapter because the standard GCC compiler on the Mac doesn't support ARC. However, you will see the use of @autoreleasepool within Xcode in Chapter 6.

For more information on memory management in general, go to www. dummies.com/go/iosprogramminglinks, and in the web resources for this chapter, check out the iOS Memory Management link. In the same set of resources, the link labeled Autorelease Pools explains more about that topic, and the link labeled Transitioning to ARC shows you how to transition to ARC from the old memory-management method.

Handling Exceptions

In Objective-C, exceptions deal with unexpected conditions in your program — for example:

- ✔ An alloc statement fails because your system runs out of memory.
- ✔ Bad input gets into your program causing (say) a divide-by-zero error.
- ✔ Your program erroneously tries to access an array with an index that's out of bounds.

Exceptions apply the OO principle of separation of concerns by decoupling the detection of error conditions from their handling. Exceptions also automate the propagation of an unexpected condition to the point where it's handled. As a result, your code isn't cluttered with exception-handling statements, which makes your code easier to write and maintain.

Objective-C extends C by providing four compiler directives for exception handling:

- ✔ @try defines an exception handling block (that is, code that could throw an exception).
- ✔ @catch() defines a block of code for handling the exception thrown in the @try block. The parameter of @catch is the exception object thrown; this is usually an NSException object.
- ✔ @finally defines a block of code that's executed whether or not an exception is thrown.
- ✔ @throw throws an exception — an NSException object or, more often, an object belonging to a subclass of NSException.

The following code shows how exceptions can be thrown, caught, and handled within a @try...@catch block.

```
@try {
        printf("I know this will fail\n");
        NSDictionary* emptyDictionary = [[NSDictionary alloc] init];
        NSException* anException =
            [NSException exceptionWithName:@"MyException" reason:@"Just for
                grins" userInfo:emptyDictionary];
        @throw anException;
}
@catch (NSException *exception) {
        NSLog(@"Exception caught with reason >%@<\n", exception);
}
```

Organizing Program Files

In the example program, I show you the interface specification as well as the implementation of the postfixAll class in one big file, with the main program thrown in for good measure. I do so for two reasons: I don't want to make you go through multiple files to understand the program. I want you to see the wrong way to do things before showing you a better way of organizing your source files that actually illustrates object-orientation principles. So here goes.

Go to the source code for this chapter and take a look at the files in the directory Postfix-Split. As shown in Figure 3-2, it contains the following files with relevant source code: NSString+Reversible.h, Printable.h, StackOfInteger.h, StackOfInteger.m, PostfixCalculator.h, PostfixCalculator.m, and main.m.

The files with the .h extension contain the Printable protocol and interface specifications for the classes StackOfInteger and PostfixCalculator. The files with the .m extension contain the implementations of these classes, as well as the main program (in main.m).

Here is the proper way to structure Objective-C files:

- Protocols, categories, and interfaces each in their own .h files
- Implementations in their own .m files

This structuring applies the object-oriented principle of separating the interface from implementation. If this structuring is followed, a program includes only the interface of the classes it needs, with the implementation of the classes hidden. This implements the OO principle of information hiding. Once you see OO, you'll see it everywhere.

```
rajiv-macbook-pro:Postfix-Split ramnath$ ls -l
total 72
-rw-r--r--@ 1 ramnath  staff   123 Jan 24 17:30 NSString+Reversible.h
-rw-r--r--@ 1 ramnath  staff   452 Jan 24 17:30 NSString+Reversible.m
-rw-r--r--@ 1 ramnath  staff   482 Aug 20 22:37 PostfixCalculator.h
-rw-r--r--  1 ramnath  staff  3226 Aug 20 22:47 PostfixCalculator.m
-rw-r--r--@ 1 ramnath  staff   198 Aug 20 22:42 Printable.h
-rw-r--r--@ 1 ramnath  staff   462 Jan 24 10:02 StackOfInteger.h
-rw-r--r--  1 ramnath  staff  1533 Aug 20 22:48 StackOfInteger.m
-rw-r--r--  1 ramnath  staff   277 Jan 24 17:35 build-commands.txt
-rw-r--r--  1 ramnath  staff  3883 Jan 24 17:33 main.m
rajiv-macbook-pro:Postfix-Split ramnath$ sh build-commands.txt
rajiv-macbook-pro:Postfix-Split ramnath$ ls -l
total 192
-rw-r--r--@ 1 ramnath  staff   123 Jan 24 17:30 NSString+Reversible.h
-rw-r--r--@ 1 ramnath  staff   452 Jan 24 17:30 NSString+Reversible.m
-rw-r--r--  1 ramnath  staff  2824 Jan 24 17:43 NSString+Reversible.o
-rw-r--r--  1 ramnath  staff   482 Aug 20 22:37 PostfixCalculator.h
-rw-r--r--  1 ramnath  staff  3226 Aug 20 22:47 PostfixCalculator.m
-rw-r--r--  1 ramnath  staff  9328 Jan 24 17:43 PostfixCalculator.o
-rw-r--r--@ 1 ramnath  staff   198 Aug 20 22:42 Printable.h
-rw-r--r--@ 1 ramnath  staff   462 Jan 24 10:02 StackOfInteger.h
-rw-r--r--  1 ramnath  staff  1533 Aug 20 22:48 StackOfInteger.m
-rw-r--r--  1 ramnath  staff  9512 Jan 24 17:43 StackOfInteger.o
-rw-r--r--  1 ramnath  staff   277 Jan 24 17:35 build-commands.txt
-rw-r--r--  1 ramnath  staff  3883 Jan 24 17:33 main.m
-rw-r--r--  1 ramnath  staff  8260 Jan 24 17:43 main.o
-rwxr-xr-x  1 ramnath  staff 19220 Jan 24 17:43 pfsplit
rajiv-macbook-pro:Postfix-Split ramnath$
```

Figure 3-2:
Files in the
sample
program.

In order to build the program, enter **sh build-commands.txt**. While you're
at it, take a look at this file. You'll see separate calls to the GCC compiler for
each .m file and a final call to link the object files together.

Analyzing Objective-C's Object-Orientation Capabilities

Now it's time to discuss Objective-C in terms of its object-orientation (OO).

As mentioned earlier in this chapter, Objective-C is really a set of extensions on C, so you can freely mix and match C and Objective-C. However,
Objective-C is a full-fledged object-oriented language. It supports the definition and use of classes, inheritance, attributes, methods, and instances.

In the sidebar "In the beginning," earlier in this chapter, I mentioned that
Objective-C derives a lot from Smalltalk. If you're an OO nut like me or end up
becoming one, you'll find it very worthwhile to spend a day or two research-
ing Smalltalk. Because everything in a Smalltalk program is an object, it
remains one of the first of the few pure object-oriented languages. You can find
out more about Smalltalk here: www.smalltalk.org.

Objective-C separates the definition of the interface of the class from its implementation, thereby promoting information hiding. This information hiding is even supported in the way you're expected (by convention) to structure Objective-C files. However, its information hiding isn't complete because you reveal a class's instance variables in the interface file, which is unlike, say, Java, where this information can be completely hidden. However, the properties extension to Objective-C tries to add another layer of abstraction to the language. The ability to have forward declaration of a class is also helpful in hiding information.

Thanks to its support of inheritance and protocols, and the `id` class, Objective-C supports polymorphism. However, Objective-C doesn't support operator overloading. Also, unlike C++, Objective-C doesn't allow multiple inheritance, which is actually a blessing in disguise because it makes class hierarchies in your program much easier to understand. Protocols can be used as an alternative way to achieve the same results. Objective-C doesn't have compile-time polymorphism (that is, *generics*), although Apple may add this capability in a later version.

Objective-C's support of polymorphism is more dynamic than how C++ or Java support polymorphism. Because Objective-C was developed very early in object-oriented technology, it's actually much more like Smalltalk than C++ or Java in that it does very little compile-time type checking. You can send a message to any type of object, and the compiler will, at most, issue a warning. If the object later turns out to have a method corresponding to the message, fine. If not, an exception is thrown.

Objective-C doesn't support abstract classes, but it does support something like abstract classes — that is, protocols.

Objective-C is almost as advanced as Java in its introspection capabilities, which allows you to look at an object and its class at runtime and inject all kinds of dynamic behavior, such as building a message on the fly and invoking it. That being said, Objective-C's introspection capabilities aren't quite as easy to use as those of Java or C#. But, hey, those languages came much later, and we knew more about language design.

Unlike C++, Java, or C#, no namespaces are in Objective-C. Naming conventions must be used to ensure that names of classes in applications and libraries don't clash.

At this point, allow me to discuss runtime support and capabilities of Objective-C. Objective-C applications are generally larger than similar C or C++ applications because dynamic typing doesn't allow methods to be inlined or removed (due to not being used). Because an Objective-C programmer has so much freedom to delegate, forward calls, build selectors on the fly, and pass them to the runtime system, you can't assume that it's safe to remove unused methods or inline method calls. This dynamism is also why certain runtime optimizations can't be applied to Objective-C programs, so they run slower than similar C++ or C programs.

Part II
Meeting the Methods and Platforms

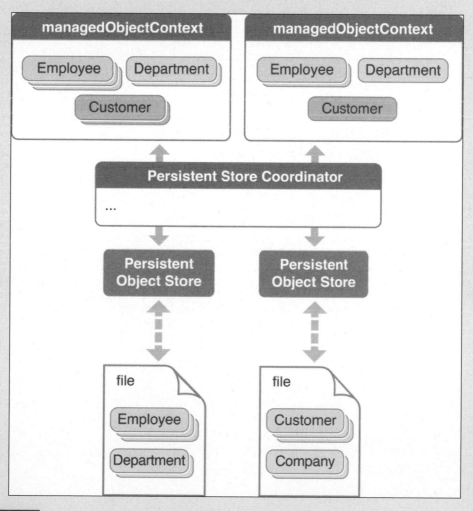

In this part . . .

- ✔ Applying basic design patterns
- ✔ Managing code with frameworks
- ✔ Working in Xcode
- ✔ Running the sample application
- ✔ Analyzing design principles in use
- ✔ Visit `www.dummies.com/extras/beginningiosprogramming` for great Dummies content online.

Chapter 4

Patterns and Frameworks

● ●

In This Chapter

▶ Capturing OO design principles with patterns

▶ Avoiding bad patterns

▶ Reusing and scaffolding for control flow

▶ Applying design patterns in frameworks

● ●

*O*ver time and after developers created many OO programs, the software development community built on these programs to create higher-level concepts and techniques. These techniques are called *patterns*.

About the same time, developers created software frameworks for specific platforms, such as the iOS framework. These frameworks provided libraries of useful functionality that an application developer, such as you, could use in his code. These frameworks also provided application templates that implemented typical flows of control in an application. Because the templates provided most of the generic code, for the most part, you only had to write your app-specific code. Finally, these frameworks used these patterns extensively.

Common Patterns of OO Design

Patterns adhere to the guiding principles of OO design: loose coupling and high cohesion. They use polymorphism by programming to an interface and by using delegation and delayed binding. As I describe the patterns in this chapter, you'll see how each pattern does all this.

The book, *Design Patterns: Elements of Reusable Object-Oriented Software*, written by the IBM "Gang of Four" (see upcoming sidebar, "Count to four!"), categorizes patterns three ways:

- ✔ *Creational patterns* capture typical ways objects collaborate to manage the lifecycle of a set of objects — that is, the way other objects create, read, update, and destroy these objects.

- ✔ *Structural patterns* capture typical ways a collection of objects are made to relate to each other when they're used to solve a particular problem.

- ✔ *Behavioral patterns capture* how related objects might interact in order to solve a particular problem.

All three of these patterns show up in the iOS framework.

Seeing basic design patterns

In this section I cover three basic patterns, one each for the three categories I mention in the previous section. These patterns are *Singleton, Façade,* and *Chain of Responsibility.* Singleton is a creational pattern, Façade is a structural pattern, and Chain of Responsibility is a behavioral pattern.

Controlling object creation using the Singleton pattern

A Singleton pattern is a creational design pattern. You use this pattern when you need one and only one instance of a class, and this instance is one that you need to access from several places in your program. In the Singleton

Count to four!

The 1994 book, *Design Patterns: Elements of Reusable Object-Oriented Software*, written by Erich Gamma, Richard Helm, Ralph Johnson, and John M. Vlissides (the "Gang of Four"), highly influenced the field of software design and became an important resource for learning object-oriented design. It captured common ways of designing classes and their *relationships* and *interactions* for solving common software design problems.

The idea was that software developers could look up a catalog of designs and say, "Aha! My current design problem looks pretty close to the design problem this pattern addresses," and then use the design pattern as a template for beginning their design.

The Gang of Four took pains to note that they didn't invent the patterns but were best practices they painstakingly discovered after designing many, many programs.

Close, but no cigar

You can solve the problem that Singleton addresses in ways other than using the Singleton pattern, though each introduces new problems:

✔ You can make the single instance a global variable.

However, giving uncontrolled access to a global variable isn't the greatest idea — some part of your program could inadvertently free it — plus doing so doesn't prevent the creation of additional instances.

✔ You can create an instance once and then pass it as a parameter to each and every called method.

However, this approach gives each method in your program a parameter unrelated to the functionality of the method. Also, this approach doesn't control instantiation — your program can still create multiple instances.

pattern, the class of the object is responsible for ensuring that only one instance is created. The class also is responsible for providing a way to access this single instance.

A typical example is a *logger* (an object that provides an interface that you can use to record the execution of a program). A logger can write to a file or, if it's an enterprise application deployed on a server, write to a socket and thereby stream the logged data to a remote monitoring program.

The following code snippet is a skeleton for the Singleton pattern. The first listing shows the header file:

```
#import <Foundation/Foundation.h>

@interface Singleton : NSObject{
    // Member variables
    ...
}
    +(Singleton*) CreateInstance;
    // Other operations
    ...
@end
```

As the header file indicates, `CreateInstance` is a class-level method. Also, `CreateInstance` returns an instance of the class. In fact, `CreateInstance` is intended to be a special method in this class in that it should be used exclusively for creating an instance of the class. The class can certainly have other operations of its choosing, but it must have at least one method like `CreateInstance` for creating instances.

Here is the implementation of the `CreateInstance` method along with a skeleton of the class:

```
#import "Singleton.h"

@implementation TTTSymbol
    static Singleton *singletonInstance = nil;

    +(Singleton *) CreateInstance{
        @synchronized([Singleton class]){
            if (singletonInstance == nil){
                singletonInstance = [[Singleton alloc] init];
            }
            return singletonInstance;
        }
        ...
    }

    // Other operations

@end
```

First, you can see that the class contains a static variable of its own type called `singletonInstance` that is initialized to `nil` upon declaration. The class may have other static and instance variables, but `singletonInstance` is special.

Here's what this special method does:

✔ When first called, `singletonInstance` is `nil`, so the `CreateInstance` method does the following, in the order shown:

  1. Creates a new instance.

  2. Assigns this instance to the variable `singletonInstance`.

  3. Returns this new instance.

✔ During subsequent calls to `CreateInstance`, `singletonInstance` is no longer `nil`, so no new instance is created. Instead, the instance created and saved during the first call is returned.

Voilà! Only one instance is created, and it's then reused forever.

This pattern has another feature: The `CreateInstance` method is enclosed within a `synchronized` block. This block locks the class and prevents access to it while the `CreateInstance` method is executing (and, for that matter, holds up `CreateInstance` until other currently executing methods of the class are done).

This `synchronized` block is needed because iOS programs are multithreaded, and more than one thread could be trying to create an instance of the Singleton. If several threads are allowed to proceed, more than one object could end up being created. The synchronized block limits access to the method to one thread at a time. As a result, the first thread getting through safely creates the instance, and subsequent threads receive the instance that's already created.

Now, analyze Singleton from an OO perspective. Note that by using the `CreateInstance` method, the Singleton pattern hides how the single instance is created and managed. This is an illustration of the OO principle of *information hiding*. Through its use of information hiding, the Singleton class is also loosely coupled to any class that uses Singleton. Note, however, that a class implementing the Singleton pattern needs to do two things: It must implement the domain methods of the class as well as the management of the single instance of this class. Consequently, a Singleton class isn't as cohesive as it could be.

You can find an iOS example that uses Singleton in Chapter 7.

Simplifying use of a set of objects using Façade

Good OO design usually results in many smaller, highly cohesive classes. This design makes each class more reusable and the set of classes more customizable; however, for client programs that don't need the reusability but simply want to use the objects in a standard way, having to deal with all the classes adds complexity. The Façade pattern provides a single, simplified interface for using the functionality provided.

Façades are often used for simplifying access to the facilities of a subsystem.

The next set of code uses the Façade pattern to draw a pie chart utilizing Circle, Line, and Point classes to represent the pies. (*Note:* I created these Circle, Line, and Point classes to illustrate Facades, so they aren't classes from the iOS or any other framework.)

The code begins with the following interface file of the `PieChart` class. The initializer `initWithViewAndSegments` sets the enclosing view of the pie chart, the center coordinates, the radius, the number of slices, and the proportion of each slice. There's also a `draw` method that draws the pie chart inside its enclosing view.

```
#import <Foundation/Foundation.h>

@interface PieChart : NSObject{
    // Member variables
    @private (UIView *) enclosingView;
    @private int radius;
    @private int numberOfSlices;
    @private float[] pieProportions;
}
    -(id) initWithViewAndSegments :(UIView *) enclosingView
                                  :(Point *) center
                                  :(int) radius
                                  :(int) numberOfSlices
                                  :float[] pieProportions;
    -(void) draw;

    // Other operations

@end
```

You can see how easy it is for a client program of the `PieChart` class to draw a pie chart. All the program has to do is initialize the chart using `initWithViewAndSegments` and then call `draw`.

Now compare the preceding use of a Façade to the implementation of the draw method (pseudocode shown here), which is what someone directly using `Circle` and `Line` objects to draw the pie chart would have to do:

```
@implementation PieChart
    ...

    -(void) draw{
        Circle *pieChartCircle =
            [[Circle alloc] initWithViewRadiusAndOrigin
                                                :enclosingView
                                                :radius :center];
            pieChartCircle.draw; // draw the circle
            for (int k = 0; k <= numberOfPies-1; k++){ // for each pie
                Point *endPoint; // end point of radius that bounds a pie
                float slopeOfLine;

                // Calculate slopeOfLine from pieProportions[k].
                // 100% => 360 degrees
                ...

                // Calculate endPoint of radial line from origin, slope
                // and length (= radius)
                ...

                // Draw the line
                Line *radialLine =
                    [[Line alloc] initWithCoordinates :enclosingView
                                                :center
                                                :endPoint];

                oneLine.draw;
            }
        }
    ...
```

To be thorough, I show the interfaces for `Circle`, `Line`, and `Point` here:

```
@interface Circle : NSObject{
    // Member variables
    @private UIView *enclosingView;
    @private int radius;
    @private int centerX;
    @private int centerY;
}
    -(id) initWithViewRadiusAndOrigin :(UIView *) enclosingView
                                                :(int) radius
                                                :(Point *) center;

    -(void) draw;
```

```
    // Other operations

@end

@interface Line : NSObject{
    // Member variables
    @private Point *start, *end
}
    -(id) initWithCoordinates :(UIView *) enclosingView :(Point) *start
                                                :(Point) *end;

    -(void) draw;

    // Other operations

@end

@interface Point : NSObject{
    // Member variables
    @private int x, y;
}
    -(id) initWithCoordinates :(int) x :(int) y;
@end
```

In regard to OO techniques and principles, you can clearly see that Façade uses delegation extensively. Also, if a Façade is well designed, it illustrates the OO principles of information hiding, high cohesion, and low coupling very well.

You can find an example that uses the Façade pattern in Chapter 7.

Although this isn't the case for the PieChart class, façade objects often create natural singletons because only one façade object is usually required. The lesson here is that patterns are often combined in a solution for a particular situation.

Properly passing the buck using Chain of Responsibility

In many situations, there's a hierarchy or chain of active objects, with each object linked back to a previous object in the hierarchy or the chain. In this case, you can use a behavioral pattern called *Chain Of Responsibility*.

Imagine a situation in which an event takes place at an object at the end of the chain or at a leaf node in the hierarchy. (I'm using event in a general sense here and don't specifically mean, for example, user-interface events.) This object will be the first object notified of the event. It may choose to do something about the event, or it may choose to simply send the event back up the chain to be handled by one of the objects preceding it in the chain. The intent is for the buck (so to speak) to stop somewhere in the chain or hierarchy or, if all else fails, for the objects to pass on handling the event at the root of the hierarchy.

> # Passing the buck
>
> The expression "passing the buck" is said to have originated from poker. A knife with a buckhorn handle was used as a marker to indicate the person whose turn it was to deal. If that player didn't want to deal, he could pass the buck to the next player.

Chain Of Responsibility is very visible in frameworks like iOS. Specifically, it's seen within a view hierarchy within an iOS program that needs to handle user-interface events like mouse clicks and touches (see Chapter 9).

Chain Of Responsibility is also implicitly seen in exception handling within any language that supports exceptions.

At least from a client program's perspective, Chain of Responsibility is an interesting example of both loose and tight coupling. The object that sends the command up the chain has no interest in, or any idea about, which object handles the command. Because of this, the transmitter of the event is loosely coupled with the handler of the event. However, the command object and the actual handler are certainly tightly coupled.

Understanding the Model-View-Controller

The Model-View-Controller (MVC) is a very well-known design pattern used in applications, in particular, web applications, and certainly in iOS. You may remember that I introduced MVC in Chapter 1 as an important pattern in iOS and mentioned it again in Chapter 2 when discussing OO techniques. Here, I give you more details about MVC.

The idea behind this pattern is to isolate the domain logic of the application from the way the application is presented to the user (that is, the application's user interface) so that these two very important components of any application can be designed, implemented, and maintained separately.

✔ The *model* is a class or collection of classes that captures the domain classes of an application. For example, model classes for a book-selling website might be classes such as Customer, Book, Shopping Cart, Invoice, Shipment, and so on. Typically, the persistent state of the app resides in the model objects.

Model objects represent a problem domain. Their value comes from the fact that they're reusable in similar problem domains. A model object should not be concerned with the transactions that take place within the application (which is the role of controllers) or with user-interface issues (which is the role of the views).

✔ *Views* handle the presentation aspects of the application and also serve as the conduit through which users interact with it.

✔ *Controllers* implement the application logic, and in doing so, stitch models and views together.

Figure 4-1 shows how the model, view, and controller interact.

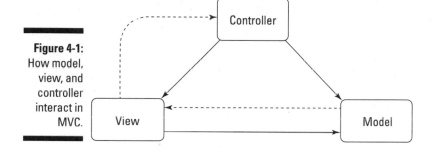

Figure 4-1: How model, view, and controller interact in MVC.

Typically, MVC apps stay passive and waiting (as though for Godot) until a transaction is initiated from a view. This transaction is then handled by the controller:

✔ If any domain objects are involved in the interaction with the view, the controller

- Updates these domain objects.
- Causes all other views to be appropriately updated in response to changes in the model.

✔ Transactions that directly cause changes to the model may also take place outside the view. If that happens, it's again the controller's responsibility to update the views.

Making model objects persistent

Most applications (and iOS apps are no exception) deal with long-lived data whose lifecycle is independent from the lifecycle of the app. The app may start up and shut down, but the data it created and managed lives on, ready to be used for the next run of the app. For example, think about how you use an editor to create and edit documents. You bring the editor up, open and edit a few documents, perhaps save them, and exit the editor. The documents are retained on the file system ready for the next use of the editor. Similarly, you might have an iOS app that manages your contacts. Your contacts app starts, and then the contacts are loaded and manipulated. Even after the app exits, your contacts live on and prosper.

An app generally deals with persistent data as follows:

1. When the app starts, and as the app is running, existing data (typically stored in a database or on the file system) is loaded into model objects in memory as needed.

2. New objects may be created and updated, and objects may also be deleted.

3. The data is written back to the database or the file system either periodically (for example, when you save a document) or when the app exits.

The objects that exist in memory correspond to (or are said to be *mapped* to) data elements in the database or file system. Therefore, when data is loaded into an object, database keys or other information that will identify where the data is stored is also loaded into the object. When the object is deleted or modified in memory, you know what to remove or change in the database or file system.

Two patterns that suggest how to make model objects persistent — whether a database, a file system, or another data store — are Active Record and Data Mapper.

Implementing persistence using Active Record

Active Record is a simple pattern, in which the class of the in-memory model object is extended with methods that handle the persistence of the class.

Following is an example that uses a table named PERSONTABLE to persist objects of a Person class in a relational database as the data-store. This is the interface file of the Person class:

```
@interface Person : NSObject <Persistable> {

    // Model attributes

    @private NSString * Name;
    @private NSString * SSNo;
}
    -(id) init;
    -(id) initWithOIDNameAndSSNo :(NSString *) OID :(NSString *) aName
                                                   :(NSString *) aSSNo;

    -(NSString *) getName;
    -(NSString *) getSSNo;
    -(void) setName :(NSString *) aName;
    -(void) setSsno :(NSString *) aSSNo;

    -(void) setAsRetired;

    // Other operations, if any

@end
```

Only the domain methods are shown in this interface. The additional methods needed for persistence are defined in the `Persistable` protocol:

```
typedef enum {
    NEW, EXISTS, CHANGED, DELETED
} STATE;

@protocol Persistable

    // Properties required by the protocol

    @required
    @property (copy) NSString *OID; // Unique ID in the Database

    @required
    @property (readonly) STATE state;

    + (id) findByOID :(NSString *) OID;

    - (void) insert;
    - (void) update;
    - (void) delete;

    - (void) persist;
@end
```

This protocol declares two required attributes:

✔ **The `OID` attribute:** This attribute holds the persistent ID of the object that will uniquely identify the object within a persistent data-store.

✔ **The `state` attribute:** This attribute indicates whether the object

- Was newly created in memory (state is `NEW`).

- Exists in the database (state is `EXISTING`).

- Was modified in memory after being fetched from the data-store (state is `CHANGED`).

- Is marked for deletion (state is `DELETED`).

The protocol then declares a collection of methods that the class needs to implement. You use the class method `FindByOid` to bring an object from the database into memory. (Such methods are known as *finder* methods, and you can have many different kinds of them, such as a `findByName`, `findBySSNo`, and so on.) Pseudocode for implementing this method in the `Person` class is shown here:

```
+ (id) findByOID :(NSString *) anOID {
    Person *returnedPerson;

    // SQL statement to retrieve object from the database
    // Save retrieved NAME and SSNO in local variables aName and anSSNo
```

```
... SELECT NAME, SSNO, from PERSONTABLE
    where OID = :anOID INTO :aName, :anSSNo;

aPerson = [[Person alloc] initWithOIDNameAndSSNo :anOID :anSSNo];
aPerson->state = EXISTING;
return returnedPerson;
}
```

The logic of this method is as follows:

✔ The embedded SQL SELECT statement fetches the Name and Social Security number attributes of the object from the database and saves these values in the local variables aName and anSSNo.

✔ These variables along with the OID instantiate and initialize an object of the Person class and return it.

Next, you see the implementation of the other methods from the Persistable protocol, in the Person class. The persist method is called whenever the object needs to be saved to the database, as shown here:

```
- (void) persist {
    // Check the state of the object

    // If it is a new object i.e. state = NEW call [self insert]
    // to create an entry in PERSONTABLE

    // If state = EXISTS do nothing

    // If state = CHANGED, call update to update the database

    // If state - DELETED, call delete to remove the information
    // in the database

}
```

The persist method uses the state variable to invoke the right methods for the object's persistence.

✔ If the object is newly created, a record is inserted in the object's table using the insert method, as shown here:

```
- (void) insert {
    INSERT INTO PERSONTABLE (OID, NAME, SSNO) VALUES :OID :Name :SSNo
    ...
}
```

✔ If the object is retrieved from the database and then modified in memory, the update method is called.

```
- (void) update {
    UPDATE PERSONTABLE SET VALUES NAME = :Name, SSNO=:SSNo
        WHERE OID = :OID
    ...
}
```

✔ If the object is retrieved from the database and then marked for deletion in memory, the delete method is called.

```
- (void) delete {
    DELETE FROM PERSONTABLE WHERE OID = :OID;
    ...
}
```

Note that the domain methods as well as the finder methods should set the state of the object appropriately. As a result, init sets the state of the object to NEW, findByOID sets the state to EXISTING, setAsRetired could potentially set the state to DELETED, setName, and setSSNo set the state to CHANGED (if the original state was EXISTING), and so on. The domain methods and the persistence methods are, therefore, coupled to some degree.

When you use Active Record to store objects in a relational database, it typically maps an object to a database table, with the object's persistent variables mapped to fields in that table. All of the lifecycle-management logic of the object — deciding when to fetch it from the database, whether to allow duplicate instance in memory corresponding to the same object in the database, when to save, when to delete objects permanently— are the application's responsibilities.

The next pattern (Data Mapper) moves the responsibility of managing objects out of an application and into a separate component.

Managing persistent objects using Data Mapper

Interposing a class that mediates between the in-memory object and the database is an approach for making the responsibility of managing persistent objects easier. This pattern is known as *Data Mapper*. Figure 4-2 shows the interaction between classes in a simple version of the Data Mapper. Basically, all persistent operations that access the database (that is, create, retrieve, update, and delete) are the responsibility of the Data Mapper. The application simply makes the appropriate requests of the Data Mapper.

The *Data Mapper* pattern is an abstraction with which you can handle persistent objects when their lifecycle management is complex. In fact, with Data Mapper, the objects in memory don't even need to know that there's a database present; they don't need SQL or any knowledge of the database schema.

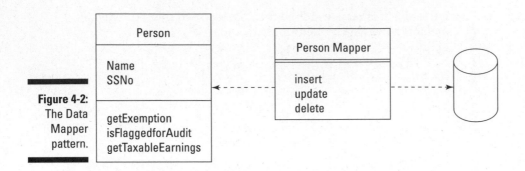

Figure 4-2:
The Data
Mapper
pattern.

Implementing a good Data Mapper is complicated. For example, the methods in Active Record suggest that a single invocation (such as a finder method) results in one SQL query. This isn't always true. Loading an object with multiple contained objects, for instance, could require loading the line items as well. If the objects are complex, a find request could load an entire graph of objects. Mappers may need to handle classes that turn into multiple fields in multiple tables, classes with inheritance, and relating objects once they're fetched from the data store. The data-store mapping layer needs to understand which objects have changed, which new ones have been created, and which have been destroyed. If multiple updates are made to the persistent records of a set of objects, then all these manipulations would have to take place inside a transaction.

The Data Mapper pattern often lets Active Record handle single objects, while Data Mapper takes care of the more complicated requirements, such as inheritance, deep retrieval and linking together of objects, queries based on complex relationships, transactions encompassing a working set of objects, and so on.

Data Mapper acts like a true *object manager* while delegating object-level operations to Active Record. This makes for a better OO design overall because Mapper cohesively handles the manager responsibility, while Active Record handles the simple persistence of the object (also cohesively). Also, the management policy is separated from the persistence mechanism. Therefore, the management policy and the persistence mechanisms are loosely coupled.

Finally, the Data Mapper pattern (with some variations) has become a core part of iOS with the provision of the Core Data component in iOS. I discuss Core Data in Chapter 6. For more details, go to www.dummies.com/go/iosprogramminglinks and, in the web resources for this chapter, check the link labeled Core Data.

Avoiding anti-patterns

If you use the process and rules of OO design (which I introduce in Chapter 2 and explain with a detailed example in Chapter 7), your designs will be more robust. However, even with a sound process and appropriate guidelines, and even if you're an experienced developer, you could get things badly wrong. In this section I discuss anti-patterns, which are specific ways you could get things wrong.

Several of these anti-patterns are discussed in the book, *AntiPatterns: Refactoring Software, Architectures, and Projects in Crisis,* by William Brown, Raphael Malveau, Skip McCormick, and Tom Mowbray. Scott Thomas, although never an author of this book, also contributed to the work on anti-patterns, specifically anti-patterns in other software-related development areas, such as project management.

Anti-patterns cover a range of pitfalls from organizational design and project management to programming. Here are a couple of anti-patterns relevant to OO design:

- ✔ **The so-called Base Bean anti-pattern:** This is where a class inherits from another class because the superclass contains functionality needed in the subclass.

    For example, suppose you're implementing a dictionary class where you can look up the meanings of words. A hash table, where the words are hashed to locate their meanings is a reasonable data structure to use within a dictionary. However, making your dictionary inherit from a hash table isn't good design. Your dictionary ends up having methods in its interface that have no connection with words and their meanings. Conversely, your class has methods that have everything to do with dictionaries, but nothing at all to do with hash tables.

    Base Bean usually occurs when a software developer confuses an IS-A relationship, which is appropriate for representing a true subclass via inheritance, with a HAS-A relationship, which is better served by a containment relationship. In other words, a Dictionary can *have* a Hash Table but *is not* a Hash Table.

    Note that the OO design process described in Chapter 2 requires you to try to agree on a short, crisp definition for every potential class before elevating it to become a candidate class. This helps you avoid the Base Bean anti-pattern.

- ✔ **The Anemic Domain Model:** Some groups, particularly the Enterprise Java community, think of domain model classes as simply consisting of getters and setters for the attributes in the class, with no domain behavior in the class (for example, validations, calculations, business rules, and the like). This kind of design is contrary to OO thinking.

Applying patterns to application design

Design patterns aren't canned solutions that you can simply take and plug into your code. However, they provide highly regarded ways of providing certain capabilities, so they're a great place to start your design.

Recognizing patterns in your design will also help you map your design to your implementation framework (that is, iOS). For example, in the Tic-Tac-Toe game in Chapter 7, you see that a *game session* manager is needed to control and keep track of the multiple games played in a single session. This session manager accesses a model consisting of the state of the game and displays data from this model (such as the accumulated scores) in a view on the screen. Tic-Tac-Toe has the natural occurrence of a model (the session), a view (the view showing the data of the session), and a controller (the session manager). These three classes directly map to an iOS model, a set of iOS views, and an iOS view controller, respectively.

Understanding Frameworks

A software framework is a set of components containing common code that provides generic functionality. In order to make an app using a framework, this generic functionality must be transformed into app-specific functionality. You do this by selectively specializing classes and overriding methods and using a mix of inheritance, late binding, and delegation.

Inversion of control

Customization of functionality occurs within a framework using a paradigm known as *inversion of control.*

Inversion of control distinguishes frameworks from software libraries that provide computational capabilities that your application can invoke, such as the string manipulation routines provided by the `java.lang` package.

Inversion of control means that a developer who uses the framework doesn't dictate the way the program runs (its flow of control); instead, it's dictated by the framework itself, as the default behavior. This default behavior is extended or modified by code the developer supplies. The user supplies this code in the form of classes that do the following:

✔ Extend the base classes of the framework (which are usually abstract classes) and either override certain methods or provide implementations of virtual methods.

✔ Implement specific interfaces that are then passed to and invoked by the framework.

Apple's iOS is a framework. It provides a set of base classes that you extend with your own classes and code. These base classes also provide default functionality, such as for event and exception handling. Finally, iOS also provides application templates that capture an overall sequence (that is, control flow) of computation. Once again, you customize these templates by plugging in your classes and code.

Basic concepts

To explain the basic ideas behind frameworks, allow me to show you a very simple framework (call it Printing For Dummies, or PFD, framework).

The PFD framework enables you to write programs that transfer (or *spool*) documents to a printer and then print them. It also allows you to extend the printing capabilities of your system by providing you with a way to spool new types of documents and add new types of printers.

First, this framework defines a protocol (`PrinterMethods`) for printing, as follows:

```
@protocol PrinterMethods
    - (id) initWithConfiguration :(NSString *) printerConfiguration;
    - (void) spool :(NSString*) path;
    - (void) print;
@end
```

The `spool` method sends a document to a printer queue (a special directory on the file system known to the printer), whereas the `print` method does the actual printing. The `initWithConfiguration` method sets the printer's configuration so that it can accept print jobs. For example, this method might set the USB port number for a local printer or the IP address for a network printer.

The framework provides a class called `PrinterBase` that implements this protocol with an empty function, as shown here:

```
@interface PrinterBase:NSObject <PrinterMethods>{
    // Nothing
}

@end

@implementation PrinterBase

    - (id) initWithConfiguration :(NSString *) printerConfiguration{
        return self;
    }
```

```
- (void) spool :(NSString*) path {
    // Does nothing
}

- (void) print{
    // Does nothing
}

@end
```

You can find this class in the files `PrinterBase.h` and `PrinterBase.m`, which are provided in the source code for this chapter. Go ahead and navigate to the source directory and compile `PrinterBase.m` from the command line in a Terminal window, as follows:

```
gcc -c PrinterBase.m -o PrinterBase.o
```

Keep the object file, `PrinterBase.o`, handy for the next step.

The framework also provides a built-in `PCLPrinter` class that can print documents already formatted to printers that use the Printer Command Language developed by Hewlett-Packard as a printer protocol. The `PCLPrinter` class looks like this (interface first, and a skeleton of its implementation):

```
@interface PCLPrinter:NSObject <PrinterMethods>{
    @private NSString *Configuration;
}

@implementation PCLPrinter

    - (id) initWithConfiguration :(NSString *) printerConfiguration{
        Configuration = printerConfiguration;
        NSLog(@"Printer configuration %@\n", Configuration);
        return self;
    }

    - (void) spool :(NSString*) path {
        NSLog(@"Spooling file for PCL printing %@\n", path);
    ...
    }

    - (void) print{
        NSLog(@"Printing file on PCL printer\n");
        ...
    }

@end
```

This class implements the methods of the PrinterMethods protocol. That is, it also implements the methods initWithConfiguration, spool, and print. Unlike the methods in PrinterBase, these methods actually do something.

Flow of control

The framework provides an app template with a straightforward built-in flow of control. When a print app is launched, an instance of a class that implements the PrinterMethods protocol is created. Then the spool method of that instance is called, which pulls the file with the specified pathname over to the printer queue. Then the print method is called and reads the file from the printer queue and prints it. The app template generates code for an application that uses a specific printer class. For example, the code for a printer app that uses the PCLPrinter class will look similar to the following:

```
int main(int argc, char* argv[]){
    NSString *configuration = [[NSString alloc] initWithUTF8String:argv[1]];
    NSString *fileName = [[NSString alloc] initWithUTF8String: argv[2]];
    PrinterApplicationMain([PCLPrinter class], configuration, fileName);
}
```

This generated main function embeds the PCLPrinter class in its code and then uses a function named PrinterApplicationMain. This function is part of PrinterBase and is compiled into and provided by the framework. The PrinterApplicationMain function is as follows:

```
void PrinterApplicationMain(Class PrinterClass,
                            NSString *configuration,
                            NSString *fileName){
    PrinterBase *printer =
        [[PrinterClass alloc] initWithConfiguration:configuration];
    [printer spool :fileName];
    [printer print];
}
```

This method is passed the *class* of a specific type of printer. It instantiates an object of this class, and then it implements the desired control flow (described previously) of a printer application. That is, it spools the file and then prints it. Once again, when you previously compiled PrinterBase, this function was compiled and made ready for use.

It's time to build the classes for PCLPrinter and its main program, which are also provided in the source code for this chapter. You compile it from the command line as follows:

```
gcc -c PCLPrinter.m -o PCLPrinter.o
gcc -c PCLPrinterMain.m -o PCLPrinterMain.o
gcc PCLPrinterMain.o PCLPrinter.o PrinterBase.o -o pclprinter -lobjc \
    -framework Cocoa
```

You then launch the `pclprinter` executable as follows:

```
pclprinter 192.168.1.70 /Users/somepath/somefile.pcl
```

You now see the following output:

```
pclprinter 192.168.1.70 /Users/somepath/somefile.pcl
2013-09-26 19:08:29.457 pclprinter[9735:707]
        Printer configuration 192.168.1.70

2013-09-26 19:08:29.459 pclprinter[9735:707]
        Spooling file for PCL printing /Users/somepath/somefile.txt
2013-09-26 19:08:29.460 pclprinter[9735:707] Printing file on PCL printer
```

Say that you want to print Postscript files on a PCL printer. To do so, you create your own class; go ahead and name it **PostscriptPrinter**. To save some work, you reuse the `PCLPrinter` class already in the framework by inheriting from it; then you override its spool method to convert the file from Postscript to PCL and reuse the `PCLPrinter` print method. The interface and implementation files of the `PostscriptPrinter` class are shown here:

```
...
#import "PCLPrinter.h"

@interface PostscriptPrinter : PCLPrinter {

}
    - (void) spool :(NSString*) path; // overriding spool

@end

@implementation PostscriptPrinter
    - (void) spool :(NSString*) path {
        NSLog(@"Converting from Postscript to PCL before spooling %@ \
                to /spool/job01.pcl \n",
            path);
        [super spool:@"/spool/job01.pcl"]; // then send to PCL printer
    }
@end
```

Here is the `main` program generated for a printer app built for the `PostscriptPrinter` class:

```
#import "PostscriptPrinter.h"

int main(int argc, char* argv[]){
    NSString *configuration = [[NSString alloc] initWithUTF8String:argv[1]];
    NSString *fileName = [[NSString alloc] initWithUTF8String: argv[2]];
    PrinterApplicationMain([PostscriptPrinter class],
                        configuration,
                        fileName);
}
```

The only difference between this `main` function and the `main` function of the `PCLPrinter` app is that the `PostscriptPrinter` class is sent to `PrinterApplicationMain`. So, go ahead and build this program using the following commands:

```
gcc -c PostscriptPrinter.m -o PostscriptPrinter.o
gcc -c PostscriptPrinterMain.m -o PostscriptPrinterMain.o
gcc PostscriptPrinterMain.o PostscriptPrinter.o PCLPrinter.o PrinterBase.o \
    -o psprinter -lobjc -framework Cocoa
```

Now run it as follows (feel free to change the command-line arguments):

```
psprinter 192.168.1.70 /Users/somepath/somefile.ps
```

You now have the following:

```
2013-09-26 20:21:26.352 psprinter[9985:707] \
                    Printer configuration 192.168.1.70
2013-09-26 20:21:26.354 psprinter[9985:707] \
            Converting from Postscript to PCL before spooling \
            /Users/somepath/somefile.ps to /spool/job01.pcl
2013-09-26 20:21:26.355 psprinter[9985:707] \
            Spooling file for PCL printing /spool/job01.pcl
2013-09-26 20:21:26.355 psprinter[9985:707] Printing file on PCL printer
```

This framework is limited, but it demonstrates two key elements of how frameworks, such as the iOS framework, operate:

- Using the `PCLPrinter` class and its components, it shows how a framework provides reusable functionality.

- Using the generated `main` program, its components, and the `PostscriptPrinter` class, it shows how control flow templates are provided and utilized.

Chapter 5

Setting Up to Develop iOS Apps

*i*OS applications are almost exclusively developed in Objective-C. At one time, you could install the iOS framework along with an Objective-C compiler and build iOS apps the old-fashioned way — with a text editor and the command line. Nowadays, most folks like to make their lives a little easier, so they use an integrated development environment (IDE) for their iOS development. The IDE for iOS development is Xcode.

In this chapter, I show you how to officially become an iOS developer so you can get access to Xcode. I then show you how to install Xcode and how to verify whether you installed it correctly. Then I show you how to build a simple application and how to import and run the source code of the Tic-Tac-Toe application.

Becoming an iOS Developer

This section explains what you need and how you can become an iOS developer. If you're a new developer, you need the tools of the trade:

> ✔ A Mac desktop or laptop system to develop on.
>
> It must be a machine with an Intel processor, running OS X Mountain Lion or Mavericks with at least 6GB of free space. In terms of memory, 4GB is the minimum, but 8GB is better (Xcode likes to feast on memory).
>
> ✔ An Apple developer registration.

You can easily register as an Apple developer, and there's no fee for getting started. You can then develop iOS applications and test them on the simulator to your heart's content.

However, if want to test your apps on real devices or allow a few users to test them on their devices, or if you want to apply to have your app put in the Apple Store, you must pay an annual fee of $99 for an individual license or $299 for an enterprise license. This fee must be paid in local currency wherever the iOS Developer Program is available.

Paid members get early access to beta versions of the iOS and SDK — a nice perk. For example, I was one of the privileged few able to have iOS 7 on my iPhone when it was announced.

I'll now take you through the major steps to register as an Apple developer (paid or unpaid) and to obtain the tools you need to start developing apps. The exact steps you'll take depend upon things such as whether you already have an Apple ID, whether you already have a credit card registered, whether you're revisiting any of the pages, and so on.

When you're ready, follow these steps:

1. **Go to the Apple Developer website at** `https://developer.apple.com`, **scroll all the way to the bottom of the page, and click the Register button (see Figure 5-1).**

Figure 5-1:
How to get on the Apple Developer website.

To register, you can also go to `https://developer.apple.com/programs/register`.

The Apple Developer registration page appears, as shown in Figure 5-2.

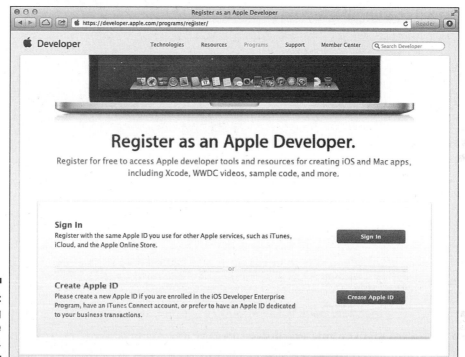

Figure 5-2:
Registering
as an Apple
developer.

2. **Sign in using your Apple ID or create a new one.**

   You may already have an Apple ID — say, the one you use for iTunes. You can use that one, or you can create a new one just for development. If you want to create a new Apple ID, click Create Apple ID and complete the steps to create a new one.

3. **When you have your Apple ID, sign in and create your developer profile.**

4. **To enroll in a paid developer membership, go to** `https://developer.apple.com/programs`.

   The Apple Developer page appears, showing all the developer programs Apple supports (see Figure 5-3).

Figure 5-3:
The Apple
developer
programs.

If you plan to create apps and test them in the simulator without paying to register as a developer, skip to Step 13 and download and install Xcode.

 5. **Click the iOS Developer Program box.**

    The enrollment page appears (see Figure 5-4).

 6. **Click Enroll Now.**

    You'll see an information page that outlines the steps to become a developer (see Figure 5-5).

 7. **Select Continue. If a screen appears asking you to sign in again, do so.**

 8. **Click Individual to enroll.**

    Here, I'm assuming you're enrolling for your own personal app, rather than as a company.

    The license agreement page appears.

 9. **Check the I Agree box at the bottom of the page and click Agree.**

    A profile page appears.

 10. **Fill out your professional profile and click Register.**

Figure 5-4:
Enrolling
in the iOS
developer
program.

Figure 5-5:
Steps for
enrolling
in the iOS
Developer
Program.

You'll be asked to fill out several profile items (see Figure 5-6), such as your experience with iOS, what kinds of apps you plan to develop, and what other platforms you plan to develop for. If you navigate away from this page, you can go back to it by following this link: `https://developer.apple.com/register/professionalProfile.action`.

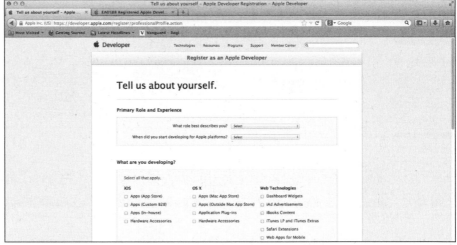

Figure 5-6:
Filling out your developer profile.

11. **After you complete your profile, a page appears asking you to fill in your credit card information. Provide the required information.**

    If credit card information is already on file, you can skip this step.

12. **Follow the steps to purchase the iOS Developer Program.**

    First, you add the program to your shopping cart; then you follow the steps to check out and pay for the program. When you're finished, you're taken back to the iOS Developer Center (Figure 5-7).

13. **From the iOS Developer Center (refer to Figure 5-5), download Xcode and other developer resources, as I describe in the next section.**

    If you're not at the iOS Developer Center and need to get to it, use this link: `https://developer.apple.com/devcenter/ios`.

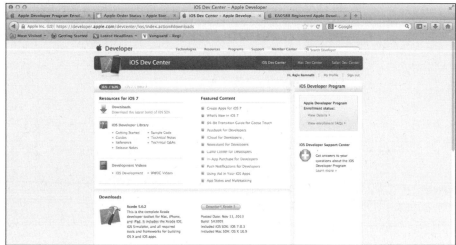

Figure 5-7:
The iOS Dev
Center.

Installing, Verifying, and Understanding the Xcode Development Environment

From the iOS Dev Center page (refer to Figure 5-5), you can download all kinds of developer resources — documents, videos, and even working examples with source code. Most importantly, you can download the available versions of Xcode, Apple's development environment for iOS (currently available for iOS 7 and a beta version of iOS 7.1).

Installing Xcode

Now it's time to download the complete Xcode developer toolset for Mac, iPhone, and iPad. The toolset includes the Xcode IDE, the iOS Simulator, and other required tools and frameworks for building iOS apps.

Before beginning, be sure you're signed in with your Apple ID and are at the iOS Developer Center at `https://developer.apple.com/devcenter/ios` (refer to Figure 5-7). Then follow these steps:

1. **Click Downloads and then click the Download Xcode 5 button.**

   A page with the heading Xcode appears (see Figure 5-8). From this page select the button View in Mac App Store (in the section titled Download Xcode 5). You're taken to the Xcode page on the App Store where Xcode is shown as a free app (see Figure 5-9).

Figure 5-8:
The Xcode download page.

Figure 5-9:
Xcode page on the Mac App Store.

2. **Install Xcode from the Mac App Store.**

   Select the Free button beneath the Xcode icon at the upper-left of the page (see Figure 5-9). At this point, you're asked for your Mac Keychain password; provide it. Xcode will be downloaded and installed. When Xcode has been installed, the button will change to Installed, as shown in Figure 5-10.

Figure 5-10: Xcode page on the Mac App Store after installation.

3. **In your Mac's Applications folder, locate the Xcode 5 application.**

   At the time of this writing, the application was named `Xcode5.app`.

Create a shortcut (an *alias* on the Mac) for Xcode on your desktop so that you don't have to navigate to its location every time you need to start it.

Verifying the development environment

After Xcode is installed, it's time to check that it's properly set up and working correctly.

Installations on a Mac almost always work. Apple has well-specified standards for developing and installing applications. Also, Apple manufactures all Macs and can control the quality and compatibility of all components. However, it's a good idea to make sure that everything is in good working condition before proceeding further.

To make sure Xcode is working properly, follow these steps:

1. **Locate the Xcode 5 application and double-click it.**

   When running Xcode for the first time, you're asked to accept a license agreement.

2. **Accept the license agreement.**

   A dialog box asking for your Keychain password appears. This is the standard dialog box that appears on the Mac whenever you try to install software or update a system setting, so you've probably seen this dialog box before.

3. **Enter your Keychain password (see Figure 5-11).**

   The Welcome to Xcode window appears (see Figure 5-12). Of course, if you're doing this for the first time, you won't see any existing projects.

4. **Click Create a new Xcode Project.**

   A set of application templates appears.

   These templates are wizards for creating different types of apps (see Figure 5-13). I describe these templates in Chapter 6 and show talk about how to use them in Chapter 7.

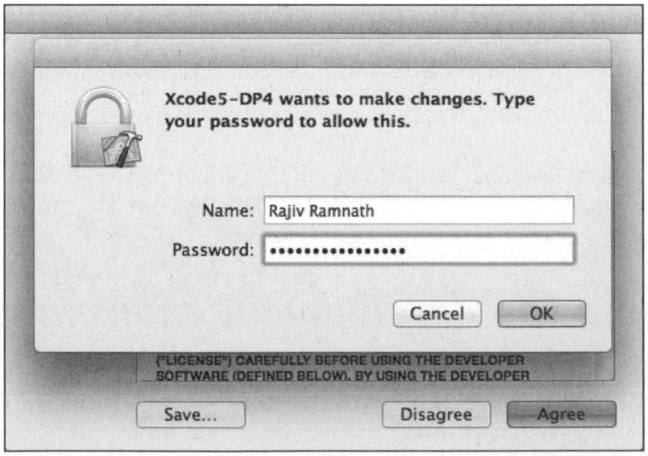

Figure 5-11:
Entering the
Keychain
password.

Xcode5-DP4 wants to make changes. Type your password to allow this.

Name: Rajiv Ramnath

Password: ••••••••••••••

Cancel   OK

("LICENSE") CAREFULLY BEFORE USING THE DEVELOPER
SOFTWARE (DEFINED BELOW). BY USING THE DEVELOPER

Save...   Disagree   Agree

Figure 5-12:
Welcome to
Xcode.

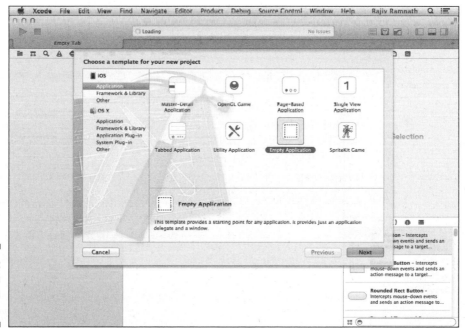

Figure 5-13:
Selecting an
application
type.

5. Double-click Empty Application.

The Choose Options for Your New Project dialog box appears, where
(you guessed it), you're asked to choose options for your new project.
In Figure 5-14, I chose the Test application and provided my Company
Identifier as com.rr. I also made Test the Class Prefix (which means that
the names of all the classes I use in this application and the names of the
files in which they'll be stored will automatically get the prefix Test).

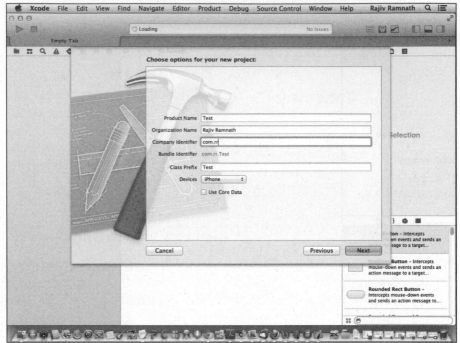

Notice that I selected iPhone in the Devices list. This selection is not significant for verifying that Xcode works. You can select iPad or leave the default selection (Universal) as is.

6. Click Next.

A Mac OS file save window appears (see Figure 5-15) so you can create a folder for your app.

7. Select where you want to save the project in the Mac file system.

8. Click Create (which tells Xcode to save the project in the default directory).

The workspace for your project appears (see Figure 5-16).

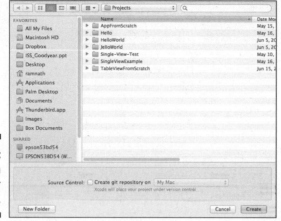

Figure 5-15:
Creating a
folder for
the app.

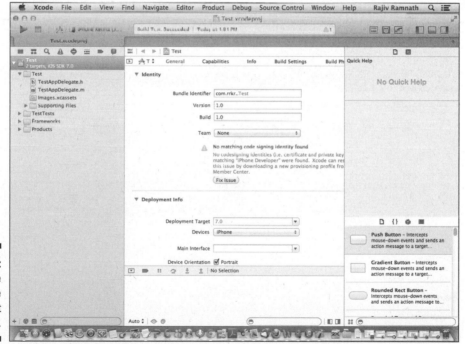

Figure 5-16:
Xcode
workspace
for the Test
application.

9. **To build and run the Test application, select Run from the Product menu (see Figure 5-17).**

   If everything is correct (and why wouldn't it be?), Xcode builds the app, starts the simulator, and installs the app on the simulator. The result of this final step is shown in Figure 5-18.

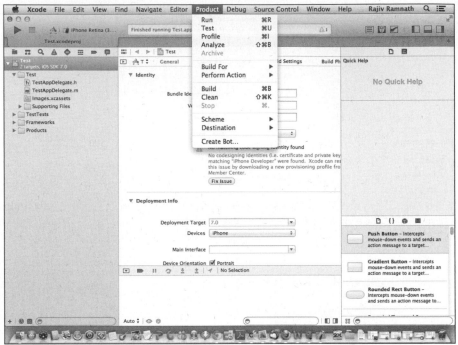

Figure 5-17:
Running an
application.

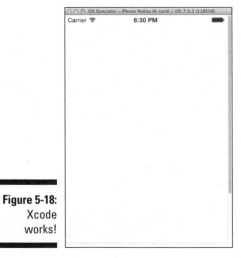

Figure 5-18:
Xcode
works!

That's it. Xcode is installed properly, and you're all set to start developing
iOS apps.

Understanding the elements of an Xcode workspace

The application workspace in Xcode is where you'll do most of your work, including the Navigator area, the Editor area, the Utility area, and the Debug area (see Figure 5-19).

Navigator area

The Navigator area consists of a collection of navigators each of which allows you to examine a different aspect of the application.

The navigator that you see when the project workspace is first shown looks like a hierarchical file browser. This is the Project navigator that shows all the files in the project, including the files with code that Xcode generates (based on the template used), as well as the files containing code you create.

The Project navigator is only one of several navigators in this area. As you slide your mouse across the icons at the top, tooltips for the Project, Symbol, Find, Issue, Test, Debug, Breakpoint, and Log navigators appear. Click each one to see what happens.

Navigator area   Editor area   Utilities area

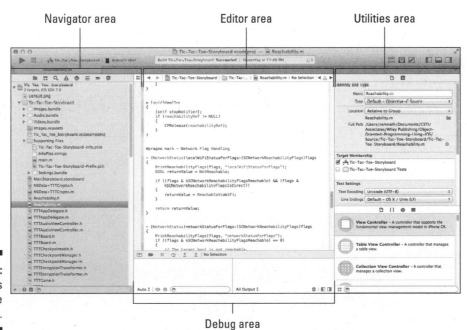

Figure 5-19:
Components
of an Xcode
workspace.

Debug area

You can hide or show the entire Navigator area by choosing View⇨Navigators ⇨Show/Hide Navigator or by pressing ⌘-0.

Editor area

The Editor area is where you do the actual development — that is, where you write the code or configure parameters of the app.

Utilities area

Choose View⇨Utilities⇨Show/Hide Utilities or press ⌘-Option-0 to show and hide the Utilities area. The icons at the top of this area are *inspectors.* As you slide your mouse across the icons for the inspectors, tooltips appear that display text such as: Show the File Inspector and Show the Quick Help Inspector. More inspectors will show, depending on what is selected in Navigator area. There are actually six inspectors — File, Quick Help, Identity, Attributes, Size and Connection. These inspectors allow you to provide and change information about the current selection.

The Utilities area also lists the iOS Framework classes and libraries you need for your project.

Debug area

At the bottom of the Utilities area, you will find the Debug area. If you don't see it, click View⇨Show/Hide Debug Area or press Shift-⌘-Y. As its name signifies, you use this area when debugging your app — to inspect variables, see exceptions thrown, view output from any print or log statements in your app, and so on.

Importing and Running the Tic-Tac-Toe Sample Program

You know how to set up and go through your IDE. It's time to complete the last steps to the Tic-Tac-Toe sample application — namely, importing and running it. When that's all done, the framework necessary for subsequent chapters is set up (including for Chapter 8, which goes into the advanced capabilities of Xcode).

Importing Tic-Tac-Toe and running it on the simulator

To import Tic-Tac-Toe, go to this book's website (www.dummies.com/ extras/beginningiosprogramming) and download the zip archive containing this app. Save the archive file in a suitable directory on your Mac and unzip it. Then follow these steps to bring the Tic-Tac-Toe project into Xcode:

1. **From the File menu, select Open.**

2. **Browse to the folder where you saved the Tic-Tac-Toe project.**

3. **Select the root directory and click Open.**

   The project opens in an Xcode workspace.

Sometimes when the project opens, only the Editor area is shown. If that happens, you can open the other areas from the View menu (as I explain in the earlier section, "Understanding the elements of an Xcode workspace").

Running the program is straightforward:

1. **Make sure an iPhone Retina 3.5 inch or iPhone Retina 4 inch is selected as the simulator (see Figure 5-20).**

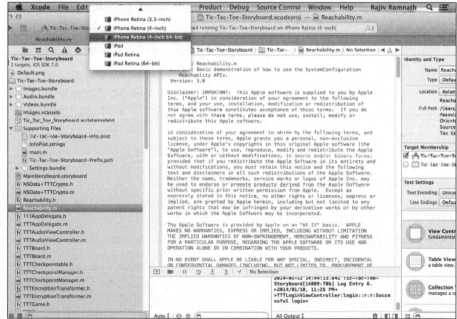

Figure 5-20: Selecting a simulator to run your app.

2. **Click the Product menu, and from the drop-down menu select Run (refer to Figure 5-17, shown earlier in this chapter).**

   The iOS simulator starts, and after a splash screen appears, Tic-Tac-Toe opens (as shown in Figure 5-21). Enjoy!

If you've linked an iOS device to your computer before (for example, to synch it with iTunes), Xcode may try to run Tic-Tac-Toe on that device but fail because the device hasn't been set up as a development device. If that happens, set the active scheme to be a simulator using the selector at the top of the Xcode window, as shown in Figure 5-20.

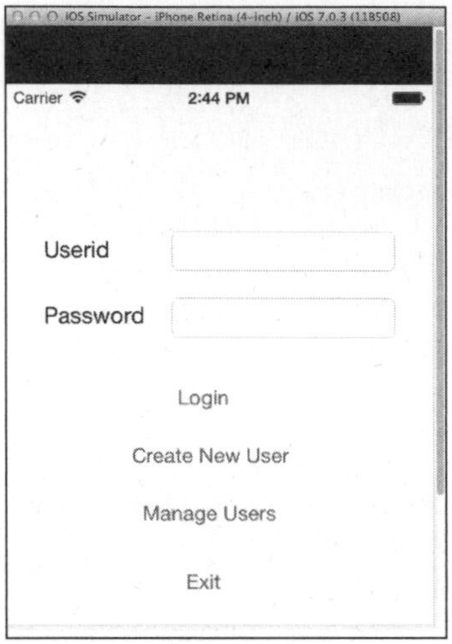

Figure 5-21:
Tic-Tac-
Toe run-
ning in the
simulator.

Deploying an App on an iOS device

After an app runs on a simulator, it's ready to run on an actual device. However, Apple tries to carefully control the app development and distribution process. So, Apple has thrown in two additional hoops you must jump through before you can run an app on a real device.

✔ You must be a paid Apple developer.

✔ You must create a development provisioning profile for the device.

Creating and installing a development provisioning profile

I begin this section by explaining provisioning profiles and their related components — certificates, the device ID, and the app ID.

When you're registered in the iOS Developer program, you need to request and get a developer certificate. This developer certificate contains information about the developers of the app (that is, about you) and is needed to sign any apps that you develop.

A provisioning profile then needs to be created that links information about the developers (that is, the developer certificate) with the app, via its app ID. A *development* provisioning profile then extends the provisioning profile to include the identity of the device on which the application will run via the unique device identifier (or UDID) of the device.

This development provisioning profile is then used to generate a provisioning file during the compilation process of an iOS app and is put on the device.

You can create certificates, provisioning profiles, and provisioning files in different ways. The old way was via a combination of the Keychain Access utility and the Apple Developer Portal. You had to first create a certificate signing request (or CSR) by using the Keychain Access application on your Mac, which is stored in the Utilities folder. The next step, creating the development profile, was done via the web at the iOS Developer Center (`https://developer.apple.com/devcenter/ios/index.action`).

The Keychain is a secure information store on iOS and Mac devices used to save passwords, certificates, and other information.

All of this made for a confusing process because Apple's own documentation (`https://developer.apple.com/library/ios/#documentation/IDEs/Conceptual/AppDistributionGuide/Introduction/Introduction.html`) is unclear, to say the least.

I describe this old way in Chapter 14 because, in some situations, you may want to take that route.

However, you can now get certificates and create profiles and provision files much more easily via Xcode, starting with Xcode 4.6 and iOS 5. This process is much smoother, and that's what I describe in detail in this chapter.

Here's how to create the provisioning profile via Xcode:

1. **Connect your device to your Mac via the USB port.**

2. **Open Xcode and choose Window⇨Organizer. If the Devices tab isn't selected, select it.**

   You see something similar to Figure 5-22 (where I'm configuring my son Arman's iPad mini).

3. **Select your device in the panel on the left; then in Xcode's Organizer window, click Use for Development.**

4. **Sign in with the Apple ID associated with your iOS Developer Program membership (see Figure 5-23).**

   Xcode automatically registers your device for development.

   Xcode also needs to add the development profiles and certificates to your keychain, so allow it to access your keychain (see Figure 5-24).

5. **Navigate to the Library section of the window and select Provisioning Profiles.**

6. **Click the Refresh button at the bottom-right corner of the window.**

7. **Enter your username and password and click Log In.**

   After you sign in to your account, a prompt appears asking whether you wish to request your development certificate.

8. **Click the Submit Request button.**

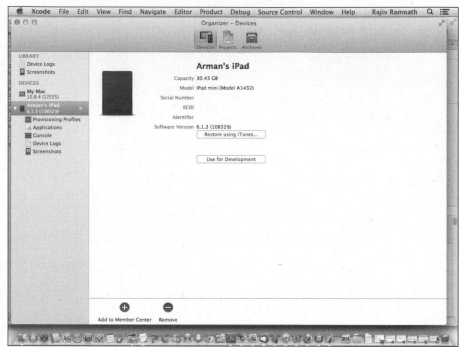

Figure 5-22:
Configuring
a device for
development.

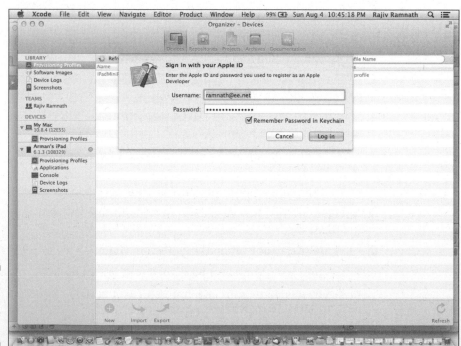

Figure 5-23:
Signing in
with your
Apple ID.

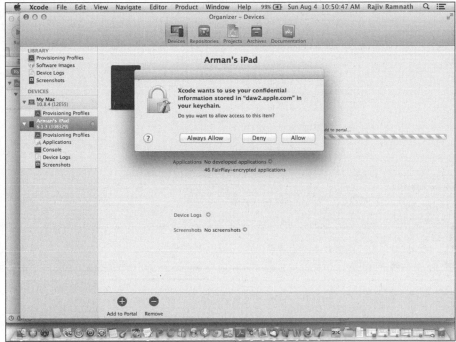

Figure 5-24:
Saving
informa-
tion in your
keychain.

The development certificate is added to your keychain and later to your team provisioning profile.

An App ID is requested as part of the device provisioning process. This is a two-part string used to identify the apps from a single development team, consisting of a Team ID and a Bundle ID string, separated by a period (.).

- Apple provides the Team ID, which is unique to a specific development team.

- You supply the Bundle ID. It's intended to match either the Bundle ID of a single app or a set of Bundle IDs for a set of apps.

If the same App ID is used for multiple apps, these apps can share keychain data.

The App ID you set up for the device is important because it must match the Bundle ID of the app.

9. **Open the Tic-Tac-Toe project, go to the Editor area, click General, and create the Bundle ID.**

   You do this by setting the prefix of the Bundle to match the App ID you set for the device.

   For example, I had set the App ID as `com.rr.*`. Given this, I set the Bundle ID prefix for the Tic-Tac-Toe app to be `com.rr` (see Figure 5-25).

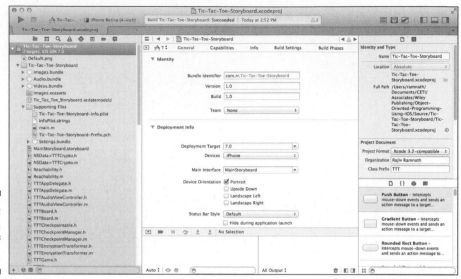

Figure 5-25:
Setting the
Bundle ID of
the app.

Running the app

When you're ready, just select the device from the Scheme drop-down menu and then select Product➪Run.

Tic-Tac-Toe is built and deployed to the device and starts running (see Figure 5-26).

Figure 5-26:
Tic-Tac-Toe
on an iPad
mini.

Chapter 6

Developing an App on iOS

· ·

In This Chapter

▶ Understanding the lifecycle of an iOS app

▶ Configuring your app using the built-in Settings app

▶ Managing your app's data using files and iOS

▶ Using the built-in app templates in iOS

▶ Using patterns to understand how the iOS framework works

· ·

*I*f you were to read only one chapter in this book, this would be the one to read. Here's why: In Chapter 1, I describe iOS and lay out the components of the iOS framework. This chapter focuses on the app and how it works. It starts with the components of an app and how they fit together and then describes how it runs and its lifecycle from start up to shutdown.

This chapter explains the capabilities iOS provides for integrating apps into the iOS ecosystem — in a sense, making the app a complete iOS citizen. Making an app complete includes, for example, integrating the app with the settings database on the device, using the Address Book, following Apple's behavior guidelines, sharing the app's data, and responsibly managing its lifecycle.

This chapter also covers essential elements of the iOS Framework, such as Core Data. Finally, it analyzes the components of an app and the iOS framework from an object-oriented perspective.

Dissecting an iOS App

In this section, you find out about the typical components of an app and how they interact as it runs. Figure 6-1 shows these components. As you can see from this figure, the components of an app can be grouped into model, view, and controller components.

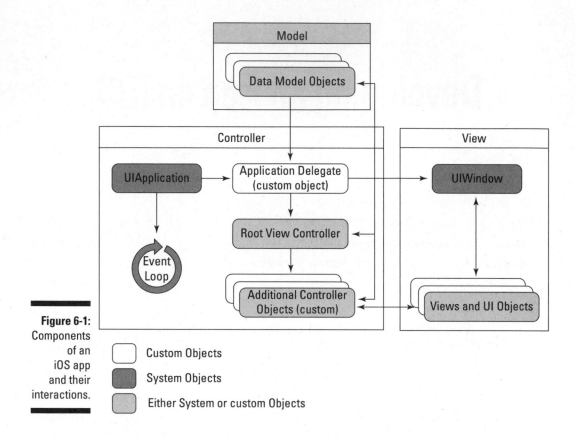

Figure 6-1:
Components
of an
iOS app
and their
interactions.

The model components are the Objective-C classes that implement the domain logic of the application as well as manage long-lived state. Some of these classes might also be persistent; that is, they may save their state across runs of the app on the file system or in a database.

The view classes represent the user interface of the app. They handle showing information to the user. These classes also handle interactions with the user; that is, they handle touches on the screen, keyboard input, and so on.

The controller classes are responsible for managing the execution of the app. Once the app is running, these controller classes also are the bridge between the views with the model. These classes consist of the Application Delegate, the root view controller, and app-specific view controllers.

The preceding model, view, and controller classes don't simply materialize out of thin air when an app starts. App execution actually begins with a `main` function that is then responsible for instantiating all the other classes.

The following code for the main program of the Tic-Tac-Toe application shows you how app execution begins (see file main.m in the folder Supporting Files):

```
...
#import "TTTAppDelegate.h"
int main(int argc, char * argv[]){
    @autoreleasepool {
        return UIApplicationMain(argc, argv, nil,
                                NSStringFromClass([TTTAppDelegate class]));
    }
}
```

Running this main function causes the following:

1. A (singleton) instance of the class UIApplication is created.

2. The UIApplication object, in turn, creates an instance of the app-specific application delegate (that is, a subclass of UIApplicationDelegate) and, in a separate thread, calls its initialize method.

3. The UIApplication object executes an event loop, where it listens for two kinds of events:

   • User-interface (UI) events, such as touches on a screen.

     The UI events are sent to the window object (see Step 4).

   • System events, such as for a low battery or when the app will be sent to the background because the device receives a phone call.

     System events are sent to the application delegate by the UIApplication object.

4. The application delegate creates the window for the app (an instance of the class UIWindow), along with a Root view controller that manages the window.

   The application delegate also creates a manager for the app's model. This manager manages the Core Data objects for the app. (Turn to Chapter 7 for information about Core Data.)

5. The Root view controller creates additional view controllers as specified in the storyboard of the app. Creation of the view controllers results in the creation of their views. These views become part of a view *hierarchy* — an inverted tree of views and subviews.

When the app commences and is in steady state, only the event loop runs. This event loop listens for events and calls your code appropriately to respond to them. Once the app starts, it's completely event-driven and does computation only when iOS or a user asks it to do so.

Understanding an App's Lifecycle

Your app goes through a set of states, known as a *lifecycle.* If you need a refresher on life cycles before moving on, please refer to Chapter 1 where I first introduce them. Also, Figure 6-2 shows the states of an app's lifecycle.

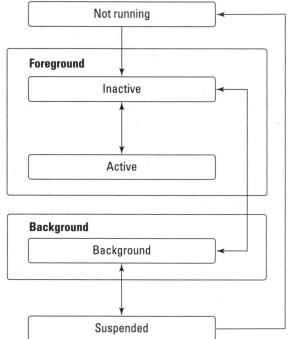

Figure 6-2:
Lifecycle of
an iOS app.

Apps can be in these states:

✔ When an app is in the *Not Running* state, either the app hasn't been launched or the system terminated it.

✔ When an app starts, it goes through a short transition through the *Inactive* state. It's actually running but needs to execute some setup steps before it's ready to accept user inputs or system events.

✔ An app in *Active* state is running in the foreground and receiving events. This is the normal mode for foreground apps — apps that interact with the user through a user interface.

✔ When an app is in the *Background* state, its user interface isn't visible, but it *is* running. Most apps transition through this state on their way to being suspended. An app may need (and request) extra execution time and so may stay in this state for a time. Certain apps run only in the background. These apps, in fact, are launched directly into the background. Such an app enters the background state directly and doesn't go through the Inactive state.

✔ If an app hasn't interacted with the user for a while, iOS may move an app to a *Suspended* state. The app is in the background but is *not* running any code. It does stay in memory, though. If a low-memory condition occurs, the system may purge apps in the Suspended state without notice.

When an iOS app starts, you may not — ever — exit the app completely. In fact, only the iOS system can terminate the app (this behavior is a requirement per Apple's standards).

As your app goes through these states, certain standard methods of the application delegate object, known as *lifecycle methods* are called by iOS. These lifecycle methods are essentially a way to make your app aware of these state transitions, so it can add app-specific behavior at each transition.

Now, allow me to walk you through these methods using Tic-Tac-Toe. Along the way, I'll give you a brief description and, in some cases, provide a code sample.

Start by opening the file `TTTAppDelegate.m`. Each of the lifecycle methods are there, from `didFinishLaunchingWithOptions` to `applicationWill Terminate`. These methods begin with the line `#pragma Lifecycle methods`, so you can find them easily.

Note the `NSLog` statement at the start of each of these methods. Here's one such statement from `applicationDidBecomeActive`:

```
NSLog(@"In applicationDidBecomeActive");
```

Put a breakpoint on each logging statement, as shown in Figure 6-3. Click next to the `NSLog` statement in the column to the left of all the statements.

Now, run the Tic-Tac-Toe app (doesn't matter whether you run on the simulator or an actual device). The log statements appear in the console in the following order:

1. `willFinishLaunchingWithOptions`: The app breaks at this method even before it appears.

   This method is your app's first opportunity to run custom code before the app's windows appear.

2. `didFinishLaunchingWithOptions`: This method is the second opportunity to perform initialization before your app becomes visible to users.

3. `applicationDidBecomeActive`: This method lets your app know that it's about to become the foreground app.

   Use this method for any last-minute preparation.

Figure 6-3:
Setting
breakpoints
in the
lifecycle
methods.

Once the app is running and showing its first screen, press your device's
Home button. Almost immediately, log messages from the following methods
appear:

1. `applicationWillResignActive`: Lets the app know that it's transitioning from being the foreground app.

   Use this method to put your app into a quiescent state.

2. `applicationDidEnterBackground`: Lets you know that your app is
   now running in the background and may be suspended at any time.

Now, find your app on the home page and touch to make it restart. It starts
where it left off, and log messages appear for the methods `application`
`WillEnterForeground` and `applicationDidBecomeActive`. The first
method lets the app know that it's moving out of the background and back
into the foreground but that it isn't active yet. The second method lets the
app know that it's now active.

Now for the last method. Press the Power button on your device so that it
begins to shut down. A log message from the following method appears on
your console: `applicationWillTerminate`. It lets you know that your app
is closing down. This method isn't called if your app is in the suspended state.

These methods obviously aren't there to just log the transition of the app
through its states. They're there so that you can add custom code as the
app transitions to save and reload its data, release and regain resources, and
so on. Chapter 12 covers how to do so within the context of the Tic-Tac-Toe
application.

For more about app states, go to the web resources for each chapter of the book at www.dummies.com/go/iosprogramminglinks and check out the Dealing with App States link. Also, on the same page, click the link labeled Application Delegate Protocol to get more details on the application delegate object.

Interacting with the App Through Its User Interface

As I mention in the previous section, the application object takes each incoming UI event and routes it to its main window. Note that the Application monitors its own window's current status (such as whether it's in the foreground or the background) to decide whether it should send an event to the main window. The main window, in turn, keeps track of its sub-windows and their status. Upon receiving an event from the application object, the main window distributes the event to the most appropriate views in its hierarchy.

Some types of views handle events. Most of the time, however, a custom object must be written to handle events. This custom object is typically a view controller object (an instance of the class or a subclass of UIViewController).

View controllers are the key bridging elements of an app. In fact, you can think of them as the skeleton on which apps are built. iOS provides several types of view controllers (all subclasses of UIViewController), including the Navigation view controller and the Tab Bar, Page View, and Split View view controllers, as well as popovers. iOS has more view controllers for specific functions, such as for controlling the camera.

Because of the core role of view controllers in an iOS app, I recommend that you start with view controllers when developing an app. The importance of view controllers is also reflected in the sample application templates provided in Xcode (discussed in the section, "Visiting the App Templates in Xcode," later in this chapter). These templates differ only in the kinds of view controllers (and related views) they contain.

I discuss view controllers and views in detail in Chapter 9.

Dealing with Data

The previous sections describe how an app starts and how its UI works. In addition, almost every app has data on which it operates. This data can come in various forms within iOS — as files, as Core Data objects, as data from other applications, and from the web. These include built-in applications written by Apple that come with each device, such as the Address Book, as well as apps written by third parties, such as developers like you. This section covers these and other facilities that iOS provides for working with data.

For more about how to deal with data, go to www.dummies.com/go/iosprogramminglinks and check out the Data Management in iOS link, where you will find a complete overview of the data management capabilities in iOS.

Using JSON

JavaScript Object Notation (JSON) has become the *de facto* standard in terms of representing data. You can use JSON to transfer data across the web and as the format for saving and retrieving long-lived data. JSON is both human-readable and easy for machines to understand. Data in JSON can be in one of two structures:

- ✔ An object comprising an un-ordered set of name-value pairs. Each name-value corresponds to an attribute of the object. Each name-value pair can be nested, in case the attribute being represented is hierarchical in nature.

- ✔ An ordered array of values. Each value in the array can be a scalar (a Boolean, string, or number value), an object, or an array.

In Tic-Tac-Toe, JSON represents the state of a game. This state consists of the following:

- ✔ The current player (player 1 or player 2) is represented as an integer (0 for Player 1, and 1 for Player 2).

- ✔ The state of the game — whether it's active or complete; if it's complete, whether it's won or drawn; and if won, by whom.

   The states are also represented as integers, with Inactive being –1, Active being 0, Won being 1, and Draw being 2.

- ✔ The state of the grid — that is, what symbols are present in each of the squares on the grid. Note that the symbols are represented as the integer values 0, 1, and 2, which stand for Blank, X, and O, respectively.

- ✔ The current symbol (the one that will be played on the next move). Here (and just to vary the example), I represent the symbol as the string "X" or the string "O" or a blank (" ").

- ✔ The play count (the number of moves made to the current point in the game) is represented as an integer.

Say that a game is in the state shown in Figure 6-4. In this code, I show the JSON object corresponding to this game:

```
{
  "TTTGameKeyCurrentPlayer" : 0,
  "TTTGameKeyState" : 0,
  "TTTGameKeyGridState" : "2,1,2,2,1,0,1,2,1",
  "TTTGameKeyCurrentSymbol" : "X",
  "TTTGameKeyPlaycount" : 8
}
```

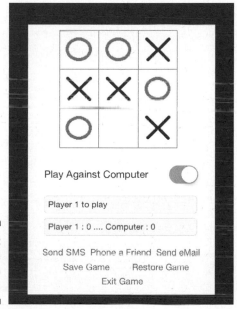

Figure 6-4:
An active
Tic-Tac-Toe
game.

JSON easily maps to the available data structures (such as array, structures, and objects) in pretty much every programming language. The object form of JSON easily maps to programming language objects or structures, whereas the array form of JSON can map to an array, vector, list, or sequence, basically whatever data structure can hold an ordered collection of objects.

In Tic-Tac-Toe, the JSON object corresponding to the state of the game is mapped to a NSDictionary, because a NSDictionary object also consists of nested name value pairs. As a result, when you have to save the state of the game, you get its state as an NSDictionary object and then convert it to a JSON string. When you retrieve the state of the game, you do the opposite — you read in JSON data and convert it to an NSDictionary object and then use the NSDictionary to restore the game to the saved state.

The following example shows this conversion from a dictionary object to JSON and from the JSON data object to a string (from the method `saveGame` in the Game Session view controller — files `TTTGameSessionView Controller.m` and `.h`):

```
- (IBAction) saveGame:(id)sender {
    NSDictionary* savedGameDictionary = [activeGame toDictionary];
    NSError *error;
    NSData *jsonData =
        [NSJSONSerialization dataWithJSONObject:savedGameDictionary
                            options:NSJSONWritingPrettyPrinted
                            error:&error];
    NSString *savedGameString =
        [[NSString alloc] initWithData:jsonData
        encoding:NSUTF8StringEncoding];

    NSString *savedGamesFilePath =
        [NSHomeDirectory()
            stringByAppendingPathComponent:@TTTGAMESESSIONSAVEDFILEPATH];

    [savedGameString writeToFile:savedGamesFilePath
                                atomically:YES
                                encoding:NSUTF8StringEncoding
                                error:NULL];
}
```

The important method here is in the method `dataWithJSONObject` from the `NSJSONSerialization` class.

You can see the reverse operation (that is, from a JSON string to an `NSDictionary`) in the `restoreGame` method in the same view controller:

```
- (IBAction) restoreGame:(id)sender {
    NSLog(@"Restoring game");
    ...
    NSError *restoreError = nil;
    NSMutableDictionary *savedDictionary =
        [NSJSONSerialization JSONObjectWithData:[savedGameString
                                dataUsingEncoding:NSUTF8StringEncoding]
                                options:NSJSONReadingMutableContainers
                                error:&restoreError ];

    activeGame = [[TTTGame alloc] initFromDictionary:savedDictionary];
    TTTGameGrid *gameGrid = [activeGame getGameGrid];
    if (![activeGame isActive])[boardView disableInput];
    [boardView setGrid:gameGrid];
    [gameView redraw];
}
```

Here the key method is the JSONObjectWithData, which does the reverse operation of creating the Objective-C NSDictionary from JSON data.

For complete information about JSON (from the source, so to speak), go to the web resources for this chapter at www.dummies.com/go/iosprogramminglinks and check out the JSON link.

Saving data using files

If you've done any programming in any language (C, C++, Java, C#, you name it), I'm sure that you've used files to read data from and write data to. Objective-C allows you to work with files as well. I use files in Tic-Tac-Toe as the means for storing and restoring the state of an active game.

Files in iOS are organized into directories. Each app gets its own directory (see Figure 6-5) where the app resides and its data can be stored. This directory is known as the app's *sandbox*.

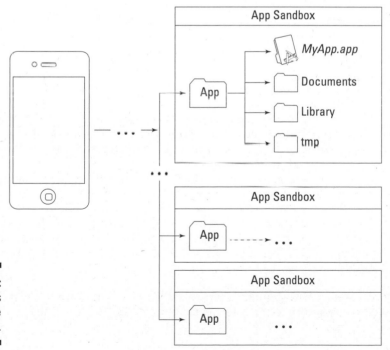

Figure 6-5:
How files
in iOS are
organized.

An app is prohibited from accessing or creating files outside its sandbox. When an app needs to work with the user's contacts or music, the system needs to (and does) allow the file-related operations needed to read from or modify these data stores, which are outside the app's sandbox.

This sandbox directory is organized in a set of subdirectories. Apple specifies how each of these subdirectories should be used, as follows:

✔ The *<app name>*.app directory is where the app's executable and all the files in its bundle reside (such as the X and O images for Tic-Tac-Toe).

✔ The Documents directory holds data that your app can't re-create, such as user-generated documents or content. This is the directory where the Tic-Tac-Toe app saves games, keeps its SQLite files, and so on. iTunes backs up this directory, so when you connect your device to your Mac, the data here will be saved.

✔ The Inbox directory within the Documents directory has special meaning. This directory stores files that *other* apps ask your app to open. For example, the Mail program places e-mail attachments associated with your app in this directory. Your app can read and delete files in this directory but can't create new files or write to existing files.

✔ The Library directory is used for files that aren't user data files but need to be backed up. With the exception of a subdirectory named Caches (which is specifically for data the app temporarily wants to save for faster access), the files here are backed up by iTunes.

✔ The tmp subdirectory saves temporary data that doesn't need to persist between app runs. Your app should remove files from this directory when they're no longer needed. The system may also purge lingering files from this directory when your app isn't running or disk space is low. The contents of this directory are *not* backed up.

Now, look at a quick example in Tic-Tac-Toe that shows how to write to and read from files. In this example, I use a file to save and restore the state of a game. When a user touches Save Game (see Figure 6-6), the current state of the game is saved to a file named `SavedGames.data` in the Documents directory in the app's sandbox (the path to this file was set using #define as the constant `TTTGAMESESSIONSAVEDFILEPATH` in the file `TTTGameSession ViewController.h`).

If the user exits without finishing the game, she can return to the game session screen and return to the saved game by selecting Restore Game.

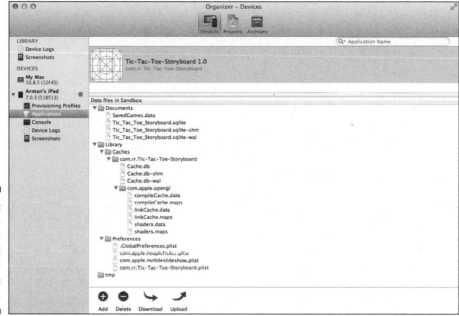

Figure 6-6:
The direc-
tory struc-
ture and
files in Tic-
Tac-Toe's
sandbox.

Now for some code. The following code shows saveGame:

```objc
- (IBAction) saveGame:(id)sender {
    NSDictionary* savedGameDictionary = [activeGame toDictionary];
    NSError *error;
    NSData *jsonData =
        [NSJSONSerialization dataWithJSONObject:savedGameDictionary
                            options:NSJSONWritingPrettyPrinted
                            error:&error];
    NSString *savedGameString =
        [[NSString alloc] initWithData:jsonData
                            encoding:NSUTF8StringEncoding];

    NSString *savedGamesFilePath =
        [NSHomeDirectory()
            stringByAppendingPathComponent:@TTTGAMESESSIONSAVEDFILEPATH];

    [savedGameString writeToFile:savedGamesFilePath
                            atomically:YES
                            encoding:NSUTF8StringEncoding
                            error:NULL];
}
```

Writing to a file is easy. You just build the pathname of the file using the method `stringByAppendingPathComponent` on an object representing the app's home directory (which you get by calling the function `NSHomeDirectory`). Then `[savedGameString writeToFile:savedGamesFilePath ...]` does the actual writing.

Reading from a file is straightforward, too. Here's the code for `restoreGame`:

```
- (IBAction) restoreGame:(id)sender {
    NSString *savedGamesFilePath =
        [NSHomeDirectory()
            stringByAppendingPathComponent:@TTTGAMESESSIONSAVEDFILEPATH];
    NSString *savedGameString =
        [NSString stringWithContentsOfFile:savedGamesFilePath
                encoding:NSUTF8StringEncoding
                error:NULL];

    NSError *restoreError = nil;
    NSMutableDictionary *savedDictionary =
        [NSJSONSerialization JSONObjectWithData:[savedGameString
                            dataUsingEncoding:NSUTF8StringEncoding]
                            options:NSJSONReadingMutableContainers
                            error:&restoreError ];

    activeGame = [[TTTGame alloc] initFromDictionary:savedDictionary];
    TTTGameGrid *gameGrid = [activeGame getGameGrid];
    if (![activeGame isActive])[boardView disableInput];
    [boardView setGrid:gameGrid];
    [gameView redraw];
}
```

You've already seen how a path to the file is created using the `NSHomeDirectory` function to get the home directory object, and then using this object's method `stringByAppendingPathComponent` to create the string. Next, you read the entire file into a string using `[NSString stringWithContentsOfFile:savedGamesFilePath ...]`, and then you're free to process the string as needed. (I left the JSON serialization statements in both the `saveGame` and `restoreGame` snippets so that you can see the file operation within context.)

To find out more about reading and writing files, go to the web resources for this chapter at `www.dummies.com/go/iosprogramminglinks` and check out the Locating Items in an App's Sandbox link.

The file operations shown are easy to use but aren't very refined. Especially note that the Objective-C standard capability for reading from a file is to load the entire file into an object. Loading an entire file into an object is obviously convenient, but it's certainly not the only way to work with files.

For example, you want to be able to read from and write to text files a line at a time. However, iOS doesn't provide easy ways to do so because Objective-C language was created exclusively for development of applications on the Mac and iOS devices, rather than a general purpose language like Java. Consequently, Apple, the primary developer of the MacOS, iOS, and Objective-C, included file-handling methods specifically tailored to the requirements of Cocoa and iOS applications, instead of providing a complete set of general-purpose file-handling capabilities. If you need to get crazy with files, just drop into C.

Moving up to Core Data

In Chapter 4, I present patterns (such as Active Record) for making objects persistent in a database. These patterns deal with standard ways to manage the lifecycle of persistent objects (that is, objects that remain across multiple runs of an app). iOS implementation of ORM is shown in the Core Data framework, which provides standard ways to deal with the common tasks associated with the lifecycle of objects, from their creation, through their modification, through their persistence, to their destruction.

Core Data classes and objects are used within the app's model. These objects are also known as *managed objects* because instances of model objects are handled by a manager object known as the *managed object context*. This context object is a container that serves as a factory for new model objects. Managed objects are also known as *entities,* and I use the terms managed object and entity interchangeably.

This context object also handles the persistence of the model objects by working through an object termed the *persistent store coordinator.* The persistent store coordinator mediates between one or more context objects, and these objects are generally stored in a SQLite database. Figure 6-7 shows how the context and the persistent store coordinator interact.

SQLite is an open-source software library that implements a file-based SQL database engine with transaction support. SQLite is probably the most widely used database on mobile devices. For more information, go to `http:// sqlite.org`.

Now, I show you how to define and use Core Data classes and objects.

When I created the project for the Tic-Tac-Toe app, I set it to use Core Data by checking off the Core Data check box in the window in which I named the project (see Figure 6-8).

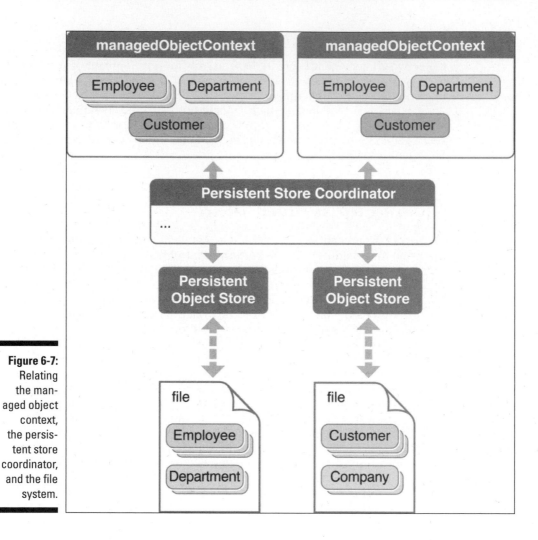

Figure 6-7:
Relating the managed object context, the persistent store coordinator, and the file system.

Checking the Core Data check box brings the Core Data stack of methods into the app delegate class, as shown in Figure 6-9.

It's best to add Core Data at the start of the project. Adding Core Data to an existing project does require a little bit of work. If you need to add Core Data to an existing project, go to `www.dummies.com/go/iosprogramminglinks` and check out the Adding Core Data to an Existing Project link.

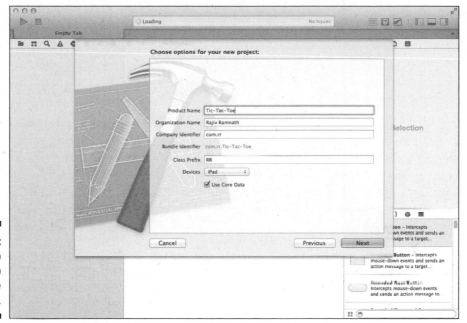

Now, take a look at each of these methods, beginning with the interface file for the Tic-Tac-Toe app delegate, `TTTAppDelegate.h`:

```objc
#import <UIKit/UIKit.h>
@interface TTTAppDelegate : UIResponder <UIApplicationDelegate>
    @property (strong, nonatomic) UIWindow *window;
    @property (readonly, strong, nonatomic)
        NSManagedObjectContext *managedObjectContext;
    @property (readonly, strong, nonatomic)
        NSManagedObjectModel *managedObjectModel;
    @property (readonly, strong, nonatomic)
        NSPersistentStoreCoordinator *persistentStoreCoordinator;

    - (void)saveContext;
    - (NSURL *)applicationDocumentsDirectory;
@end
```

The Core Data methods in the implementation file (`TTTAppDelegate.m`) act as getters for these attributes and are as follows:

- The method `(NSManagedObjectContext *)managedObjectContext` returns the managed object context for the application.

- The method `(NSPersistentStoreCoordinator *) persistentStoreCoordinator` returns the persistent store coordinator for the application. This method needs to be customized with the pathname to the data store, as shown in the following listing. Also, notice the code toward the end of the method where the SQLite file is marked for encryption (see Chapter 12 for more details on encrypting Core Data files).

```objc
- (NSPersistentStoreCoordinator *)persistentStoreCoordinator{
    if (_persistentStoreCoordinator != nil)
        return _persistentStoreCoordinator;

    // Create the URL for the password file
    NSURL *storeURL =
        [[self applicationDocumentsDirectory]
            URLByAppendingPathComponent:
                @"Tic_Tac_Toe_Storyboard.sqlite"];
    NSError *error = nil;
    _persistentStoreCoordinator =
        [[NSPersistentStoreCoordinator alloc]
            initWithManagedObjectModel:[self managedObjectModel]];
    if (![_persistentStoreCoordinator
        addPersistentStoreWithType:NSSQLiteStoreType configuration:nil
        URL:storeURL options:nil error:&error]) {
        ...
    }
```

```
    ...
    // Encrypt the SQLite file
    NSDictionary *fileAttributes =
        [NSDictionary dictionaryWithObject:NSFileProtectionComplete
                    forKey:NSFileProtectionKey];
    if (![[NSFileManager defaultManager] setAttributes:fileAttributes
                            ofItemAtPath:[storeURL path]
                            error:&error])
    {
        ...
    }

    return _persistentStoreCoordinator;
}
```

✔ `(NSManagedObjectModel *)managedObjectModel` returns an object that describes the *schema* or description of all the objects in the model. This method also needs to be initialized with the pathname for the model description file, as shown here:

```
- (NSManagedObjectModel *) managedObjectModel{
    if (_managedObjectModel != nil) return _managedObjectModel;
    NSURL *modelURL = [[NSBundle mainBundle]
                        URLForResource:@"Tic_Tac_Toe_Storyboard"
                        withExtension:@"momd"];

    _managedObjectModel =
        [[NSManagedObjectModel alloc] initWithContentsOfURL:modelURL];
    return _managedObjectModel;
}
```

Now, you're ready to create the model. When you created the project and selected Core Data, you most likely already had a model file (just look for a file with an xcdatamodel extension automatically created by Xcode and named the same as your project).

If you don't already have a model file, don't worry. In Xcode, choose File⇨New⇨File and add a model file, as shown in Figure 6-10. Name it anything you like. However, you have to insert the filename (along with a .sqlite extension in the persistentStoreCoordinator method, as shown here:

```
NSURL *storeURL =
    [[self applicationDocumentsDirectory]
        URLByAppendingPathComponent:@"Tic_Tac_Toe_Storyboard.sqlite"];
```

You also need to insert the name of the file in the `managedObjectModel` method, as shown here:

```
NSURL *modelURL =
    [[NSBundle mainBundle] URLForResource:@"Tic_Tac_Toe_Storyboard"
                          withExtension:@"momd"];
```

Now you're all set to create the model, which is stored in the SQLite database. Rather than a step-by-step guide to creating a model, I show you one from Tic-Tac-Toe.

Click the model file `Tic_Tac_Toe_Storyboard.xcdatamodeld` to open the model used in Tic-Tac-Toe in a model definition screen on the right. You can see this model in either a detail view (see Figure 6-11) or a graphical view (see Figure 6-12) by using the button at the window's lower-right to switch between views. You can add a new entity by clicking the Add Entity button at the bottom-left, or you can add a new attribute to an entity by first selecting the entity and then adding an attribute. Or you can set or change the type of an attribute using the pop-up menu as shown in Figure 6-11.

When you have the model to your liking, it's time to create the classes for the managed objects. So, choose your trusty File➪New➪File menus (which you'll be using a lot) and add a `NSManagedObject` subclass (see Figure 6-13).

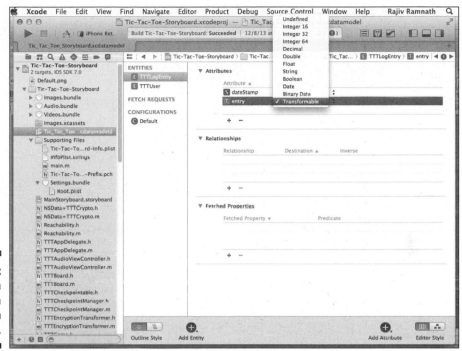

Figure 6-11:
Editing a
Core Data
model in
Detail view.

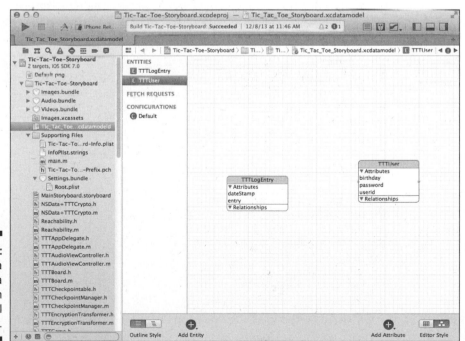

Figure 6-12:
Editing a
Core Data
model in
Graphical
view.

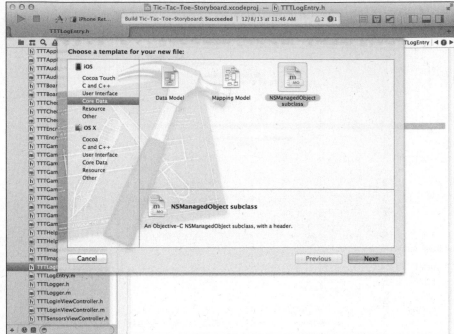

Figure 6-13:
Adding a
managed
object
subclass.

Tic-Tac-Toe has two managed object subclasses. The more interesting one
is the managed class named User (see files TTTUser.h and TTTUser.m).
Here's the interface file for this class:

```objc
#import <Foundation/Foundation.h>
#import <CoreData/CoreData.h>
@interface TTTUser : NSManagedObject

    @property (nonatomic, retain) NSString * userid;
    @property (nonatomic, retain) NSString * password;
    @property (nonatomic, retain) NSDate * birthday;

@end
```

You can see that the properties of this class match the attributes of the corresponding model. Here's the implementation (.m) file:

```objc
#import "TTTUser.h"
@implementation TTTUser
    @dynamic userid;
    @dynamic password;
    @dynamic birthday;
@end
```

The @dynamic annotation means that the accessor methods are provided by
the NSManagedObject superclass.

Next, you find out how to use Core Data. I used it two ways: to store users' data (userids, passwords, and birthdates) utilizing `TTTUser` objects and to store log entries using the `TTTLogEntry` object. I show you examples of both. As always, you can follow along in Xcode; just refer to the User Manager class (files `TTTUserManager.h` and `.m`) and the Logger class (files `TTTLogger.h` and `.m`).

The following code (from the `log` method of the Logger class) shows how an instance of a model class is created and saved, using calls to the `insert NewObjectForEntityForName` method and the `save` method of the `managedObjectContext`, respectively:

```objc
-(void) log :(NSString *) anEntry{


    ...
    TTTLogEntry *logEntryObject =
        [NSEntityDescription insertNewObjectForEntityForName:@"TTTLogEntry"
                        inManagedObjectContext:self->managedObjectContext];

    [logEntryObject setDateStamp :aDateStamp];
    [logEntryObject setEntry :anEntry];

    NSError *error = nil;
    [managedObjectContext save:&error];
}
```

The following code from the User Manager class shows how objects are fetched from the data store:

```objc
- (NSMutableArray*) getAllUsersFromDB {

    NSMutableArray* retVal-nil;
    NSEntityDescription *userEntityDescription =
        [NSEntityDescription
                         entityForName:@"TTTUser"
                         inManagedObjectContext: managedObjectContext];
    NSFetchRequest *request = [[NSFetchRequest alloc] init];
    [request setEntity: userEntityDescription];

    NSError *error = nil;
    NSArray *results =
        [managedObjectContext executeFetchRequest:request error:&error];

    if (!results || error) return nil;

    retVal = [[NSMutableArray alloc] initWithArray: results];
    return retVal;
}
```

Note the call to `entityForName` to extract the description (that is, the schema) of the User entity and the call to the `executeFetchRequest` of the managed object context that fetches all the results. These are the two important statements in this method.

That's it for Core Data. For more information about this topic, go to www. dummies.com/go/iosprogramminglinks and check out information on the Core Data Technology Overview, Core Data Programming Guide, and Core Data Model Editor links.

Accessing the Address Book

The iOS framework provides functions that enable your app to work with the databases that come with iOS devices. One such database is the *Address Book*, which includes people and their contact information. iOS devices also provide a Contacts app that allows users to manage this database by adding new contacts, updating them, deleting them, and so on.

The information in an Address Book is accessible to other apps, albeit in a controlled manner. For example, your app can present users with the contacts from the Address Book, allow them to select a contact, and then use the information of the selected contact. I sometimes use this functionality in Tic-Tac-Toe to gloat over my glorious Tic-Tac-Toe score via an e-mail to someone in my contact list.

To better understand, take a look at the Game Session view controller (TTTGameSessionViewController.m and .h) and follow along. First, you use the view controller to implement the ABPeoplePickerNavigation ControllerDelegate protocol, as shown here:

```
@interface TTTGameSessionViewController:
                            UIViewController
                            <MFMailComposeViewControllerDelegate,
                            MFMessageComposeViewControllerDelegate,
                            ABPeoplePickerNavigationControllerDelegate,
                            TTTCheckpointable> {
 ...
}
```

The method sendScoresByEmailWithContact (reproduced next) is the action method that initiates the process by presenting the Address Book picker and allowing the user to select the contact:

```
- (IBAction) sendScoresByEmailWithContact:(id)sender{
    ABPeoplePickerNavigationController *picker =
        [[c alloc] init];
    picker.peoplePickerDelegate = self;
    [self presentViewController:picker animated:YES completion:nil];
}
```

This method also sets its object (the Game Session view controller) as the delegate for the picker. When the picker finishes selecting an entry from the Address Book, the delegate method `shouldContinueAfterSelecting Person` is called:

```
- (BOOL)peoplePickerNavigationController:
        (ABPeoplePickerNavigationController *)peoplePicker
        shouldContinueAfterSelectingPerson:(ABRecordRef)selectedPerson {
    NSString* oneEmail=nil;
    ABMultiValueRef emails = ABRecordCopyValue(selectedPerson,
                                                kABPersonEmailProperty);
    if (ABMultiValueGetCount(emails) > 0) {
        oneEmail =
            (__bridge_transfer NSString*)
                ABMultiValueCopyValueAtIndex(emails, 0);
    }
    CFRelease(emails);
    [self dismissViewControllerAnimated:YES
        completion:^{[self sendScoresByEmailWithAddress:oneEmail];}];
    return NO;
}
```

The e-mail address of the contact selected using the picker is extracted from the variable `selectedPerson` using the property `kABPersonEmailProperty`. Note also that the contact may have several e-mails, and only the first one (at index 0 in the extracted list) is used.

Next, the Picker view controller is dismissed using `dismissViewController Animated`. Here comes the cool part: Setting the completion parameter to the method `sendScoresByEmailWithAddress` causes this method to be called right after the Address Book picker is dismissed. This process, in turn, causes the Mail app to fire up, with the address filled in, all ready for you to send your scores (see Figure 6-14).

Finally, look at the two methods `bridge_transfer` and `CFRelease`. They are necessary because the Address Book API isn't integrated with the new Automated Reference Counting (ARC) memory management mechanism (refer to Chapter 3).

For more about using the Address Book, go to the web resources for the chapters in this book at www.dummies.com/go/iosprogramminglinks) and check out the Address Book Programming link.

Figure 6-14:
Sending
e-mail with
the address
prefilled.

Setting options for your app

Apps often present a variety of customizable options to users that define how the apps work. These options are usually known as the *settings* for the app and include options such as the user's name, a startup image for the app, and the beginning level of play for a game (for example, novice, expert, and so on).

Understanding the Settings app

Rather than require developers to implement settings functionality in every app, iOS provides a Settings app with capabilities that can be extended to accommodate new apps as needed. Select the appropriate settings via the Settings app, and then when running, the app can read these settings. You can also change the settings from within the app and synch these changes with the Settings app.

Now for a walk through the Settings app (if you're already an iPhone or iPad user, you're probably familiar with this app). In Figure 6-15, the Settings app presents a hierarchical set of pages for navigating app settings in a spilt screen format. The main page of the Settings app shows the preferences for the overall system and lists the apps, including apps others may have developed, with customizable preferences.

Selecting a third-party app takes the user to the preferences for that app, as shown for Tic-Tac-Toe in Figure 6-16.

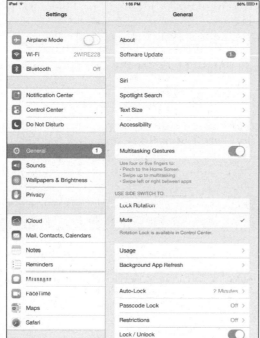

Figure 6-15:
The Settings app showing General settings for the device.

Figure 6-16:
Settings for Tic-Tac-Toe.

As you can see, Tic-Tac-Toe has two Settings options: Player Name (the name of the main user — for example, the owner of the device) and Play Against Computer. Here's what you do to specify the settings I chose:

1. **In Xcode, create a Settings bundle for the app's project by choosing File⇨New⇨File.**

   A window showing a set of file templates appears.

2. **Under iOS, located on the left side of the screen, select Resource, then select Settings Bundle (see Figure 6-17), and click Next.**

   A Save As screen appears.

Figure 6-17:
Adding a Settings bundle to your app's project.

3. **Associate the file with the project and save it.**

4. **Create a property list file by choosing File⇨New⇨File, select Resource (refer Figure 6-17), and then select Property List.**

5. **Name the file** Root.plist, **associate this file with the project, and save it.**

   Future versions of Xcode may create this file for you within the Settings bundle.

6. **Move the property list file to this Settings bundle.**

   I tried to figure out how to perform this step within Xcode and gave up. Finally, I found the Settings bundle in the project directory for your app, edited the name to remove the .bundle extension, which reveals it as a directory, manually moved the file into this Settings bundle directory, and then reentered the .bundle extension.

7. **In Xcode, edit the** `Root.plist` **file (as shown in Figure 6-18) to set Item 0 as a text field named Player Name and a default value of** *<Enter Player Name>*.

The next time you build and install this app (on a device or on the simulator), you'll see an entry for Tic-Tac-Toe Storyboard in the Settings app, with the two items just described.

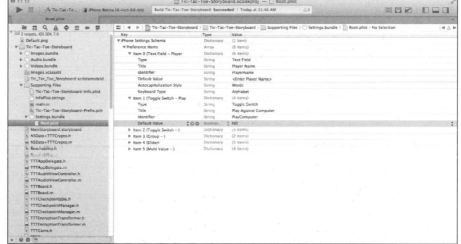

Figure 6-18: Adding preference items to the `Root.plist` file.

The User Defaults component and the NSUserDefaults class

The Settings app is actually the frontend to the User Defaults component managed by iOS, which keeps track of user preferences for all the installed apps, as well as for system attributes, such as the volume setting.

Your app can access these settings through the `NSUserDefaults` class, as I show next.

Reading and writing preferences in your app code

The code for Tic-Tac-Toe settings turns out to be quite simple, as the following code shows (from the method `initializeGameSession` in `TTTGame SessionViewController.m`):

```
NSUserDefaults *tictactoeDefaults =
                    [NSUserDefaults
    standardUserDefaults];
firstPlayerName = [tictactoeDefaults
    stringForKey:@"PlayerName"];
if (firstPlayerName == nil) firstPlayerName = @"Player 1";


playComputer = [tictactoeDefaults


    boolForKey:@"PlayComputer"];
```

The method `standardUserDefaults` returns an instance of `NSUserDefaults`, which is a dictionary object containing the defaults for your app as name-value pairs. The statement `[tictactoeDefaults stringForKey:@"Player Name"]` returns the value of the player name, whereas `[tictactoeDefaults boolForKey:@"PlayComputer"]` returns whether Tic-Tac-Toe is played against a computer or between two people.

You may choose to modify these settings from within the app, which means that the changed settings must be written back to the `NSUserDefaults` subsystem. The following code from the method `synchronizeDefaults` in `TTTGameSessionViewController.m` shows you how to do so. You must get an `NSUserDefaults` object, change the value for the appropriate key in this object, and then call the `synchronize` method. That's it!

```
- (void) synchronizeDefaults {
    NSUserDefaults *tictactoeDefaults =
                [NSUserDefaults standardUserDefaults];
    [tictactoeDefaults setObject:[NSNumber numberWithBool:playComputer]
                             forKey:@"PlayComputer"];
    [tictactoeDefaults synchronize];
}
```

To find out more about the Settings app, go to the web resources for this chapter at `www.dummies.com/go/iosprogramminglinks` and check out the link aptly named The Settings App. On the same page, you'll also find the NSUser Class Reference link, where you can find information about the `NSUserDefaults` class.

Sharing data across apps

The Address Book and the Settings database aren't the only databases that are shareable across apps. iOS provides many options for sharing information among the applications installed on a device. Using Universal Record Locators (URL), your app can access data from the web, as well as pass information to other installed applications, such as Mail, iTunes, and YouTube. Your own application can declare its own URL scheme, allowing any application to collaborate and share data with your app. I briefly describe some facilities here:

✔ iOS apps can gain access to event information from the Calendar database on the device. Your app can fetch events within a date range, be notified when events change, and even directly create, edit, and synch events with a remote calendar. Access to the calendar is provided by the Event Kit framework, details of which you can find by going to `www.dummies.com/go/iosprogramminglinks` and checking the Event Kit Programming link.

✔ The `UIActivityViewController` class is a built-in view controller. You can use it to provide various built-in, standard services, such as a pasteboard for copying and cutting data from your app and pasting it in another one (and vice versa), for posting to social media sites from within your app, and for sending messages via e-mail and SMS. For more about the `UIActivityViewController` class, go to www.dummies.com/go/iosprogramminglinks and check out the UIActivityViewController link.

✔ iOS provides a *keychain* as one of the facilities it offers. A keychain is an encrypted container that holds things like passwords and other information that needs to be secure on an app. Applications with the same app ID prefix can gain shared access to the elements of the keychain that they're supposed to jointly create and manage. For more about keychains, go to www.dummies.com/go/iosprogramminglinks and check out the Keychain link.

✔ Apple's iCloud is a cloud storage service where you (and your app) can store data and automatically have this data synchronized with all your devices. iCloud provides an application programming interface (API). To find out more about the iCloud, go to www.dummies.com/go/iosprogramminglinks and check out the iCloud link.

✔ As with other frameworks for mobile devices (such as the Android framework), iOS apps can access the web through web services programming interfaces provided by the `NSURL` and `NSURLConnection` classes. Most web services today use JavaScript Object Notation (aka JSON), and parsing JSON is handled in the iOS framework by the `NSJSONSerialization` class (as shown in the earlier section "Saving data using files." Chapter 12 has an example showing how to use a geocoding web service. To find out more about URLs and JSON, go to www.dummies.com/go/iosprogramminglinks and check out the NSURL, NSURLConnection, and Handling JSON links.

Using Other iOS Capabilities on a Device

You can design your app to take advantage of several additional iOS capabilities, all of which I cover in detail in subsequent chapters.

✔ **Location and mapping services:** Location services inform apps of their locations in a variety of ways from GPS devices that are accurate to within 15 feet to Wi-Fi that comes close to matching GPS accuracy. Mapping services allow you to write apps that can show information on maps. I cover both these services in detail in Chapter 12.

✔ **Sensors on devices:** Sensors, such as accelerometers that can sense straight-line motion, gyroscopes that can sense rotational motion, and magnetometers that can sense closeness to metal objects are covered in Chapter 13.

✔ **Other built-in apps:** Other built-in apps that provide capabilities such as e-mail, SMS, telephony, cameras, and audio and video players are also covered in Chapter 13.

Visiting the App Templates in Xcode

Xcode provides several templates for building apps, as shown in Figure 6-19. These templates provide a quick and convenient way to start building several of the common types of iOS apps.

You see these templates when you choose File➪New➪Project to create a new iOS development project in Xcode. These templates aren't complicated. Also, you can start with any one of them and then add other templates as needed. For example, I started with an Empty Application template and then added everything else.

Figure 6-19: iOS project templates in Xcode.

With that introduction, here are the templates:

✔ The Single View Application template provides a view controller and a storyboard with the single view.

✔ The Utility Application template provides a starting point for an application with two views — a main view and an alternate view.

- For iPhone, this template sets up a button with the default name Info (this name can be changed). Touching the Info button causes the app to change from the main view to an alternate view.

- For iPad, it sets up a bar button with the default name Info (this name can be changed) that shows the alternate view in a popover.

✔ The Empty Application template is just that: It provides only an application delegate and a window on which to build.

✔ The Master-Detail Application template is a starting point for an application that shows a list of items on a page. When you click one of the items, details about that item appear.

- On an iPhone, an item's details appear on a separate screen.

  Figure 6-20 shows an iPhone simulator example from Tic-Tac-Toe, where the master list and detail are split across two pages.

Figure 6-20:
A Master-Detail Application on an iPhone simulator.

- On an iPad, the details appear in a split view.

  Figure 6-21 shows the Settings app on an iPad mini, where the master list and the detail appear in a split view.

✔ The Tabbed Application template starts an application with a tab bar. It comes preconfigured with a Tab Bar view controller and view controllers for the views that are selected by the tab bar items.

✔ The Page-Based Application template provides a starting point for a page-based application that uses a Page view controller.

Some application templates have certain options that others don't have. For example, the Single View Application template, the Tabbed Application template, and the Page-Based Application template don't come with the option to include Core Data.

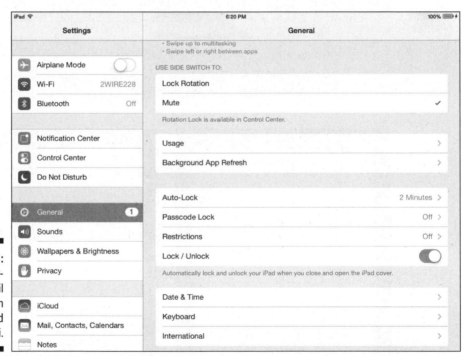

Figure 6-21:
A Master-Detail Application on an iPad mini.

Deconstructing the iOS Framework Using OO Principles and Design Patterns

So far in this chapter, you've been fire-hosed with information about the iOS framework and how to build and use an iOS app. Next, I discuss this information from the perspective of object-orientation (OO) — refer to Chapter 2 for the basics on OO.

Seeing object-oriented concepts and techniques in iOS

The iOS framework and an iOS app are poster children for object-orientation — all the OO concepts and techniques, such as classes, inheritance and subclassing, and methods are used in the framework and in the assembly of an iOS app.

I don't go into all the uses of OO in the framework and the app in this section. However, I do want to draw your attention to several examples of OO. You can find the concepts behind most of these examples in Chapter 2. In the cases where a concept or technique isn't covered in Chapter 2, I've at least made mention of the concept (once again in Chapter 2) and provided references there.

A lot of app building is facilitated via subclassing, as shown here:

- ✔ View controllers are the dominant components of iOS apps. So that building view controllers is made easy, iOS provides a great deal of built-in view controller functionality that you can use simply by subclassing. You'll see that each view controller class in Tic-Tac-Toe, from `TTTAudioViewController` to `TTTSensorsViewController` is subclassed from `UIViewController`.

- ✔ You can create custom views by subclassing from the View class. An example of creating a custom view in Tic-Tac-Toe is the Board class (`TTTBoard`), which is subclassed from `UIView`.

- ✔ Subclassing is also used to customize functionality within Core Data. For example, see the use of `TTTEncryptionTransformer` (which is subclassed from `NSValueTransformer`).

Subtyping (or reuse of an *interface*) is different from subclassing (which is reuse of *implementation*) and is used in the various protocols that the Tic-Tac-Toe classes implement. In particular, the view controllers use subtyping as a way to act as delegates to a variety of other components. For example:

- ✔ `TTTAudioViewController` implements the `AVAudioRecorder Delegate` and `AVAudioPlayerDelegate` protocols to handle playing and stopping recordings.

- ✔ `TTTGameSessionViewController` implements several protocols — namely, `MFMailComposeViewControllerDelegate`, `MFMessage ComposeViewControllerDelegate`, and `ABPeoplePickerNavigation ControllerDelegate` — so it can serve as the delegate to the mail, SMS, and Address Book pickers, as well as `TTTCheckpointable` so that it can save game settings.

- ✔ Tic-Tac-Toe even defines its own protocol — `TTTCheckpointable` — for classes that would need to save data if the operating system were to force the app to shut down.

Note especially that protocols and delegation are what allow you to use polymorphism.

In setting up the delegate for the Address Book picker, you'll see examples for delayed binding.

Inversion of control (which occurs when the iOS framework calls components of your app, rather than the other way around) occurs in the setting up of event handling in the various screens and views. Inversion of control is also particularly visible in how the lifecycle of an iOS app is handled. In this case, the system calls the lifecycle methods — `applicationWillResignActive`, `applicationDidEnterBackground`, `applicationWillEnterFore ground`, `applicationWillTerminate`, and others — in the app delegate whenever the app starts up, is sent to the background, comes back to the foreground, or is terminated.

Seeing patterns in iOS

Because I cover the Model-View-Controller (MVC) pattern in several previous chapters (Chapters 2, 4, 7, and 9), I don't cover it in this section, except to say that it's the dominant behavioral pattern for iOS apps, and it's used in every view controller. However, in this section, I do talk about other patterns mentioned in this chapter.

In regard to construction or creational patterns, the Singleton pattern is apparent in the creation of Application and App Delegate objects (there's exactly one of each of these objects) and in the Managed Object Context. These singletons are created via a Factory class. That is, the Singleton pattern is combined with the Factory pattern. The Façade pattern is used in the Objective-C file-handling routines to provide a simplified interface to the underlying C-based capabilities.

A prime example of structural patterns is in use of the Composite pattern in the view hierarchy. Rather than treating composite views and views without children separately, iOS treats them all as one class of object, specifically in the way events are handled, by having every view inherit from the `UIResponder` class.

Critiquing the iOS framework from the perspective of OO principles

The three key principles behind good object-oriented design are separation of concerns, low coupling, and high cohesion.

The iOS framework attempts to adhere to these principles by separating into several smaller frameworks and libraries and then attempting to provide reasonably well-structured and cohesive classes and protocols around distinct areas of functionality (such as user-interface handling rather than, say, file handling), with low coupling among these classes and frameworks.

However, iOS is a large framework developed over several years (20 years or more, if you include the MacOS, which served as the basis for iOS) by tens, if not hundreds, of people. Also, Objective-C, unlike Java, was designed from the ground up as a new language and was meant to be an OO layer on C. As a result, some of the framework's components are hard to understand and use.

I found the file-handling API surprisingly hard to figure out and use. For one thing, the `NSString` class provides methods that deal with file handling, essentially making the `NSString` class, which is a scalar class, (that is, a class meant to hold one value and small amounts of data) a façade for files that will hold large data sets and be a mediator between memory and disk.

Here are examples of overloading the `NSString` class:

```
[savedGameString writeToFile:savedGamesFilePath
              atomically:YES
              encoding:NSUTF8StringEncoding
              error:NULL];
```

and

```
NSString *savedGameString =
        [NSString stringWithContentsOfFile:savedGamesFilePath
                  encoding:NSUTF8StringEncoding
                  error:NULL];
```

Imagine, for example, an inexperienced programmer trying to read a large document from a disc into a string and running out of memory.

Because iOS apps are user-driven, you need to separate presentation of the user interface from actions that occur because of users' interactions with the interface. These apps give users a set of capabilities and allow users to pick what they want to do, instead of controlling or sequencing what the user does.

However, in some situations, this separation of UI and action is unnecessary and results in a loose coupling technique (such as delegation), whereas the interaction should be tightly coupled. Pickers and delegate combos, such as the Address Book picker and delegate, are prime examples of this anti-pattern.

The Address Book picker doesn't simply present a UI and return the selected contact in a modal dialog. Instead, it sends the selected contact to a delegate method. So, in order to provide the contact selected from the Address Book to the Mail app, I had to create an inline callback of sendScoresByEmail WithAddress:oneEmail and include it as a parameter to peoplePicker NavigationController.

```
- (BOOL)peoplePickerNavigationController:
    (ABPeoplePickerNavigationController *)peoplePicker
    shouldContinueAfterSelectingPerson:(ABRecordRef)selectedPerson {
  NSString* oneEmail=nil;
  ABMultiValueRef emails =
      ABRecordCopyValue(selectedPerson, kABPersonEmailProperty);
  if (ABMultiValueGetCount(emails) > 0) {
      oneEmail = (__bridge_transfer NSString*)
      ABMultiValueCopyValueAtIndex(emails, 0);
  }
  CFRelease(emails);
  [self dismissViewControllerAnimated:YES
      completion:^{[self sendScoresByEmailWithAddress:oneEmail];}];
  return NO;
}
```

Chapter 7

Illustrating Object-Oriented iOS App Design

In This Chapter

▶ Creating a simple software development process for your project

▶ Identifying use cases and scenarios and creating an object-oriented design for an app

▶ Transferring a design to and implementing it on the iOS framework

*P*rior chapters in this book focus mostly on explaining OO design, except for a little hands-on work in Chapters 3, 5, and 6 (on Objective-C, Xcode, and an introduction to the iOS Framework, respectively). In this chapter you will see how to take the idea behind your app and design and implement it using OO techniques. That is, you find out how to design an iOS application from scratch.

Customizing an SDLC for iOS App Development

Before starting on the development of your app, I strongly recommend that you think about and design your development process (also known as your software development lifecycle, or SDLC). In other words, you need to decide *how* you'll develop the app (rather than what you will develop). First, you must decide how predictive and structured or how flexible and agile the SDLC will be. As I explain in Chapter 2, this choice depends upon the following:

▶ How critical is my app's mission?

▶ How likely is it that the app will change?

▶ How skilled is the team (for current purposes, the team consists of you and me)?

▶ How big is the system?

▶ How comfortable is the team, (once again, you and me) with change?

To answer these questions, you must first understand what you're building (you're building a Tic-Tac-Toe game), why you're building it (to learn how to build apps using iOS), and with whom you're building it (you're building it with me). Here are some responses to the preceding questions:

- **Mission critical:** The app isn't mission critical; no one is likely to be injured playing Tic-Tac-Toe, which means you could use an agile process.

- **Likelihood of change:** How likely are the requirements of the app to change? We both know what Tic-Tac-Toe is, so the game part of the app is pretty well understood. This means you could use a predictable, structured process.

- **Team's skill:** With you on board, the team is pretty skilled. Given that we're both pretty skilled, I think we could work together in a very agile manner, although if we went about app development in a well-structured manner, it wouldn't do any harm.

- **Size of system:** The system is small. In fact, you might be hard-pressed to call the app a system. A small system could easily accommodate an agile process.

- **Team's comfort with change:** You are, after all, reading this book to find out how to develop iOS apps, and you probably wouldn't like it if I made all kinds of changes to the app as we go along. So, you probably want me to tell you up front what I'm going to build and to stick with the plan. I'd say this calls for a structured process.

Some of these responses suggest an agile process. However, most of them support use of a systematic, structured process. So that's the process you'll use in this chapter to understand iOS app development — using Tic-Tac-Toe as the example. Specifically, you'll do the following:

- Develop use cases for the Tic-Tac-Toe app.

- Design the user interface using pen-and-pencil sketches.

- Produce an OO design of the app and its logic.

You begin with an OO design without considering the implementation platform — iOS. Doing so makes the design process easier and results in a good design from an OO perspective.

Once you have the initial design, you map the design onto the iOS platform. Finally, you implement the design — that is, you write the code for the app.

Think of this process as being one for a fancy dessert recipe that you must translate according to what's in your kitchen.

Developing Use Cases

Your first step is to identify what the app must do. In techie-speak this is known as capturing the app's *functional* requirements. Functional requirements are typically captured as use cases. A *use case* is a description of a specific interaction between an *actor* (an entity external to the system, such as a user or another system) and the system being designed.

Developing use cases begins with creating a written description of the app. Here is a simple description of Tic-Tac-Toe:

Tic-tac-toe, also spelled tick-tack-toe, or noughts and crosses, as it's known in Britain and some of the Commonwealth countries, is a pencil-and-paper game for two players. These two players take turns marking the empty spaces in a three-by-three grid, one player using the symbols X and the other player using the symbol O. The X player usually goes first. The player who succeeds in placing three of his marks to fill a horizontal, vertical, or diagonal row wins the game.

Now, here's a narrative that extends the preceding description about playing Tic-Tac-Toe on an iOS device.

Tic-Tac-Toe for iOS implements the Tic-Tac-Toe paper game as an iOS app. Users can play the game against the computer. Multiple games can be played in each session, with either the computer playing first or the user playing first on an electronic board shown on the device's touchscreen. Scores for each session are accumulated. If the user quits the session, scores are reset.

The next step in developing use cases is to identify the actors and write down their interactions with the app. In Tic-Tac-Toe, there are either two actors who are the players of the game or one human actor who is playing against a computer (which is considered a system actor). The interactions of the actors with the game are as follows:

1. A player starts a game session.

2. A player makes a move (that is, places an X or an O in any empty square).

3. The game ends in either a win or a draw. When the game ends, the players are notified of the result.

4. A player continues a game session and starts another game.

5. A player terminates the session, which could happen in the middle of the game or after a game is over.

Here's the general format of a use case (once again, for a specific interaction with the system):

- ✔ Title of use case
- ✔ Actor or set of actors interacting with the system
- ✔ Starting point of the interaction, also known as the *assumptions* necessary for the interaction
- ✔ Short description of the interaction
- ✔ Outcomes of the interaction

Consequently, the use cases for Tic-Tac-Toe are as follows:

- ✔ **Use Case 1:** Player starts a game session.

  Actor: Player.

  Assumptions: The app is running. One of the players is presented with a user interface option to start a new session.

  Description: This use case describes the interactions that take place when a player creates a new Tic-Tac-Toe session. Starting a session automatically starts a new game.

  Outcomes: Scores are set to 0 for both players. A new game starts, and the players see a blank three by three grid to play on.

- ✔ **Use Case 2:** Player makes a move.

  Actor: Player (could be Player 1 or Player 2).

  Assumptions: A game session and a game are active (see Use Case 1).

  Description: Player 1 makes the first move. His move consists of placing an X in an empty square on the game grid. Player 2 goes next by placing an O in an empty square. The players then alternate until the game ends.

  Outcomes: After each move, an X or an O appears in the appropriate square on the grid.

- ✔ **Use Case 3:** The game ends, and the players are notified.

  Actor: Player (could be Player 1 or Player 2).

  Assumptions: A game session and a game are active. A player (Player 1 or Player 2) just made a move (see Use Case 2).

  Description: If the move results in every cell in a row, column, or diagonal being filled with the same symbol (either an X or an O), the game ends. The last player to make a move wins, and his tally is incremented accordingly. If the move doesn't result in a win but all the cells are filled leaving the next player with no place to play, the game ends in a draw.

Outcomes: The players are notified of the outcome and the updated scores and are asked whether they want to continue the session by playing another game.

✔ **Use Case 4:** Player continues a session.

Actor: Player (could be Player 1 or Player 2).

Assumptions: A game session is active. A game has just ended (see Use Case 3), and the players are asked whether they want to continue the session by playing another game.

Description: A player elects to continue the session by starting a new game.

Outcomes: A new game begins within the same session.

✔ **Use Case 5:** Player ends a session.

Actor: Player (could be Player 1 or Player 2).

Assumptions: A game session is active. A game has just ended (see Use Case 3), and the players are asked whether they want to continue the session by playing another game

Description: A player elects not to play another game, so the session terminates.

Outcomes: The session terminates. Scores are reset. The user is presented with an option to start a new session (see Use Case 1).

I used a simple notation to demonstrate use cases, but there are many formal formats for documenting use cases. You can find one to suit your taste by searching the web. Just enter the keywords *Use case template* in your favorite search engine. You can also find some resources in Chapter 15.

Creating the User Interface

Now that the use cases have been defined, you're ready to start sketching the user interface for the app. You can use drawing software, if you really want to, but I've found that using pencil and paper is just fine. You can even use a whiteboard or blackboard and then take a picture of the board.

Figure 7-1 shows a sketch of the app's startup screen welcoming you to Tic-Tac-Toe and inviting you to start a new game.

WELCOME
TO
TIC-TAC-TOE !

Start a New Session

Figure 7-1:
UI sketch
for start-
ing a new
Tic-Tac-Toe
session.

Figure 7-2 shows the user interface when the game is underway. Note that both players have made a few moves and it's Player 1's turn to play.

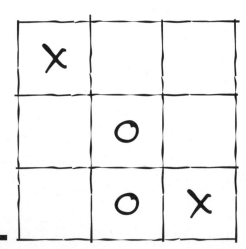

Figure 7-2:
An active
Tic-Tac-Toe
game.

Player 1 to play

Scores: Player 1: 8   Player 2: 6

Figure 7-3 shows what happens when a game ends and the players are asked whether they want to play a new game in the same session.

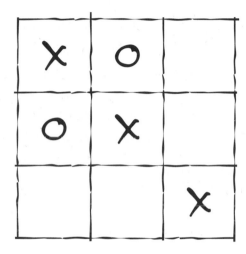

Game Over!

Scores:

Figure 7-3:
Game ends!
Play a new
game?

Play New game?

Yes   No

The screen flow for the game is shown in Figure 7-4 (which is built from Figures 7-1, 7-2, and 7-3). Note that the screen flow is from Figure 7-1 to Figure 7-2 and then to Figure 7-3.

I recommend developing the use case and the user interface (UI) together. You may want to follow this process, as I do at times:

✔ **Write down the concept for your app.** Then start by sketching a few screens or writing a use case or two or, if necessary, by going back and refining the concept for the app. Basically, if you get stuck while doing one thing, switch to doing another.

✔ **Be prepared to iterate.** Even at this high-level point in your, the process is by no means linear. Design involves lots of back-and-forth activity and erasure of previous work, along with wads of balled-up paper and pictures of whiteboards in the wastebasket. Keep in mind that in OO design and development, the end result is clean, but the process is sometimes messy.

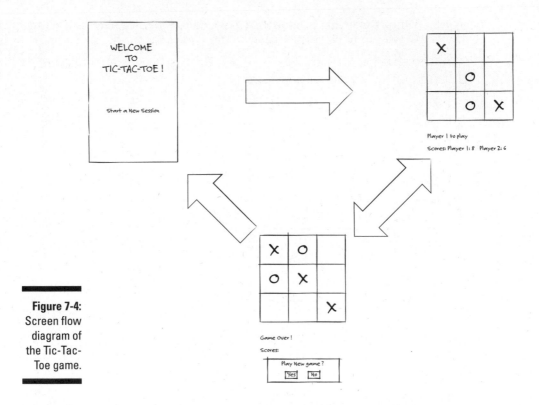

Figure 7-4:
Screen flow
diagram of
the Tic-Tac-
Toe game.

Illustrating Object-Oriented Design

Your next step in designing your app in an object-oriented way is to extract software elements from the text descriptions of the app. That is, you need to extract objects, classes, responsibilities of these classes, and collaborations among these classes, from the app's description and use cases. In the following three sections, I show you how to extract these elements from the description of Tic-Tac-Toe, along with the use cases and sketches from the previous section.

These extracted classes, responsibilities, and collaborations make up your initial design of the app. Once you have this initial design, you can start translating it into code, as I describe in the section, "Implementing an Object-Oriented Design on iOS," later in this chapter.

Classes and responsibilities

Start by extracting nouns from the description of the app and its use cases. These become potential objects, classes, and attributes of your app. Next, you extract verbs from the description and use cases. These become candidate responsibilities (potential methods of classes).

The following list shows how I identified, defined, and extracted nouns for the Tic-Tac-Toe app; then I do the same for verbs.

✔ **Nouns:** Nouns that you may find in the descriptions and use cases of the Tic-Tac-Toe app are pencil, paper, game, nought, cross, player, X, O, space, symbol, grid, mark, vertical row, horizontal row, diagonal row, human user, human, computer, session, board, touchscreen, and score.

Next, write down a one-to-two line definition of each noun in the context of the app that you're trying to build. Then compare these definitions. If you find that two nouns are defined in the same way, remove one of them. You might also decide to merge two definitions (and therefore the corresponding nouns) into one. When you complete this process of definition, removal, and merging, you're left with a set of nouns that will serve as your candidate classes. Following is an example of this process from Tic-Tac-Toe (using a subset of the nouns and verbs, to avoid taxing your patience):

• Remove the nouns *pencil* and *paper* as physical things not relevant to an iOS-based game.

• Observe that *symbol* and *mark* mean the same in the context of Tic-Tac-Toe, so delete mark and retain symbol.

• Observe that *nought* and *O* mean the same thing in the context of a Tic-Tac-Toe game and that *cross* and *X* mean the same, as well. So, remove the ill-favored British terms nought and cross, and leave O and X. Also, be aware that O and X appear to be either instances or subclasses of *symbol*.

• Compare *user* and *player*. Retain *player* as the player in the game. Depending on the context, *human user* and *human* can be the same. These nouns, along with computer, are instances or subclasses of *player*.

• *Board* and *grid* are similar enough in meaning that one of them can be removed. For current purposes, I kept grid and, in fact, gave it a new name: *game grid*.

• What about *touchscreen?* It refers to a physical component of the phone, so you might be inclined to remove it. On the other hand, something needs to handle the visual display of the board. It could be the board itself. Or you could separate the data structure that represents the board from its visual manifestation, and that's what I did. But I renamed it *board* to help address the first issue that arises with it.

- Consider *row* as a component of *game grid* and *vertical row, diagonal row,* and *horizontal row* as being different subclasses or instances of *row* (but you don't know which yet).

- Retain *game,* for obvious reasons.

- Consider *session* as the manager of games, with score being an attribute of the session for the two players.

✔ **Verbs:** Candidates for verbs in the Tic-Tac-Toe app are *take turn, mark, goes, place, win, implement, play, playing first, display, accumulate, quit, reset.*

  - Remove *take turn* and *goes* as being close enough to *play,* which you retain. For now, retain playing first and the missing *playing second* as potential refinements of play. The final design will ultimately show you that these last two verbs aren't needed.

  - When used as a verb in the context of Tic-Tac-Toe, *mark* can be seen as similar to *play.* That is, when you play by making your move, you're marking a location on the grid. So, remove mark and retain place, but rename it *place symbol.*

  - Remove *implement* because it isn't a responsibility relevant to the game; instead, it's relevant to the process of building the game.

  - Retain *display, accumulate, exit,* and *reset* as valid responsibilities.

You now have the following potential classes, instances, and responsibilities:

✔ **Classes:** Symbol, Player, Human, Computer, Board, Row, Game Session, and Game (with the attribute Score).

✔ **Instances:** O, X of the class Symbol.

✔ **Responsibilities (which will become methods):** play, place, display, accumulate (scores), quit, and reset.

Now it's time to tentatively assign responsibilities to classes as logically as possible:

✔ Allocate the Game Session class the responsibilities, play new game, accumulateScores, quit, and reset.

✔ Allocate the Game class the responsibilities, play.

✔ Class Board has Display responsibilities.

✔ Class Game Grid has Place.

✔ Symbol, Player, Human, Computer, and Row have no responsibilities. But don't delete them just yet. You find out what needs to be done with them in the next section.

Collaborators and missing classes and responsibilities

It's time to take a walk through several use cases to ensure that each use case is supported by a class and its methods (more accurately, an instance of a class and its methods). As part of this process, you also find out about the collaborations between classes. Because the Tic-Tac-Toe app isn't complicated, this exercise is simple and somewhat generalized.

For Tic-Tac-Toe, you can simply create a high-level scenario by combining multiple use cases; however, when you build a complex app, be sure to have detailed scenarios, each exploring a new set of interactions with the app. Here's your generalized scenario:

1. A player starts a new game session.

2. The first player places his, or its, symbol (the X) in an empty location on the board.

3. The second player does likewise. That is, he places his symbol (the O) in an empty location on the board.

4. Repeat Steps 1 and 2 until either

    • One player has three of his (or its) symbols in a row, column, or diagonal. This could happen at the end of Step 1 or at the end of Step 2.

    • There are no more locations to play, so the game ends in a draw.

5. Accumulate the scores for the players.

    • Both players' scores stay the same when the game ends in a draw.

    • The number 1 is added to the winning player's score.

    • No change is made to a losing player's score.

6. If the player wishes, both players return to Step 1 to start a new game; otherwise, they quit.

Now go through each step to see which class handles it.

Ouch. You run into trouble in the first step! There's no class to support the responsibility of starting a new game session. It looks like this responsibility can belong in the Game, and certainly not in the Board class, so you need to create a new Game Manager class to create a new game session.

Game Manager and Game Session are therefore collaborators — because Game Manager creates an instance of Game Session.

In the following, Steps 2 and 3 describe what happens when a symbol is placed on a board:

1. A symbol must be placed at a location and be visible on the Board. Creation of the Symbol itself is covered by Symbol. Board can cover *placement* of the symbol, if you add a place Symbol method to it. Location is a noun that wasn't considered earlier. You evaluate whether it's a candidate class, but decide that it's an attribute of the Board, and not a class by itself.

2. Board then must signify to Game that a play has been made.

3. When Play is invoked in the Game, the Game Grid is updated (so it needs the responsibility of setting a symbol at a location. Call this responsibility setSymbolAtLocation.

   You now have to evaluate whether the game ended with a win or a draw. This looks like a Game responsibility and that Game will collaborate with Game Grid to see whether a row, column, or diagonal is complete. Game needs a responsibility, so checkResult and Game Grid will have the responsibilities isRowFilled, isColumn Filled, isLeftToRightDiagonal-Filled, and isRightToLeftDiagonalFilled. Also, note that the classes Board, GameGrid, and Game are now collaborators.

4. Finally, you have to switch to player 2. Let Game handle this logic.

5. Rinse. Repeat the preceding steps.

At first blush, it looks as though the Game class should be responsible for accumulating scores, but it represents only a single game, and scores are accumulated across games in a session. So Game isn't suitable, so you try Game Session:

- ✔ Game Session now creates a new game, decides on and sets the players, plays the game, and accumulates the scores.

- ✔ Game Session can also handle playing a new game or quitting the game, which adds a nice symmetry.

The updated scores must be shown somewhere. What about showing them using the Board class? That doesn't work because Board shows the Tic-Tac-Toe playing surface — that is, the board. However, you can create a Game View class and add a Show Scores method to it. Game Session will use Game View to show updated scores.

Moreover, Game View can manage the entire visual aspect of the game. So, let it display the score and the players' alternating access to the Board.

Now you have the following classes, responsibilities, and collaborators:

- ✔ **Game:** Represents a single Tic-Tac-Toe game.
  - *Responsibilities:* play, checkResult
  - *Collaborators:* GameSession, GameView, Grid.
- ✔ **Board:** Represents the Tic-Tac-Toe board.
- ✔ **Game View:** Represents the visual display of a Tic-Tac-Toe game.
  - *Responsibilities:* placeSymbol, showScores
  - *Collaborators:* Game
- ✔ **Game Grid:** Represents the three-by-three Tic-Tac-Toe grid.
  - *Responsibilities:* setSymbolAtLocation, getSymbolAtLocation, isRowFilled, isColumnFilled, isLeftToRightDiagonalFilled, isRightToLeftDiagonalFilled, getEmptySquares
  - *Collaborators:* Game
- ✔ **Game Session:** Represents a Tic-Tac-Toe playing session consisting of multiple games.
  - *Responsibilities:* playNewGame, quit, decidePlayers, accumulateScores
  - *Collaborators:* Game, Game View
- ✔ **Symbol:** Represents a Tic-Tac-Toe symbol either an X or an O.
  - *Responsibilities:* None
  - *Collaborators:* Game

Notice that the names of the responsibilities are similar to the names of the methods, which follows standard Objective-C naming conventions.

Finally, for each class, run through this checklist for a proper class:

- ✔ Does the class have a suitable name?
- ✔ Does it have a cohesive description?
- ✔ Does it have responsibilities?
- ✔ Does it have collaborators?
- ✔ Does it and its components maintain state?

All the Tic-Tac-Toe classes just identified meet these criteria.

Contracts and signatures

You're making good progress. You have classes and methods, and you know which classes collaborate in the game. The next step is to clearly specify (or at least understand) what each method is supposed to do, and what it needs in order to do so. In this section, you go class by class, method by method, starting with Game (although the order in which you address each class doesn't matter).

✔ The first method in Game is *play*. This method is called when an X or an O is played on a location. The location is identified by its coordinates. This method needs a Game Grid, a Symbol, and a coordinate (that is, x, y) position. So, its signature is play(Game Grid, Symbol, x, y).

The play method can return one of two types of values. It could return an error code indicating whether the move was legal or illegal. Or it could return the state of the game after the move — that is, Win, Draw, or Active. Just assume that play will return a Boolean, either true for success or false for failure (for example, if someone tried to play a square that was already filled). You also create three additional methods that will indicate whether the game ended with a win or a draw, or if it's still active.

✔ The second method in Game is checkResult. It needs to examine the Grid, so its signature is checkResult :Grid. You want it to set the state of the game to a Win (for the player who just played), to a Draw, or to Active. You also want it to set the state of the game, so rename this method checkResultAndSetState :Grid.

✔ You need methods that will return the state of the game, so add three methods: isActive, isWon, and isDrawn to the class.

Going systematically through all the classes gives you this set of methods and signatures (I've used a notation similar to that of Objective-C):

✔ **Game:**

• *(Bool) play Grid: Symbol: x: y:* Returns success or failure.

• *checkResultAndSetState Grid:* Returns nothing.

• *isActive:* Returns true or false.

• *isWon:* Returns true or false.

• *isDrawn:* Returns true or false.

✔ **GameView:**

- *placeSymbol Symbol: X: Y:* Returns success or failure.

- *showScores PlayerOneScore:* PlayerTwoScore: Returns nothing.

✔ **GameGrid:**

- *setSymbolAtLocation Symbol: x: y:* Returns nothing.

- *Symbol getSymbolAtLocation x: y:* Returns success or failure.

- *isRowFilled row:* Returns YES if a row is filled with the same symbol.

- *isColumnFilled, column:* Returns YES if a column is filled with the same symbol.

- *isLeftToRightDiagonalFilled:* Returns YES if the left-to-right diagonal (from 0,0 to 2,2) is filled with the same symbol.

- *isRightToLeftDiagonalFilled:* Returns YES if the right-to-left diagonal (from 0,2 to 2,0) is filled with the same symbol.

- *getEmptySquares:* Returns a list of (x, y) coordinates of the empty squares.

✔ **Symbol:**

- *None*

✔ **GameSession:**

- *playNewGame:* Returns nothing.

- *quit:* Returns nothing

- *accumulateScores WinningPlayer:* Returns nothing.

So, there they are — classes and methods with method signatures. You ask, "Am I done with designing? Can I start implementing?" My answer is, unfortunately, not yet, as I explain next.

If you were the Paladin of computing (Have Compiler, Will Travel) developing an application from scratch, you might be able to start writing code. But, sad to say, you aren't. Instead, it's time to put on the mantle of a modern-day "Knight in iOS Armor" and fit your design within the iOS framework. Namely, you need to take advantage of the framework where possible while also compromising where the framework doesn't quite fit your design (or at least not without lots of extra work). In the next section, you see an example of how to convert your initial OO design to one that fits into the iOS Framework.

Implementing an Object-Oriented Design on iOS

If you've been following along, you now have a good OO design; however, it isn't a design that will work on iOS. In this section, you find out how to transform your initial OO design into one that works with iOS.

First, in Xcode, open the Tic-Tac-Toe project associated with this chapter so that you can follow along as I explain how to implement it (refer to Chapter 5 for instructions on loading an existing project).

The core pattern within any iOS app is the Model-View Controller-View (as I explain in Chapters 4 and 6, this is Apple's take on the tried-and-true Model-View-Controller, or MVC, pattern). In this pattern, views are the user-interface elements of the application. Models represent the domain logic of the application, and view controllers stitch the two together.

Some developers see the model as only the data that an application manages, whereas I see it as the application's domain model — it includes the data as well as the application's core behavior. In this respect, the Tic-Tac-Toe game is the model, not just the grid within the game.

Because the model will likely be the most stable part of a program, implementing at least its core parts early will speed up the rest of the process.

As I explain in Chapters 4 and 6, when you create the model, you do so from the requirements or other descriptions of the app. You then validate the model by walking through it using scenarios that describe how the app is intended to be used.

Implementing the model

Now that you know what a model is, it's time to create one. To identify the classes in the model, look at the list of classes you identified during the OO design process (as discussed in the earlier section, "Illustrating Object-Oriented Design") and identify the subset of classes that are *core* to the app. Incidentally, model classes won't have display or user-interface elements. The core elements of Tic-Tac-Toe are Game, Grid, and Symbol. These taken together implement the domain logic of Tic-Tac-Toe, and so make up the model.

Take a look at how each of the model classes appears when implemented, starting with the largest and most important class in the model — the Game class (called TTTGame in the app, per the iOS convention of keeping class names unique in the absence of namespaces).

Here is the interface file of the Game class (`TTTGame.h`):

```
//
//
. . .
#import <Foundation/Foundation.h>
#import "TTTSymbol.h"
#import "TTTGameGrid.h"

typedef enum {
    Inactive, Active, Won, Draw
} STATE;

typedef enum {Player1, Player2} PLAYER;

@interface TTTGame : NSObject{
    @private STATE gameState;
    @private TTTSymbol *currentSymbol;
    @private PLAYER currentPlayer;
    @private PLAYER winningPlayer;
    @private NSString *PlayerOneName, *PlayerTwoName;
    @private TTTGameGrid *gameGrid;
    @private int playCount;
}
    -(id) init;
    - (TTTGameGrid *) getGameGrid;
    - (void) setPlayerNames :(NSString *) FirstPlayer
                            :(NSString *) SecondPlayer;
    - (NSString *) getPlayerOneName;
    (NSString *) getPlayerTwoName;
    - (NSString *) getCurrentPlayerName;
    - (NSString *)  getWinningPlayerName;
    - (TTTSymbol *) getCurrentSymbol;
    - (void) checkResultAndSetState;
    - (BOOL) play :(int) x :(int) y;
    - (BOOL) isActive;
    - (BOOL) isWon;
    - (BOOL) isDrawn;
    - (int) getPlayCount;
@end
```

The methods in the design are almost identically reflected in the implementation. The differences between the methods in the design and the methods in the implementation are as follows:

✔ Several extra methods are in the implementation.

✔ The signature of the play method in the actual code is different from the signature in the design.

✔ There is a method called init.

To find out why those differences exist, begin by determining why all the accessor methods are there. Notice that the Game class doesn't have visual elements and display responsibilities, which is exactly right for a model class.

The views, however, need to display the Tic-Tac-Toe grid and the play-by-play progress of the game. Therefore, the view controllers need to pass the symbol currently being placed, the names of the players, and the grid from the Game class on to the views. To enable the view controllers to pass the necessary data to the views, accessor methods are provided for the model classes.

Now in the play method in the implementation has 2 parameters (the x and y coordinates) while its counterpart in the had 4 parameters (grid, symbol *and* the coordinates x and y).

grid isn't needed because it's a member variable of the game and doesn't need to be passed in. symbol is also not needed. A quick look at the following implementation of play reveals why symbol doesn't need to be passed as a parameter. The implementation of the Tic-Tac-Toe game always uses X for the starting symbol (for Player One) and O for Player 2's symbol. Therefore, you can hardwire the code to always start with X and then alternate between O and X. Note that although the method becomes simpler, the class becomes a little more complex because it "secretly" uses a characteristic of Tic-Tac-Toe.

```
- (BOOL) play :(int) x :(int) y {
    BOOL successfulPlay=false;
    if ([gameGrid getSymbolAtLocation :x :y] == [TTTSymbol SymbolBlankCreate]){
        successfulPlay = true;
        playCount++;
        [gameGrid setSymbolAtLocation :x :y :currentSymbol];
        [self checkResultAndSetState];
        if(gameState == Active){// if the game is still active
            // Swap symbols and players
            if(currentSymbol == [TTTSymbol SymbolXCreate]){
                currentSymbol= [TTTSymbol SymbolOCreate];
            } else {
                currentSymbol= [TTTSymbol SymbolXCreate];
            }
            if(currentPlayer == Player1) currentPlayer = Player2;
            else currentPlayer = Player1;
        }
    return successfulPlay;
}
```

You may be wondering whether having extra accessors, particularly the gameGrid accessor, is a bad thing. And is incorporating a secret in your code poor design? If so, just hold those questions until I discuss them and other design decisions in the section, "Analyzing the OO and Design Principles Used in Tic-Tac-Toe," later in this chapter.

The final difference is the method called init. This method initializes the game — creates a GameGrid, sets the state of the game to Active, the current player to Player1, and the current symbol to an X. Here is the code for init:

```
-(id) init { //Constructor
    gameGrid = [[TTTGameGrid alloc] init];
    gameState = Active;
    currentSymbol = [TTTSymbol SymbolXCreate];
    currentPlayer = Player1;
    return self;
}
```

It's time to move on to the Game Grid class, called TTTGameGrid in the implementation. Here's its interface:

```
//
//  TTTGameGrid.h
. . .
#import <Foundation/Foundation.h>
#import "TTTSymbol.h"

#define GAMEGRIDSIZE 3

@interface TTTGameGrid : NSObject{
    @private TTTSymbol *grid[GAMEGRIDSIZE][GAMEGRIDSIZE];

}
    -(id) init;
    -(void) setSymbolAtLocation: (int) x :(int) y :(TTTSymbol *) value;
    (TTTSymbol *) getSymbolAtLocation: (int) x :(int) y;
    -(BOOL) isRowFilled: (int) row;
    -(BOOL) isColumnFilled: (int) column;
    -(BOOL) isLeftToRightDiagonalFilled;
    -(BOOL) isRightToLeftDiagonalFilled;
@end
```

The methods of the Game Grid class methods are exactly as designed. The implementation of the class (in TTTGameGrid.m) isn't complicated either, which is why the method implementations aren't inserted here. Just for grins, though, here's checkResultAndSetState, the most complex method in TTTGameGrid:

```
- (void) checkResultAndSetState{
    if([gameGrid isRowFilled:0]||
       [gameGrid isRowFilled:1]||
       [gameGrid isRowFilled:2]||
       [gameGrid isColumnFilled:0]||
       [gameGrid isColumnFilled:1]||
       [gameGrid isColumnFilled:2]||
       [gameGrid isLeftToRightDiagonalFilled]||
       [gameGrid isRightToLeftDiagonalFilled]){
            winningPlayer = currentPlayer;
            gameState = Won;
    }else if (playCount==9){
        gameState = Draw;
    } /* else, leave state as is */
}
```

checkResultAndSetState and the other methods in GameGrid are pretty straightforward. Although the methods aren't complex, GameGrid clearly illustrates the concept of abstraction and information hiding. For example, you can change the *implementation* of GameGrid without the classes outside it — like Game — having to change *how* they use GameGrid. (You see more on this and other OO design points in the section, "Analyzing the OO and Design Principles Used in Tic-Tac-Toe," later in this chapter.)

Now, move on to Symbol. Here is the interface file of the Symbol class (named TTTSymbol):

```
//  TTTSymbol.h
. . .
#import <Foundation/Foundation.h>

#define MARKBLANK 0
#define MARKX 1
#define MARKO 2

@interface TTTSymbol : NSObject{
    @private int value;
}
    +(TTTSymbol*) SymbolXCreate;
    +(TTTSymbol*) SymbolOCreate;
    +(TTTSymbol*) SymbolBlankCreate;
    -(NSString *) toString;
    -(UIImage *)  getBitmapForSymbol;
@end
```

This class encapsulates the Tic-tac-Toe symbols X and O. Note the two variations of the Singleton pattern applied in the implementation of this class.

✔ One variation is in the factory methods for the symbol instances SymbolBlankCreate, SymbolXCreate, and SymbolOCreate.

✔ The second variation of the Singleton pattern is in getBitmap ForSymbol.

   You find more on using the Singleton pattern in the section, "Analyzing the OO and Design Principles Used in Tic-Tac-Toe," later in this chapter.

The last class in the Tic-Tac-Toe model is `Square` (named `TTTSquare`). Here is its interface file:

```
//
. . .
//
#import <Foundation/Foundation.h>

@interface TTTSquare : NSObject{
    @private int x;
    @private int y;
}
    -(id) initWithXY: (int) initX :(int) initY;
    -(int) x;
    -(int) y;
@end
```

You use this class as a data structure to represent a square within the game grid. You also use this class to represent each square that is returned when a collection of the empty squares in the grid is requested. This class implements a pattern known as *Data Transfer Object,* which I explain in the last section of this chapter.

Now that the model is ready, you can build the rest of the application. So read on!

Creating storyboards and views

One of the very convenient features Apple added to Xcode 4 is the Storyboard feature, which is a *declarative* (that is a non-programming) means of *specifying* (but not implementing) the screen flow of an app. The Storyboard feature can also be used to define most of the views of the app. A storyboard consists of a representation of the screens in an app and the transitions between them. The individual screens are called *scenes,* and the transitions between the screens are called *segues.*

For more on how to work with storyboards, scenes, and segues, check the Storyboards and Scenes link in the web resources for the chapters in this book at www.dummies.com/go/iosprogramminglinks.

As you can see from the screen flow diagram of the app (refer to Figure 7-4), the Tic-Tac-Toe app transitions between two main states:

- ✔ A user is about to start a game session (refer to Figure 7-1).
- ✔ The players are playing a Tic-Tac-Toe game in an active game session (refer to Figure 7-2).

These states also correspond to the start and end of Use Case 1. These two screens will be the basis of the two scenes in the storyboard of the app, with a segue named `segueToGameSession` from Scene 1 to Scene 2. You can see all of this in Figure 7-5.

Within each scene are views. Scene 1 is the main screen of the app, and it has two buttons, Start a New Tic-Tac-Toe Session and Exit. The gameplay screen (Scene 2) shows a drawing area for the Tic-Tac-Toe board (highlighted in blue in Figure 7-6) and two text fields where the status of the game is displayed.

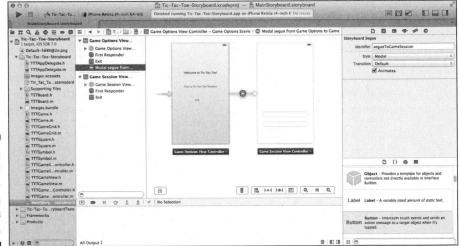

Figure 7-5:
Storyboard
for Tic-Tac-
Toe showing
the scenes
and a segue.

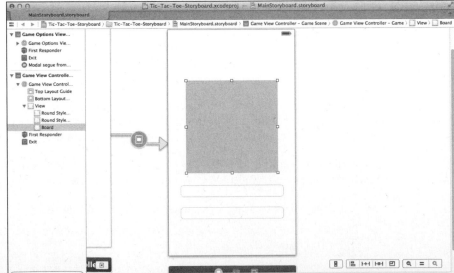

Figure 7-6:
Scene 2
in the Tic-
Tac-Toe
storyboard.

In Figures 7-1 and 7-2, shown earlier in this chapter, you can see that a good deal of the Tic-Tac-Toe user interface is done declaratively. Of course, you'll need more code to complete the implementation of the views and to orchestrate the flow of the user interface from scene to scene, which you read about in the next section.

Making the app active

So far in this section, you've read about the app's model and should have a good idea about what the app's user interface look like (that is, its views). But views and a model doth not an app make. View controllers must stitch models and views together and make the app actually work.

The view controllers are where the app's use cases are implemented.

Following the object-oriented design principle of cohesion, I created separate view controllers for the two scenes. (By *cohesion,* I mean ensuring that the things a class does relate to each other and to the intent of the class. Refer to Chapter 2 for more on cohesion.)

I call these two view controllers the Game Options view controller and the Game Session view controller. Both view controllers are subclasses of `UIViewController`, the base class in the iOS Framework from which all view controllers are derived. Note that they also bound the classes of these view controllers to their respective scenes through the Identity inspector in Xcode's Utilities area (refer to Chapter 5). Also, events in these scenes are bound to actions in their respective view controllers.

You implement the Game Options view controller (class name `TTTGameOpti onsViewController`). The Game Options view controller is also designated the *root* view controller, and the iOS runtime launches it when the app starts up. Along with this view controller, the view it manages (that is, Scene 1) is also created and presented.

The primary role of the Game Options view controller is to implement the first part of "Use Case 1: Player starts a game session." As a result, the Touch Down event in the `Start a New Tic-Tac-Toe Session` button is bound to the `IBAction` annotated `startNewGame` method (see `TTTGameOption sViewController.m`). Clicking `Start a New Tic-Tac-Toe Session` invokes this method, as shown here:

```
- (IBAction)startNewGame{
    [self performSegueWithIdentifier:@"segueToGameSession" sender:self];
}
```

`startNewGame` is known as an *action* method because its purpose is to respond to a user action, such as touching a button (I explain action methods in Chapter 9). The method is simplicity itself. It just segues the app from Scene 1 to Scene 2, causing the Game Session view to come up, showing the Tic-Tac-Toe grid and the two status display areas. This action launches the Game Session view controller (implemented by the class `TTTGameSessionViewController`) along with its view.

The Game Session view controller is the workhorse of the Tic-Tac-Toe app because it implements the remaining part of Use Case 1 and all the other use cases. Its view comprises three parts:

✔ A board where the Tic-Tac-Toe grid and the played Xs and Os are shown

✔ A text field that shows the game status (either the next player or the final result)

✔ A text field that shows the accumulated scores of the two players in the current session

Figure 7-7 shows the views that the Game Session view controller manages.

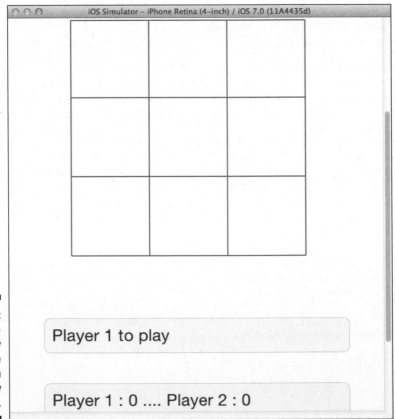

Figure 7-7:
View managed by the Game Session view controller.

The board is a custom view that's implemented by the TTTBoard class, which is a subclass of UIView. Here is the interface file for the TTTBoard class:

```
//
//
. . .
#import <UIKit/UIKit.h>
#import "TTTGameSessionViewController.h"

@class TTTGameGrid;

@interface TTTBoard : UIView{
    @private BOOL enabled;
    @private TTTGameSessionViewController *gameSession;
    @private TTTGameGrid *grid;
    @private float width;        // width of one block
    @private float height;       // will be same as width;
}
    - (void)drawRect:(CGRect)rect;
    - (void) setGrid: (TTTGameGrid *) aGrid;
    - (void)touchesBegan:(NSSet *)touches withEvent:(UIEvent *)event;
    - (void) setGameSession: (TTTGameSessionViewController *) aGameSession;
    - (float) getWidth;
    - (float) getHeight;
    - (void) invalidateBlock: (int) x :(int) y;
    - (BOOL) isInputEnabled;
    - (void) disableInput;
    - (void) enableInput;
@end
```

Next, I explain what the important methods in this class do, and how they work:

✔ TTTBoard is specialized from UIView in that it overrides the drawRect method from UIView and implements its own method. This drawRect method is the one that draws the Tic-Tac-Toe grid along with all the played symbols when the board changes (that is, after each move).

The drawRect method is automatically called by the iOS runtime system or, more specifically, by the view manager within iOS when the view needs to be rendered.

✔ TTTBoard implements several of its own methods, such as accessor methods to get its height, width, and status, to set its grid and view controller and to enable and disable input.

✔ TTTBoard overrides and implements its own touchesBegan method in order to respond to the placement of symbols.

Via the storyboard of the app, this board is wired to and can be referenced by the outlet boardView in the Game Session view controller. The two text fields in this view are wired to (and therefore can be referenced by) the outlets turnTextField and scoreTextField in the Game Session view controller. These three outlets are declared in TTTGameSessionViewController:

```
@property (nonatomic, retain) IBOutlet TTTBoard *boardView;
@property (nonatomic, retain) IBOutlet UITextField *scoreTextField;
@property (nonatomic, retain) IBOutlet UITextField *turnTextField;
```

Here's what the Game Session view controller does:

1. The iOS runtime launches the Game Session view controller when Scene 1 segues to Scene 2.

2. The iOS runtime calls the viewDidLoad method of Game Session after all its views are successfully loaded and rendered, as shown here:

```
- (void)viewDidLoad{
    [super viewDidLoad];
    // Do any additional setup after loading the view.
    [self initializeGameSession];
    [self playNewGame];
}
```

3. viewDidLoad, in turn, calls initializeGameSession (which initializes the game session) and playNewGame, which sets up a new game.

   The game is *event driven* in that the Tic-Tac-Toe program sets up and displays the board and then responds to the placement of symbols. This response begins with the touchesBegan method of TTTBoard, as shown here:

```
- (void)touchesBegan:(NSSet *)touches withEvent:(UIEvent *)event{

    [super touchesBegan:touches withEvent:event];

    NSSet* touchesInView = [event touchesForView:self];
    UITouch* touchInGrid = (UITouch *)[touchesInView anyObject];
    CGPoint touchPoint = [touchInGrid locationInView:self];
    float x = touchPoint.x-TTTBOARDLOCATIONINVIEWX;
    float y = touchPoint.y-TTTBOARDLOCATIONINVIEWX;

    [gameSession boardTouchedAt:x :y];
}
```

4. touchesBegan receives the touch event, extracts the window coordinates of the touch points in the event (touchPoint.x and touchPoint.y), translates them to grid coordinates (x and y), and passes these grid coordinates to the Game Session view controller via the controller's boardTouchedAt method.

5. The `boardTouchedAt` method translates the touch point to Tic-Tac-Toe grid coordinates and calls `humanTakesATurn`, which calls methods of the `Game` class (named `TTTGame`) to execute the logic behind a move.

   This logic is pretty straightforward. Once the move is made, methods in the `Game` class check to see whether the move causes a row, column, or diagonal to be filled with the same symbol:

   • If so, the game is terminated as a victory for the player making the last play.

   • If not, these methods check to see whether the board is filled.

     If the board is filled, the game is declared a draw.

If the game is won or there's a draw, the game terminates (its state is set to won or drawn, as the case may be). Game Session displays appropriate messages and asks whether another game should be started, in which case the cycle begins anew at `playNewGame`.

Finally, if neither of these cases is true, the game stays active and simply waits for the next move.

Analyzing the OO and Design Principles Used in Tic-Tac-Toe

I created the Tic-Tac-Toe application to illustrate object-oriented (OO) techniques and principles as well as the process of OO design and development. So I'll analyze it from that perspective. (This analysis is arranged according to the order of the OO concepts in Chapter 2.)

✔ *Language constructs,* such as classes, objects, inheritance, methods, and polymorphism

✔ *Principles* of OO design, namely, information hiding, low coupling, and high cohesion

✔ *Techniques,* such as delayed binding, delegation

✔ *Patterns*

✔ *Frameworks,* specifically the iOS framework

Tic-Tac-Toe uses many of the building blocks of OO as implemented in Objective-C. The program uses these classes: Board, Game, Game Grid, Square, and Symbol, and two view controllers — Game Options view controller and Game Session view controller (note that the exact class names have no spaces and are prefixed with `TTT`). Objects of each of these classes are instantiated, and the game is implemented as collaborations among these objects, manifested as messages being sent between objects that result in invocations of their methods.

Each of the classes inherits from a base class in the iOS framework — Game, Game Grid, Square, and Symbol from `NSObject`, `Board` from `UIView`, and the two view controllers from `UIViewController`. Considering this inheritance, you should expect to see examples of polymorphic behavior in Tic-Tac-Toe, and it doesn't disappoint. Here are two examples:

- ✔ The Board class (named `TTTBoard`) inherits from `UIView`.

   Board overrides the `drawRect` that it inherits from `UIView`. This view is rendered by the iOS framework (specifically, the iOS window manager), which recognizes this view as an instance of `UIView`. However, the (custom) `drawRect` method is invoked.

- ✔ `touchesBegan` is another method from `UIView` that's overridden in Board.

   Here again, the iOS window manager thinks it's dealing with an instance of a `UIView` class, whereas the object is actually an instance of Board.

Using objects only through their interface enforces a certain degree of information hiding. By accessing objects only through their interface, the using objects know no more than the externally accessible methods and their signatures of the used objects. See how each class in Tic-Tac-Toe, for the most part, can be understood by its interface alone. However, Objective-C does force you to reveal the member variables of a class in an interface file, which doesn't unnecessarily need to be revealed. In general, the OO design process also facilitates proper separation of class responsibilities and enables low coupling among classes and high cohesion within each class.

One interesting example of separation of concerns within the app (but which you don't see in the design process) is the new memory management paradigm in iOS — *Automated Reference Counting (ARC)*. Thanks to this paradigm, an object doesn't have to worry about how its collaborating objects are dealing with shared information.

Tic-Tac-Toe also uses delegation. For example, the `Start a Tic-Tac-Toe Session` button in Scene 1 is delegating handling of the `Touch Down` button press event to the method `startNewGame` in the Game Options view controller. The framework also uses delegation. For example, it delegates the start up of the app to an instance of an app-specific class — the app's own `Applicaton Delegate` class (named `TTTAppDelegate` in the file `main.m`).

```
//
. . .
//
. . .

#import <UIKit/UIKit.h>

#import "TTTAppDelegate.h"

int main(int argc, char * argv[])
{
    @autoreleasepool {
        return UIApplicationMain(argc, argv, nil, NSStringFromClass([TTTAppDeleg
            ate class]));
    }
}
```

Use of design patterns in Tic-Tac-Toe

Design patterns are formal ways of documenting a solution to a design problem (I discuss design patterns in Chapter 4). Tic-Tac-Toe uses two patterns: Singleton and Model-View-Controller.

Singleton pattern

The Singleton pattern is used in the Symbol class. Note how I customized this pattern in the Tic-Tac-Toe application:

✔ Rather than the one instance returned by the textbook Singleton pattern, three instances (one each for the X, O, and blank symbols) are allowed in the Symbol class. These instances are managed by the three static, or class, methods. One of these methods is shown here:

```
+(TTTSymbol*) SymbolXCreate{
    @synchronized([TTTSymbol class]){
        if (SymbolX == nil){
            SymbolX = [[TTTSymbol alloc] init];
            SymbolX->value = MARKX;
        }
        return SymbolX;
    }
}
```

✔ The technique used in the Singleton pattern to create only one instance is used in the method `getBitmapForSymbol` to get the images for the X, O, and blank symbols:

```
- (UIImage *) getBitmapForSymbol{
        @synchronized([TTTSymbol class]){
            if (!bitMapsInitialized){
                NSString* imagePath =
                    [[NSBundle mainBundle]
                        pathForResource:
                            @"Images.bundle/x" ofType:@"png"];
                imageX = [[UIImage alloc]
                    initWithContentsOfFile:imagePath];
                imagePath =
                    [[NSBundle mainBundle]
                        pathForResource:
                            @"Images.bundle/o" ofType:@"png"];
                imageO =
                    [[UIImage alloc] initWithContentsOfFile:imagePath];
                imagePath =
                    [[NSBundle mainBundle]
                        pathForResource:
                            @"Images.bundle/blank" ofType:@"png"];
                imageBlank =
                    [[UIImage alloc] initWithContentsOfFile:imagePath];
                bitMapsInitialized=true;
            }
        }
        UIImage *imageSelected = imageBlank;

        if (self == [TTTSymbol SymbolXCreate]) imageSelected = imageX;
        else if (self == [TTTSymbol SymbolOCreate])
            imageSelected = imageO;
        return imageSelected;
}
```

✔ Because iOS apps can be multithreaded, Singleton is modified to deal with multiple threads by using the `@synchronized` annotation.

Model-View-Controller pattern

Model-View-Controller (MVC), shown in Figure 7-8, is the most important pattern within iOS. It's frequently used in applications, particularly web applications.

The pattern isolates the domain logic and core objects of the application (aka the model) from the application's user interface. In this way, these important components (that is, the model and the views) can be designed, implemented, and maintained separately. The controller is placed between the model and the user interface. It receives user actions (such as *The user clicked here*) and translates those commands into actions on the model and then takes the resulting model updates and notifies the user interface to update itself.

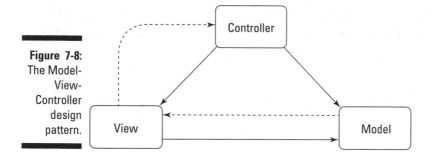

Within iOS, controllers are called *view controllers.*

The Tic-Tac-Toe model consists of the classes Game, Grid, and Symbol. These classes encapsulate the domain logic of the game.

The Game, Grid, and Symbol classes are implemented so that they're completely independent of the application's user interface. You could use these classes just as they are in a command-line–driven, console-app version of Tic-Tac-Toe. Note that the logic of a game session is currently embedded in the Game Session view controller. You could also abstract a class representing a game session and make it part of the model.

The two major views in Tic-Tac-Toe are represented by Scene 1 and Scene 2 in the Tic-Tac-Toe storyboard (refer to Figure 7-5). Objects that represent these views are instances of UIView and are created behind the scenes (no pun intended) by the iOS runtime. The buttons, text fields, and Board class that represent the Tic-Tac-Toe grid are subordinate views within these main views.

Finally, note that the Game View class (named TTTGameView and implemented in the files TTTGameView.h and TTTGameView.m) is also a view. It encapsulates the user-interface elements in Scene 2 (the board and the two text fields that show the scores and the game status, respectively).

Corresponding to the two scenes are two view controllers in Tic-Tac-Toe: the Game Options view controller and the Game Session view controller. (Refer to the previous section where I explain how these two view controllers manage the app's logic and tie together the model objects and the views.)

Data Transfer Object pattern

The Data Transfer Object (DTO) pattern is used when several bits of information that need to be transferred from one part of the system to another part are encapsulated into an object. You see the DTO pattern in the method getEmptySquares, defined in the Game Grid class and used to return the list of empty squares on the board. Every instance of the Square class (see TTTSquare.m and the corresponding interface file TTTSquare.h) is a DTO.

Façade pattern

You use the Façade pattern to simplify the use of the functionality provided by a set of classes. A façade provides a simpler set of methods to interact with these classes. Rather than you having to learn how to use the individual classes, a program can use these classes through a façade. You see an example of a façade in the Game View class, which simplifies the interaction between the Game Session view controller and the Scene 2-based view it handles.

Other concepts

Other, mostly language-specific, examples of OO concepts are utilized. A simple example of abstraction and loose coupling shows up in the use of `#define` and `#typedef` constructs to enumerate the values allowed by a variable. You can see `#typedef` constructs in the definition and State and Player types in Game. Here's the code from `TTTGame.h` that defines the State type (named `STATE`) and the Player type (`PLAYER`):

```
typedef enum {
    Inactive, Active, Won, Draw
} STATE;

typedef enum {Player1, Player2} PLAYER;
```

The `enum` construct also provides type safety, as opposed to an approach that might use integer constants to represent both player and state.

Here's an example of `#define` statements used to define the size and location of the board drawing area (from `TTTBoard.h`):

```
#define TTTBOARDLOCATIONINVIEWX 10
#define TTTBOARDLOCATIONINVIEWY 10
#define TTTBOARDSIZE 200
```

By using #defines, the size of the board and its location on the window are defined in one place in the file. You can modify these values simply by editing these constants, rather than by changing the values in all the places in the code where they're used.

As you begin to understand the Tic-Tac-Toe code, you'll see tradeoffs, compromises, and even flaws in the OO design. Some of these, such as the visibility of member variables in the interface files, are a consequence of using Objective-C.

Other compromises are made by the iOS framework. For example, some actions on events are implemented by delegate objects (such as the callbacks to button clicks). However, rather than implement delegates, you can implement some events by overriding base classes and using inheritance-driven polymorphism, such as processing touch events on the Board and drawing of the board, both done by overriding methods – `touchesBegan` and `drawRect`, respectively.

I made other compromises; I list them here with the intention of starting a discussion about them:

✔ The Game Session view controller handles all three subviews — the Board and the two text fields. This view controller handles the game session logic and the game logic. Could I (and should I) split the responsibility of this controller with another? For example, would it be better to create an additional view controller to handle the playing of a single game?

✔ Game View is only a partial façade over the views that the Game Session view controller handles. It abstracts the text fields from the following:

- The Game Session view controller (via `setGameStatus` and `showScores`)

- The symbol placement on the Board (via `placeSymbol`)

However, the Board is coupled directly to the Game Session view controller in how it responds to events — such as touches. Take a look at how the `touchesBegan` method, shown here, directly invokes `boardTouchedAt` on `gameSession`:

```
- (void)touchesBegan:(NSSet *)touches withEvent:(UIEvent *)event{

        [super touchesBegan:touches withEvent:event];

        NSSet* touchesInView = [event touchesForView:self];
        UITouch* touchInGrid = (UITouch *)[touchesInView anyObject];
        CGPoint touchPoint = [touchInGrid locationInView:self];
        float x = touchPoint.x-TTTBOARDLOCATIONINVIEWX;
        float y = touchPoint.y-TTTBOARDLOCATIONINVIEWX;

        [gameSession boardTouchedAt:x :y];

    }
```

In order for Game View to be a complete façade over the game play views, Game View should take care of the event handling, as well. Would doing this make the components of the program more cohesive and easier to understand? Or would the addition of another layer of indirection make understanding the program more difficult?

✔ The Game class is subtly coupled with the Board class because an instance of Board and an instance of Game from within the same game share the same Game Grid instance.

The following lines from `playNewGame` within the Game Session view controller illustrate this point:

```
- (void) playNewGame{
    activeGame = [[TTTGame alloc] init];
    . . .
    TTTGameGrid *gameGrid = [activeGame getGameGrid];
    [boardView setGrid:gameGrid];


    . . .
}
```

Here, Board needs the Game Grid to redraw itself and Game needs the same Game Grid to play the game. You could also hold the Game Grid instance in the Game class and provide accessor methods in the Game class to access the cells. I see good and bad points for both approaches. If you like, try this alternative approach and see whether it works for you.

Part III
Making Your iOS Apps Fit for Consumption

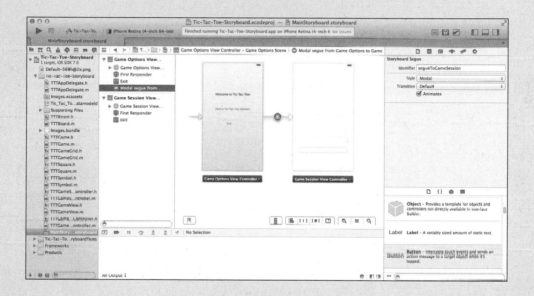

Visit www.dummies.com/extras/beginningiosprogramming for great Dummies content online.

In this part...

✔ Using the integrated development environment

✔ Polishing your application

✔ Creating the user interface

✔ Accelerating performance

✔ Increasing reliability

✔ Controlling access

✔ Visit `www.dummies.com/extras/
beginningiosprogramming` for great Dummies
content online.

Chapter 8

Effectively Using Xcode

∙ ∙

In This Chapter

▶ Developing your app's UI using Xcode storyboards

▶ Analyzing and refactoring your app's code using Xcode tools

▶ Managing your app's lifecycle using Git

▶ Adding and removing files from your device

▶ Tracking and debugging your app

∙ ∙

Developers who programmed in the early days of C and C++ used command-line tools and obscure Unix commands to compile, run, debug, and test their programs. Those tools were easy to use but limited in their support of large or complicated programs. They certainly didn't support use of frameworks or visual software development. Nowadays, of course, we have IDEs like Xcode.

Xcode is a comprehensive and powerful integrated development environment (IDE) that makes large-scale iOS development much easier. It allows you to specify several aspects of your app graphically — such as the UI and its linkages to code. It provides a visual debugger and a framework for testing your app thoroughly before release.

In Chapter 5, I introduce Xcode (version 5) and its capabilities. This chapter builds on that information to specifically explain important capabilities of Xcode for iOS app development. I begin with an overview of Xcode and then explain Xcode's features for developing, testing, debugging, and managing iOS apps, including Xcode's features for tracing an app's progress using logging and instrumentation.

My goal is to give you the knowledge necessary to effectively leverage your IDE's capabilities to build enterprise-class, commercially viable iOS apps.

Xcode and IOS — A Beautiful Friendship

Xcode consists of a comprehensive set of developer tools for creating iOS applications for the iPhone and iPad (and for Mac, as well). It comes with a workspace of tools for building, testing, deploying, and maintaining apps. These tools consist of interactive utilities such as these:

- A file-browser-like component that you can use to navigate to all the components of your app
- Graphical tools for designing the screen flow and layouts for each screen without writing code
- An editor for writing and editing code
- Inspectors for editing classes
- Graphical tools for connecting views, and view controllers, and so on (see Figure 8-1)
- A testing framework
- Integration with source code control systems like these:
  - Subversion (http://subversion.apache.org)
  - Git (http://git-scm.com)

Navigator Area · Editor Area · Utilities Area

Figure 8-1: Components of an Xcode workspace.

Debug Area

Xcode: History 101

From its beginnings as an IDE for the NeXt platform, Xcode has gone through many, many iterations and (mostly) improvements. Changes include

✔ A shift to Apple's own Objective-C compiler to provide better incremental help and diagnostics

✔ Project organization and presentation

✔ New features like storyboards

For details on changes from Xcode 4.0 and higher, go to www.dummies.com/go/iosprogramminglinks and check out the What's New in Xcode link.

It's clear that Xcode provides a comprehensive set of tools for managing the soup-to-nuts lifecycle of an iOS app.

In the following sections, I explain these capabilities. In keeping with the theme of this book, the underlying thread will be the object-oriented development process.

Setting up your app's project

In this section, I'm assuming that you created your app's use cases and laid out the screen flow for the app as shown in Chapter 7. (Figure 8-2 shows the Tic-Tac-Toe screen flow, which is a typical screen flow for an app.) I also assume that you've done an initial OO design and know the classes you need and the methods and collaborators for each class (again, as shown in Chapter 7). With those tasks done, you're ready to start making your app.

You now need to create an iOS project for your app in Xcode. So, go ahead; fire up Xcode. When the Xcode splash screen appears, select Create a New Xcode project.

If you aren't the first (or only) user of Xcode on your computer, the splash screen may not appear, in which case, you're taken directly to a screen that looks like Figure 8-1. If that happens, simply choose File➪New➪Project to create a new project.

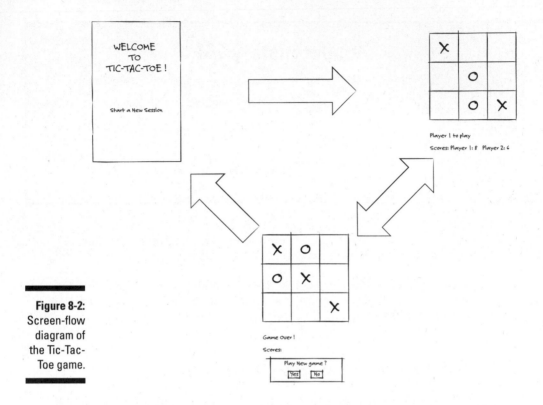

Figure 8-2:
Screen-flow
diagram of
the Tic-Tac-
Toe game.

A screen filled with application templates appears, as shown in Figure 8-3.

Click each application template to see a brief explanation of what it's designed for.

The Empty Application template is a bare-bones template, which means you must create all your app's components from scratch — views, view controllers, model classes, and so on. For current purposes, that's the route you take.

Click the Empty Application template. A screen appears where you can name the app and set the class name's prefix string for the classes in your project. (Objective-C doesn't support namespaces; therefore, each class must have a unique name.) In my example, I named the app Tic-Tac-Toe-Chapter-8 and used TTT as the prefix for the class name. As a result, all the class names in this project start with TTT. I set the target device as iPad, and left the other fields with their default values.

After you provide the information and click Next, you're asked to select the folder where the project will be stored. If you just click Next, the app's project workspace appears, as shown in Figure 8-4. In this figure, note that I expanded all the folders using the Project Navigator in the Navigator area (refer to Figure 8-1). You need to do the same to reproduce what this figure shows.

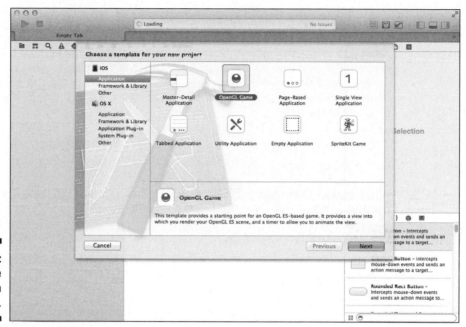

Figure 8-3:
Xcode
application
templates.

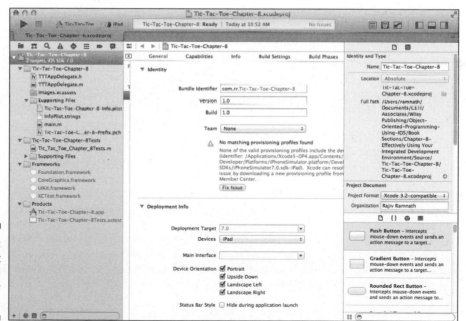

Figure 8-4:
Project
workspace
for an empty
application.

Creating your app's screen flow

After you create the project, you're ready to create a storyboard that captures the screen flow for the app. As I explain in Chapter 7, storyboards give developers a declarative (non-programming) way to lay out the screen flow of an app, as well as define the layout of each screen in the app. A storyboard consists of the following:

- ✔ A graphical representation of each screen in an app
- ✔ A specification of the transitions between screens known as *segues*

When you use the Empty Application template to create the project, you need to add a storyboard file. To do so, follow these steps:

1. **Choose File➪New➪File.**

    The screen shown in Figure 8-5 appears, where you can select a template for the new file.

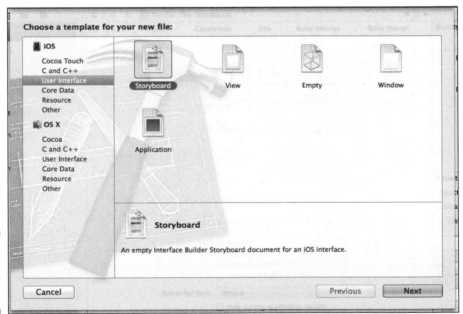

Figure 8-5:
Selecting a
template for
a new file.

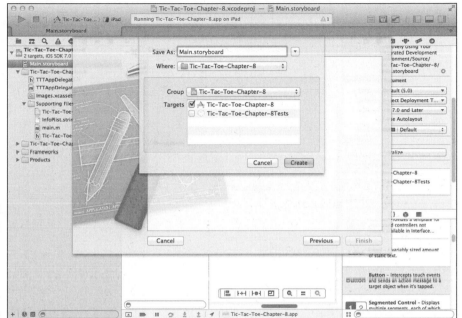

Figure 8-6:
Naming and setting the membership of a storyboard.

2. **Select User Interface on the left panel under iOS and then select Storyboard to add a storyboard file.**

   Figure 8-6 shows that I named this file `Main.storyboard`, but feel free to pick any name you want as long as it has the `.storyboard` extension. Leave the Where box as is, so that the storyboard will be saved in the same folder as the rest of your project's files.

   In the figure, you see I placed a check mark beside Tic-Tac-Toe-Chapter-8, which is the app build target in this case. This step makes the storyboard a member of the app build target, so when the app is built, the storyboard is included in the build.

   Make sure you check the app build target; otherwise, you'll get weird errors that will take hours to debug. However, if you forget to check the target when you add the storyboard, you can do so later.

If you forget to make the storyboard a member of the app target, you can do so by selecting the storyboard using the File inspector, located on the right side of the workspace (see Figure 8-7). While you're in the File inspector, take a look at what else is there. Notice that you can build the storyboard for different targets and have different background colors (try changing the Global Tint to a different color to see how your app looks). You can also manage it in a source code control repository because a storyboard file is actually kept in XML.

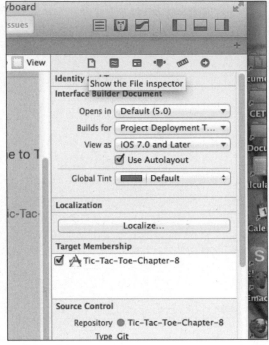

Figure 8-7:
Using the
File inspec-
tor to set the
member-
ship of a
storyboard.

After you add the storyboard, you need to configure the project to use it, as follows:

1. Edit the `.plist` **file.**

Open the file with the `.plist` extension — `Tic-Tac-Toe-Chapter-8-Info.plist` (plist stands for *property list file*).

2. Add a new row to the Information Property list.

Move your mouse past the last row of the Information Property list. Right-click and select Add Row.

3. Set the value for the new row.

If you select the new row that you just added, it becomes a drop-down list. Select the entry `Main storyboard file base name`. Move your mouse to the right, under the Value column, and set the value for the new entry you just added to `Main`.

Figure 8-8 shows the final result.

4. Edit the app delegate file.

Using the Project navigator, locate the app delegate file (in this case, `TTTAppDelegate.m`) and locate the method `didFinishLaunching WithOptions` (see the following code).

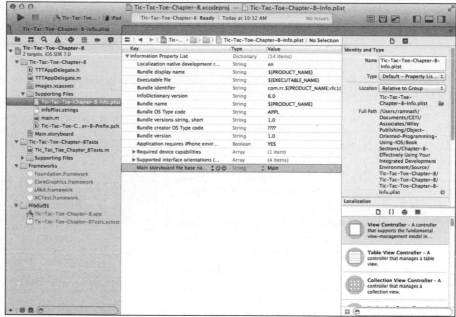

Figure 8-8:
Linking the
storyboard
in the
.plist
file.

5. **Edit the** `didFinishLaunchingWithOptions` **method.**

   Comment out (or simply delete) all the lines except for the `return YES` statement.

   ```
   - (BOOL)application:(UIApplication *)application
         didFinishLaunchingWithOptions:(NSDictionary *)launchOptions
   {
       // self.window - [[UIWindow alloc]
                       initWithFrame:[[UIScreen mainScreen] bounds]];
       // Override point for customization after application launch.
       // self.window.backgroundColor = [UIColor whiteColor];
       // [self.window makeKeyAndVisible];
       return YES;
   }
   ```

6. **Right-click the storyboard file and choose Open As⇨Source Code.**

   The storyboard appears, shown in XML.

   Now it's time to set up the scenes and the screen flow. To add a scene, follow these steps:

1. **Edit the storyboard file.**

   Select the storyboard file for the project (for this project the file is named `MainStoryboard.storyboard`).

   A blank canvas appears.

2. Show the Object Library.

In the Utility area (refer to Figure 8-1), click the little cube shown at the lower-right of the screen below the panel labeled Text Settings. The cube will become blue.

Hover the cursor over the cube, and a tooltip displaying Show the Object Library appears.

A collection of classes appears, with the first class being View Controller (see Figure 8-9).

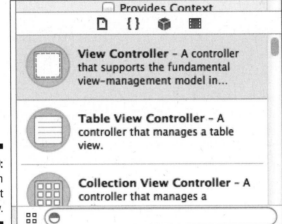

Figure 8-9: Classes in the Object Library.

3. Add a view controller to the storyboard:

    a. Select View Controller and drag it onto the canvas.

    b. Zoom the scene to 100% (by right-clicking on a blank area on the storyboard canvas).

    c. Scroll down the Object Library until you see typical UI classes (buttons, labels, and the like).

    d. Drag and drop a label (a class named UILabel) where you need to on the screen. Double-click the label and enter **Welcome to Tic-Tac-Toe!**

    e. Drag and drop a button (a class named UIButton) where you need to on the screen. Double-click the button and enter **Start a New Session.**

4. Add the second scene.

    a. Drag in a view controller to create a scene.

    b. Drag in a view (a class named UIView).

c. Drag in two text fields (each of a class named `UIText`).

One text field shows the game status, and the other one shows the accumulated scores of each player in that session.

After you're familiar with the UI elements, you can get an element by clicking a row in the list of elements and typing the name of the element you're looking for.

5. **Stitch the scenes together.**

In the screen flow for Tic-Tac-Toe, the goal is to click the Start New Session button to bring up the second screen. Place the cursor on the Start New Session button and Control-drag from there to the second scene.

When you release the cursor, you're prompted to make a selection that sets the segue's type.

6. **Select Modal.**

A segue from Start New Session in the first scene to the second is created. The resulting storyboard should look like Figure 8-10. And you haven't written a lick of code.

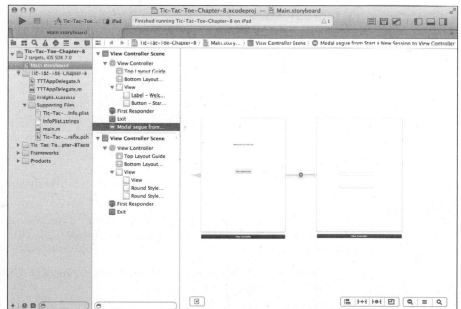

Figure 8-10:
A storyboard with two screens and a connecting segue.

You can now test the screen flow:

1. **Go to the main menu, click Product, and select Run.**

   The program starts and the first scene appears.

2. **Click Start New Session.**

   The second scene appears. "Magic," you say. "The magic of iOS story-boards," I say. Of course, you still have to write the code to implement the game's functionality, but, hey, every little bit helps.

The view controllers that you dropped into the storyboards to create the scenes will, by default, use the base view controller classes. These, obviously, have no app-specific functionality. To add this functionality, you do the following:

✔ Create your own view controller (which is a subclass of the base view controller).

✔ Implement app-specific methods and link the scene view controllers to those classes.

To see an example of an app-specific view controller, follow these steps:

1. **Open the Tic-Tac-Toe-Chapter-8 project in Xcode (which has a complete, runnable implementation of Tic-Tac-Toe).**

   Files corresponding to two view controller classes appear:

   - `TTTGameOptionsViewController`
   - `TTTGameSessionViewController`

2. **Click the storyboard file named** `MainStoryboard`**.**

   The storyboard canvas appears, along with its two screens and the segue, as shown in Figure 8-11.

   Zoom out until you see the entire storyboard; 25% should do it (refer to Figure 8-9).

3. **Click one of the scenes to select it (the outline of the screen will turn blue); then in the Inspector pane on the right, click the Identity inspector.**

   - The first scene is shown as a custom class with its `Class` field set to `TTTGameOptionsViewController`.

   - The `Class` field for the second scene is set to `TTTGameSessionViewController`.

   These fields are set manually; that is, you type the class names. After you set the linkages, the iOS runtime instantiates and uses the app's view controllers as the scenes become active.

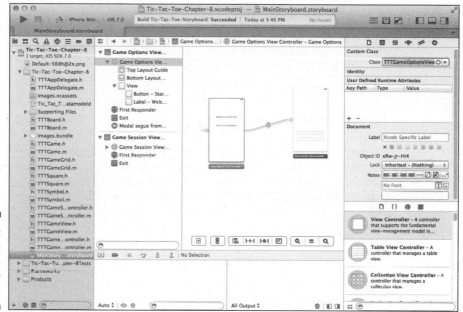

After setting the view controller's custom class, you can use the Attributes inspector to specify additional custom settings. For example, a view controller can be the manager of the first scene in the storyboard. You can also set other characteristics of the scene, such as the appearance of the title bar.

There are also multiple kinds of segues. The segue that you created earlier automatically transitioned the app from the Game Options scene to the Game Session scene when the Start New Session button was clicked. However, you may want to control the transition. For example, say that you want to check some entered values and then transition to the second scene only if the values are valid. To do so, you use what is known as a *manual* segue that's linked from the top-level view controller to the view controller of the second scene. The segue in the Tic-Tac-Toe app is a manual segue.

To use a manual segue, you must give it a name; I named this segue segueToGameSession.

You execute a manual segue by using the performSegueWithIdentifier method in your program's code, as shown in the following snippet from the startNewGame method in TTTGameOptionsViewController (note that the string "segueToGameSession" in the code matches what's shown in the Identifier field in the Attribute inspector.

```
- (IBAction)startNewGame{
    [self performSegueWithIdentifier:@"segueToGameSession" sender:self];
}
```

Finally, you can set cool visual effects for the transition.

For complete details on how to work with storyboards, scenes, and segues, go to www.dummies.com/go/iosprogramminglinks and check out the Working with Storyboards link.

Writing your app's code

Before I show you what Xcode provides for writing code, let me tell you what structure your app will have. You may recall that in earlier chapters, I mention that the Model-View-Controller (MVC) is the dominant pattern in an iOS app. In fact, an app can be thought of as a collection of MVCs working together.

You can implement most of the *view* functionality of an MVC component using storyboards and scenes. After you implement the views, the controller and model logic needs to be implemented. For this, you must write code.

Incidentally, some custom views also need actual code (for example, the Tic-Tac-Toe board). So let me start with how to create a custom view. First, you have to add such a view to a scene (as shown in the previous section). Then you set the class of the view to a custom subclass using the Identity inspector (see Figure 8-12).

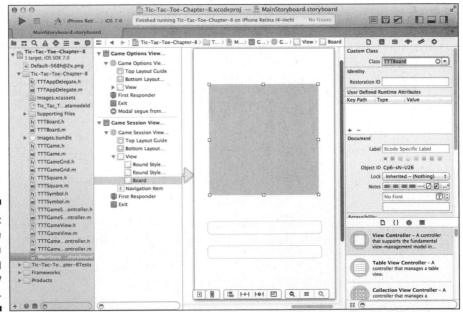

Figure 8-12: Setting the class of a view using the Identity inspector.

Of course, you need to implement the class for this custom view. In addition to the custom view classes, you need to write the code for the model and the controllers (or view controllers in iOS terminology). For all of these elements, you need to create Objective-C classes. To create a class, any class, follow these steps:

1. **Choose File⇨New⇨File.**

   The set of file templates appears (refer to Figure 8-5).

2. **Select Cocoa Touch and Objective-C class, then click Next.**

   A dialog box for naming the class appears.

3. **Name the class and set the superclass. Then click Next.**

   A dialog box for saving the file appears. This dialog box also allows you to set the project target for the file.

4. **Set the target of the file to be the current project and save the file in the project's folder.**

   Check the box next to the target (see Figure 8-13) to make the class you added a member of the target. Note that the default directory shown is the project's folder. Just stay with the default.

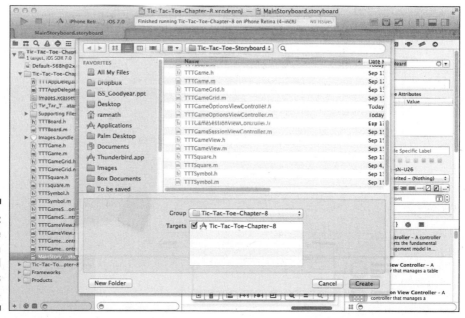

Figure 8-13:
Creating the files for a class and setting its target.

   5. **Click Create.**

   Two files are added to the project — an interface file (.h) and an implementation file (.m) — both with boilerplate code specific to the kind of
   class they represent (for example, the superclass of the new class).

Now you can knock yourself out writing code. Of course, my job in this
chapter is to show you how to use the Xcode IDE to do so.

In order to edit a file in the project, click the filename in the Project navigator.
The text in the files appears in the Editor area in Xcode (where the storyboard canvas was in the previous section). The Xcode editor allows you to
type and format your code as you do with other interactive editors. It also
has a lot of cool features (similar to the features found in other IDEs, such
as Eclipse). For example, as you type code, the editor provides suggestions
for completing variable declarations, commands, method calls, and the like.
Figure 8-14 shows a sampling of the Xcode editor's autocomplete capabilities.

Figure 8-14:
Auto-
complete
capabili-
ties of the
Xcode
editor.

The Xcode editor also incrementally checks the syntax of your code as you go. These incremental checks of syntax and the autocomplete feature are examples of how Xcode's incremental compiler tools (clang and llvm) work together to interpret your code and provide context-sensitive help.

Xcode also interprets your Objective-C code so that it can provide you with graphical help for user-interface wiring.

To see an example of user-interface wiring to code, take a look at the following snippet from the interface file `TTTGameSessionViewController.h`, where three properties are declared, each of type `IBOutlet`:

```
@property (nonatomic, retain) IBOutlet TTTBoard *boardView;
@property (nonatomic, retain) IBOutlet UITextField *scoreTextField;
@property (nonatomic, retain) IBOutlet UITextField *turnTextField;
```

A variable with the tag `IBOutlet` is known as an outlet, and used within a view controller to hold a reference to a view element (such as a text box) inside the view hierarchy managed by the view controller. When Xcode sees that a variable has been tagged in this manner, Xcode recognizes this variable as an outlet and allows you to graphically link a view element to it. Here's how to link an outlet to a text field:

1. **Control-click and drag the mouse from the view controller to the UI element.**

   A pop-up menu showing the outlets in the view controller appears.

2. **Select the right outlet for the UI element.**

See Figure 8-15 for an example of how `turnTextField` is wired to the text field used to show the game's status.

Note that the pop-up menu shows only the candidate outlets that are compatible with the UI element. In the preceding example, `boardView` isn't shown as a potential outlet for the text field. This is because `boardView` is of type `TTTBoard`, which isn't compatible with the text field, which is of type `UITextField`.

You can also graphically wire a method to a UI element to make the method the action for a user-interface event such as a button click. An example of an action method is shown here (from the file `TTTGameOptionsViewController.m`):

```
- (IBAction)startNewGame{
    [self performSegueWithIdentifier:@"segueToGameSession" sender:self];
}
```

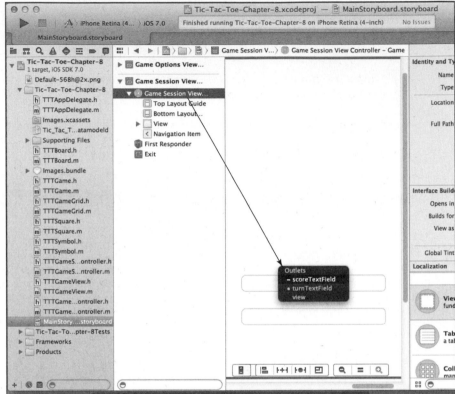

Figure 8-15:
Wiring
an outlet
to a view
element.

This kind of wiring is shown in Figure 8-16. Here, you Control-drag from the UI element to the view controller and then select the appropriate method from the pop-up menu that appears.

You can view the wirings between an outlet to a UI element or from a UI element to its actions by selecting the element and then clicking the Connections inspector.

Working in other editors

I hope that, like me, you're impressed with the cool Xcode editor, but if not, you can open Xcode files in any external editor. Here's how:

1. Select a file.

2. Choose File⇨Open with External Editor.

The MacOS default editor for that type of file appears.

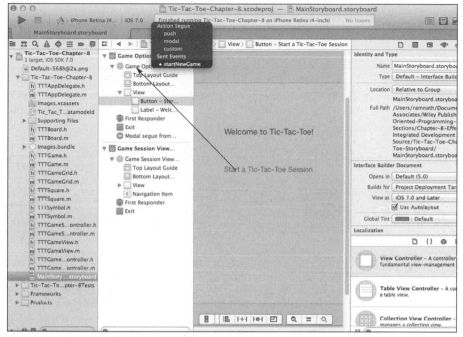

Managing and maintaining your app's components

This section describes the capabilities in Xcode that help you improve the quality of your code and manage it better. These capabilities include using the static analyzer to identify potential problems in your code and tools for refactoring your code.

Using the static analyzer

The *static analyzer* examines and analyzes your source code and points out any issues it finds, such as these:

- ✔ Accessing uninitialized variables
- ✔ Dereferencing null pointers
- ✔ Leaking allocated memory and unused variables
- ✔ Library usage flaws that result from violating policies required by the libraries

You run the static analyzer by choosing Product⇨Analyze. After the analyzer runs, any errors it finds appear in the Issue navigator, as shown in Figure 8-17. They are as follows:

- ✔ The first error the static analyzer points out occurs in the Game class (see TTTGame.m): I used the instance variable gameGrid in the init method without properly initializing self (the current, newly created instance) by calling [super init]. Adding the call to the superclass's init (see following code) fixes the error.

```
-(id) init { //Constructor
    self = [super init]; /// Initially missing
    gameGrid = [[TTTGameGrid alloc] init];
    gameState = Active;
    currentSymbol = [TTTSymbol SymbolXCreate];
    currentPlayer = Player1;
    return self;
}
```

- ✔ The second error is in the GameGrid class, where the static analyzer (rightly so) points out that foundIndex is never used after it's set.

```
-(BOOL) isRightToLeftDiagonalFilled{//Right diagonal has the same symbol
    int foundIndex=-1;
    BOOL isFilled=false;
    BOOL foundMismatch=false;
    for(int index = GAMEGRIDSIZE-1; (index >= 0)&&(!foundMismatch);
        index--){
        if(grid[0][GAMEGRIDSIZE-1] !=
           grid[GAMEGRIDSIZE-1-index][index]){
            foundMismatch=true;
            foundIndex=index; // Unused variable
        }
    }
    isFilled = (!foundMismatch) &&
               (grid[0][GAMEGRIDSIZE-1] !=
                           x[TTTSymbol SymbolBlankCreate]);
    return isFilled;
}
```

I left the preceding errors in the code so that you can run the analyzer yourself and see the same results. Note that neither error causes the program to fail, so (for example), the debugger wouldn't catch them. For more on the analyzer, see the link labeled Static Analyzer in the web resources for the book at www.dummies.com/go/iosprogramminglinks.

Restructuring your code using refactoring tools

You can use the refactoring tool in Xcode to clean and restructure your code. With this tool, you can

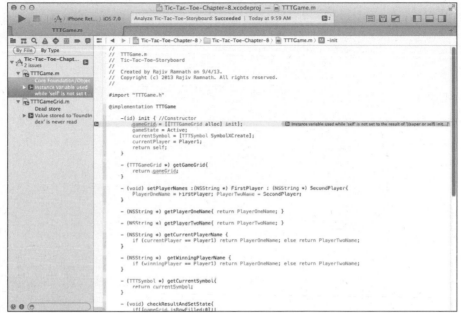

Figure 8-17:
Errors found
by the static
analyzer.

✔ Rename a symbol (such as a variable or a method) to better reflect what the method does.

✔ Take inline code and make it a method.

✔ Create a superclass (a skeleton of one, at any rate).

✔ Move methods from a class up to a superclass or from a superclass down to a subclass.

The refactoring process is straightforward, which will become clear if you join me by taking the following steps in which a method name is changed:

1. **In the Source editor (see Figure 8-18), select a piece of source code that you want to refactor — in this case,** `getBitmapForSymbol`.

2. **Rename it** `getBitmap` **because it's a method of the** `Symbol` **class.**

3. **Choose the appropriate refactoring command. In this example, I chose Edit⇨Refactor⇨Rename.**

   Xcode prompts you for the new name.

4. **Enter the new name.**

5. **Click Preview.**

   A preview of the changes appears (see Figure 8-19).

6. **Deselect changes you don't want to make and click Save.**

The first time you try to do any refactoring, you'll be prompted to enable (or disable) Automatic Snapshots. I recommend that you enable snapshots, at least the first few times that you refactor code. Incidentally, I discuss snapshots in the next section.

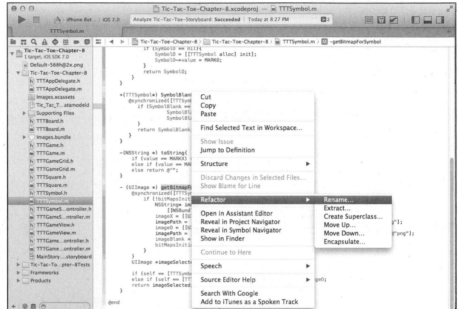

Figure 8-18: Refactoring a method name.

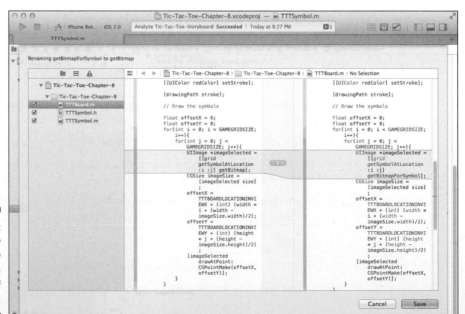

Figure 8-19: Preview window showing the effects of refactoring.

For more details on refactoring, go to the link labeled Refactoring in the web resources for this book at www.dummies.com/go/iosprogramminglinks.

Managing versions of your project

When you're taking an app through active development, you'll often try out a few ideas to see if they work, while planning to revert back to your old code if the ideas don't pan out. Xcode provides a useful snapshot capability to help you do this experimenting easily. You can save named images of your project as you go, and when you need to revert back to one, you can just select and revert back to it. Figure 8-20 shows you how to create a snapshot. After you initiate the snapshot, you're asked to give it a name. Do so and click Create Snapshot, and the snapshot is saved.

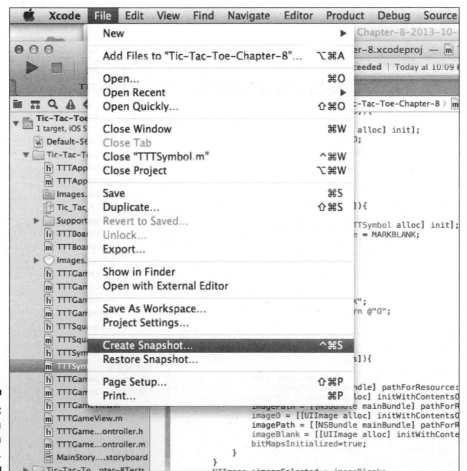

Figure 8-20: Creating a snapshot in Xcode.

You initiate the restore process by choosing File➪Restore Snapshot. A list of snapshots appears. Select one of them, and you see the difference between the snapshot and the current state of the project (as shown in Figure 8-21). If you want to revert to the selected snapshot, click Restore, and the snapshot becomes the current state of the project.

Snapshots become inaccessible if you change or move the project name because they're stored based on the encoding of the project name. So, if you change the project name, you lose the snapshot history. Also, be aware: Recovering snapshots isn't easy. To find out what to do if you need to recover a snapshot, go to the link labeled Recovering Snapshots in the web resources for the book at www.dummies.com/go/iosprogramminglinks.

Although the snapshots feature is great for individuals experimenting with their app, it doesn't provide enough support for large-scale software development by teams. For that, you need to use a robust source-code management (SCM) system that enables checking in and checking out individual files, creating and merging development branches, and so on.

Currently, the most popular (and free) SCM is Git (https://github.com). Xcode provides built-in support for integrating your project with Git. However, you first must create a repository in your project folder. Xcode creates it for you if you check the box labeled *Create git repository* at the time you select the folder for the project. (I didn't do that because I want to show you how to bring Git into your project *after* you create it.)

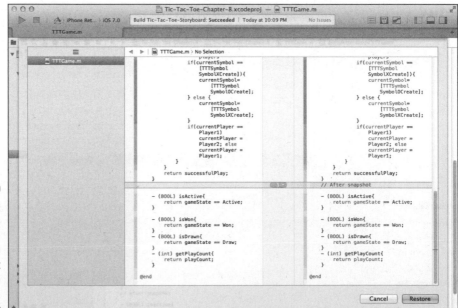

Figure 8-21:
Comparing the snapshot with the current state of the project.

To create a Git repository for your project, navigate to the project folder and create a file named `.gitignore` with the following content (this file is located in this chapter's project folder; please feel free to copy it and use it for any of your projects):

```
OS X Finder
.DS_Store

# Xcode per-user config
*.mode1
*.mode1v3
*.mode2v3
*.perspective
*.perspectivev3
*.pbxuser
*.xcworkspace
xcuserdata

# Build products
build/
*.o
*.LinkFileList
*.hmap

# Automatic backup files
*~.nib/
*.swp
*~
```

This file describes which types of files should not be version-controlled — such as files with compiled object code, executables, and temporary files used by Xcode.

Having a minimal `.getignore` file is essential for the proper operation of Git and Xcode. Certain files are constantly changed by Xcode, which will cause many Git operations, such as merging branches, to fail.

Exit from Xcode if it's running.

From a Terminal window, navigate to the project directory and issue the following commands from the command line (bravely and without hesitation):

```
git init
git add .
git commit -m "Initial commit of project"
```

These commands create the repository with the files that you currently have in your project. Now, bring up Xcode and, on the taskbar, click the Source Control menu, and you'll see the repository as well as the various commands you can use to work with Git.

Figure 8-22 shows what happens when you click Commit to save changes. Note that you can select which files to commit. In fact, you can even select changes to be committed at the individual method level. Also, note that unlike creating snapshots, committing files creates versions of only the changed files. This approach is more efficient than snapshots that copy the entire project.

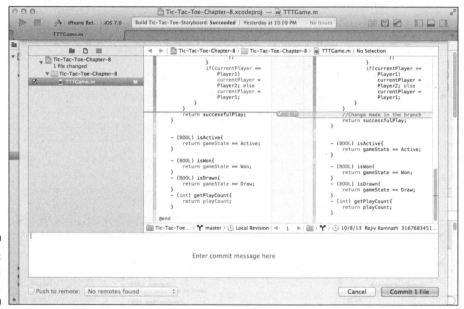

Figure 8-22:
Committing files to Git.

Figure 8-23 shows the project history after several changes are committed.

Other capabilities in Git include creating a branch (essentially a snapshot) of all the files in your project and merging the main repository to a branch, and vice versa. This branching capability is often used in place of creating snapshots. At any time, you can switch back to a branch. Figure 8-24 shows you how.

Figure 8-23:
Git project
history.

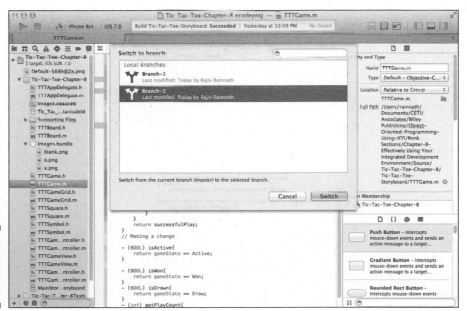

Figure 8-24:
Switching
to a branch
in Git.

The integration of Xcode with Git is somewhat minimal in that certain useful SCM functions are missing, such as being able to revert back to specific versions of files. Xcode also doesn't show the proper hierarchy of branches. That is, if you create a branch from the main trunk and another branch from the first branch, it shows all the branches at the same level, as opposed to a hierarchical structure, which clearly shows that the branch structure is `Main->Branch-1-> Branch-2`.

Incidentally, using local Git repositories (or, for that matter, snapshots) doesn't help much when teams need to develop code collaboratively. To do that, you must create or link to a Git repository on a server. The easiest place to create a Git repository is on GitHub (`https://github.com`). Using remote repositories is beyond the scope of this book. However, go to `https://help.github.com` for information on how to do so. Also, for an extensive, but now dated, tutorial on Git, go to the link labeled Git Tutorial in the web resources for this book at `www.dummies.com/go/iosprogramminglinks`.

Using external tools within Xcode

You can access several external tools from Xcode. One is the FileMerge tool, which allows you to compare and merge two text documents (and, of course, source code). You launch this tool by choosing Xcode⇨Open Developer Tool⇨FileMerge. Select two files, and you see the differences between them (see Figure 8-25).

Figure 8-25:
Comparing
files in
FileMerge.

All the standard Unix command-line tools, such as *make,* are available for download from Apple. This means you can build and manage your iOS programs completely outside Xcode. For more details, go to the link labeled Unix tools for Xcode at www.dummies.com/go/iosprogramminglinks.

Fine-Tuning Your App in Xcode

In this section, you find out how to configure your app so that it's built for specific iOS versions, as well as how to use advanced capabilities such as iCloud, in-app purchasing, maps, and so on. You discover how to use the iOS simulator, add resources (such as image files) to your device, extract data saved by your app on the device, and debug your app; as well as how to collect data about how fast your app is running, how many resources its consuming (such as memory), and so on.

Configuring your app

In this section, I show you how to configure the settings of your app (such as the package name). I also show you how to provide resources to your app (such as images).

Settings

You can see the settings of your app in the Editor area by clicking the app's name in Xcode (see Figure 8-26). Start with the General tab and then click all the tabs to see what's in each of them.

- ✔ On the General tab, you can change the package (or bundle) identifier (which you set when you created the project), the version of iOS you want to build the app for, the libraries you want to link to, and so on.

- ✔ On the Capabilities tab, you can turn on additional capabilities for your app — such as using iCloud, In-App purchasing, and maps.

- ✔ The Info tab shows another group of settings, such as the orientations your app is built to deal with and the language it uses.

- ✔ As its name implies, the Build Settings tab shows the build settings — the target platforms, the compiler settings, and so on. You can add custom C and C++ symbol definitions here.

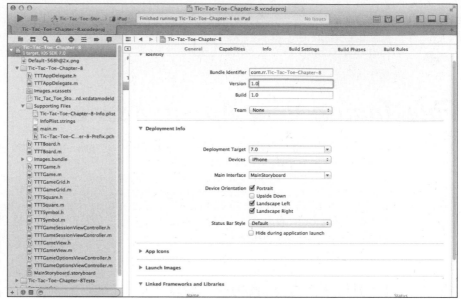

Figure 8-26:
General
settings for
your app.

✔ The Build Phases tab is where you add additional libraries to be linked into the app. This tab also shows all the source files that will be compiled for your app; if any are excluded, here's where you remove them. You can also change the order in which the files are compiled, if there are dependencies.

✔ Regarding the Build Rules tab, Xcode processes your files based on a set of rules for each file type. For example, `plist` files are copied into the product using the `CopyPlistFile` script.

Resources

The second aspect of configuration involves the resources needed for your application to run properly, such as images. For example, Tic-Tac-Toe uses images to display the X and O (and the blank) symbols. These images are put into a special folder called a *bundle* and compiled into your application's executable file. You create a bundle by choosing File➪New File, selecting a Settings Bundle file template, and naming the file. This bundle, which is really a folder, is placed in your project, and you can fill it with images and other files by dragging them from your Finder and dropping them into the bundle.

From within your program, you can access bundle elements as shown here (taken from the `getImageForSymbol` method in the `Symbol` class, in the file named `TTTSymbol.m`):

```
...
if (!bitMapsInitialized){
    NSString* imagePath = [[NSBundle mainBundle]
                           pathForResource:@"Images.bundle/x" ofType:@"png"];
    imageX = [[UIImage alloc] initWithContentsOfFile:imagePath];
          ...
}
```

Digging into the Simulator

The iOS Simulator enables you to simulate all the iOS devices on several versions of iOS and find major problems in your app before you put it on an actual device. Each device and software version is its own simulation environment with its own settings and files. Having used simulators for software development on other mobile platforms, I can honestly say that Apple's iOS Simulator is by far the best in terms of look and feel and performance. In addition to being one slick piece of software, it provides additional ways to test your app with developer tools available only for the Simulator. There are, of course, several limitations, which I also briefly talk about.

The easiest way to run your app in the Simulator is to launch it from your Xcode project by first setting the device type and the iOS level in the Scheme pop-up menu, and then choosing Product➪Run. The app automatically builds and then installs and runs on the chosen device (see Figure 8-27).

Because the available simulators reflect the iOS devices on the market, not all combinations of device and iOS versions are available as simulators.

At times, you may want to launch the iOS Simulator directly — for example, to test how your app launches from the home page or to test a web app in Safari. You can access the home page on the Simulator by choosing Hardware➪Home.

The Simulator's home page doesn't have all the apps that are installed on a real device. Those that are installed are mostly ones that your app will typically interact with. For example, Game Center is installed so that you can test via the Simulator to see whether a game you're developing is using Game Center correctly.

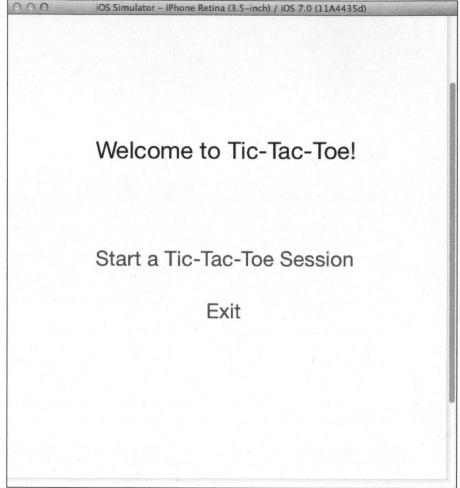

○ ○ ○   iOS Simulator – iPhone Retina (3.5–inch) / iOS 7.0 (11A4435d)

Welcome to Tic-Tac-Toe!

Start a Tic-Tac-Toe Session

Exit

Figure 8-27:
Tic-Tac-Toe
running
in the
Simulator.

To download older simulators, choose Xcode➪Preferences and click
Downloads. In Components, find the legacy simulator version and click Install.

For more about the iOS Simulator, go to the link labeled iOS Simulator at
www.dummies.com/go/iosprogramminglinks.

Exploring your iOS device from Xcode

Chapter 5 covers how to install and run your app on a device. In this section,
I discuss a few more useful capabilities within Xcode for managing your device.

First, you need to become familiar with the Organizer window, specifically the Devices tab in that window (see Figure 8-28). You open the Organizer by choosing Window⇨Organizer.

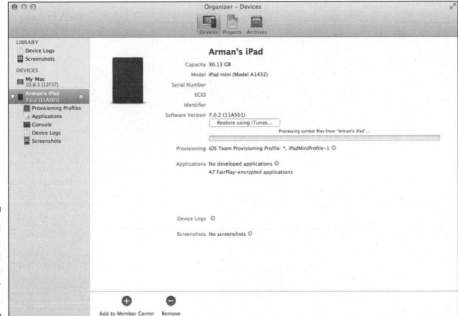

Figure 8-28:
Seeing devices in the Organizer window.

Figure 8-28 shows the root node of a tree of information. Clicking the root node shows a summary of information about the device. Clicking on each leaf node shows details about the device, such as the screenshots taken of the device.

Other information about an application is shown in the Organizer window. Figure 8-29 shows you the following:

- ✔ The provisioning profiles on the device
- ✔ The device log
- ✔ The private files of an application
- ✔ Screenshots from your application
- ✔ The console area of your app on the device

Provisioning profiles   Device log

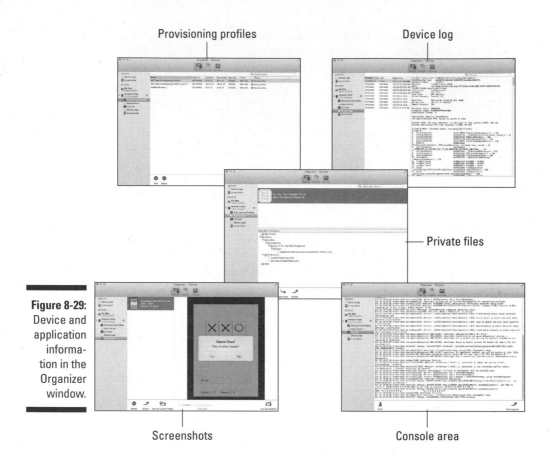

Private files

Figure 8-29:
Device and
application
informa-
tion in the
Organizer
window.

Screenshots   Console area

Viewing the private files of an application is especially important. As part of
the security architecture of iOS, each app runs in its own sandbox on the iOS
device. In other words, each app has its own folder on the iOS file system
where it can read and write files. You can copy and paste this folder into your
Mac and inspect it.

1. **Open the Xcode organizer with your device connected.**

2. **Click the Devices tab, click the little arrow next to your device, select
   Applications, and choose the app that you want to inspect.**

3. **Click the Download button, which becomes active when you select
   your application.**

   The device file system is now copied to your Mac, so you can inspect it
   to your heart's content.

If Xcode doesn't recognize your iPhone in the Scheme pop-up menu (even though it's connected to the computer), check to be sure the Use for Development option is enabled. Click the iPhone's icon beneath the Devices heading and click the Use for Development button.

Debugging your app

A simple way to watch your application run is by logging. Objective-C provides a simple static method named NSLog to log app execution. Using it is easy: Just embed calls to NSLog(@"<any string>"); where you like in your code and watch these lines as they appear (typically in a console window).

In Xcode, the console window is located at the bottom of the project workspace, but it's sometimes hidden. So, make it appear as shown in Figure 8-30 and watch your NSLog statements as they execute.

Figure 8-30: Showing the console window in the Debug area in Xcode.

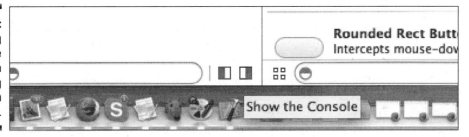

If you don't have your Console window open in Xcode, you can see your NSLog output in the Console pane of your device in the Organizer window (see the bottom right corner of Figure 8-29).

Of course, you have a full-blown visual debugger at your disposal in Xcode. Figure 8-31 shows the debugger in action (or actually, in *in*action because it's stopped at a breakpoint).

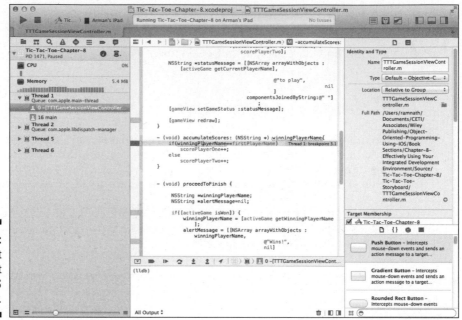

Figure 8-31:
Stopping at
a breakpoint
in the iOS
debugger.

You can right-click on a breakpoint and set conditions for the breakpoint. For more information on breakpoints, go to the link labeled Breakpoints in the web resources for this book at www.dummies.com/go/iosprogramminglinks.

Using instruments to collect data

Xcode provides a developer tool called *Instruments* that allows dynamic tracing and profiling of iOS code to help you understand the joint behavior of both the app code and the operating system. To use this tool, follow these steps:

1. Choose Xcode⇨Open Developer Tool⇨Instruments.

The Instruments window appears showing a collection of templates.

You can also access Instruments by clicking and holding the Play button and clicking Profile.

2. **Select Blank Template.**

   The Instrumentation window appears showing a blank area with the message *Drag recording instruments here from the Library to set up the Trace Document* (see Figure 8-32). If the window with the instruments library does not show, click on the little arrow below the above message (labeled Library).

3. **Drag and drop one or more instruments from the Library window into the instrumentation canvas.**

   The selected instruments appear in the Trace Document area

4. **Select an application to target for the instrumentation.**

   Figure 8-33 shows you how to select a target for the instrumentation — In this case, the Tic-Tac-Toe-Chapter-8 application.

   Figure 8-34 shows the data collected after an instrumentation run.

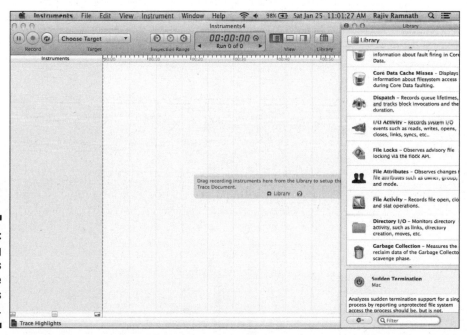

Figure 8-32:
Adding instruments in the Trace Documents area.

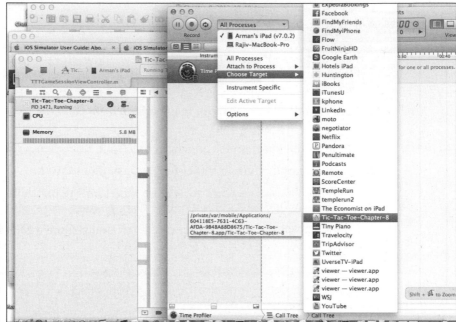

Figure 8-33:
Selecting a target for instrumentation.

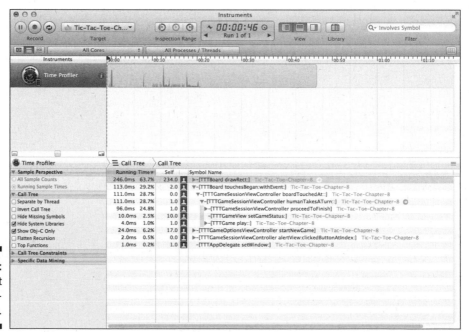

Figure 8-34:
Looking at instrumentation data.

I had to check Hide System Libraries and Objective-C Only in order to see useful data about my app.

Getting Help

As I mentioned at the beginning of this chapter, Xcode is a comprehensive and powerful integrated development environment (IDE) with a rich set of tools to make your development go smoothly, and to remove roadblocks when your development doesn't go smoothly. However, it's a complex system, and much of its functionality is hard for the uninitiated to find.

Plenty of help is available, starting with Xcode itself (see Figure 8-35 on how to invoke Xcode's built-in help features).

Apple's docs are also on the web, and they're kept current. The complete documentation of Xcode is here: `https://developer.apple.com/technologies/tools/features.html`.

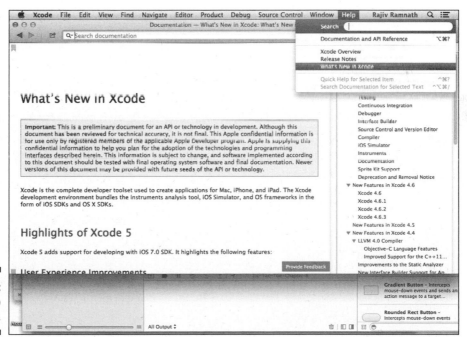

Figure 8-35: Built-in help in Xcode.

Chapter 9

Developing Your App's User Interface

. . . .

In This Chapter

▶ Understanding how user interfaces are built in iOS

▶ Using the common user-interface elements provided by the iOS framework

▶ Understanding the OO principles underlying user interfaces

. . . .

*T*his chapter focuses on developing the user interface (or UI) of your iOS app. I briefly discuss the theory behind how the UI works. Then I explain how iOS implements user interfaces, starting with the Application object, and how user-interface events (such as touches) are transmitted down the responder chain.

I go over the Model-View-Controller (MVC), which is layered on the responder chain and is the dominant pattern used in iOS user interfaces. Next, I cover several components that Apple makes available in the iOS framework that you can use in developing your apps. Finally, I tie these patterns and components to OO techniques, concepts, and design principles.

Understanding How User Interfaces Work in iOS

In this section, I explain event-driven programming, an approach that is fundamental to developing applications with rich graphical user interfaces. I also explain how iOS handles events.

Comprehending event-driven programming in iOS

Applications with highly interactive (or *rich*) user interfaces implement a programming model known as *event-driven programming*. Programs that primarily do computations and calculations in order to accomplish a task have a main function that orchestrates these computations and calculations. Event-driven programs are different. Their purpose isn't to accomplish a computational goal but to make a buffet of capabilities available to the user or external systems, and then react to these events.

Rather than orchestrating computations, therefore, the main function in event-driven programs runs *event loops*. The event loop catches events as they're posted from external sources and processes them by handing them off to appropriate objects, which results in the correct methods in these objects being called. User-interface events are generated by devices that interface with the operating system — such as a mouse or touchscreen — to enable human interaction with the application.

Event-driven programming isn't just about dealing with user interaction. Sensors also post events that your program may need to handle. Other components of the system can also post events, such as the component that monitors the battery level.

Understanding the Application and the Application Delegate objects in UI processing

Just to briefly recap what I say in Chapter 6, when an iOS application starts, it runs a function called main that creates a Singleton UIApplication object. This object is responsible for routing external events as well as overall management of a running application.

The UIApplication object creates an Application Delegate object. This delegate object is particular to your app and was created especially for it by Xcode. In Tic-Tac-Toe, the Application Delegate is named TTTAppDelegate (see files TTTAppDelegate.h and .m in the sample project). The primary job of the delegate object is to initialize the application and present its initial window. This delegate is also notified (by the UIApplication object) when specific application-level events occur, such as when the application needs to be interrupted (because of an incoming message) or moved to the background (because the user touched the Home button).

User-interface events are handled differently, however. Rather than going through an Application Delegate, the Application object takes each incoming UI event and routes it to the object (known as a *Responder*) containing the view on which the action occurred (see Figure 9-1). To do so, the Application object monitors its window's current status (such as whether it's in the foreground or the background).

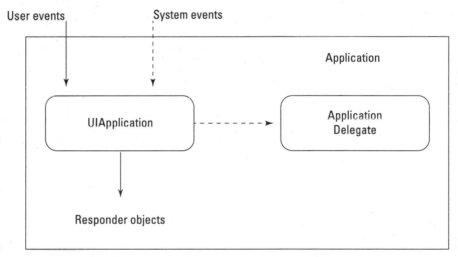

Figure 9-1:
How the Application object in iOS deals with events

A window in iOS is an instance of a class named `UIWindow`. Because iOS applications are limited to a single window, a `UIWindow` object has a limited role in iOS. This window occupies the entire screen and doesn't interact with the user, so it doesn't have a title, controls, or other adornments — such as scroll bars. A `UIWindow` contains a hierarchy of view objects (instances of `UIView` or its subclasses). At launch time, an application creates its window and adds its views, either by executing code written by the developer of the app or by interpreting its storyboard.

Although a Window object doesn't interact with users, it plays an important role in drawing its views and distributing events to these views.

Think of the window as being at the root of a hierarchy of views, with views higher in the hierarchy enclosing other views. When a window becomes active (because an app comes into the foreground), the Window object displays the app's content by going down the view hierarchy, asking each view in turn to draw itself inside the view in which it's contained.

A window distributes incoming events to the most appropriate views in its hierarchy using *action messages*. For example, for touch and gesture events, the recipient of the action message (and its contained event) is the view touched by a user's finger. For events like keyboard events that have no target, the recipient is whichever view is the *first responder*. The first responder is the object that should be asked first to respond to the event. For example, when you click in a text box, focus is set on that view, and it becomes the first responder and starts responding to keyboard events. The single `UIWindow` is in charge of assigning and keeping track of the first responder.

Figure 9-2 shows the class hierarchy for windows, views, and responders. To find more about windows and views, go to the web resources for this book at `www.dummies.com/go/iosprogramminglinks` and check out the Windows and Views link.

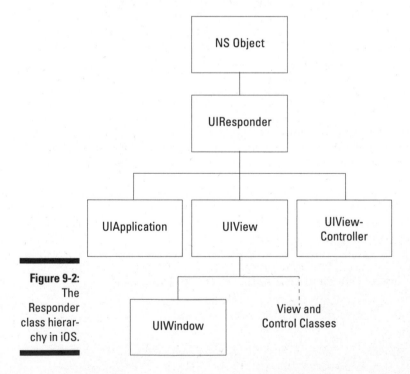

Figure 9-2:
The Responder class hierarchy in iOS.

A chain of responders is behind the designated first responder. If the first responder can't handle an event, the event is forwarded to the next responder in the chain. The message travels up the chain, toward higher-level objects, until it reaches the `UIWindow` object. If it isn't handled there, the app discards it. In most cases, the responder chain consists of views. However, when a designated view controller is managing a view, the view controller becomes the next responder in the chain.

Now that you know how to draw views and dispatch and handle UI events, it's time to revisit the Model-View-Controller design pattern within the context of iOS and to discuss views, the view hierarchy, user-interface events, and action messages in more detail.

Revisiting the Model-View-Controller Design Pattern

I introduce the Model-View-Controller (MVC) in Chapter 2, where I say that it's a well-known design pattern in mobile applications and especially in web applications. In Chapter 4, I explain, in detail, the idea behind this pattern, which is to isolate the domain logic of the application from its user interface so that these two very important components can be designed, implemented, and maintained separately.

Model objects represent a problem domain — such as the Tic-Tac-Toe game and its rules. A model is valuable because it's reusable in similar problem domains.

A model isn't concerned with user-interface issues. This is the role of the *views,* which handle the presentation aspects of the application, and also serve as the conduit through which users interact with the application.

Controllers implement the application logic, and in doing so, stitch models and views together.

Figure 9-3 shows how the model, view, and controller interact in the standard MVC pattern. The solid lines show which objects act on the other; the dashed lines indicate linkages between objects.

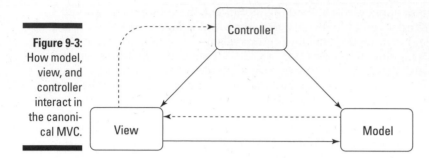

Figure 9-3:
How model,
view, and
controller
interact in
the canoni-
cal MVC.

MVC is the basis for user-interface development in iOS. Models are implemented as plain old Objective-C classes. (Now that POJO is an accepted
abbreviation for "plain old Java objects," should we accept POOCC?)

In iOS, controllers are called *view controllers.* They implement the logic
of the app and serve as the link between its data and its user interface. In
iOS, a view controller or a group of cooperating view controllers manage
how content is shown on an app and connect this content to the logic of
the app.

For Apple's introduction on how iOS implements MVC, go to www.dummies.
com/go/iosprogramminglinks and check out the MVC in iOS link.

View controllers are the key bridging elements of an app. They also consti-
tute the skeleton on which apps are built. iOS provides several types of view
controllers (all subclasses of the base UIViewController class). These
include the Navigation view controller, the Tab Bar, Page View, and Split View
view controllers, as well as popovers. iOS also has even more view controllers for specific functions, such as for controlling the camera.

The centrality of view controllers is also why the recommended process
for developing apps in iOS starts with view controllers, and why the sample
application templates provided in Xcode (and discussed in Chapter 6) essentially differ in the kinds of view controllers and related views they contain
(except, of course, for the Empty Application template, which comes with
only an app delegate).

For more on view controllers in iOS, go to www.dummies.com/go/
iosprogramminglinks and check out the View-Controllers in iOS link.

A *view* is an object that draws itself within a rectangular area of a window and that can respond to user actions such as the tap of a finger. A view must be situated in the view hierarchy of a window — an inverted tree structure with the window at the root. Note that each view is completely enclosed in its parent view, with the window containing all the views. For more on views and the view hierarchy, go to `www.dummies.com/go/iosprogramminglinks` and check out the link labeled The View Hierarchy.

UI events in iOS are the result of (finger) touches on a view (or of the user shaking the device). A `UITouch` object representing each touch is packaged in the event sent to the responder. This object contains information such as the view being touched, the location of the touch, a timestamp, and a phase. The phase is necessary because a touch object goes through a sequence of phases during a touch — in the following order:

- ✔ `UITouchPhaseBegan`: Finger touched a view.

- ✔ `UITouchPhaseMoved`: Finger moved on that view or moved to an adjacent view.

- ✔ `UITouchPhaseEnded`: Finger lifted from a view.

Via the main event loop (see "Comprehending event-driven programming in iOS," earlier in this chapter), the application object receives touch events in its event queue. It then packages them as `UITouch` objects within `UIEvent` objects and dispatches them to the appropriate responder. In order for the responder to handle events, it must override four methods (declared in the `UIResponder` base class), as follows:

- ✔ `touchesBegan` is called for touches in the Began phase.

- ✔ `touchesMoved` is called for touch objects in the Moved phase. That is, after the touch, the user's finger continues to press while dragging on the screen.

- ✔ `touchesEnded` is called for touch objects in the Ended phase. That is, the user lifts her finger after the touch.

- ✔ `touchesCancelled` is called when (say) an incoming phone call cancels touch events that took place before the phone call.

Figure 9-4 shows how touches and events are handled in iOS. For more on events and touches, go to `www.dummies.com/go/iosprogramminglinks` and check out the Events link.

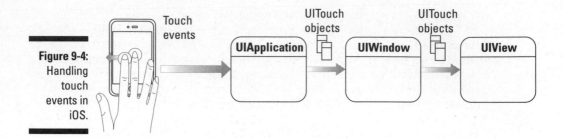

Certain specialized UI elements (like text fields) use a different mechanism for user-interface interactions. Rather than reporting events to their respond-ers, who then have to decide how to act on these events, the UI elements send actions (or action messages) to their responders that these responders act upon. The information stored in an action message consists of two items: a selector, which identifies the method to be invoked, and a target, which is the object that receives the message. A method that will handle an action message must look like the following:

```
- (IBAction)doSomething:(id)sender;
```

For more on action messages, go to www.dummies.com/go/ iosprogramminglinks and check out the Action Messages link.

All this may sound complicated, but just note that delegation is the common theme in handling events. Essentially, events and actions are recognized in views and then handling of the event or action is delegated to a responder. Keep in mind that delegation needs to be specified differently in different UI elements, and figuring out how to develop an iOS UI will be a breeze.

Understanding the UI Components Available in iOS

In this section, I describe what iOS provides in terms of user-interface com-ponents. Figure 9-5 shows you a varied set of UI elements on an iOS screen and the typical location of each element on the screen of a device. As you can see, the window is the background screen, and an instance of a Navigation Bar component is at the top. Also, a view consisting of the Date Picker con-trol and the Text Field control overlays the window. Finally, an instance of the Tab Bar component, composed of bar items, is at the bottom of the screen.

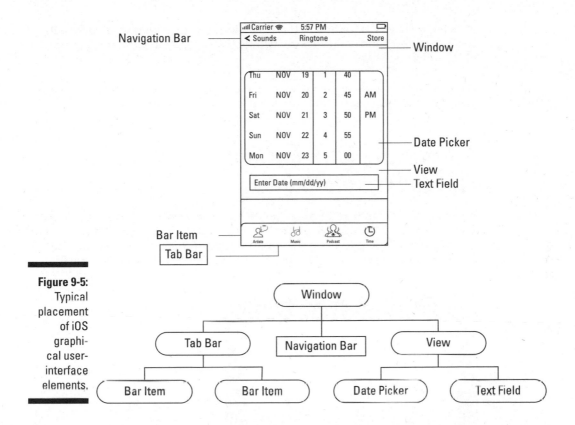

Figure 9-5: Typical placement of iOS graphical user-interface elements.

Figure 9-5 also shows iOS UI elements in a tree-like hierarchy. As shown in this figure, a window is the root of three view hierarchies. The first is the Navigation bar at the top, along with the elements it contains. The second is the Tab bar at the bottom, with its contained elements. The last view on the screen (which is between the Navigation bar and the Tab bar) is the app-specific view hierarchy that is, in a sense, the main view hierarchy of the app.

For more on the iOS view hierarchies, go to www.dummies.com/go/iosprogramminglinks and check out the iOS View Hierarchy link.

Each element on the screen is a view. That is, the navigation bar is a view as are its components, so are the tab bar and its components, and finally so are the window, the overlaid view, the date picker, and the text field. iOS provides classes that you use to create these views. I discuss these classes next and provide examples of code with their use, starting with the simpler classes (Text Field, Label, and Button), moving on to the more complex ones

(Alert and Picker), and then to the even more complex ones that come with their own view controllers. These include the Navigation view, the Tab Bar view, and so on.

For a detailed reference on iOS views, go to www.dummies.com/go/ iosprogramminglinks and check out the iOS Views link.

Interacting with buttons, text fields, and labels

Buttons, labels, and text fields are among the simplest views available in iOS. The iOS classes for these views are UIButton, UILabel, and UITextField, respectively. These classes are liberally sprinkled through the Tic-Tac-Toe application; an example of their use in Tic-Tac-Toe is shown in Figure 9-6.

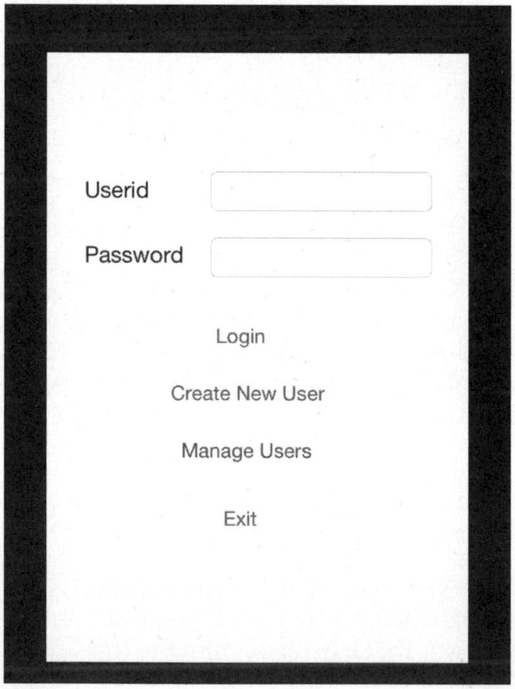

Figure 9-6:
Labels, text fields, and buttons.

Userid

Password

Login

Create New User

Manage Users

Exit

Note the labels Userid and Password, the text fields next to them, and the buttons Login, Create New User, Manage Users, and Exit. You can examine these elements from within Xcode, as well. For example, Figure 9-7 shows the Login button in the Identity inspector.

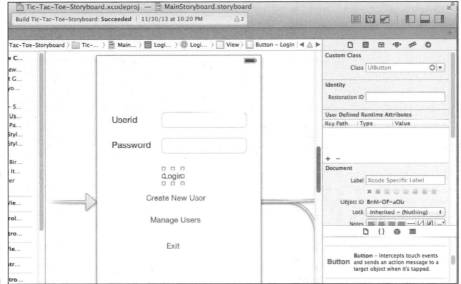

Figure 9-7: Inspecting the Login button using the Identity inspector.

Every button event is bound to an action method. When the button is touched and the event is posted, the action method is called. The Connections inspector shows that the Touch Up Inside event of the Login button is bound to the login action method in the Login view controller (see Figure 9-8).

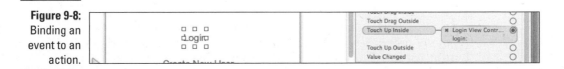

Figure 9-8: Binding an event to an action.

The following code shows the definition of the login method. Feel free to bring up this method in Xcode (in the file TTTLoginViewController.m) and follow along.

```
- (IBAction)login:(id)sender{

    NSString* oneUserid = [useridTextField text];
    NSString* onePassword = [passwordTextField text];
    useridTextField.text = @"";
    passwordTextField.text = @"";
    TTTUserManager* myUserManager = [TTTUserManager CreateUserManager];
    if ([myUserManager useridPassWordMatch :oneUserid :onePassword]){ //
        Login successful
        ...

        // Segue to GameOptions scene
        [self performSegueWithIdentifier:@"SuccessfulLogin" sender:self];
    }else{
        [self showMessage :@"Login Failed!" :@"Check userid and
          password"];
        ...
    }
}
```

Note the IBAction in the declaration of the login method. This is actually nothing more than a macro that translates to void, but it marks login as an action method for Xcode to display appropriately (for example, when you try to tie the Login button to this method in the storyboard).

Next, note the variable useridTextField. This variable refers to the User ID text field in the view. Because useridTextField refers to a UI element, it's known as an *outlet,* and its declaration as a property in TTTLoginViewController.h reflects this, as shown in the following code:

```
@property (nonatomic, retain) IBOutlet UIButton *loginButton;
...
@property (nonatomic, retain) IBOutlet UITextField *useridTextField;
...
```

An outlet property named loginButton is declared and bound to the Login button, as well. This outlet could be used to get access to the button to dynamically change its properties — for example, to disable it until something is actually typed in the Userid field.

Text fields, such as the Userid text field, mostly provide ways to put data into the program. The text field can be read into the program by accessing its contents via the outlet. You can also use this outlet to change the contents of the text field, as illustrated here:

```
        NSString* oneUserid = [useridTextField text];
        ...
        useridTextField.text = @"";
```

Users enter data into a text field via a keyboard that pops up when they touch the text field (see Figure 9-9).

Figure 9-9:
Entering
data into a
text field via
a keyboard.

Because this keyboard often obscures other parts of the view (such as a button that needs to be clicked when users finish entering data in the text field), it needs to be dismissed when the user finishes entering text. In order to trigger actions tied to text fields, text fields also post events that can be linked to actions. In Figure 9-10, you can see that the Did End On Exit event in the text field for entering the User Id is linked to the doneEnteringText method in the Login view controller (see file TTTLoginViewController.m).

Figure 9-10:
Binding an
event of a
text field to
an action.

The code for this method is

```
-(IBAction)doneEnteringText:(id)sender{
    UITextField *theField = (UITextField*)sender;
    ...
    [theField resignFirstResponder];
}
```

This code grabs whatever field is posting the event (through the `sender` parameter) and asks it to resign as the first responder. This resignation (often accompanied by a deep sigh!) will hide the keyboard again.

Finally, it's time for labels. Labels are similar to text fields, except, of course, they don't allow users to enter information and change their value. However, the *program* can change a label's value or set its properties by wiring it to an outlet and referring to it via this outlet (see Figure 9-11).

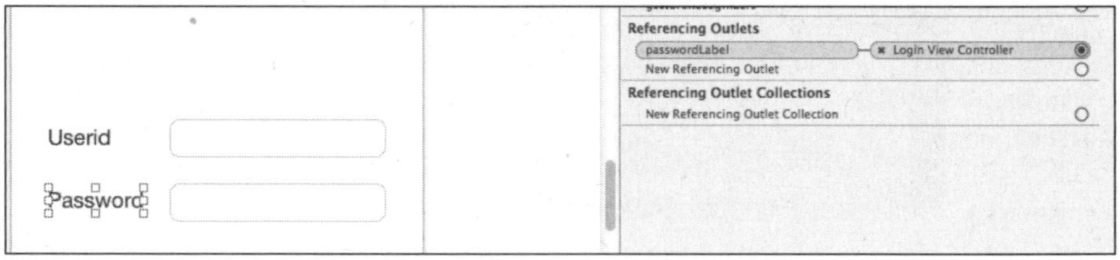

Figure 9-11:
Wiring a label to an outlet.

Here's how to wire a label to an outlet:

```
(IBAction)doneEnteringText:(id)sender{
    UITextField *theField = (UITextField*)sender;
    // [passwordLabel setText:@"Tell me all!"];
    [theField resignFirstResponder];
}
```

Just uncomment the statement `[passwordLabel setText:@"Tell me all!"];` and run the app. If you touch any of the text fields on the login screen and then press Return on the keyboard (so that the keyboard goes away), the Password label changes to Tell me all!

Alerting the user

Alert views interrupt users while they're using an app, requiring them to stop what they're doing and either dismiss the alert or select an action. Note that an Alert view appears on top of the content on an app's screen — after all, the alert's purpose is to catch the user's attention. Figure 9-12 shows an Alert view from Tic-Tac-Toe. Clicking Yes clears the old game and starts a new one. Clicking No ends the game.

Figure 9-12:
The Alert view in Tic-Tac-Toe.

As with most iOS views, you use delegation to implement an alert. However, the specification of the delegate is done programmatically — that is, not through the interface builder, as for buttons. The following code illustrates how to do so (taken from the GameView class; implemented in TTTGameView.m and .h):

```
- (void) promptToProceed :(TTTGameSessionViewController *)
        GameViewController {
    UIAlertView *alert = [[UIAlertView alloc] init];
    [alert setTitle:@"Game Over!"];
    [alert setMessage:@"Play Another Game?"];
    [alert addButtonWithTitle:@"Yes"];
    [alert addButtonWithTitle:@"No"];
    [alert setDelegate:GameViewController];
    [alert show];
}
```

After alert is instantiated in the typical Objective-C manner (using alloc followed by init), the title and message properties are set, and the Yes and No buttons are added as subviews to the Alert view using the method addButtonWithTitle. Just before the alert is shown (using the show method), the Game Session view controller is set as the delegate to the alert using the setDelegate method.

Because the Game Session view controller is set as the delegate to the alert, an action in the Game Session view controller class is triggered when a button of the alert is touched.

Any delegate to the alert must implement the `UIAlertViewDelegate` protocol, and therefore, a method named `clickedButtonAtIndex` as the delegate action method for the alert. Check `TTTGameSessionViewContro ller.m`, and you'll see this `clickedButtonAtIndex` method, which is also shown in the following code:

```
- (void)alertView:(UIAlertView *)alertView
        clickedButtonAtIndex:(NSInteger)buttonIndex{
   if (buttonIndex == 0){
      [self playNewGame];
   } else if (buttonIndex == 1) {
      return;
   }
}
```

The Yes button was added first, so its index is 0. As you can see, touching this button starts a new game. The No button was added second, so its index is 1. Touching it does nothing. Incidentally, did you notice the coupling between the delegate method and the method that created the alert? If not, don't worry. You find out more about it in the last section of this chapter where I discuss the OO design principles in user-interface development.

Selecting items using pickers

A picker view is a compact and visually appealing way to present a range of values in one or more dimensions to users (such as a date, where the dimensions are month, day, and year) and to let them select a set of values, with one value from each range.

The base class for a picker view is `UIPicker`. Pickers that are built from the base class need two delegates: one to implement the `UIPickerViewDelegate` protocol to provide the data shown on the picker and handle user interactions, such as the delegate for the Alert view; and another one, known as a *data source delegate,* to provide the dimensions of the picker (the number of columns and the number of rows in each column). Despite its name, data source delegate protocol isn't the protocol for actually providing the data. Instead, to provide the data for the picker, the delegate must implement the `UIPickerViewDataSource` protocol.

Because you'll see something very similar for the Table view in the next section, I don't go into the details of the picker protocols here. For now, I'll just describe a subclass of `UIPicker`, named `UIDatePicker`, which has the data source and view delegate already so complete that you can use a date picker almost like a text field. To see how the date picker is used, look at the User Detail view controller (`TTTUserDetailViewController.m` and `.h`).

Figure 9-13 shows the screen for the view managed by the User Detail view controller.

Figure 9-13: Using a date picker.

The interface file has an outlet for the birthday date picker, as shown here:

```
@property (nonatomic, retain) IBOutlet UIDatePicker *birthdayPicker;
```

In the implementation file, you see the following:

```
- (IBAction) saveChanges:(id)sender{
    ...
    NSDate *birthday = [self.birthdayPicker date];
    NSLog(@"Birthday selected is %@", birthday);
    ...
}
```

You can see that the value set in the picker is being read via the outlet connected to it. Easy as pie.

Incidentally, for a detailed reference on pickers, go to www.dummies.com/go/iosprogramminglinks and check out the link named The Picker View.

Showing columnar data using a Table view

The Table view is a complex view needing complex delegates. It presents data in multiple rows, with each row divided into columns. You can see a Table view in Tic-Tac-Toe in the Manage Tic-Tac-Toe Users screen, as shown in Figure 9-14.

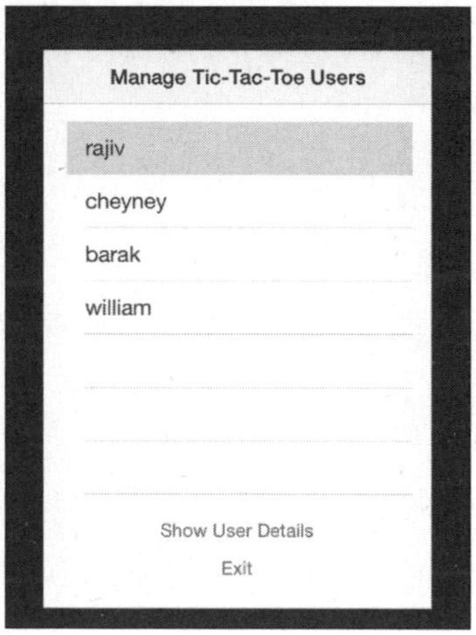

Figure 9-14: A Table view showing a list of Tic-Tac-Toe users.

You can add a Table view as you do a view in a storyboard. You can also set several attributes of the view in the storyboard via the Attributes inspector. However, in order for content to appear in a table, it must have a data source delegate — that is, a class that implements the UITableViewDataSource protocol. For the table shown in Figure 9-14, the data source delegate is the User Manager view controller (implemented in TTTUserManagerViewController.m and .h). This delegate is also configured via the storyboard, as shown in Figure 9-15.

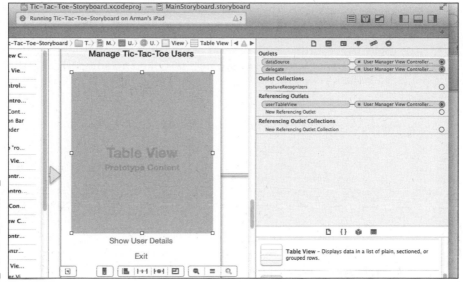

Figure 9-15:
Setting the
delegates
for a Table
view.

The following code shows the `cellForRowAtIndexPath` data source method:

```
#pragma Table View Data Source methods

    - (UITableViewCell *)tableView:(UITableView *)tableView
            cellForRowAtIndexPath:(NSIndexPath *)indexPath{
        static NSString *userTableIdentifier = @"UserItem";

        UITableViewCell *cell =
            [tableView dequeueReusableCellWithIdentifier:userTableIdentifier];

        if (cell == nil) {
            cell = [[UITableViewCell alloc]
                    initWithStyle:UITableViewCellStyleDefault
                    reuseIdentifier:userTableIdentifier];
        }

        cell.textLabel.text =
            [[userTableData objectAtIndex:indexPath.row] userid];
        return cell;
    }

    - (NSInteger)tableView:(UITableView *)tableView
            numberOfRowsInSection:(NSInteger)section{
        return [userTableData count];
    }
```

In the preceding code, the key method in the `TableViewDelegate` protocol (the one that specifies how interactions with the Table view are handled) is the method `didSelectRowAtIndexPath`, as shown next. The content of the selected row (that is, the userid of the user) is read from the selected cell. Utilizing the userid, the user object is looked up and cached in the member variable `selectedUser`.

```
#pragma Table View Delegate methods

- (void)tableView:(UITableView *)tableView
        didSelectRowAtIndexPath:(NSIndexPath *)indexPath {
    UITableViewCell *cell = [tableView cellForRowAtIndexPath:indexPath];
    NSString *cellText = cell.textLabel.text;
    ...
    selectedUser = [userManager getUserGivenUserid:cellText];
}
```

Going through the other views in the iOS framework

So far I've shown you several view elements, with a view (pun intended) to showing you the range of techniques and patterns used in implementing views. However, these aren't the only UI elements available. The Web View and the Image View classes are covered in Chapters 12 and 13, respectively. Other elements are as follows:

✔ Action sheets display a collection of vertically arranged buttons representing a set of alternative choices.

✔ An activity indicator is a spinning wheel signifying that an action is still in progress.

✔ Similar to an activity indicator, a progress view shows the extent to which a task has executed.

✔ A search bar provides a text box to enter a search term and buttons to start and cancel the search.

✔ A scroll view allows users to see content that goes beyond the visible boundaries of a view.

These views are all shown in Figure 9-16.

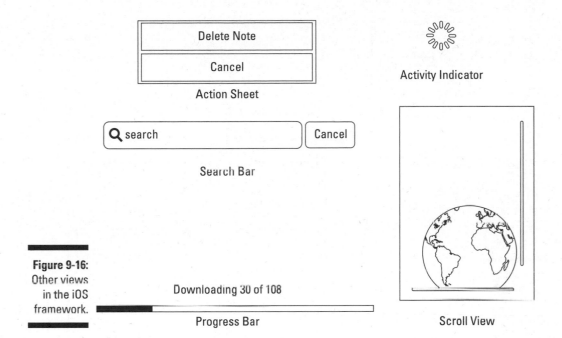

Delete Note

Cancel

Action Sheet

Activity Indicator

Q search   Cancel

Search Bar

Figure 9-16:
Other views
in the iOS
framework.

Downloading 30 of 108

Progress Bar

Scroll View

For more about all these views, go to www.dummies.com/go/
iosprogramminglinks and check out the iOS Views link.

Navigating through a stack of screens using a Navigation controller

An app often must allow a user to navigate down a hierarchy of data. For
example, a screen may need to show a list of countries; and when you select
a country, show a list of cities in the country; and when you click on a city,
show details about the city. A Navigation controller is a UI component provided by the iOS framework for navigating through such a hierarchy.

You can see an example of a Navigation in Tic-Tac-Toe when you select
Manage Users on the first screen of the app. When you select a user and
then touch Show User Details, the details about that user appear. Figure 9-17
shows the screen flow for this sequence. Notice that on the User Details
screen, a Navigation bar with a Back button appears, which enables you to
return to the list of users.

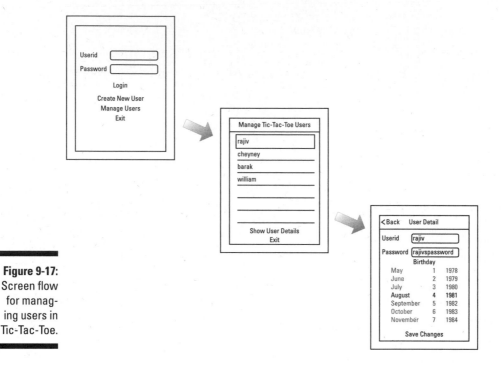

Figure 9-17:
Screen flow
for manag-
ing users in
Tic-Tac-Toe.

You could implement this flow by customizing your own view controllers and views. However, iOS provides packaged capability that allows you to do so more easily using a Navigation controller.

iOS provides templates for many kinds of things — from entire applications to complex user interfaces. Sometimes using the templates is harder than building the functionality from scratch. Feel free to do what works best for you.

I used a Navigation controller to implement the Manage Users screen flow previously introduced in this chapter, and I'll show how I did so. First, though, look at the section of the Tic-Tac-Toe storyboard shown in Figure 9-18, where you see three view controllers. The first is a Navigation controller connected to the Login screen of Tic-Tac-Toe by a modal segue from the button Manage Users. The Navigation view controller is connected by a segue to a second view controller named User Manager (class name `TTTUserManagerViewController`) that has an embedded Table view. Note that this is a *Relationship* segue. This kind of segue can originate *only* from a Navigation controller. When you add the segue, add the target view controller — the one labeled Manage Tic-Tac-Toe Users — as the Root view controller (see Figure 9-18).

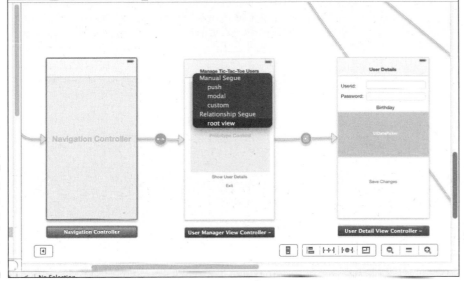

Figure 9-18:
Setting up a
Navigation
controller
with mul-
tiple views.

Finally, The User Manager view controller is, in turn, connected to the next view controller (this one is named User Details) by a Push segue.

Setting up this chain is simply a matter of dropping in the Navigation view controller and two other view controllers and wiring them together with segues, starting from the Navigation view controller.

Even though the wiring is simple, it sets up the complex, hierarchical navigation functionality within this set of view controllers. The first of these views, the Navigation controller, is launched from the Login screen by a segue originating at the button Manage Users. When the program runs and you push Manage Users from the Login screen, it doesn't linger on the screen of the Navigation view controller. In fact, the Navigation view controller has *no* screen. Its job, when activated, is simply to transition control to the view controller connected to it via the Relationship segue — that is, the User Manager view controller that's identified as the Root view controller. Finally, this User Manager view controller is connected to the User Details view controller by a Push segue originating from the Show User Details button.

Note that you can test the navigation from end to end simply by wiring the view controllers in the storyboard, without writing a single line of code. So, go ahead and test the navigation.

More code is needed, however, to complete the preceding scenario; that is, the app shows you a list of users, and you pick one of the users and touch the Show User Details button, at which point the next screen pops up with the detailed information about the user — his name, password, and birthday.

The implementation of the scenario described in the previous paragraph begins with the method `prepareForSegue` in the `TTTUserManagerViewCo ntroller`:

```
-(void)prepareForSegue:(UIStoryboardSegue *)segue sender:(id)sender{
    ...
    TTTUserDetailViewController* userDetailsViewController =
                                    segue.destinationViewController;
    [userDetailsViewController setUserObject:selectedUser];
}
```

This method is called *after* the segue has executed and after the destination view is created but just before it's presented. Consequently, using the method `segue.destinationViewController`, you can get a reference to the User Manager view controller instance and then call a method on it (in this case, the `setUserObject` method) to pass the `TTTUser` object that corresponds to the selected user into the User Detail view controller.

When a user is selected and Show User Details is touched, the app transitions to the User Details screen (and shows the user details). In addition to the user details, note the Back button that appears at the upper-left corner of the User Details screen. Touch the Back button, and the User Details view controller slides out of the way, and the User Manager screen reappears.

The rest of the code in these two view controllers contains only the table-handling code described earlier.

Drawing using 2-D Graphics

Using the built-in controls for defining your app's user interface is fun and easy. However, there's a back-to-basics way to draw your user interface within a view using the iOS Quartz Graphics framework that provides you with 2-D graphics capability, as illustrated in the drawing of the Tic-Tac-Toe board. To see an example of using 2-D graphics, refer to the Board class (files `TTTBoard.m` and `.h`). The interface file of the Board class is shown here:

```
@interface TTTBoard : UIView {
    ...
}
    ...
@end
```

Note that I overrode the `drawRect` method of the base View class, as shown here:

```
// Drawing code
- (void)drawRect:(CGRect)rect {
    int gridSize = TTTBOARDSIZE;

    UIBezierPath *drawingPath = [UIBezierPath bezierPath];
    // draw vertical lines
    for(int i-0; i <= 3; i++) {
        int x = TTTBOARDLOCATIONINVIEWX + [self getWidth]*i;
        [drawingPath moveToPoint:CGPointMake(x, TTTBOARDLOCATIONINVIEWY)];
        [drawingPath addLineToPoint:CGPointMake(x, TTTBOARDLOCATIONINVIEWY +
            gridSize)];
    }
    // draw horizontal lines
    for(int j = 0; j <= 3; j++) {
        int y = TTTBOARDLOCATIONINVIEWY + j * [self getHeight];
        [drawingPath moveToPoint:CGPointMake(TTTBOARDLOCATIONINVIEWX, y)];
        [drawingPath addLineToPoint:CGPointMake(TTTBOARDLOCATIONINVIEWX +
                                                gridSize,
                                                y)];
    }
    [[UIColor redColor] setStroke];
    [drawingPath stroke];

    // Draw the symbols

    float offsetX = 0;
    float offsetY = 0;
    for(int i = 0; i < GAMEGRIDSIZE; i++){
        for(int j = 0; j < GAMEGRIDSIZE; j++){
            UIImage *imageSelected =
                [[grid getValueAtLocation :i :j] getBitmapForSymbol];
            CGSize imageSize = [imageSelected size];
            offsetX = TTTBOARDLOCATIONINVIEWX +
                    (int) (width * i + (width - imageSize.width)/2);
            offsetY = TTTBOARDLOCATIONINVIEWY +
                    (int) (height * j + (height - imageSize.height)/2);

            [imageSelected drawAtPoint:CGPointMake(offsetX, offsetY)];
        }
    }
}
```

The lines relevant to 2-D graphics drawing are extracted from the method, as shown here:

```
UIBezierPath *drawingPath = [UIBezierPath bezierPath];
    ...
[drawingPath moveToPoint:CGPointMake(TTTBOARDLOCATIONINVIEWX, y)];
[drawingPath addLineToPoint:CGPointMake(TTTBOARDLOCATIONINVIEWX +
                                            gridSize,
                                            y)];
    ...
[[UIColor redColor] setStroke];
[drawingPath stroke];
    ...
[imageSelected drawAtPoint:CGPointMake(offsetX, offsetY)];
```

OO and design principles in user interface development

Plenty of OO information is in this chapter. In regard to techniques, inheritance is used to specialize every controller. Especially note the Board class (TTTBoard.m and .h) and how the drawRect method is overridden to show the Tic-Tac-Toe board.

Delegation is used in handling every user inter-face event. For example:

✔ Action methods (labeled with the annota-tion IBAction) are the delegates for handling interactions with buttons and text fields.

✔ Delegate methods handle the conse-quences of button selections made in alerts.

✔ The Table view has two kinds of delegates. The Data Source delegate provides the data shown in the table, and the Table View delegate handles the interaction with the table when rows in the table are selected.

The primary pattern in this chapter is the vener-able Model-View-Controller (MVC). Every view controller and view combination is a reflection of MVC.

Although the chapter includes more than enough evidence of high-quality OO design, with most classes exhibiting high cohesion and low coupling, there's one iffy piece of coupling in the Alert View class: The order in which the buttons are added in the *construction* of the alert is very important in *handling* the alert by the delegate.

You must know in which order the buttons are added when the alert is instantiated because this order determines which is the Yes button (button at position 1) and which is the No button (button at position 2). The method that constructs the alert is coupled with the method that handles the alert. Not good! A better option is to have the ability to access the button by the label.

Although it's not covered in this book, the visual design (the look and feel of the UI) is also an important consideration for your app. To find the Apple UI guidelines for visual design, go to www.dummies.com/go/iosprogramminglinks and check out the UI Guidelines link.

First, the `UIBezierPath` class lets you define a path consisting of line segments. The methods used here for adding line segments are `moveToPoint` and `addLineToPoint`. Next, the color of the pen is set using `setStroke`; then the line is rendered using the method `stroke`. Finally, the last statement — `[imageSelected drawAtPoint:CGPointMake(offsetX, offsetY)];` — draws an image (in this case, any of the Tic-Tac-Toe symbols, including the Blank symbol) on the grid.

To learn more about Quartz 2-D graphics, go to `www.dummies.com/go/ iosprogramminglinks` and check out the Quartz 2-D Graphics link.

Chapter 10

Making Applications Fast and Responsive

*A*n app that's fully accepted by users must meet two kinds of requirements: functional and nonfunctional. The former describes *what* the app must do (that is, the functions it must perform); the latter provides guidelines on *how* the app must work (for example, how fast it should operate, how reliable it must be, and so on).

While functional requirements are about describing the right app, nonfunctional requirements are about how to build the app correctly. In this chapter, I focus on nonfunctional requirements.

After discussing nonfunctional requirements, I talk about how to design software to meet nonfunctional requirements. I describe how app design actually takes place at multiple levels, from the architecture of the system, to the design of the objects and interactions, to the choice of algorithms.

Finally, I explain how you can apply these concepts to make apps for mobile devices. I focus on two nonfunctional requirements: performance and responsiveness. (I cover two more, security and reliability, in the next chapter.)

I explain how to make iOS apps run fast by showing you techniques and tools for optimizing your app's performance. I then discuss an important facet of performance known as responsiveness and how to achieve it using threading.

Becoming Familiar with Nonfunctional Requirements

As I mention in the introduction, nonfunctional requirements (NFR) provide guidelines on how to build an app correctly (such requirements are also known as *quality requirements* or *design requirements*).

Let me start with a categorization and examples of NFR. Say that you're building a wayfinding app that will plot a route from one location to another. Here are the general categories of NFR and examples for each, specifically in the context of the wayfinding app:

- ✔ **Performance:** This is essentially how fast your app works. A performance requirement for the wayfinding app could be that it plot a route in less than 20 seconds.

- ✔ **Responsiveness:** This requirement ensures that your app is ready to respond to a user's input or an external event no matter what it's doing currently. For example, does your app allow the user to switch to another function even while it's busy calculating a route.

- ✔ **Scalability:** Scalability is how well your app deals with increasing use, or size of data. For example, you might require that the time your app takes to plot a route is linear with the distance between the two points.

- ✔ **Usability:** This relates to how easily people can use your app. A measure of usability could be the time it takes for end users to become familiar with your app's functions, without training or help.

- ✔ **Reliability:** This is the percentage of time that your app works correctly to deliver the desired results, despite potential failures in its environment. For the wayfinding app, it's the percentage of time that it correctly plots the route, given that the network may not be available or that bandwidth may be limited. You might require that your app work with a reliability of 99 percent, which means that in a given 24-hour day, it can fail to plot a route for no more than one percent of the day, or about 15 minutes.

The term *availability* can be used interchangeably with reliability. I prefer to use reliability in this book because most people are more likely to understand that word.

- ✔ **Security:** Say that your app saves all the previous routes it calculated and lets you reuse a saved route rather than recalculate it. If security isn't a requirement, you can store all app data in unencrypted files and on the SD card. If security is an issue, however, you can encrypt the files and store them in the app's private file area so that their content isn't easily accessible and so that they're deleted when the app is uninstalled.

- ✔ **Modifiability:** This requirement governs how easily your app may be changed. For the wayfinding app, this requirement might state that the app can use more than one map without needing to be rebuilt.

✔ **Maintainability:** This relates to the ease at which your app finds bugs and fixes them. For example, if a map is incorrect, can you fix the problem simply by downloading a correct map or do you have to purchase the next version of the app.

Cost is also often important. When you build an app, you must decide which nonfunctional requirements apply to your app. You also have to refine your NFRs so that you can test them. For example, for a performance NFR, you must be able to measure the speed of your application at the appropriate places (such as while the screen appears).

Certain nonfunctional requirements are especially important for mobile devices. These requirements are performance and responsiveness, which I discuss in the sections "Optimizing an Application's Performance" and "Ensuring Responsiveness in Your Apps," later in this chapter. Also, Chapter 11 covers security and reliability.

Don't attempt to meet all possible nonfunctional requirements in an app. Why spend resources implementing features that users won't value? Instead, define and, wherever applicable, quantify the extent to which you want to meet the NFR. Also, NFR always involves trade-offs. Meeting a single nonfunctional requirement can sometimes cause your app not to meet another one. For example, performance and security are often at cross-purposes. Increased security is often implemented by encrypting and decrypting stored data. However, having to decrypt data in order to use it, and encrypt it after the app is done using it takes time, thereby reducing the app's performance. The trick with meeting NFRs is to find the right balance.

Designing Your App at Multiple Levels

When you design an app, you have to design it at more than one level. You first have to decide on the design decisions that will affect all the components of the app. These are called *architectural* decisions. Architectural decisions need to be made first and are very hard to change once you start building your software because they affect many, if not most, of the components of your app.

An example of an architectural decision is the decision to build the app on the iOS framework. A second, related, architectural decision is to use Objective-C as the development language. You can clearly understand why this decision has to be made early. You can also see that moving away from this decision (say, by deciding to build an Android app) will essentially cause you to throw most of your work away and restart almost from scratch.

You often have little choice in making certain architectural decisions. For example, if you want to make apps run on iOS devices, your best choice currently is to use the iOS Framework and Objective-C.

Apple provides the highest level of support for Objective-C, so developing apps in Objective-C is significantly easier than using C or C++ (although this can be done). In this case, the architectural decision to use Objective-C is a no-brainer.

After the architecture is set (yes, like cement), you're ready to begin the second level of design, as follows:

- ✔ Partitioning your application into classes
- ✔ Allocating methods to classes
- ✔ Mapping the design of the architecture formulated at the first level of design

These generic steps are discussed in detail in Chapters 6 and 7. Incidentally this level of design is certainly difficult to modify once decided upon, but certainly it's not as hard to change as the architecture.

In the third level of design, you have the choice of using

- ✔ Algorithms (say, for sorting).
- ✔ Data structures (using a hash table to find a value in a contact list — for example, a phone number — corresponding to a key, such as the name of the contact).

Abstracting the data structures and algorithms inside classes or methods so that they're compartmentalized really helps when you try to change their structures.

- ✔ Low-level coding practices (such as what you name variables, how you write loops, and so on).

Code is relatively easy to change; all you need is a good editor, a few hours to hack your way through the existing code, and strong coffee to keep you awake throughout the process.

Optimizing an Application's Performance

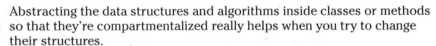

In this section, I talk about app performance in iOS, using the example Tic-Tac-Toe application introduced in earlier chapters.

Architectural choices related to performance include decisions such as whether to use a database (that is, Core Data) or files, whether to build screens using 2D graphics or widgets, and whether to access the network every time your app needs data or to store certain data locally.

Core Data is slower in some cases; however, it's faster if you're retrieving bits of data that are already stored.

The following list describes the requirements-driven architectural decisions made in the Tic-Tac-Toe application earlier in the book, and the reasons for making them:

- ✔ **Programming language:** The app uses Objective-C because of its built-in support and easy app development. These choices outweigh gains in performance you might make by writing native (C or C++) code, especially considering that the app docsn't have an extraordinary need for high performance.

- ✔ **Data storage:** User preferences are stored via the built-in preference classes because of their programming convenience. The app uses Core Data to store login and password information because this information is so frequently stored and retrieved, a task that Core Data excels in. For example, use of this information is much higher than for the number of registered users added, a task that Core Data is slower in doing.

- ✔ **Graphics:** For speed, the app uses raw 2D graphics rather than widgets for the board. (The graphics in the Tic-Tac-Toe app are uncomplicated, so widgets would work as well.)

Note that early on in the Tic-Tac-Toe app, a couple of deliberate decisions were made about data structures and algorithms. The primary data structure decision is to represent the grid as a two-dimensional array and to encapsulate it inside a class named Grid so that you can change this implementation if it turns out to be too slow. (The design process shown in Chapter 7 concludes that the grid should be its own class, which serves as a validation for the design process.)

Less computation in your coding practices will improve your app's performance. Here are some actions you can take to do so:

- ✔ **Save intermediate results in variables and then reuse them, especially in loops.** Here's a simple example of this technique, taken from the androidTakesATurn method in the TTTGameSessionViewController class:

```
...
// Play at that square
pickedX = [picked x];
pickedY = [picked y];

[activeGame play:pickedX :pickedY];
[gameView placeSymbol:pickedX :pickedY];
...
```

✔ **Avoid internal getters and setters.** Access member variables directly when within the class, instead of using the getters and setters. Doing so avoids the overhead of an additional method call. You can see this process in the GameGrid class, where the locations in the two-dimensional array member variable grid are accessed directly instead of using the accessor methods setValueAtLocation(...) and getValueAtLocation(...), which is how the grid is accessed *outside* the class by client classes such as Board and Game.

✔ **Avoid creating unnecessary objects.** Instances of the Objective-C NSString class (though appearing to be elementary data types) are objects, so limit their number, as well. This tactic is illustrated in the Symbol class in Tic-Tac-Toe, where you use the Singleton pattern so that only one instance of an X, an O, and a Blank symbol is ever created; also, symbols are defined as enumerated types rather than as strings.

✔ **Know the framework libraries well, and use them wherever possible instead of writing your own code.** Because the library-implemented code is optimized (for example, by using assembler code), using it is more efficient than writing equivalent code, even after the compiler tries to optimize it.

An excellent set of old-but-gold techniques around low-level coding practices for efficiency is Jon Bentley's rules for writing efficient programs. You can find summaries of these techniques at various places on the web by entering *Jon Bentley writing efficient programs* in your favorite search engine. You can also check out the Jon Bentley on Writing Efficient Programs link in the web resources for this chapter at www.dummies.com/go/iosprogramminglinks.

Using Instrumentation for Code Optimization

You can expend a lot of time optimizing code, only to see no real improvement in the performance of your program. To make your optimization efforts pay off, develop the habit of *profiling* (or instrumenting) your app's code to determine the level of its performance and where it's spending most of its time. Follow these steps to profile your code:

1. **Within Xcode, choose Xcode⇨Open Developer Tool⇨Instruments.**

   The Instruments screen appears showing all the available instrumentation templates (see Figure 10-1).

Figure 10-1:
Selecting an
instrument.

2. **Select Time Profiler.**

   An Instruments screen appears with the selected instrument in the left panel — in this case, the Time Profiler — a blank display area in the middle, and the Library of instruments in a panel on the right (see Figure 10-2).

   A button with the text All Processes appears at the top of this screen. (Hover the cursor over this picker, and you see the Choose Target to Record Trace Data From tooltip.)

3. **Select the device you want to run the instrumentation on.**

4. **Click the Choose Target button.**

   A list of running applications appears.

5. **From the list of applications, select the Tic-Tac-Toe app.** The label for what used to be the Choose Target button changes to Tic-Tac-Toe.

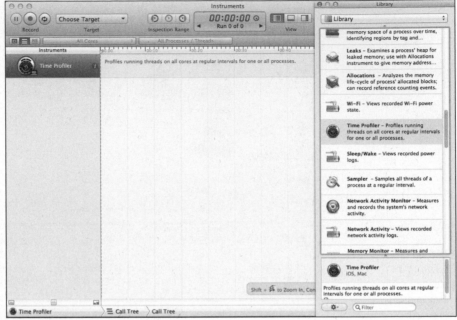

Figure 10-2:
Instruments
screen after
selecting
the Time
Profiler.

6. **Press the red Record button at the top-left corner of the Instruments screen.**

   Your app starts, and the Time Profiler starts recording timing information. The Record button changes to Stop.

7. **Play four or five games, taking each game as far as possible.**

8. **Click the Stop button to stop profiling.**

Now things get interesting. A panel on the profiler window just below the Instrumentation panel (see Figure 10-3) shows a list of methods, in the order of their contribution to overall execution time. As you review this list of methods, you start to come across methods from Tic-Tac-Toe. You see that drawRect is consuming large chunks of time. Drill into this method by clicking the arrow to the left, as shown in Figure 10-3, and notice that getBitMapForSymbol is the true culprit.

This is certainly cool, but let me now show you something even cooler. Double-click the method, and you see the source code of the method, showing the percentage of time contributed by each statement. You can clearly see that the memory allocation and initialization of the X, O, and Blank image objects are taking most of the time in this method (see Figure 10-4).

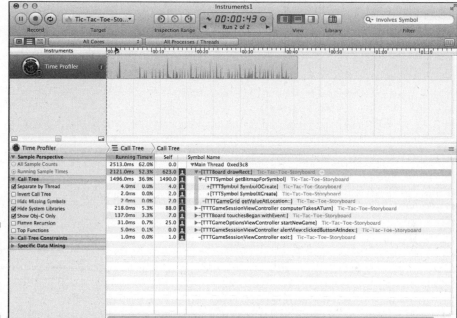

Figure 10-3:
Seeing time consumed in each method.

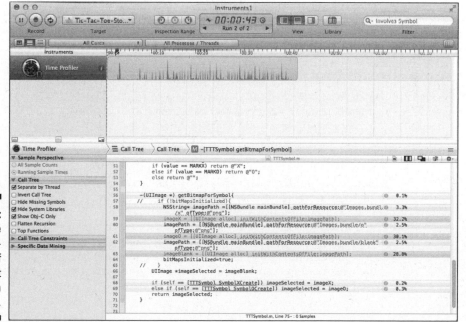

Figure 10-4:
Seeing the percentage of time spent in each statement.

The fact that these images are the same for every move (and, in fact, for every game) gives you a clear path to optimizing this code. You can create a set of static variables to hold these images, along with a Boolean flag bitMapsInitialized that indicates whether these variables have been initialized, as shown in the following code:

```
static BOOL bitMapsInitialized = NO;
static UIImage *imageBlank=nil;
static UIImage *imageX=nil;
static UIImage *imageO=nil;
```

Then you change the code in getBitmapForSymbol to load the images only once, as shown here:

```
-(UIImage *) getBitmapForSymbol{
    if (!bitMapsInitialized){
        NSString* imagePath =
            [[NSBundle mainBundle]
                pathForResource:@"Images.bundle/x" ofType:@"png"];
        imageX = [[UIImage alloc] initWithContentsOfFile:imagePath];
        imagePath =
            [[NSBundle mainBundle]
                pathForResource:@"Images.bundle/o" ofType:@"png"];
        imageO = [[UIImage alloc] initWithContentsOfFile:imagePath];
        imagePath =
            [[NSBundle mainBundle]
                pathForResource:@"Images.bundle/blank" ofType:@"png"];
        imageBlank = [[UIImage alloc] initWithContentsOfFile:imagePath];
        bitMapsInitialized=true;
    }
    UIImage *imageSelected = imageBlank;

    if (self == [TTTSymbol SymbolXCreate]) imageSelected = imageX;
    else if (self == [TTTSymbol SymbolOCreate]) imageSelected = imageO;
    return imageSelected;
}
```

Figure 10-5 shows a profile run after the optimization is in place. The time expended in getBitmapForSymbol has dropped from about 1500 milliseconds to around 6. Not only that, the overall runtime has dropped by a third.

The optimized code is in the class already, just commented out. I left in both the un-optimized and optimized codes to make illustrating this example easier. Incidentally, this particular example is a real one. The performance issue was identified and solved, thanks to yours truly for actually using the Time Profiler.

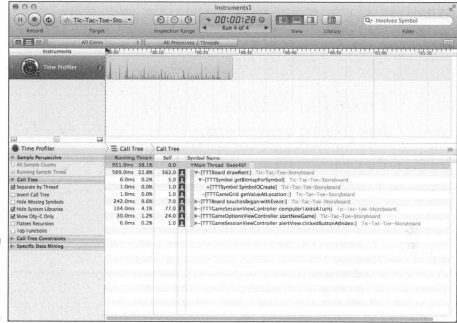

Figure 10-5:
Profiler
run after
optimization.

Though this section explains how to use the profiling tools to judiciously micro-optimize an application's performance, your app could run on multiple hardware platforms (such as iPad, iPhone, or iPod Touch). Each device runs on different processors at different speeds, with different computational add-ons (such as a video coprocessor) that affect the speed of your app differently. If performance on a specific platform is especially important to you, profile and optimize for that platform.

Ensuring Responsiveness in Your Apps

One nonfunctional requirement of special concern in mobile apps is responsiveness. Mobile app developers must ensure that their apps don't even appear to freeze, become sluggish, or fail to respond to user input.

Ensuring responsiveness isn't the same as optimizing performance.

Even though your app may operate as fast as possible, it must appear as though the user controls it, even when it's actively working. For example, refreshing a web page might take a long time because the network or the server providing the page is slow. Obviously, your app can't do anything about speeding the refresh, but whenever this type of operation takes place, your app must not freeze — and it should, for example, allow the user to abandon the sluggish activity.

Ensuring responsiveness by using threading

The primary technique to achieve responsiveness is *threading*. The idea is to move the operation that's likely to take a long time from the main thread and execute its operations on separate (additional) threads using the thread functionality in iOS.

The following simple pseudocode shows you how a thread can be used to load an image from a network:

```
- (void) viewDidLoad {
    CreateThread {
        Image b = [self loadImageFromNetwork]; // user written method
        // do something with the image
        ...
    }
    // While the image s loading do something more or even exit the method
        ...
}
```

Now, I'll show you a couple of examples, one from Tic-Tac-Toe and one from the iOS framework.

Implementing threading for responsiveness in Tic-Tac-Toe

To illustrate responsiveness and how to use threading for it, I'm implementing computer play in Tic-Tac-Toe — that is, you'll have the option to play against the computer in Tic-Tac-Toe. The computer, in this case, isn't very smart, and you'll beat it most every time. (Making a smart Tic-Tac-Toe player out of the computer isn't the goal of the program; illustrating responsiveness is.)

Although the computer isn't going to actually play very smartly, it will make every effort to look like it's thinking before it actually plays, which it does by waiting for random amounts of time before making each move.

So here goes (and please follow along in Xcode; all the code I show here comes from `TTTGameSessionViewController.m`). First, I enhance the Game Session screen to allow you to set an option to play the computer using a `UISwitch` control. The new screen looks like the one shown in Figure 10-6.

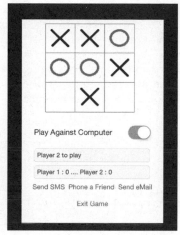

To save this setting, I created a `BOOL` property called `playComputer` and an `IBAction` callback for the `UISwitch` that sets this variable. This method is called `changeOpponent`. The property declaration and synthesis of the property is shown here:

```
@property (nonatomic) BOOL playComputer; // In TTTGameSessionViewCOntroller.h

@synthesize playComputer; // In TTTGameSessionViewCOntroller.m
```

The code for the `IBAction` callback is

```
- (IBAction) changeOpponent:(id)sender{
    NSLog(@"Value %d", changeOpponentSwitch.on);
    playComputer = changeOpponentSwitch.on;
    if(playComputer) [self scheduleComputersTurn];
}
```

This method does a couple of things. First, it sets the `playComputer` flag appropriately. It also starts the computer by calling `scheduleComputersTurn`.

Now let me show you how the computer does the playing, starting with `scheduleComputersTurn`:

```
- (void) scheduleComputersTurn {
    int randomDelay = arc4random()%TTTDELAY;
    [boardView disableInput];
    NSLog(@" Delay = >%d< seconds", randomDelay);
    [self performSelector:@selector(computerTakesATurn) withObject:nil
                                                afterDelay:randomDelay];
}
```

What's going on in this code is pretty clear. You generate a random delay between zero and TTTDELAY seconds. (TTTDELAY is a #defined constant in TTTGameSessionViewController and is set to 10.)

You can find out more about arc4random and about generating random numbers in general by following the Generating Random Numbers on iOS link in the web resources page for this book at www.dummies.com/go/iosprogramminglinks.

The performSelector method (shown here) then makes computer play happen (by calling computerTakesATurn) in the background, and on a separate thread:

```
[self performSelector:@selector(computerTakesATurn) withObject:nil
                                              afterDelay:randomDelay];
```

You might logically ask, "How can I test whether computerTakesATurn is really happening in the background on a separate thread?" After you've made a move and the computer is "thinking," click the Exit button. You'll see that the screen is still responsive and that the game exits right away.

Just for grins, illustrate lack of responsiveness. Comment out the call to performSelector just shown and replace it with a call to sleep for the same random delay and a direct call to computerTakesATurn, as shown in the following code:

```
- (void) scheduleComputersTurn {
    int randomDelay = arc4random()%TTTDELAY;
    [boardView disableInput];
    NSLog(@" Delay = >%d< seconds", randomDelay);
    //[self performSelector:@selector(computerTakesATurn) withObject:nil
                                              afterDelay:randomDelay];
    sleep(randomDelay);
    [self computerTakesATurn];
}
```

Now play the game again. You'll see that when the computer is thinking (this time in the foreground and on the main thread), the app is totally unresponsive.

Threading for responsiveness in iOS components

Certain iOS framework components automatically move long-lived operations to separate threads (so that you don't have to do it). Take a look at the method `helpWithWebView` in `TTTHelpViewController.m`, as shown here:

```
- (IBAction) helpWithWebView: (id) sender{
    NSString *wikpediaURLString = @"http://en.wikipedia.org/wiki/Tictactoe";
    NSURL *wikepediaUrl = [NSURL URLWithString:wikpediaURLString];
    NSURLRequest *requestObj = [NSURLRequest requestWithURL:wikepediaUrl];
    [helpWebView loadRequest:requestObj];
}
```

`loadRequest` actually launches a separate thread to load the URL so that the application remains responsive while the page is being loaded. You can test this in the same way you tested game playing for responsiveness. Click Help in WebView (see Figure 10-7) and before the page loads, click Exit. The screen immediately exits.

Figure 10-7: Testing Help in WebView for responsiveness.

Other Performance Considerations for iOS Apps

Now that you've seen the main techniques and tools for improving performance, I'd like to present more considerations for performance specific to iOS apps.

- ✔ Reduce the amount of memory used by your app by creating only necessary objects, eliminating memory leaks, and using small images and resources. The amount of free memory available and the performance of your app are strongly correlated.

  You can use Instruments to help quantify memory use as well as to find leaks.

- ✔ Reduce power consumption by optimizing your app's use of the CPU, networking, location, and sensor services. Try not to use polling when you check for data or the status of an operation. Instead, set up a listener in a separate thread that will notify you when the data is available or when the status changes. Also turn off the sensors when they aren't needed.

  You can use the Energy Diagnostics instrument to analyze energy use. For more on this instrument, check out the Energy Diagnostics link in the web resources for this chapter at www.dummies.com/go/ iosprogramminglinks.

- ✔ Connect to external servers only when needed, transmit the smallest amount of data needed, and use compact data formats (JSON rather than XML). Transmit data in bursts.

- ✔ The main thread is where your app handles touch events and other user input. Creating separate threads to perform long-running or potentially unbounded tasks leaves the main thread free to continue processing user input.

- ✔ Modify your code to use floating-point math wherever possible. Hardware-based floating-point computations are typically much faster than their software-based fixed-point equivalents.

- ✔ Apple provides a service called iCloud to which users can back up the data of their apps. You can configure your app to back up to iCloud. Because backing up to iCloud is a time-, network- and energy-consuming operation, ensure that your app handles backing up to iCloud as efficiently as possible. You do so by placing temporary files in specific directories where temporary files are supposed to be written (that is, <Application-Home>/Library/Caches and <Application-Home>/ tmp). Files in these locations aren't backed up to iCloud.

  I talk about handling files in Chapter 6.

You can find more information about improving the performance of iOS apps on the iOS developer website starting with the Basic iOS Performance Tips link in the web resources for this book at www.dummies.com/go/ iosprogramminglinks.

Chapter 11

Making Your App Reliable and Secure

● ●

In This Chapter
▶ Applying nonfunctional requirements to iOS apps
▶ Making your app robust in the face of failure
▶ Making your application secure

● ●

*T*he approach and effort required to create an Objective-C program for personal use or for a small prototype app for limited distribution are very different than they are for developing an app for consumer or enterprise use. All apps must deliver the expected functionality; however, consumer and enterprise apps must deliver this functionality with as close to 24/7 reliability as possible. These apps must also be secure; that is, they should prevent unauthorized or malicious users from gaining access to their services, and they must protect all valuable data.

This chapter focuses on reliability and security and shows you ways to meet these two nonfunctional requirements. I discuss two aspects of reliability: how to test your app to eliminate as many bugs as possible and how to design your app so that it remains stable during changing circumstances, such as when other apps try to take over or when the device's capabilities fail (for example, networking failures). I then get into how to systematically make your app secure.

Making Your App Reliable Through Testing

At all stages of your app's development, including after it's built, you need to ensure its reliability, which you do through more (and more) testing. Testing can serve two purposes. First, of course, it helps you find and eliminate problems in your app. Second, testing can provide you with visible benchmarks.

As you eliminate problems, you see improvements in your app, such as fewer bugs and better speed and responsiveness. Each step of the way, the progress your app is making is clear.

Understanding the fundamentals and levels of testing

This section covers some of the fundamentals related to levels of testing and creating test cases. As you follow along, I'll relate these fundamentals to object-oriented (OO) development, although you can apply them to all kinds of software testing.

Understanding the levels of testing

While you're testing your app, test it at multiple levels. Test each class and its methods. Test how the classes work together. Finally, test the final, completely put-together app from its user interface. Here's a broader description of these levels of testing:

- ✔ **Unit testing:** Testing at the level of an individual class or of a small set of related classes is known as *unit testing*. Individual developers typically do this kind of testing — for example, before checking it into source control for others to use in their programs. In unit testing, you create an instance of a class and call all its methods with different input values and then check whether the methods work properly.

  Generally, unit testing in iOS is done on a model object (such as an object of the Game class in the Tic-Tac-Toe app). However, even testing a single screen to see whether all the UI elements work properly can be thought of as unit testing.

- ✔ **Integration testing:** As the name indicates, the purpose of integration testing is to ensure that the different software modules work together properly.

- ✔ **System testing:** In this case, the system as a whole is tested by people acting as potential users of the app.

If you're the only one developing an app and are wondering how the preceding levels relate to you, the answer is that you get to play all the roles. For example, you may be a single developer unit testing your components, an integration tester pulling together two components developed independently (for example, the Game class and the Game Session view controller), and a system tester testing the complete app.

You must try to find and fix as many bugs as you can. To catch as many as possible, test as many paths through your code as possible.

The extent to which you can test all paths through your code is known as *test coverage*. Test coverage is often measured as a percentage of the total lines of code that were actually exercised in your tests. You must try to maximize test coverage to catch as many bugs as possible.

Edsger Dijkstra, one of the original gurus of computing, once said, "Testing shows the presence, not the absence of bugs." By this, he meant that just because you can't find any more bugs doesn't mean you've found all of them. So, never become complacent about finding bugs.

As you develop your software, I suggest creating and maintaining a test plan — that is, a list of test cases, with each test case being a single test for your system (such as, "Login with invalid username or password") along with suggested inputs followed by the expected outcome. Here's a test case:

1. Test: Log in with invalid username or password.

2. Suggested inputs:

   a. A user ID that's not yet created for Tic-Tac-Toe

   b. A user ID consisting of an empty or blank string

   c. A password consisting of an empty or blank string

   d. An incorrect password for a user ID

3. Expected outcome: App should show a "Login Failed" message.

Testing thoroughly means testing systematically. It also means emphasizing testing for those things that can go wrong, instead of testing whether something goes right. Here are some simple guidelines for what to test and how to do so:

✔ **Test with valid inputs to ensure that your code works.** However, limit your testing with valid inputs to, say, one set of good values followed by tests of special cases (for example, the following boundary conditions). I've found it helpful to break "good values" into categories. For example, for a method that takes an integer input, I make sure to cover negative and positive numbers, along with zero. They may all be good values, but covering all of these logical groupings makes for better tests.

✔ **Test boundary conditions.** Say that your program expects inputs in the range 1–100. Be sure to test with 0, 1, 2, 99, 100, and 101. Note that 1, 2, 99, and 100 are valid inputs that should give correct outputs, whereas 0 and 101 are invalid inputs near the boundary and should generate error conditions, and so should not processed.

Note that I deliberately left an error in the Tic-Tac-Toe grid that the technical editor found (see Figure 11-1). If you touch outside the right boundary of the grid, Xs and Os miraculously appear in the left column.

Figure 11-1:
Touching near the boundaries of the Tic-Tac-Toe grid causes errors.

✔ Test methods with complex code more than simple code. Complex code is typically code that exhibits one or more of these characteristics:

  • It has mathematical computations.

  • It consists of more than 10 lines.

  • It has complicated loop conditions.

  • It has complicated logic consisting of nested if statements or other conditional logic.

  • It has multiple exit points.

✔ **Ask someone else to test your app.** Because you know where the problems might lie and what boundary conditions to test, you can test your own app efficiently. However, you're likely to have blind spots and may assume your code works just fine when actually it isn't.

Large organizations do this kind of end-user testing, known as *beta testing,* at a scale of thousands of users. Beta testing is so useful for individual developers that I cover it in Chapter 14.

✔ Be sure to test for nonfunctional requirements such as performance, responsiveness, usability, and so on. These kinds of tests require some thought, but you can measure, for example, usability by counting the number of clicks to get to each point in your app and then trying to keep this number to a minimum. You can also test performance using Xcode instruments (which I explain in Chapter 10).

✔ **Repeat relevant tests after each change.** You want to be sure that things you fixed or that were previously working are still working correctly. Do a complete system test after a significant amount of code is changed. Definitely redo all system tests before releasing a new version of your app.

This kind of testing is known as *regression* testing.

Using automated testing

Manually repeating regression tests each time your app's functionality changes is inefficient. Most of the tests usually pass, so a great deal of effort goes into validating stuff that works rather than catching stuff that doesn't work (which is the real goal of testing). Automated testing makes regression testing efficient. Using automated testing, you can create a bunch of tests once and run them again and again with very little manual intervention.

Automated tests also help you do *continuous integration,* which is a model of development where you commit, build, and test your code after small changes, rather than waiting for a long interval. Continuous integration is a very good approach to building bug-free software, because you find bugs almost as soon as they're introduced into code, and at a time when fixing them is easy.

You can find tools to automate tests for most established software-development platforms. These automated tools fall into two general categories: tools for unit testing and tools for user interface-driven testing. Both types of tools usually have a management tool to manage test cases. In the following subsections, I explain both types of testing and present an example of each.

Automating unit testing in iOS

Automating unit testing involves writing code to test a class. This code creates instances of a class, calls all the methods of that instance with a range of values, and compares the results with the expected results, again through code. The unit-testing program also similarly tests all class (or static) methods of the class.

Convenience functions are typically provided to make coding a little easier. A typical convenience function is the `assert` function that tests whether the value returned by a method being tested is equal (or not equal) to an expected value.

Xcode provides a unit-testing framework called the *XCTest framework* that allows you to write unit tests for iOS (and for the Mac, for that matter).

Now, take a look at an XCTest example in Tic-Tac-Toe. Open the Tic-Tac-Toe project for this chapter and find the folder `Tic-Tac-Toe-Storyboard Tests` in the Project navigator. This folder was automatically created when the project was created (if it doesn't exist, choose File⇨New⇨Target and create a Cocoa Touch Unit Testing Bundle, as shown in Figure 11-2).

Figure 11-2:
Adding a unit-testing bundle to your project.

In this folder, you see a file named `Tic_Tac_Toe_Storyboard_Tests.m`. It contains all the unit tests. Here's the code in this file, which includes the code of the unit tests:

```objc
//   Tic_Tac_Toe_Storyboard_Tests.m...

#import <XCTest/XCTest.h>
#import "TTTGame.h"

@interface Tic_Tac_Toe_Storyboard_Tests : XCTestCase

@end

@implementation Tic_Tac_Toe_Storyboard_Tests

- (void)setUp{
    [super setUp];
    // Put setup code here. This method is called before the invocation of
        each test method in the class.
}

- (void)tearDown{
    // Put teardown code here. This method is called after the invocation of
        each test method in the class.
    [super tearDown];
}
```

```
- (void)testGameIsActive{
    TTTGame *testGame = [[TTTGame alloc] init];
    [testGame play:0 :0];
    [testGame play:1 :0];
    [testGame play:0 :1];
    [testGame play:1 :1];
    [testGame play:2 :2];
    XCTAssertEqual([testGame isActive], YES);
}

- (void)testGameSuccessfulFinish{
    TTTGame *testGame = [[TTTGame alloc] init];
    [testGame play:0 :0];
    [testGame play:1 :0];
    [testGame play:0 :1];
    [testGame play:1 :1];
    [testGame play:0 :2];
    XCTAssertEqual([testGame isActive], NO);
}
@end
```

This file has two unit tests: testGameIsActive and testGameSuccess
fulFinish. Both of them create an instance of TTTGame and then play a few
moves. Then testGameIsActive uses XCAssert to test whether the game
is still active, and testGameSuccessfulFinish tests whether the game
has ended.

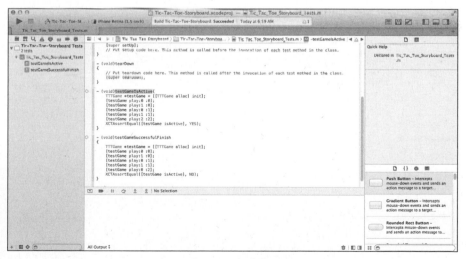

Figure 11-3:
The Xcode
Test
navigator.

To run these tests, go to the Test navigator (see Figure 11-3) and choose
Product⇨Test (the entire Tic-Tac-Toe app actually loads as part of this test).
The two unit tests pass successfully and are marked with green check marks
(see Figure 11-4).

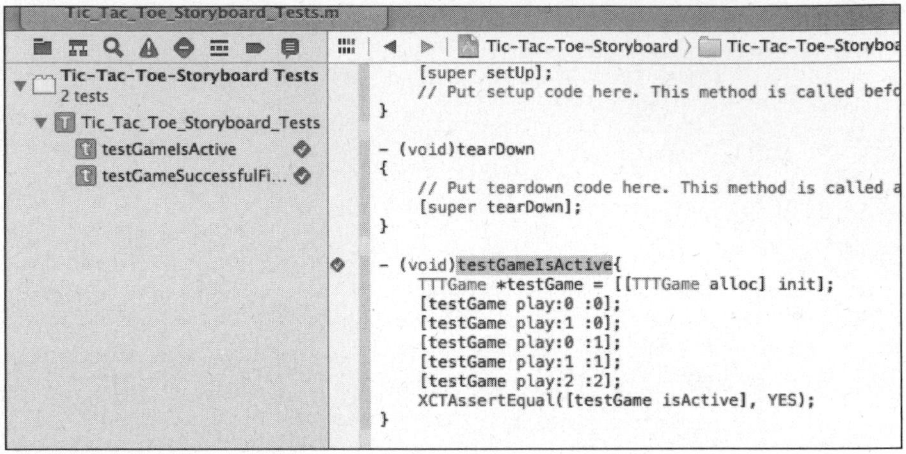

Figure 11-4:
Test navigator showing tests that passed successfully.

Now change the XCAssert statement in testGameIsActive to XCTAssertEqual([testGame isActive], NO). Run the tests again. This time you see that the first test fails (and is shown with a red check mark) and that the XCAssert statement is highlighted with the error message (see Figure 11-5).

Figure 11-5:
Test navigator showing a failed test.

That's it for automated unit tests. For more information on this topic, go to www.dummies.com/go/iosprogramminglinks and check out the Automated Unit Tests link.

Automating UI-based testing in iOS

Apple has also provided an automated means for system-testing through your app's user interface. These tests mimic a user's interactions with an app. By using a programming language, you can create regression tests that a user can run again and again with minimal effort.

You can create and run automated UI-based tests through JavaScript test scripts that you write and then run them using the Automation instrument (also known as *UI Automation*) within the Instruments developer tool. These scripts specify user actions to be performed in your app as it runs. As you run your tests, you can log time-stamped information about the test. As in the XCTest framework, you can verify the results of user actions and declare whether a test has passed or failed.

Interestingly, you can create tests simply by running your application within the tool and then recording your interactions. Once you have such a trace, you can extend or modify your test by adding JavaScript code.

To access the Automation instrument, choose Xcode⇨Open Developer Tool⇨Instruments and select the Automation instrument template (see Figure 11-6). Then, follow these steps to create a test:

Figure 11-6:
Selecting the Automation instrument template.

1. **Select the Automation instrument template and click Choose.**

   An Instruments window appears. This window has an area where you can create scripts along the left side of the screen.

2. **Click the Add button and then select Create to create a new script (as shown in Figure 11-7).**

   A new script (named New Script) is created.

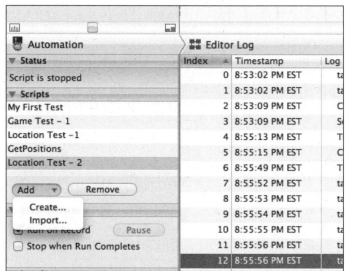

Figure 11-7:
Creating a new script.

3. **Double-click on New Script and give it a name of your choice.**

4. **Connect a device to the computer.**

5. **Select the device in the list of targets.**

6. **Make the Tic-Tac-Toe application the target of the instrument.**

   For the following steps, refer to Figure 11-8.

7. **Click the red button located at the bottom of the Instruments window to start the Tic-Tac-Toe app on your device.**

   Play with it for a while, clicking various screens until you're satisfied.

   As you click around Tic-Tac-Toe, you'll see a script captured (before your very eyes) in the Scripts window.

8. **When you're done, click the black square (the button to the right of the red button) to stop the recording.**

   You can stop the recording at any time during the capture.

9. **Click the arrow to the left of the red button to replay the script.**

   Voilà. The app magically starts again and runs through all the steps you put it through earlier.

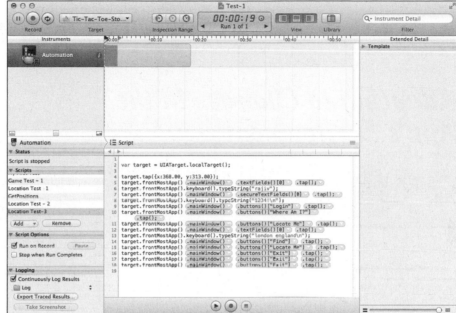

Figure 11-8:
Capturing
an
Automation
script.

Incidentally, you must tweak the captured script to make it work correctly, including adding delays so that you can see the results of actions that take a little time to execute. You may also want to add `UIALogger.logStart` messages to give this test a grouping in the Editor Log. In addition, you may also want to declare that the test passed (or failed) after it runs. You can see these extensions in the final script:

```
UIALogger.logStart("Location Test - 3");
var target = UIATarget.localTarget();

target.frontMostApp().mainWindow().textFields()[0].tap();
target.frontMostApp().keyboard().typeString("rajiv");
target.frontMostApp().mainWindow().secureTextFields()[0].tap();
target.frontMostApp().keyboard().typeString("1234!\n");
target.frontMostApp().mainWindow().buttons()["Login"].tap();
target.frontMostApp().mainWindow().buttons()["Where Am I?"].tap();
target.frontMostApp().mainWindow().buttons()["Locate Me"].tap();
target.delay(5);
target.frontMostApp().mainWindow().textFields()[0].tap();
target.frontMostApp().keyboard().typeString("london england\n");
target.frontMostApp().mainWindow().buttons()["Find"].tap();
target.delay(5);
target.frontMostApp().mainWindow().buttons()["Locate Me"].tap();
target.delay(5);
target.frontMostApp().mainWindow().buttons()["Exit"].tap();
target.frontMostApp().mainWindow().buttons()["Exit"].tap();
target.frontMostApp().mainWindow().buttons()["Exit"].tap();
UIALogger.logPass("Passed");
```

For more information on the Automation instrument and how to use it, go to www.dummies.com/go/iosprogramminglinks and check out the UI Automation link.

Adapting to Changes in the App's Environment

Your app might *think* it's king of the castle, lording over the screen and unabashedly consuming memory and CPU cycles, but it'll get its comeuppance every so often because iOS needs to run other apps or take care of dire situations such as low memory. iOS may require your app to give way to another app, limit resources, or deny it access to services (such as network access) that are no longer available. In some cases, iOS will notify your app of the changed situation and give it time to deal with the new state of things. In other cases, your app must check whether a capability is available before trying to use it. I discuss all these issues in this section.

Implementing reliability while navigating your app's lifecycle

As I discuss in Chapters 1 and 6, your app goes through a set of states as it runs. These states (shown in Figure 11-9) are known as states of the app's lifecycle.

Here's more information about the states (once again, refer to Figure 11-9):

- ✔ When an app is in the *Not Running* state, either the app hasn't been launched or the system shut it down.

- ✔ When an app starts, it transitions through a short state, called the *Inactive* state. It's actually running, but it's performing other functions and isn't ready to accept user input or events.

- ✔ An app in an *Active* state is running in the foreground and receiving events. This is the normal mode for foreground apps — apps that don't have to run in the background without a user interface.

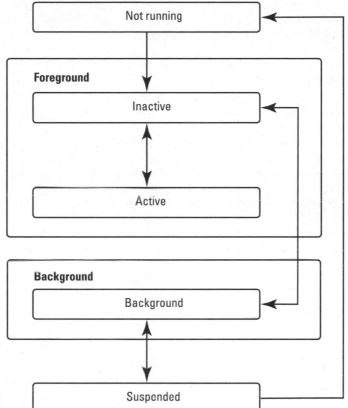

Figure 11-9:
Lifecycle of
an iOS app.

- ✔ When an app is in the *Background* state, its user interface isn't visible, but it *is* running. Most apps transition through this state on their way to being suspended. An app may need (and request) extra execution time and may stay in this state for a time. In addition, certain apps run in the background. These apps, in fact, are launched directly into the background. Such an app enters the Background state directly and doesn't go through the Inactive state.

- ✔ The iOS system may move an app to a *Suspended* state. Here the app is in the background but is *not* running code. It does stay in memory, though. If a low-memory condition occurs, the system may purge apps in the suspended state without notice. Note that, according to Apple's standards, *only* the iOS system can kill an app.

As your app goes through the states of its lifecycle, certain standard methods of the app, known as *lifecycle* methods are called by iOS. As it goes through these states, you can add app-specific behavior at each transition within the app's lifecycle.

The reliability implications of this lifecycle are that whenever the app transitions from being active in the foreground to being in the background, to being suspended and then terminated, it has to

✔ Give up all resources it's holding (such as network connections and file pointers).

✔ Save any state it wants to preserve when it's restored to active duty or starts up again (this process is also known as *checkpointing*).

But giving up resources and saving state as the app exits is only half the story. As the app goes through its startup sequence and runs through its functions (in concrete terms, loads and exits each view controller), it should register what it needs to give up and what state it needs to preserve so that the resources are released and the state is saved if the app exits.

I show you an implementation of registering and checkpointing next, as always, within the context of Tic-Tac-Toe.

In Chapter 6, I explain how to establish app settings using the Settings application and then read and save these settings from within your program. If you need to refresh your memory on how to do so, please refer to `TTTGameSes sionViewController.m` (specifically, look at `initializeGameSession` to see where the settings are being read and `exit` to see how they're being saved back).

Say that a game is being played and the user presses the Home button on his device or receives a call, either of which puts the Tic-Tac-Toe app in the background. In this case, you want all changed settings to be checkpointed immediately — because you don't know whether the app will reappear.

When an app is sent to the background, the lifecycle method `applicationWillResignActive` is called. What you want to do is save the state from the currently running view controller. However, `applicationWillResignActive` is a method at the level of the app (that is, not at the level of a specific view controller), which means it needs to handle the checkpointing state from any view controller, without knowing which one is currently active — not that it has a handle to the current view controller, in any case.

Therefore, you set up a scheme by which a view controller can register with a checkpoint manager when it starts up. This checkpoint manager is invoked by the app's lifecycle methods at appropriate state transitions. This manager then checkpoints the states of things registered with it.

The following shows you the code of the Checkpoint Manager class (class name `TTTCheckpointManager`). First comes the interface of this class, in the header file `TTTCheckpointManager.h`:

```
#import <Foundation/Foundation.h>

@interface TTTCheckpointManager : NSObject{
    @private NSMutableDictionary *managedObjects;

}

    +(TTTCheckpointManager *) CreateManager;
    -(void) registerObjectWithKey :(NSString *) key
                                 :(NSObject *) objectToBeManaged;
    -(void) unregisterObjectWithKey :(NSString *) key;
    -(void) checkpoint;

@end
```

Exactly one instance of Checkpoint Manager class must exist for an iOS app. In other words, this class is implemented as a singleton, and only `CreateManager` may be used to instantiate an object of this class.

The `registerObjectWithKey` method is called by any view controller (or, for that matter, any object) seeking to be managed. You'll see that the Checkpoint Manager class has a member variable of type `NSMutableDictionary`. This variable holds the objects that have requested to be registered. When the object no longer needs to be managed, `unregisterObjectWithKey` is called by the object. Finally, every appropriate lifecycle method (such as `applicationWillResignActive`) must call the method `checkpoint`. When this method is called, all objects registered with the Checkpoint Manager are saved.

Here's the implementation of the Checkpoint Manager:

```
#import "TTTCheckpointManager.h"

@implementation TTTCheckpointManager

    static TTTCheckpointManager *singletonManager=nil;

    +(TTTCheckpointManager *) CreateManager{
        @synchronized([TTTCheckpointManager class]){
            if (singletonManager == nil){
                singletonManager = [[TTTCheckpointManager alloc] init];
                singletonManager->managedObjects =
                    [[NSMutableDictionary alloc] init];
            }
            return singletonManager;
        }
```

```
    }

    -(id) init{
        return self;
    }

    -(void) registerObjectWithKey :(NSString *) key
                                 :(NSObject *) objectToBeManaged{
        [managedObjects setObject :objectToBeManaged forKey:key];
    }

    -(void) unregisterObjectWithKey :(NSString *) key{
        [managedObjects removeObjectForKey :key];
    }

    -(void) checkpoint{
        NSEnumerator *enumerator = [managedObjects keyEnumerator];
        id oneKey;
        while ((oneKey = [enumerator nextObject])) {
            NSObject *oneObject = [managedObjects objectForKey:oneKey];
            SEL checkpointMethodSEL = NSSelectorFromString(@"checkpoint");
            [oneObject performSelector:checkpointMethodSEL];
        }
    }
@end
```

The only method of any complexity in this class is checkpoint. All it does, though, is iterate through the objects in the dictionary and call the checkpoint method on each of them.

Each object needing to be checkpointed must implement a checkpoint method that handles its specific checkpointing needs. The Game Session view controller class certainly does so, as shown here:

```
- (void) checkpoint{
    [self synchronizeDefaults];
}
```

Now that you can customize what gets checkpointed, you can use it for other lifecycle-triggered actions, as well. Examine the Login view controller (TTTLoginViewController.m), and you'll see that I used the checkpoint method to clear the user ID and password entry fields when the Login screen is sent to the background.

Before I close this section, it's worth noting that the Xcode framework has a built-in scheme for preserving the state of view controllers and views. For more information about this scheme, go to www.dummies.com/go/iosprogramminglinks and click the State Preservation and Restoration link. This facility is somewhat complicated and also doesn't provide support for state preservation and restoration of domain objects, which is why it isn't covered here.

Dealing with missing or transient capabilities

To make your app reliable, the final consideration is to ensure that it deals well with missing capabilities on the device (such as the availability of specific sensors or the lack of a video camera) or transient failures in these capabilities (such as access to the network).

For the former, your app checks whether a certain capability is available before it tries to do anything with that capability — for example, checking whether a certain type of sensor exists before trying to use it. The method listCapabilities in TTTSensorsController.m shows how your app can discover what is currently available. I explain this method in detail in Chapter 14, so I won't go into detail here. However, snippets from this method are shown here, starting with testing for the camera; also, drill down to check whether video or only still pictures are available:

```
// Testing for the camera
BOOL cameraAvailable =
    [UIImagePickerController
        isSourceTypeAvailable:UIImagePickerControllerSourceTypeCamera];
if (cameraAvailable == YES)
    [textVal appendString:@"Camera is available\n"];

NSArray *cameraTypes =
    [UIImagePickerController availableMediaTypesForSourceType
                        :UIImagePickerControllerSourceTypeCamera];
int count = [cameraTypes count];
for (int i = 0; i < count; i++) {
    NSString *cameraCapability = [cameraTypes objectAtIndex:i];
    if (CFStringCompare ((CFStringRef) cameraCapability,
                        kUTTypeMovie,
                        0))
        [textVal appendString:@"Video capability is available\n"];
    if (CFStringCompare ((CFStringRef) cameraCapability, kUTTypeImage,
        0))
        [textVal appendString:@"Still capability is available\n"];
}
```

Finally, here's how you test for the availability of the audio player:

```
// Testing for availability of audio
AVAudioSession *audioSession = [AVAudioSession sharedInstance];
if (audioSession.inputAvailable == YES)
    [textVal appendString:@"Audio input device is available\n"];

[listOfSensorsView setText:textVal];

...
```

Next, here's how you test for the network:

```
...
// Testing for the network

NSMutableString *textVal = [[NSMutableString alloc] init];
NSString *networkReachability=nil;

Reachability *reachFacade =
    [Reachability reachabilityForInternetConnection];
NetworkStatus status = [reachFacade currentReachabilityStatus];
if (status == NotReachable) networkReachability = @"No network\n";
else if (status == ReachableViaWiFi)
    networkReachability = @"Wifi available\n";
else if (status == ReachableViaWWAN)
    networkReachability = @"WAN available\n";
[textVal appendString:networkReachability];
```

Considering Security in an iOS App

Eternal vigilance is the watchword for developing mobile devices and applications. However, implementing random security techniques in your app as a result of blind panic is hardly a good development strategy. Instead, as you design your app, think systematically about where and how to apply the security principles described in this chapter, and then implement the necessary security using a combination of the techniques described in this chapter.

In this section, you take a holistic look at developing secure iOS apps, starting with why security is especially important for mobile apps; then you look at security principles and general security techniques. Finally, you examine iOS security specifics.

Recognizing the importance of security

Security is an increasingly important consideration for mobile devices (and their applications) for three primary reasons:

✔ **Mobile devices store valuable personal information.** Most people's mobile devices eventually become repositories for all types of personal information — such as their geographical location, contact names and addresses, financial transactions, and credit card information. Theft of this information can result in significant financial loss.

✔ **Mobile devices have a greater security footprint than applications on your desktop.** Mobile devices have more areas of vulnerability than desktop computers, and even laptop computers. Mobile devices are designed to interact with the outside world via the Internet and other networking capabilities, such as Wi-Fi and Bluetooth, so they're exposed to all the consequent dangers. For example, when a user accesses the Internet from a browser on a mobile device, all browser-based vulnerabilities certainly apply — such as phishing, spyware, and viruses (collectively known as *malware*). However, malware poses a greater risk to mobile devices than to desktop computers because websites built to support mobile users are notorious for being security risks themselves, which means, of course, that they present a risk to the devices that access them.

Because apps are now the primary means of using a device, they create a security risk. Keep in mind that mobile apps are authored by a range of organizations and developers and are installed from diverse locations. An app can read and create user data on the device. If your app creates private data and leaves it on the device in an insecure manner, a malicious piece of code (such as another app) can read it.

✔ **Mobile devices aren't as capable of protecting themselves as desktop computers are.** Although mobile devices are exposed to a wider set of vulnerabilities than desktop computers are, mobile devices are *less* capable of protecting themselves because the techniques and best practices used to protect desktop computers (such as strong encryption of data) often aren't feasible on mobile devices because of their limited computing power and memory.

Lack of computing power isn't the only issue. Here are some other reasons mobile devices are more vulnerable than desktop computers:

✔ **Small physical form factor:** Because of their size, mobile devices are easy to misplace or steal. Someone with dishonest intentions can easily disassemble them and access their internal components that contain private information (for example, memory cards).

✔ **No user login required by default:** A mobile device typically isn't set to require a login or other type of authentication in order to use it. A person who steals a user's device has immediate access to all the information on it and to other systems the user has used the device to connect to, such as banks.

✔ **Weak password protection:** If a login is required on a device, the password itself can be a security threat. Using keyboards on mobile devices is difficult. Users find that it's not easy to type all the characters needed for long, strong passwords. For this reason, users tend to use shorter, simpler passwords, which makes the device easier to break into.

Building complex layers of security into mobile devices and applications is also difficult because mobile users are especially sensitive to user experiences on the devices. Mobile users have been known to reject devices that don't have user-friendly interfaces; worse, users might be inclined to circumvent security features and thereby leave themselves completely vulnerable.

✔ **Limited screen size that impedes readability:** Because of the small screen sizes of mobile devices, URLs that a device might access often aren't completely visible. If a dangerous URL is a small variation of a safe URL (as commonly happens in phishing attacks), the user may not notice the variation, thereby providing private information to the malicious site.

✔ **Environmental distractions:** Because users often use mobile devices in crowded spaces, such as buses, or while engaged in other activities, such as walking or driving (a *bad* idea), they become distracted and give less than optimum attention to security warnings.

For example, some financial portals show users personalized images to verify that they're on legitimate websites. Someone using a desktop in an office is likely to notice that this image is missing after being directed to a site that's spoofing the legitimate site. A user on a mobile device, on the other hand, may be distracted and *not* notice the missing image while simultaneously navigating a shopping mall or attempting to maintain her balance on a speeding train.

When your application is *demonstrably* safe, secure, as well as useful, it becomes an application that people trust and want to buy, download, and install. Although creating an application that's reliable and high-performing is certainly a significant factor in establishing trust, security plays the largest role.

Looking at security holistically

To provide security for an application, you typically start by considering specific (but random) topics, such as types of encryption and password-based logins.

However, you must first define the app's *threat model,* which defines the kinds of attacks the app must expect to handle, the assets that must be protected, and the likely degree of loss if those assets are violated or stolen. Along with the threat model, you must also understand how the device can be attacked — that is, where the vulnerabilities are. The set of places through which your device can be attacked is known as the *attack surface.* You find out more about the threat model and the attack surface in the next section.

After you define the threat model and understand the attack surface, you need to identify specific techniques to handle threats. Security techniques can be grouped into the following functional categories:

✔ **Authentication:** This includes techniques for validating and identifying who or what is using the system. You can achieve authentication through a username/password scheme (as in Tic-Tac-Toe), or you can be very sophisticated and use biometrics such as fingerprint or retinal scans. Authentication is a key element in secure systems, for three reasons. It's a means of protecting the system from unauthorized users. Also, once you know who the user is, you can control what services you make available to him. Finally, you can keep track of what he does on the device. Therefore, authentication is key to access control, maintaining an audit trail, and non-repudiation. I discuss these topics next.

✔ **Access control:** Manage who has access to which capabilities or data. Now that you know (through authentication) who the user is, allow him to do only what he's permitted to do.

✔ **Audit trail:** This is the concept of keeping track of who did what in the system, which is typically achieved by logging information to a secured file.

✔ **Data integrity:** This is ensuring that data doesn't become corrupted or harmed. An audit trail will help here and so will access control. Also, in this category are techniques that use checksums that can be used to test whether a piece of data has been inconsistently modified.

✔ **Non-repudiation:** This is ensuring that no user or agent can deny doing something after the fact. This condition is met by proper authentication and access control and by maintaining a secure audit trail. The former ensures that an intruder can't say "someone else acted as me," and the latter captures exactly when the user or agent intruded and what was done.

Another related classification of security techniques is defined by the *roles* that the preceding security techniques can play in implementing a secure system. There are four roles:

✔ **Resistance:** This makes the occurrence of a loss more difficult. Authentication, access control, and data integrity certainly help make the system resistant to attack.

✔ **Detection:** This is determining that a loss or breach has taken place so that the system can start to protect itself against further breaches, or limit the extent of the breach. Audit trails help, although somewhat after the fact.

✔ **Mitigation:** This is limiting the degree of loss or breach that takes place. Try to store as little valuable information on the device as possible.

✔ **Recovery:** This is helping a user recover from a loss, such as by recovering the data from a backup. I don't discuss iCloud backups in this book, but it greatly enables recovery of valuable information.

Use the threat model, understand the attack surface, and then use both the preceding lists to guide you in finding how to address attacks you're likely to face. This systematic approach will provide much better protection than simply adding a few ad hoc security techniques to your app.

Understanding the attack surface and developing a threat model for an app

The attack surface for iOS comprises all the places where iOS is vulnerable. In some respects, this surface is smaller than a desktop system. For example, certain applications known to be vulnerable, such as iChat, simply aren't available for iOS. Other applications are available for both desktops as well as iOS, but the versions of these applications on iOS have greatly reduced capabilities, and therefore are less vulnerable because they provide fewer avenues for attack. For example, mobile Safari, which is the browser on an iOS device, rejects certain file types allowed by desktop browsers. On the other hand, certain vulnerable features are present only on iOS devices, particularly the iPhone, such as SMS messages, and the radio device that makes cellular calls (also known as the *baseband processor*). Most importantly, for this book and for you, the reader, there are the apps themselves.

With that, allow me to explain how Apple tries to make iOS and apps safe.

Understanding the iOS security model

Apple tries to limit the attack surface of an iOS device many ways. Several of the techniques that Apple uses also limit the attack surface of your app.

Before apps are allowed to be on the Apple App Store and made available for general consumption, they must be sent to Apple for review. If approved, they're signed by Apple's private key. A trusted party, such as Apple, must sign apps or they won't run. Enterprises may also distribute apps to their employees. These apps must be signed by the employer, as well as by Apple. Also, the employees' phones must be configured to accept the apps that are signed by these two parties.

Additionally, App Store apps run in a sandbox at a low privilege level to reduce the damage they can cause. For example, an app may access only the portion of the file system that's allocated to it. An app also doesn't have access to system memory. Apple also (apparently) performs runtime checks on apps to ensure that unsigned code hasn't been injected.

A criticism of the iOS sandbox model is that it may be too permissive (unlike the Android mode, which controls access to device services in a much more fine-grained manner). For example, by using legitimate APIs, an app is able to access phone numbers and e-mails, browser search terms, location information, and Wi-Fi access point names. Also, you may have heard of jailbreaking your phone so you can put unapproved apps on it. Just know this: Jailbreaking pretty much turns off all security on the device, not just the code-signing part that prevented unapproved apps from running. Jailbreaking could also void your warranty and mean that you can no longer get technical support from Apple for your device.

Apple also has device-level security to prevent your device from being used by an unauthorized party. One security mechanism is the device's passcode. These locks can be enforced as part of an enterprise policy or set by individual users. Lock policies set by an enterprise can force passcodes to have requirements on length, composition, duration, and history. Users can also set the device to automatically wipe out itself if a wrong passcode is entered too many times.

I don't go into device configuration policies here. However, know that through signed *configuration profiles,* large enterprises may centrally manage access to VPN, Wi-Fi, e-mail, YouTube, the device's camera, installation of third-party applications, and so on.

Data security should be a focus of secure applications. Apple provides mechanisms that include a remote wipe function, data protection of certain files until the user has signed in with his or her passcode, and a good encryption library you can use in your code. In addition, data backed up through iTunes can be encrypted. A password can be set through iTunes and used to encrypt data backed up on iTunes.

Finally, Apple has a Common Crypto library that provides common cryptographic APIs for developers. This includes AES, 3DES, and RC4 encryption algorithms that use the hardware accelerator on the device to enable these algorithms to run fast.

If you use encryption in your app, the approval process for getting it in the App Store will take longer. So be prepared.

Developing a threat model for your app

Developing a threat model means identifying what kind of attacks you need to look out for on your app and what you need to protect. Developing a threat model is actually pretty straightforward:

- ✔ Make your app a good citizen. Test it well, and fix buggy code that could (inadvertently) hurt the device or affect other apps. For example, use ARC to manage memory (refer to Chapter 3 for an explanation on ARC), rather than try to actively manage memory. Make sure that all files your apps created are bounded in length, and make efficient use of the file system. Don't have your app launch other apps that are considered vulnerable.

- ✔ Protect your app from being taken over by malicious forces and being made to act as a Trojan horse from which the device or other apps can be attacked.

> Apple's standard practices of requiring that your app be signed and constraining it to run in a sandbox also protect your app. I discussed signing and sandboxing in the previous section on understanding the iOS security model.
>
> ✔ Block unauthorized and "unwashed" access to the data and services of your app.

Implementing authentication and access control

You can authenticate users many ways before allowing them to access your app. The easiest method of access is based on a user ID and password. Although this method is simple (and certainly nothing about Tic-Tac-Toe is really top secret), knowing how to implement it on iOS is useful, and it also relates to my later discussion on ensuring the integrity of data.

User ID- and password-based (or password-based or pin-based) access is only the simplest form of authentication. Systems now implement what is known as *multi-factor* authentication. A user must present two or more pieces of information — for example, private information (such as password), physical information (such as a fingerprint or voice signature), and information related to a possession (such as a smart card) — with each of these factors authenticated by the system being accessed.

In this section, you find out how to implement user ID and password authentication in Tic-Tac-Toe using secure text fields and Core Data. (Refer to Chapter 9 if you need a refresher on text fields and how to set up secure data entry. Refer to Chapter 6 for information on how to add the Core Data framework to your app and define your core data model.)

Start with the Login view controller and its user interface (see Figure 11-10). As you can see, there are two fields for text entry: User ID and Password.

Notice that, although the user ID is revealed, the password is hidden. You hide the password by setting the `secureTextEntry` attribute for this field, as shown here (taken from the `viewDidLoad` method of the Login view controller implemented in `TTTLoginViewController.h` and `.m`):

```
- (void)viewDidLoad{
    [super viewDidLoad];
    // Do any additional setup after loading the view.
    ...

    passwordTextField.secureTextEntry = YES;
    ...
}
```

Figure 11-10:
The login
screen in
Tic-Tac-Toe.

Here's the code that does the login:

```objc
- (IBAction)login:(id)sender{

    NSString* oneUserid = [useridTextField text];
    NSString* onePassword = [passwordTextField text];
    [self clearFields];
    if ([self useridPassWordMatch :oneUserid :onePassword]){
        // Login successful
        NSString * logEntry =
            [[NSArray arrayWithObjects :oneUserid,
                                        onePassword,
                                        @"Successful login",
                                        nil]
                componentsJoinedByString:@":"];
        [myLogger log:logEntry];

        // Done with login, unregister checkpoint

        [checkpointManager
            unregisterObjectWithKey :@"TTTLoginViewController"];

        // Segue to GameOptions scene
        [self performSegueWithIdentifier:@"SuccessfulLogin" sender:self];
    }else{
        [self showMessage :@"Login Failed!" :@"Check userid and password"];
        NSString * logEntry =
            [[NSArray arrayWithObjects :oneUserid,
                                        onePassword,
                                        @"Unsuccessful login",nil]
                componentsJoinedByString:@":"];
        [myLogger log:logEntry];
    }
}
```

Notice the following two things about the login method:

✔ I cleared the user ID and password fields by setting each field to the empty string as soon as I read what the user entered.

✔ The method useridPassWordMatch, which does the actual user ID and password matching, is shown here:

```
- (BOOL) user IDPassWordMatch :(NSString *) aUserId :(NSString * }
      aPassword{
    BOOL retVal=NO;
    for(int i=0; (i < [users count]) && !retVal; i++){
        TTTUser *oneUser = [users objectAtIndex:i];
        retVal = [aUserId isEqualToString:[oneUser userid]]&&
                    [aPassword isEqualToString:[oneUser password]];
    }
    return retVal;
}
```

The user IDs and passwords are stored in a database accessed through Core Data. Here is the code for addNewUser that enters the values into the database:

```
- (void)addNewUser:(NSString *)aUserId :(NSString *)aPassword {
    if ([self useridExists:aUserId]){
        [self showMessage :@"User ID Exists!" :@"Check User ID or login"];
    }else{
        TTTUser *user =
            [NSEntityDescription insertNewObjectForEntityForName:@"TTTUser"
                                  inManagedObjectContext:managedObjectContext];

        [user setUserid: aUserId];
        [user setPassword: aPassword];

        NSError *error = nil;
        [managedObjectContext save:&error];

        if (!error){
            [users addObject: user];
            NSString * logEntry =
                [[NSArray arrayWithObjects :aUserId,
                                            aPassword,
                                            @"User successfully added",
                                            nil]
                      componentsJoinedByString:@":"];
            [myLogger log:logEntry];
        } else {
            NSString * logEntry =
                [[NSArray arrayWithObjects :aUserId,
                                            aPassword,
```

```
                                           @"User unsuccessfully added",
                                           nil]
                          componentsJoinedByString:@":"];
                [myLogger log:logEntry];
         }
      }
   }
```

First, a Core Data managed object of type `TTTUser` is created (refer to Chapter 6 for more on Core Data):

```
TTTUser *user = [NSEntityDescription insertNewObjectForEntityForName:@"TTTUser"
                           inManagedObjectContext:managedObjectContext];
```

Next, this object is filled with the user ID and password, as shown here:

```
[user setUserid: aUserId];
[user setPassword: aPassword];
```

Finally, this object is saved:

```
[managedObjectContext save:&error];
```

Protecting core data files with encryption

Now comes the fun part. Did you know that data in Core Data models is stored in SQLite files and clearly shown in text? You can see the text by moving these files from your application's private directory to a folder on your computer and examining them in a text editor that allows you to open binary files (such as the open-source editor Emacs, available for the Mac as Aquamacs Emacs). Figure 11-11 shows you the contents of a file named `Tic_Tac_Toe_Storyboard.sqlite-wal`. You can see the user IDs (Bob and Rajiv) and their passwords ("blob" and "abcd", respectively). This kind of file is the *write-ahead log* (or WAL) file used by SQLite as its rollback journal, where it saves temporary data before committing it to the database. Take note that sometimes this file is deleted after the commit, and sometimes it isn't.

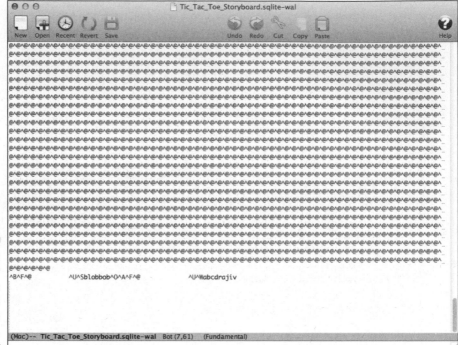

Figure 11-11:
The clear
text internals
of a Core
Data SQLite
file.

Obviously storing user IDs and passwords in clear text is a bad idea. Apple claims it provides you with a little bit of protection: When you set up the Core Data file, Apple says that you can set its parameters such that the file won't be visible if the user hasn't entered his passkey and signed in. This code (from the Core Data section of `TTTAppDelegate.m`) shows you how to set the correct Core Data parameters:

```
// Create the URL for the password file
NSURL *storeURL =
    [[self applicationDocumentsDirectory]
        URLByAppendingPathComponent:@"Tic_Tac_Toe_Storyboard.sqlite"];
...
// Encrypt the password database
NSDictionary *fileAttributes =
    [NSDictionary dictionaryWithObject:NSFileProtectionComplete
                forKey:NSFileProtectionKey];
if (![[NSFileManager defaultManager] setAttributes:fileAttributes
                                    ofItemAtPath:[storeURL path]
                                    error:&error])
```

However, if the device is jail-broken, all the sandbox protections are gone, and your file becomes visible. Also, here's the curious thing: The main SQLite data file is indeed hidden if the user hasn't signed in. But the preceding WAL file is still available and readable.

Because you can't rely on Apple's data protection, you must encrypt the data you put in Core Data. To do so, you first provide simple wrappers around Common Crypto (or CC) library functions that allow you to easily encrypt and decrypt what you write to the database. These wrappers are in an Objective-C category that extends the core `NSData` class with the encryption methods `encryptWithKey` and `decryptWithKey`, as shown here (I discuss Objective-C categories in Chapter 3):

```
#import <Foundation/Foundation.h>

@interface NSData (TTTCrypto)
    - (NSData *)encryptWithKey:(NSString *)key;
    - (NSData *)decryptWithKey:(NSString *)key;
@end
```

I don't discuss implementation of these two methods because the focus of the book isn't on encryption. However, do note that the algorithms in the example use 128-bit Advanced Encryption Standard (AES) encryption. Also feel free to look at the file `NSData+TTTCrypto.m` and the corresponding `.h` file from which the preceding interface declaration is extracted.

In addition, you declare the password attribute of the Core Data model `TTTUser` to be a `Transformable` type (see Figure 11-12) with the class `TTTEncryptionTransformer` implementing the transformation.

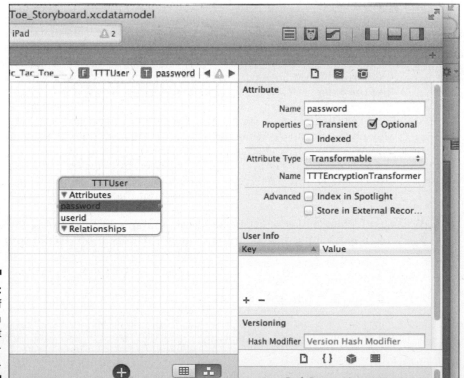

Figure 11-12:
Attribute of a Core Data entity set to Transformable.

The following code shows the two key methods:

```
...
#define TTTENCRYPTIONKEY "TTTC0D3"
...
@implementation TTTEncryptionTransformer
    ...
    - (id)transformedValue:(id)sourceValue{
        id retVal=nil;
        if (sourceValue != nil){
            NSData *UTFEncodedSourceValue =
                [sourceValue dataUsingEncoding:NSUTF8StringEncoding];
            retVal = [UTFEncodedSourceValue encryptWithKey:@TTTENCRYPTIONKEY];
        }
        return retVal;
    }

    - (id)reverseTransformedValue:(id)transformedValue{
        id retVal=nil;
        if (transformedValue != nil){
            NSData *data = [transformedValue decryptWithKey:@TTTENCRYPTIONKEY];
            retVal = [[NSString alloc] initWithData:data
                        encoding:NSUTF8StringEncoding];
        }
        return retVal;
    }

@end
```

Feel free to browse this class. It utilizes the wrappers around Common Crypto to make the use of encryption of Core Data seamless. Before the data is put into the SQLite file, it's encrypted by the transformer (see Figure 11-13). When data is read, it's decrypted and available in regular text for use within the program.

The key that encrypts (or *hashes*) the data is a two-way key (that is, the same key encrypts and decrypts the data) — in this example, the key embedded in the program code (see the file TTTEncryptionTransformer.m). For even more security, this code should be provided by the user and stored in the keychain of the iOS device. For more information, go to www.dummies.com/go/iosprogramminglinks and check out the Keychain Concepts link.

If you change the Core Data model for your app, just remember to delete the old app from the device (or the simulator) before trying to run your app again.

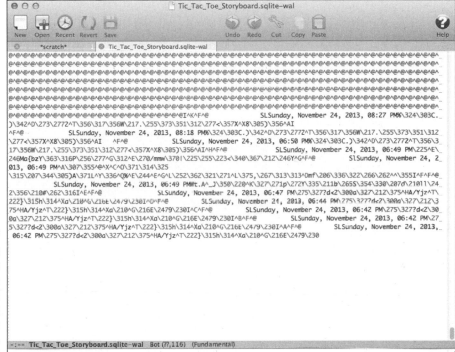

Figure 11-13:
SQLite
file with
password
and log
entry fields
encrypted.

Adding auditing to your application

In this section, you find out how to add an audit trail by logging the progress of your app and the data that's generated and used. You use Core Data and also encrypt certain elements of the data.

The key classes for logging are as follows:

✔ The TTTLogEntry class, which is a Core Data class that represents a log entry. It has two attributes, an unencrypted timestamp and the log entry, which is encrypted (that is, it's declared to be Transformable with its transformer class set to TTTEncryptionTransformer, as you saw earlier in this chapter).

✔ The `TTTLogger` class, a Singleton that encapsulates the logger. Here is the code for the log method of this class:

```
-(void) log :(NSString *) anEntry{

    NSDate *myDate = [[NSDate alloc] init];
    NSDateFormatter *dateFormat = [[NSDateFormatter alloc] init];
    [dateFormat setDateFormat:@"cccc, MMMM dd, YYYY, hh:mm aa"];
    NSString *aDateStamp = [dateFormat stringFromDate:myDate];

    TTTLogEntry *logEntryObject =
        [NSEntityDescription
    insertNewObjectForEntityForName:@"TTTLogEntry"
        inManagedObjectContext:self->managedObjectContext];

    [logEntryObject setDateStamp :aDateStamp];
    [logEntryObject setEntry :anEntry];

    NSError *error = nil;
    [managedObjectContext save:&error];
}
```

This log method is used in the Login view controller (`TTTLoginView Controller`) as follows:

```
NSString * logEntry = [[NSArray arrayWithObjects
                        :aUserId,
                        aPassword,
                        @"User successfully added",
                        nil]
                    componentsJoinedByString:@":"];
[myLogger log:logEntry];
```

Because the Tic-Tac-Toe program is just for illustration, I didn't log functionality other than to create new users and for logging in. The unencrypted code here shows what's being logged (you can see that these entries have private information):

```
2013-11-25 09:29:17.102 Tic-Tac-Toe-Storyboard[3620:60b]
    Log Entry 0. >Sunday, November 24, 2013, 06:42 PM<
            >::Unsuccessful login<
2013-11-25 09:29:17.104 Tic-Tac-Toe-Storyboard[3620:60b]
    Log Entry 1. >Sunday, November 24, 2013, 06:42 PM<
            >::Unsuccessful login<
2013-11-25 09:29:17.106 Tic-Tac-Toe-Storyboard[3620:60b]
    Log Entry 2. >Sunday, November 24, 2013, 06:42 PM<
            >::Unsuccessful login<
2013-11-25 09:29:17.107 Tic-Tac-Toe-Storyboard[3620:60b]
    Log Entry 3. >Sunday, November 24, 2013, 06:44 PM<
            >::Unsuccessful login<
2013-11-25 09:29:17.109 Tic-Tac-Toe-Storyboard[3620:60b]
    Log Entry 4. >Sunday, November 24, 2013, 06:47 PM<
            >::Unsuccessful login<
2013-11-25 09:29:17.110 Tic-Tac-Toe-Storyboard[3620:60b]
    Log Entry 5. >Sunday, November 24, 2013, 06:49 PM<
        >rajiv:abcd:Unsuccessful login<
2013-11-25 09:29:17.112 Tic-Tac-Toe-Storyboard[3620:60b]
    Log Entry 6. >Sunday, November 24, 2013, 06:49 PM<
        >rajiv:rajiv:User successfully added<
2013-11-25 09:29:17.114 Tic-Tac-Toe-Storyboard[3620:60b]
    Log Entry 7. >Sunday, November 24, 2013, 06:49 PM<
        >rajiv:rajiv:Unsuccessful login<
2013-11-25 09:29:17.116 Tic-Tac-Toe-Storyboard[3620:60b]
    Log Entry 8. >Sunday, November 24, 2013, 06:50 PM<
        >rajiv:rajiv:Successful login<
2013-11-25 09:29:17.117 Tic-Tac-Toe-Storyboard[3620:60b]
    Log Entry 9. >Sunday, November 24, 2013, 08:18 PM<
        >rajiv:rajiv:Successful login<
2013-11-25 09:29:17.119 Tic-Tac-Toe-Storyboard[3620:60b]
    Log Entry 10. >Sunday, November 24, 2013, 08:27 PM<
        >rajiv:rajiv:Successful login<
2013-11-25 09:29:17.120 Tic-Tac-Toe-Storyboard[3620:60b]
    Log Entry 11. >Sunday, November 24, 2013, 09:41 PM<
        >rajiv:rajiv:Successful login<
2013-11-25 09:29:17.121 Tic-Tac-Toe-Storyboard[3620:60b]
    Log Entry 12. >Monday, November 25, 2013, 09:16 AM<
        >rajiv:rajiv:Successful login<
2013-11-25 09:29:17.123 Tic-Tac-Toe-Storyboard[3620:60b]
    Log Entry 13. >Monday, November 25, 2013, 09:20 AM<
        >rajiv:rajiv:Successful login<
2013-11-25 09:29:17.125 Tic-Tac-Toe-Storyboard[3620:60b]
    Log Entry 14. >Monday, November 25, 2013, 09:23 AM<
        >rajiv:rajiv:Successful login<
2013-11-25 09:29:17.126 Tic-Tac-Toe-Storyboard[3620:60b]
    Log Entry 15. >Monday, November 25, 2013, 09:26 AM<
        >rajiv:rajiv:Successful login<
```

Design principles in this chapter

This chapter includes several OO techniques. First, two classes shown here are natural fits for the Singleton pattern:

- The Checkpoint Manager class (`TTTCheckpointManager`)

- The Logger (`TTTLogger`)

The Checkpoint Manager class (`TTTCheckpointManager`) is also a great example of the Observer pattern. It provides a dynamic registry capability through the `registerObjectWithKey` method using both the Login view controller (`TTTLoginViewController`) and the Game Session view controller (`TTTGameSessionViewController`) to register (and unregister). When the app "resigns active" and goes into the background, the Checkpoint Manager notifies all the registered objects to checkpoint.

Associated with use of the Observer pattern is use of a custom protocol (`TTTCheckpointable`) to ensure that the objects that need to be checkpointed implement the `checkpoint` method. Another mechanism for class extension is using an Objective-C category to extend the base `NSData` class to provide the encryption functions in the `NSData+TTTCrypto` class used by the Encryption Transformer class (`TTTEncryptionTransformer`).

In addition, delegation is used frequently. In fact, each of the preceding patterns use it. The code that puts up the successful and unsuccessful login messages also delegates handling of user input to the view controller that invoked them.

Part IV

Connecting Your Apps

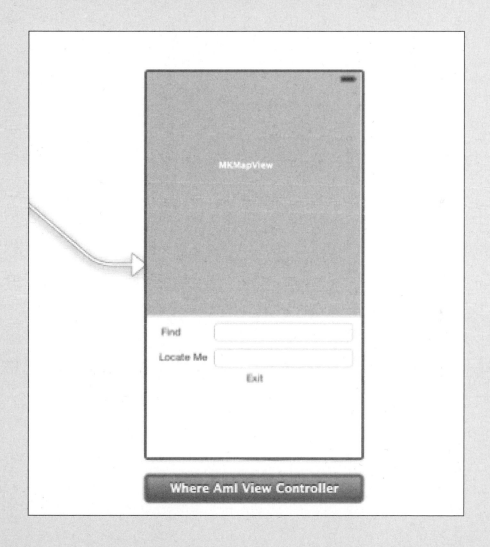

In this part...

- ✔ Accessing browsers
- ✔ Connecting to maps
- ✔ Communicating with the world
- ✔ Identifying locations
- ✔ Creating a developer account
- ✔ Publishing on iTunes
- ✔ Visit www.dummies.com/extras/beginningiosprogramming for great Dummies content online.

Chapter 12

Channeling the World Into Your Device

. . . .

In This Chapter

▶ Opening a browser from your app

▶ Incorporating a browser view into your application

▶ Using web services

▶ Finding and using your devices' location

▶ Incorporating maps into your app

. . . .

*Y*our iPhone or tablet is your portal to the world. You can interact with others, find out what's going on around you (such as shopping, dining and local points of interest) and in distant places (such as weather where you plan to visit).

Your device can do all these things because of apps that utilize three things: the web; location-based services provided by a variety of providers, especially Apple and Google; and the device's own built-in location-finding capability.

In this chapter, I illustrate how to create apps that can browse the web, call web services that provide specific assistance and information, provide maps of places of interest, show where *you* are on a map, and more.

Networking Basics

A network is any collection of interconnected computers. They can be in either Local Area Networks (or LANs) or Wide Area Networks (or WANs). LANs are computers grouped together in close proximity (for example, (in your home or workplace); WANs span across wide geographical areas, with the Internet being the largest WAN we know of.

All forms of communication have a set of rules known as a *protocol*. In computing, a protocol is a formal description of the digital formats of the messages that are exchanged and the rules for exchanging the messages — the signaling, acknowledgements, and so on. There are many such protocols, but here I focus on the three that iOS devices use to communicate:

- ✓ Bluetooth is used for close-range device-to-device communication.
- ✓ TCP/IP (Transmission Control Protocol/Internet Protocol) is the most widely used protocol for computer-to-computer communication over the Internet.
- ✓ Layered on TCP/IP is the HTTP protocol (HyperText Transfer Protocol) upon which most web-based applications are built.

  Layered on top of HTTP are some capabilities that iOS provides, such as launching a web browser. These capabilities hide even HTTP, making things even simpler.

Unless you're building a performance-critical application — such as a multiplayer game — that requires exchanging large numbers of messages in real time, the HTTP protocol is the only one you'll need. This book deals only with applications that you can build using this protocol.

Launching a browser from your app

The first (and simplest) example I show is one where your application launches the built-in Safari browser on a specific web page identified by a URL.

In Tic-Tac-Toe, I show you how to access the Wikipedia page from the Help screen of the app (see Figure 12-1).

Tic-Tac-Toe on Wikipedia

Help in WebView

Exit

Figure 12-1:
The Tic-Tac-
Toe Help
screen.

Tapping the button labeled Tic-Tac-Toe on Wikipedia brings up a Wikipedia page that describes Tic-Tac-Toe, as shown in Figure 12-2.

The code for opening a URL in the built-in Safari browser is straightforward. Here is a code snippet from Tic-Tac-Toe (taken from the `helpViaBrowser` method in `TTTHelpViewController.m`):

```
- (IBAction)helpViaBrowser: (id) sender{
    [[UIApplication sharedApplication] openURL:[NSURL
        URLWithString:@"http://en.wikipedia.org/wiki/Tictactoe"]];
}
```

One line of code. Yes, it's that simple.

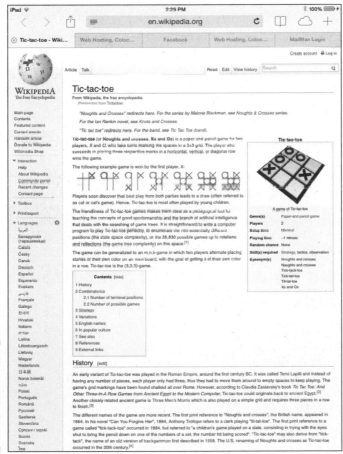

Figure 12-2:
Launching a web page in a browser from your app.

Of course, this simplicity is thanks to the UIApplication class that does all the hard work. This class provides a central coordination point for iOS apps — essentially acting as a Façade to a set of functionality provided by the operating system.

Every app gets exactly one instance of UIApplication (or a subclass) because this class is implemented as a Singleton. When an app is launched and UIApplicationMain is called (look at the main.m method in the Tic-Tac-Toe project, or for that matter in any project), a UIApplication object is created. After that, you access this single object by invoking the sharedApplication class method.

The device's browser, which opened the URL http://en.wikipedia.org/wiki/Tictactoe, is automatically redirected by the web server to http://en.m.wikipedia.org/wiki/Tictactoe. This page is the Tic-Tac-Toe web page for mobile devices (which, for example, doesn't use frames and has fewer embedded graphics).

Once you launch the browser, it completely takes over, and you don't have a good way to get back to your app. You can, of course, exit the browser by touching the Home button. But to get to the Tic-Tac-Toe app again, you must go to the Home screen and restart it, at which point, it will likely start where it left off — because it didn't really go away. However, you can't rely on this of returning to where you left off. If iOS needs to conserve resources, it may shut down your app once the browser is launched.

In other words, the preceding approach to opening a web page on an app forces you to give up control to the browser and the iOS operating system. To ensure that your app manages the web page, you must embed the browser as a view in your application, which I explain in the next section.

Embedding a browser in your iOS application using WebView

Being able to browse the web from within an app on a mobile device is a useful functionality, for users, apps, *and* websites. For users, apps set the browsing context and can take users to particular web pages; for apps, as users browse, apps can observe the pages being browsed and use that information to improve performance; and for websites, apps provide the context of the browsing (such as the location of users).

URIs and URLs

Here are technical differences between URIs and URLs:

- ✔ A Uniform Resource Identifier (or URI) is a string that identifies a resource on the web.

  Think of it is as a catalog number for a book in a library.

- ✔ A Uniform Resource Locator (or URL) is a URI *plus* a means of actually getting access to the resource and potentially acting on it.

Think of it as a catalog number, plus a shelf location in a library, plus potentially a means (such as by mail) of having a book delivered to you.

In most cases, the identifier of an item on the web is useless without knowing where and how to access it, so you can think of URLs and URIs as meaning the same thing.

Figure 12-3 shows what an embedded view looks like. As you can see, and unlike the previous example where the browser took over the entire screen, here you still have access to everything else on the screen.

Figure 12-3: Showing a web page in an embedded web view.

In the iOS framework, Apple enables you to embed a browser in your app by using the Web View component. To embed this view in a screen on a storyboard, drag and drop a component named WebView onto the screen, as you do any other UI component.

In this example, I set up an outlet in the view controller for the Web View, along with an action triggered by the Help in WebView button wired to the action `helpWithWebView`. In the following code (from `TTTHelpViewController.h`), you see the various outlets and actions:

```
#import <UIKit/UIKit.h>

@interface TTTHelpViewController : UIViewController
...
    @property (nonatomic, retain) IBOutlet UIWebView *helpWebView;
...
    @property (nonatomic, retain) IBOutlet UIButton *helpViaWebViewButton;
...
...
    - (IBAction) helpWithWebView: (id) sender;
...
@end
```

This is the code behind the `helpWithWebView` action:

```
- (IBAction) helpWithWebView: (id) sender{
    NSString *wikpediaURLString = @"http://en.wikipedia.org/wiki/Tictactoe";
    NSURL *wikepediaUrl = [NSURL URLWithString:wikpediaURLString];
    NSURLRequest *requestObj = [NSURLRequest requestWithURL:wikepediaUrl];
    [helpWebView loadRequest:requestObj];
}
```

The preceding code does the following:

1. An object representing a URL (an instance of the `NSURL` class) is created from the URL string.

2. This `NSURL` object is embedded in a `NSURLRequest` object.

3. The `NSURLRequest` object is sent to the `loadRequest` method of the web view.

And that, as they say, is that.

Using Maps and Providing Location-Based Services

A mobile device, especially a smartphone, is an integral part of many people's professional and personal lives. Because this device is also a computer that can record and remember, it retains intimate knowledge about people — such as their friends (through the address book and calling patterns), common haunts, and so on. This information can be used by your app to provide personalized and highly targeted *context-based* services that appear to be created just for a given individual.

A very important component of context is location, one that a smart iOS device is especially capable of providing because it can be located, either through a built-in GPS device or because it's visible to cellular phone towers or Wi-Fi hotspots. Because most users take these devices everywhere they go, its location is also the users' locations.

By using the iOS framework's location-finding services, you can write apps to provide location-based services. There are many kinds of location-based services — among others, providing directions to places a user isn't familiar with and information on points of interest such as dining or sights in close proximity to the user.

All of these services must have a way to do the following:

- ✔ Bring up a map.
- ✔ Navigate the map to various positions.
- ✔ Identify (from the device) the user's coordinates.

I cover how to enable these three actions in the next few sections.

To illustrate how to use location and maps from your app, I created a screen and a view controller named Where Am I (why not?). Note that the view controller is named `TTTWhereAmIViewController`, in keeping with the naming convention used in this book. The app first brings up a map inside an instance of a Map View class (named `MKMapView`) from the `MapKit` package (`#import <MapKit/MapKit.h>`).

Maps and location services are limited when run on the iOS simulator (you can see only California and Apple's location in Cupertino). To properly test maps, you must run your app on a real device. So, for this next step, locate that device and hook it up.

When you run this app on an actual device, the map responds to touch-based gestures to zoom in and out. You can also pan to different locations by dragging the map in any direction. You can enter the address of your intended destination, and the map will navigate to that address. The application determines your current location by invoking the location services on your phone and navigates the map to that location.

Installing the additional development components needed for maps

The iOS libraries added to your project don't automatically contain the Map Kit library that you need to write map applications. If you build your code based on these libraries, you'll get errors. This is not a big deal, though. You simply enable the Map capability, as shown in Figure 12-4, to link in the necessary libraries.

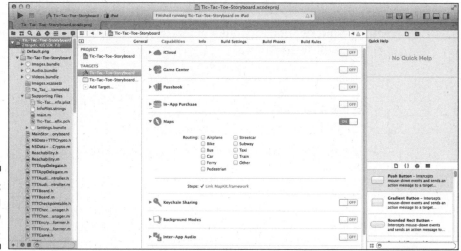

Figure 12-4: Enabling the Map capability.

You can also manually install the MapKit framework, as shown in Figure 12-5.

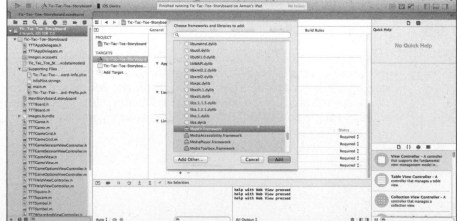

Figure 12-5: Manually adding the MapKit framework to your project.

Displaying a map using a MapView

I next illustrate how to display a map using the built-in MapView class by walking you through the Where Am I screen and view controller (once again, feel free to follow along in Xcode). Start with the screen layout for the Where Am I screen (see Figure 12-6). Note the Map View at the top and the two buttons, Find and Locate Me, next to two text fields. You can enter text in the Find text field. The Locate Me text field is, on the other hand, set programmatically when you touch Locate Me. Also note the Exit button. Finally note the segue to the Where Am I screen. If you look in Xcode, you see that this segue originates at the button named Where Am I in the Game Options screen.

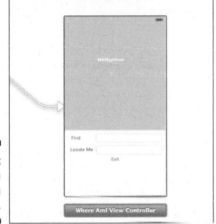

Figure 12-6:
Laying out a map using a Map View.

Now, look at the Where Am I view controller, starting as usual with the interface file:

```
#import <UIKit/UIKit.h>
#import <MapKit/MapKit.h>

@interface TTTWhereAmIViewController : UIViewController <MKMapViewDelegate> {

}
    @property (nonatomic, retain) IBOutlet MKMapView *thisMapView;
    @property (nonatomic, retain) IBOutlet UIButton *findButton;
    @property (nonatomic, retain) IBOutlet UIButton *locateMeButton;
    @property (nonatomic, retain) IBOutlet UIButton *exitButton;
    @property (nonatomic, retain) IBOutlet UITextField *locateMeTextField;
    @property (nonatomic, retain) IBOutlet UITextField *findTextField;

    - (IBAction) find:(id)sender;
    - (IBAction) locateMe:(id)sender;
    - (IBAction) exit:(id)sender;
@end
```

You see all the expected outlets (for each of the UI components on the screen) and actions (corresponding to the buttons). Now, look at the `ViewDidLoad` method:

```
- (void)viewDidLoad{
    [super viewDidLoad];
    // Do any additional setup after loading the view.
    locateMeTextField.enabled = NO; // Prevent typing in this field
    [locateMeButton setEnabled:NO]; // Disable till location found

    thisMapView.showsUserLocation = YES; // show ball at location

    myGeocoder = [[CLGeocoder alloc] init]; // Create a geocoder

    // Set this as the delegate to the location listener
    [thisMapView setDelegate:self];
}
```

In this method, you see additional setup for the Where Am I screen, after it's loaded for display. The Locate Me text field is disabled, so you can't type in it, and the Locate Me button is disabled until the device can connect to a location provider and get its location. I explain how that works in the section "Wherever you go, there you are," later in this chapter.

Next, look at the statement `thisMapView.showsUserLocation = YES`. This statement configures the map so that the user's current location is shown as a blinking ball on the map.

Finally, an instance of a `GLGeoCoder` class is created. `GLGeoCoder` is a helper class for the view that geocodes an address and also reverse geocodes a location and determines what's at that location.

Using geocoding to navigate the map

To use geocoding to navigate a map, start by locating a place on the map. The upcoming code snippet illustrates use of the `find` method, which is the action prompted by the Find button. To test this method, type the name of a unique location (for example, London, England, or New Delhi in the Find field — the name must be unique; London alone could bring up several locations, such as London, Ohio). Touch Find, and the app navigates the map to that location.

After you understand what the method calls do, you'll find that the code is straightforward. The `myGeocoder` object is an instance of the class `CLGeocoder`. The method `geocodeAddressString` of this instance takes the location name as a string and converts it to coordinates on the map:

```
- (IBAction) find:(id)sender{
    NSString *findString = [findTextField text];
    [myGeocoder geocodeAddressString:findString completionHandler:^(NSArray*
        placemarks, NSError* error){
            if ([placemarks count] > 0){
                MKPlacemark *aPlacemark = [placemarks objectAtIndex:0];
                [thisMapView
            setCenterCoordinate:aPlacemark.location.coordinate animated:YES];
            }
    }];
}
```

This information then centers the map using [thisMapView setCenterCo ordinate:userLocation.coordinate animated:YES].

The geocodeAddressString method is actually a web service call to a remote server. This remote call can take time, especially if the network is slow or spotty. If you don't want the app to hang in the meantime, you can launch the remote call in a separate thread, with a callback method defined inline to process the results when it comes back.

The MKPlacemark class is important. A MKPlacemark object stores location-related data for a given latitude and longitude, such as the country, state, city, street address, and points of interest. You can find more information about this class at the MKPlacemark link in the web resources for this chapter at www.dummies.com/go/iosprogramminglinks.

Wherever you go, there you are

iOS provides three types of location-finding capabilities as part of the iOS framework: GPS-based, cellular-tower-based, and Wi-Fi. The most accurate system is GPS (Global Positioning System), which uses a permanent ring of satellites to locate devices containing a GPS receiver. GPS is accurate to within a few meters. However, GPS doesn't work well indoors, consumes a fair bit of battery power, and sometimes takes a while to figure out where a device is located.

In addition, the cell towers that a device is communicating with (if it's a phone) know approximately where a device is to within several thousand meters — through triangulating based on signal direction and strength. Similarly, Wi-Fi access points that devices are connected to serve as approximate proxies for the device. Wi-Fi location is accurate to about a few hundred meters because, in most cases, the address of the gateway that all the access points connect to is known and serves as the proxy for the location of the device (for example, a cable or DSL modem in your house).

However, challenges remain in device location. The preceding techniques are approximations, and as a user moves around, different ones may become available or unavailable, or the provider being used may not always be the best one.

Before showing you how to get the current location of a device, you need a little background. Because the location of a mobile device changes with the location of the user, finding a location is rarely a one-time process. Location-based apps are *dynamic* apps, so as a user moves around, what these apps show changes accordingly. For that reason, most location-based apps are event-based, with the event being a detectable change in the location.

If you look at the code in the Where Am I view controller, you'll see what I mean. Now, to revisit the `ViewDidLoad` method:

```
- (void)viewDidLoad{
    [super viewDidLoad];
    // Do any additional setup after loading the view.
    ...
    [locateMeButton setEnabled:NO]; // Disable till location found

    thisMapView.showsUserLocation = YES; // show ball at location

    myGeocoder = [[CLGeocoder alloc] init]; // Create a geocoder

    // Set this as the delegate to the location listener
    [thisMapView setDelegate:self];
}
```

Notice the statement `[thisMapView setDelegate:self];`. Here, the view controller (`self`) is setting itself up as a delegate for an event in the `MapView` object. That event is a *location-changed* event. In fact, when a `MapView` is instantiated and while it's showing a map, it has a separate thread that's busily monitoring the location of the device.

When the location changes by a settable threshold, an event occurs. The `MapView` object delegates the response to that event to a delegate object — in this case, the parent view controller object (that is, the current instance of the Where Am I view controller) — by calling the delegate method `didUpdateUserLocation` with the changed location, as shown here:

```
- (void)mapView:(MKMapView *)mapView
        didUpdateUserLocation:(MKUserLocation *)userLocation {

    if ((userLocation.coordinate.latitude != 0.0) &&
        (userLocation.coordinate.longitude != 0.0)){
        // Center the map
        [thisMapView setCenterCoordinate:userLocation.coordinate
            animated:YES];

        //Save the location from userLocation
        myLocation = [userLocation location];

        // Enable Locate Me button
        if (myLocation != nil)[locateMeButton setEnabled:YES];
    }
}
```

Incidentally, `didUpdateUserLocation` is a method in the `MKMapViewDelegate` protocol shown in the definition of the Where Am I view controller (see the declaration of `TTTWhereAmIViewController` in the file `TTTWhereAmIViewController.h`).

In this method, the new location is used first to center the map using `[thisMapView setCenterCoordinate:userLocation.coordinate animated:YES]`. Then a `location` structure is extracted from the `userLocation` object and cached. Finally, now that a location is found, the Locate Me button is enabled.

Touching the Locate Me button causes the `locateMe` method to execute, as shown here:

```
- (IBAction) locateMe:(id)sender{

    // Lookup the information for the current location of the user.
    [myGeocoder reverseGeocodeLocation:myLocation
              completionHandler:^(NSArray *placemarks,
                                  NSError *error) {
        if ((placemarks != nil) && (placemarks.count > 0)) {
        // get a placemark - there should be only one most of the time
            MKPlacemark *placemark = [placemarks objectAtIndex:0];

            // Convert the location to a string
            NSString *myLocationString = [[NSArray arrayWithObjects:
                                        placemark.subThoroughfare,
                                        @" ",
                                        placemark.thoroughfare,
                                        @",",
                                        placemark.locality,
                                        @",",
                                        placemark.administrativeArea,
                                        @",",
                                        placemark.country,
                                        @" ",
                                        placemark.postalCode,
                                        nil]
                                        componentsJoinedByString:@""];
            [locateMeTextField setText:myLocationString];
            [thisMapView
                setCenterCoordinate:placemark.location.coordinate
                animated:YES];
        } else {
            // Handle errors.
            [locateMeTextField setText:@"Current location not found"];
        }
    }];
}
```

This method looks up the location saved by the `didUpdateUserLocation` callback and *reverse* geocodes it using the trusty `myGeocoder` object. In reverse geocoding, meaningful location information (such as address, city, state, points of interest, and so on) is extracted corresponding to the GPS coordinates. This information is returned in and extracted from a `MKPlacemark` object that's shown in the view. The map is also centered at this location. Figure 12-7 shows the resulting map after it's been centered.

Figure 12-7: Map centered at a location.

Now that you understand how to get a device's location and how to use that information, you need to know another important point. Before making use of its location, an app must ask for and receive permission to do so. Your app doesn't need to do anything special to ask for this location; it simply tries to use the current location of the device. The iOS framework then causes the app to prompt for this permission (see Figure 12-8).

Figure 12-8: Requesting permission to use the device's location.

Design Principles for Web- and Location-Based Apps

When you're reaching out to the web to invoke a service or read data, you're going outside the device into what is essentially the wide blue yonder. Keep in mind the things that can go wrong — such as losing connectivity or, even worse, dealing with a connection with very low bandwidth. Your application must be able to deal with such situations and still provide a good user experience.

Being nice about using remote services

Because remote calls are made to external services, you need to be aware of how to use geocoding. Here are some best-practice suggestions:

✔ Send, at most, one geocoding request for a single user action.

✔ If the user performs multiple actions that involve geocoding the same location, cache and reuse the results from the first request.

✔ Issue new geocoding requests to keep track of a moving user (therefore, the device) only after the user moves a significant distance or after some reasonable amount of time passes.

In typical situations, Apple recommends sending not more than one geocoding request per minute.

✔ When a user may not see the results right away, don't start a geocoding request. You'd just be wasting resources.

Even though the app or the location handling components in iOS may be caching location data, the device must be able to reach the network in order to return detailed `MKPlacemark` information. The geocoder caches the localized country name and ISO country code for most locations. However, if more detailed information about a country isn't available for a specific location, the geocoder may still report an error.

Using threading to deal with slow network connections

Dealing with connectivity is complicated. Dealing with situations where there is *no* connectivity is actually straightforward. The difficult part is deciding whether there is *enough* connectivity. This is because tests for connectivity will succeed if there's any connectivity at all, even if the connection is poor and has low bandwidth. However, no test will tell the app how good or bad the connectivity is.

The iOS framework tries to deal with poor connectivity by launching most remote calls over the Internet in a new thread so that, despite the slow connection, your app won't hang and stays responsive while the remote call is in progress.

In many cases, you won't have to deal directly with threads because the iOS framework does that for you. For example, when you launched the Web View in the Help screen (see the earlier section "Embedding a browser in your iOS application using WebView") or when you brought up the Map View in the Where Am I screen, the iOS framework created threads in the background to do this work so that the rest of the app remained responsive. You can test this behavior in iOS by touching the Exit button on either of the screens while the web page or the map is loading — the screen will exit immediately.

Note how the Map View finessed dealing with the lack of connectivity. It did so by automatically finding the current location in a separate thread. If there isn't access to a location-finding device, the callback method `didUpdateUserLocation` will never be invoked.

OO principles in this chapter

Both the Web View and the Map View classes use *information hiding* by not making their implementation visible and requiring the programs to use the complex capabilities of these classes only through well-defined interfaces. An interesting, and somewhat less obvious, use of information hiding is in the way threading is implemented. Note how the threading needed for each of these classes is completely encapsulated within each class. Therefore, the lifetime of the thread is the lifetime of the object, and access to the threads is only through the interface of the objects. In other words:

✔ The thread starts when the Web View or Map View object is constructed.

✔ The thread stops before these objects are destroyed.

✔ Rather than monitoring the thread directly, a callback mechanism is used to do the work necessary when the thread is complete.

At least a couple of patterns were visible in the code for this chapter. I noted the use of the Façade pattern and the Singleton pattern with the `UIApplication` object. You also saw a perfect use of delegation in registering for location events. All in all, location, mapping, and web viewing services in iOS make heavy use of OO techniques.

Chapter 13

Harnessing iOS Device Capabilities

● ●

In This Chapter

▶ Incorporating e-mail, SMS, and telephony

▶ Writing programs that use audio and video

▶ Discovering the capabilities on your device

▶ Detecting orientation, acceleration, and rotation using sensors

▶ Analyzing the OO design of components used in this chapter

● ●

*M*obile devices are powerful computing platforms and can accommodate a wide range of hardware capabilities. New iOS devices often have high-performance cameras, as well as a built-in GPS and one or more sensors.

Now that Apple has made the iOS platform developer friendly by opening up the platform to outside developers, you can design apps that can control a camera and take photographs, make phone calls and send text messages, and record and play audio and video. Also, your device can sense movement and rotation through its sensors. You can use these capabilities to detect orientation, acceleration, and rotation.

In this chapter, you find out how to incorporate these capabilities into your apps using Xcode. In some cases, you simply reuse functionality from the iOS framework or built-in apps on your system; in others, you can directly use iOS classes to create finer-grained control. I show you examples of both these strategies in this chapter.

Along the way, I point out quirks in the iOS framework, such as differences in how to handle various media (audio, video, and images). Also, dealing with sensors is complicated because not all devices have all sensors, and every sensor is different.

Finally, it's next to impossible to properly develop and test programs that use the capabilities described in this chapter on an emulator. You really need an actual iOS device. So buy, beg, borrow, or steal (well, okay, don't steal) a device if at all possible.

Integrating E-Mail, SMS, and the Phone into Your App

In this section, I show you how to write apps that send e-mail and text messages and make phone calls. As usual, I've integrated these capabilities into the Tic-Tac-Toe app.

Sending e-mail from your app

Suppose that after playing the Tic-Tac-Toe application, a user is excited about his high score and wants to send the score to a friend. From the Tic-Tac-Toe app, he selects Send eMail (see Figure 13-1).

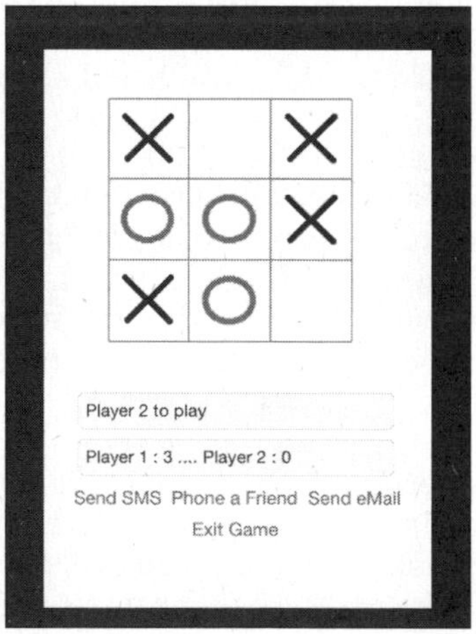

Figure 13-1: Using e-mail, SMS, and telephony from Tic-Tac-Toe.

The user can then select names from the device's address. After he does so, an e-mail composition window appears on the device with the recipient's address, subject, and the message already inserted, as shown in Figure 13-2. The user just selects Send, and off the e-mail goes.

Figure 13-2:
E-mail
composition
window.

For this example to work properly, the user must already have an e-mail account set up on his device. If not, an iOS error message appears, as shown in Figure 13-3. When he touches OK, he returns the game session screen.

Figure 13-3:
Error mes-
sage if
an e-mail
account
isn't already
set up.

You can find the code for sending e-mail in the Game Session view controller (in the file TTTGameSessionViewController). In this section, you start by looking at the method sendScoresByEmailWithAddress. (If you need a refresher on selecting a contact from the Address Book, refer to Chapter 6.)

```objc
    - (void) sendScoresByEmailWithAddress:(NSString *)address {
                    MFMailComposeViewController* mailController =
                        [[MFMailComposeViewController alloc] init];
        mailController.mailComposeDelegate = self;
        [mailController  setToRecipients:[NSArray arrayWithObjects
                                    :address,nil]];
        [mailController  setSubject:@"I rock at Tic-Tac-Toe!"];

        NSString *scoreText = [[NSArray arrayWithObjects :firstPlayerName,
                                @":",
                                [NSNumber numberWithInt:scorePlayerOne],
                                @"....",
                                secondPlayerName,
                                @":",
                                [NSNumber numberWithInt:scorePlayerTwo],
                                nil]
                                componentsJoinedByString:@" "];

        [mailController  setMessageBody:scoreText isHTML:NO];
        [self presentViewController :mailController
                            animated:YES
                            completion:nil];
    }
- (IBAction) sendScoresByEmail:(id)sender {
    MFMailComposeViewController* mailController =
                [[MFMailComposeViewController alloc] init];
    mailController .mailComposeDelegate = self;
    [mailController setSubject:@"I rock at Tic-Tac-Toe!"];
    NSString *scoreText = [[NSArray arrayWithObjects :firstPlayerName,
                                    @":",
                                    NSNumber numberWithInt:scorePlayerOne],
                                    @"....",
                                    secondPlayerName,
                                    @":",
                                    [NSNumber numberWithInt:scorePlayerTwo],
                                    nil]
                            componentsJoinedByString:@" "];

    [mailController setMessageBody:scoreText isHTML:NO];
    [self presentViewController:mailController animated:YES
                                        completion:nil];
}
```

The iOS framework has a class called MFMailComposeViewController
that serves as a view controller for the mail composition window (refer to
Figure 13-2). You create an instance of this view controller, set the subject

and message body properties, and ask the view managed by the view controller to show itself using `presentViewController`. The user still must press Send to actually send the message.

Note one interesting line in this code, though:

```
mailController .mailComposeDelegate = self;
```

If you were to say, "Aha! The Game Session view controller is setting itself as a delegate to the `mailController`," you'd be absolutely right. Setting itself up as a delegate allows the calling code, in this case Game Session view controller, to assign a callback method to be called after the e-mail is sent. Here is the code for this callback method, named `didFinishWithResult`:

```
- (void)mailComposeController:(MFMailComposeViewController*)controller
                    didFinishWithResult:(MFMailComposeResult)result
                    error:(NSError*)error;
{
    if (result == MFMailComposeResultSent) {
        NSLog(@"Email sent!");
    }
    [controller dismissViewControllerAnimated:YES completion:nil];
}
```

This method checks whether it was called with a successful result (`MFMailComposeResultSent`) and writes an appropriate log entry. It also dismisses the mail composition window and underlying view controller. You also can do more extensive error handling within this method, as you see in the SMS example in the next section.

Using the preceding iOS components to send e-mail (and SMS messages, as I explain in the next section) requires you to include the following `#import` statement in your code:

```
#import <MessageUI/MessageUI.h>
```

Don't forget to include this line; otherwise, your app won't compile.

Sending an SMS from your app

Sending an SMS from your app (see Figure 13-4) is very similar to sending e-mail.

Figure 13-4:
Sending
SMS
from the
Tic-Tac-Toe
app.

In other words, a view controller and a view for sending SMS are provided within the iOS framework. Here's how to create this view controller and view and use it to send a message:

```
- (IBAction) sendScoresBySMS:(id)sender {
    MFMessageComposeViewController *smsController =
                [[MFMessageComposeViewController alloc] init];
    if([MFMessageComposeViewController canSendText]){
        NSString *scoreText = [[NSArray arrayWithObjects:
                        @"I rock at Tic-Tac-Toe! ",
                        firstPlayerName,
                        @":",
                        [NSNumber numberWithInt:scorePlayerOne],
                        @"....",
                        secondPlayerName,
                        @":",
                        [NSNumber numberWithInt:scorePlayerTwo],
                        nil]
                        componentsJoinedByString:@" "];

        smsController.body = scoreText;
        smsController.messageComposeDelegate = self;
        [self presentViewController:smsController
                        animated:YES
                        completion:nil];

    }
}
```

As in the e-mail example in the previous section, a delegate is assigned as a callback method. This callback method is called when the message is sent, or if it couldn't be sent (for example, if the network timed out), or if the user cancelled the send. The code for the callback method is shown here:

```
- (void)messageComposeViewController:
          (MFMessageComposeViewController*)smsController
          didFinishWithResult:(MessageComposeResult)result{
  switch (result){
  case MessageComposeResultCancelled:
      NSLog(@"SMS Message Cancelled");
      break;
  case MessageComposeResultFailed:
      NSLog(@"SMS Message Failed");
      break;
  case MessageComposeResultSent:
      NSLog(@"SMS Message Sent!");
      break;
  default:
      break;
  }
  [smsController dismissViewControllerAnimated:YES completion:nil];
}
```

This method is very similar to the equivalent callback for sending e-mail. However, note that, in this method, I have tried to handle both success as well as the failure completion conditions.

Placing telephone calls from your app

Apple doesn't yet provide a good way of using telephony functionality in your app. The only thing you can do is launch the telephone application from your code, with the telephone number previously entered, if required, as shown here:

```
- (IBAction) phoneAFriend:(id)sender {
    UIApplication *applicationObject = [UIApplication sharedApplication];
    NSURL *callURL = [NSURL URLWithString:@"telprompt://614-555-1234"];
    if ([applicationObject canOpenURL:callURL]){
        [[UIApplication sharedApplication] openURL:callURL];
    } else {
        NSLog(@"Phone call failed. Probably no phone on device");
    }
}
```

In this code, I added a test that uses the canOpenURL method to check whether your device can actually make phone calls.

After the user completes the call, your application reappears. This approach isn't the greatest way to integrate telephone calling on your app, but it's the only convenient approach that's available from Apple. There are techniques to embed telephony into your app (to make it, for example, like the Skype app), but they're beyond the scope of this book.

Playing and Capturing Audio, Video, and Images

In this section, you find out how to use an audio player, a recorder, and a camera. Before beginning, however, it's important to know that iOS provides more than one framework with these capabilities, each at a different level of abstraction. When you're developing apps that use these capabilities, use the *highest-level* abstraction available that does what you need.

For example, if you just want to play movies, you can use the Media Player framework (with the class MPMoviePlayerController or the class MPMoviePlayerViewController). To easily record video, you can use the UIKit framework (specifically, the class UIImagePickerController).

For greater control over media, iOS provides the AV Foundation, which is one of several frameworks that you can use to play and create time-based audiovisual media. You can use the AV Foundation to examine, create, edit, and re-encode media files. You can also receive and process real-time input streams (for more details, see the link labeled The iOS AV Framework in the web resources for this book at www.dummies.com/go/iosprogramminglinks).

And then (as shown in Figure 13-5) there are the Core Audio, Core Media, and Core Animation frameworks, where you really get into the nitty-gritty of media encodings.

Chapter 12 also has an example of the principle of using the highest level of abstraction. In that chapter, I use the UIWebView object when displaying a web page (instead of trying to render the page using the base UIView class).

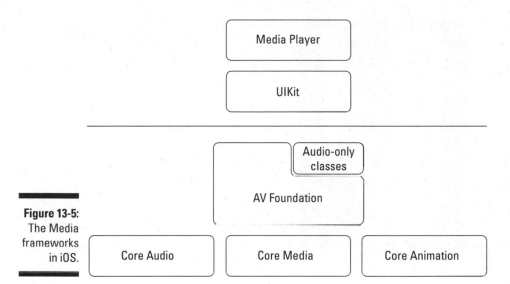

Figure 13-5:
The Media
frameworks
in iOS.

I discuss playing and recording video and audio and working with images next. In these examples, I use a higher-level abstraction as well as a lower-level abstraction from the iOS framework for video; for audio, I use a lower-level abstraction that allows finer control; and for images, I use an abstraction that's somewhere in the middle of the available abstractions.

Playing and recording video

This section starts by showing you how to use a high-level abstraction, the `MPMoviePlayerViewController` class, to play video. Here is the code (in the Video view controller, from the file `TTTVideoViewController.m`).

```
- (IBAction) playVideo:(id)sender{
    MPMoviePlayerViewController *moviePlayer =
        [[MPMoviePlayerViewController alloc] initWithContentURL:movieURL];
    [self presentMoviePlayerViewControllerAnimated:moviePlayer];
}
```

Simplicity itself! All you need is a URL that points to a movie file on the file system or to an Internet URL with which to instantiate the movie player. The player's UI handles stopping, starting, and so on (see Figure 13-6).

Figure 13-6:
Movie play-
back using
the built-in
media
player.

The member variable `movieURL` is set in the `viewDidLoad` method that's called after the display is initialized for this view controller (a sample movie is now saved in a resource file named `Videos.bundle`), as shown here:

```
- (void)viewDidLoad{
    [super viewDidLoad];
    // Do any additional setup after loading the view.
    NSString* videoPath =
        [[NSBundle mainBundle] pathForResource:@"Videos.bundle/SampleVideo"
                            ofType:@"MOV"];
    movieURL = [NSURL fileURLWithPath:videoPath];
}
```

The following example shows you how to use an abstraction that's one level lower than the preceding one. Here, I demonstrate the recording of a video using the lower-level method `recordVideo`:

```
- (IBAction) recordVideo:(id)sender{
    UIImagePickerController *imagePicker =
        [[UIImagePickerController alloc] init];
    imagePicker.sourceType = UIImagePickerControllerSourceTypeCamera;
    imagePicker.mediaTypes =
        [[NSArray alloc] initWithObjects: (NSString *) kUTTypeMovie, nil];

    imagePicker.delegate = self;
    [[UIApplication sharedApplication] setStatusBarHidden:YES];
    [self presentViewController:imagePicker animated:YES completion:nil];

}
```

When this method is called, a screen with a camera interface appears (see Figure 13-7). Using this screen, video recording can be started and stopped. When video recording is done, this screen transfers control back to the calling view controller.

Figure 13-7:
Recording
video using
the camera.

The following two methods are the callback methods called by the Image picker (notice how the Video view controller registers itself as a delegate with the `ImagePicker` object):

✔ `imagePickerControllerDidCancel` is called when the recording is cancelled. It simply dismisses the picker and shows the iOS status bar again.

```
- (void) imagePickerControllerDidCancel: (UIImagePickerController *) picker
        {
   [[UIApplication sharedApplication] setStatusBarHidden:NO];
   [picker dismissViewControllerAnimated:YES completion:nil];
}
```

✔ `didFinishPickingMediaWithInfo` starts by showing the iOS status bar again and dismisses the picker. It then saves the recorded video in the camera roll of the device. Finally, this method sets the member variable `movieURL` to point to this new video, so when you select Play Video again, the newly recorded movie plays.

```
- (void) imagePickerController:(UIImagePickerController *) picker
        didFinishPickingMediaWithInfo :(NSDictionary *) results {

    NSURL *moviePathURL =
            [results objectForKey:UIImagePickerControllerMediaURL];
    NSString *moviePath = [moviePathURL path];
    movieURL = moviePathURL;

    //Save in camera roll
    if (UIVideoAtPathIsCompatibleWithSavedPhotosAlbum (moviePath)){
        UISaveVideoAtPathToSavedPhotosAlbum (moviePath, nil, nil, nil);
    }
    [[UIApplication sharedApplication] setStatusBarHidden:NO];
    [picker dismissViewControllerAnimated:YES completion:nil];
}
```

Playing and recording audio

Now it's time to deal with audio, using classes from the AV framework (which is yet one more level down). You can find all this code in the Audio view controller (`TTTAudioViewController.h` and `TTTAudioViewController.m`) and follow along. Figure 13-8 shows this view controller's screens.

Play
Stop Playing

Record
Stop Recording
Play Recording
Stop Playing Recording

Exit

Figure 13-8:
Working
with audio in
Tic-Tac-Toe.

In this example, you go top down, starting with the `ViewDidLoad` method where member variables are initialized and an audio-visual session starts:

```
- (void)viewDidLoad{
    [super viewDidLoad];
    // Do any additional setup after loading the view.
    localRecorder = nil;
    localPlayer = nil;
    localRecordPlayer = nil;
    playFileURL = nil;
    recordFileURL = nil;
    [[AVAudioSession sharedInstance]
        setCategory:AVAudioSessionCategoryPlayAndRecord error:nil];
}
```

Here is an example of playing an audio file within an app:

```
- (IBAction) play:(id)sender{
    if (playFileURL == nil){
        NSString* audioPath =
            [[NSBundle mainBundle]
                pathForResource:@"Audio.bundle/SampleAudio-Cut"
                ofType:@"mp3"];
        playFileURL = [NSURL fileURLWithPath:audioPath];
    }

    localPlayer =
        [[AVAudioPlayer alloc] initWithContentsOfURL:playFileURL error:nil];
    [localPlayer setDelegate:self];
    [localPlayer play];
}
```

As with the `ImagePicker` example in the previous section, the Audio view controller has registered itself as a delegate. Therefore, `audioPlayerDidFinishPlaying` is called when the player finishes with the clip:

```
- (void) audioPlayerDidFinishPlaying   :(AVAudioPlayer *)player
                                        successfully:(BOOL)flag{
    NSLog(@"Done playing!");
}
```

Finally, here is how the player is stopped:

```
- (IBAction) stopPlaying:(id)sender{
    [localPlayer stop];
}
```

As you can see, the app doesn't just rely on the user interface of a built-in audio app; it has finer-grain control over the player.

Working with images

The last media type covered here demonstrates how you work with images, at an abstraction level similar to working with video recordings. As always, feel free to follow along in the Image view controller (files named TTTImage-ViewController.h and TTTImageViewController.m). Figure 13-9 shows this view controller displaying a sample image (BookFront.png in the resource file Images.bundle).

Figure 13-9:
The Image
view
controller
displaying
a sample
image.

Again, I start by showing you how variables are initialized in the ViewDidLoad method (specifically, note the initialization of the member variable localImage).

```
- (void)viewDidLoad{
    [super viewDidLoad];
    // Do any additional setup after loading the view.
    NSString* imagePath =
        [[NSBundle mainBundle] pathForResource:@"Images.bundle/BookFront"
                            ofType:@"png"];
        localImage = [[UIImage alloc] initWithContentsOfFile:imagePath];
}
```

Here you see how images are shown:

```
- (IBAction) showImage:(id)sender{
    imageView.image = localImage;
    [imageView setNeedsDisplay];
}
```

Finally, here is the `takeImage` method that contains code for taking the picture:

```
- (IBAction) takeImage:(id)sender{
    UIImagePickerController *imagePicker =
        [[UIImagePickerController alloc] init];
    imagePicker.sourceType = UIImagePickerControllerSourceTypeCamera;
    imagePicker.mediaTypes =
        [[NSArray alloc] initWithObjects: (NSString *) kUTTypeImage, nil];

    imagePicker.delegate = self;
    [[UIApplication sharedApplication] setStatusBarHidden:YES];
    [self presentViewController:imagePicker animated:YES completion:nil];
}
```

The code for taking a still image is almost identical to that for recording a video. The only difference is that the `mediaTypes` property of the `imagePicker` object is set to `kUTTypeImage` (whereas it's set to `kUTTypeMovie` when recording a video). By now, you're probably boringly familiar with the use of the view controller as a delegate object to `imagePicker` and with the purpose of the following two methods: `imagePickerControllerDidCancel` and `didFinishPickingMediaWithInfo`. This `imagePickerControllerDidCancel` is called when the user cancels the operation:

```
- (void) imagePickerControllerDidCancel:(UIImagePickerController *) picker {
    [[UIApplication sharedApplication] setStatusBarHidden:NO];
    [picker dismissViewControllerAnimated:YES completion:nil];
}
```

Figure 13-10 shows the camera while taking a still image.

Figure 13-10:
The camera while taking a still picture.

As you can see, `didFinishPickingMediaWithInfo` is called after the picture is taken. Here, I set the newly taken image into the image view of the Image view controller (see Figure 13-11).

Figure 13-11: Image embedded in an Image view.

Show Image

Take Picture

Exit

```
- (void) imagePickerController: (UIImagePickerController *) picker
              didFinishPickingMediaWithInfo: (NSDictionary *) results {
  localImage =
    (UIImage *)[results objectForKey:UIImagePickerControllerOriginalImage];
  imageView.image = localImage;
  [imageView setNeedsDisplay];
  [[UIApplication sharedApplication] setStatusBarHidden:NO];
  [picker dismissViewControllerAnimated:YES completion:nil];
}
```

One final comment before I close this section. The code for using the video recorder within an app and the code for taking images as well as the code for sending e-mail and SMS are very similar in structure. In both cases, an object of a task-specific view controller is instantiated by the view controller currently running. In the e-mail case, it's the `MFMailComposeViewController`; in the SMS case, it's the `MFMessageComposeViewController`; and in the video recording and image capture cases, it's the `UIImagePickerController`. The currently running view controller then sets itself as a delegate within the task-specific view controller. Finally, the task-specific view controller is presented, and the current view controller exits.

When the task-specific view controller (that is, the instance of the `UIImagePickerController`, the `MFMailComposeViewController`, or the `MFMessageComposeViewController`) exits, the delegate method of the original view controller is called, either to process the data returned by the recorder or the camera or to deal with errors and cancellations.

Seeing the Capabilities Available on Your Device

It's often necessary for the app to query whether certain capabilities are available on the device — for example, to see whether there's network connectivity and, if so, what kind. You also may want your app to check whether a camera is on the device and whether the camera allows both video and still pictures. In general, it's good programming practice to test for such device capabilities before trying to use them. These tests help prevent your code from crashing or hanging and, in general, improve the user's experience.

Next, I show you how to do such tests. You can find this code in the `listCapabilities` method in the Sensors view controller (relevant files are `TTTSensorsViewController.h` and the corresponding `TTTSensorsViewController.m` file), so as always, feel free to follow along.

Testing for network availability

First, I cover how you test for the network. Before you can write the code to do the actual test, you must put two additional files (`Reachability.h` and `Reachability.m`) into your project.

Apple makes these files available for download from the iOS Developer site at the Reachability Sample Code link in the web resources for this book at www. dummies.com/go/iosprogramminglinks. You can also find these files in the Tic-Tac-Toe project, but they're current only as of the date this book is published.

After you download the files into your project, you need to include `Reachability.h` in all the appropriate files (see `TTTSensorView Controller.h` for an example). You're then ready to use the functionality provided in `Reachability.m`, which includes being able to check whether a specific host is reachable, to check on available networks, and to get periodic notifications as the status networks changes.

I show you next how to figure out whether a network is reachable and, if so, which one — Wi-Fi or a wide area network (WAN, that is, a network based on a wireless service). To follow along, look at the method `listCapabilities` found in the file `TTTSensorsViewController.h`:

```
- (IBAction) listCapabilities:(id)sender{
    // Testing for the network
    NSMutableString *textVal = [[NSMutableString alloc] init];
    NSString *networkReachability=nil;

    Reachability *reachFacade =
        [Reachability reachabilityForInternetConnection];
    NetworkStatus status = [reachFacade currentReachabilityStatus];
    if (status==NotReachable) networkReachability = @"No network\n";
    else if (status==ReachableViaWiFi)
        networkReachability = @"Wifi available\n";
    else if (status==ReachableViaWWAN)
        networkReachability = @"WAN available\n";
    [textVal appendString:networkReachability];
            ...
}
```

You start by calling a Factory method named `reachabilityForInternet Connection` of the `Reachability` class to get an instance `ReachFacade` of type `Reachability`. The `reachFacade` object then has a method `currentReachabilityStatus` that can be used to check for available connections.

This method returns the best available connection. A device might have both a WAN and a Wi-Fi connection; however, there's no method to see whether both are available.

Testing for sound and camera capabilities

The method `listCapabilities` also has the code for testing for sound playing, sound recording, and a camera.

Here's the code for testing the camera for its capabilities:

```
- (IBAction) listCapabilities:(id)sender{

    ...

    BOOL cameraAvailable =
        [UIImagePickerController isSourceTypeAvailable:UIImagePickerControll
            erSourceTypeCamera];
    if (cameraAvailable == YES)
        [textVal appendString:@"Camera is available\n"];
```

```
NSArray *cameraTypes = [UIImagePickerController
                        availableMediaTypesForSourceType:
                            UIImagePickerControllerSourceTypeCamera];
int count = [cameraTypes count];
for (int i = 0; i < count; i++) {
    NSString *cameraCapability = [cameraTypes objectAtIndex:i];
    if (CFStringCompare ((CFStringRef) cameraCapability,
                         kUTTypeMovie,
                         0))
        [textVal appendString:@"Video capability is available\n"];
    if (CFStringCompare ((CFStringRef) cameraCapability,
                         kUTTypeImage,
                         0))
        [textVal appendString:@"Still capability is available\n"];
}
    ...
[listOfSensorsView setText:textVal];
    ...
}
```

The much simpler code for testing audio capabilities is

```
- (IBAction) listCapabilities:(id)sender{
    ...
    AVAudioSession *audioSession = [AVAudioSession sharedInstance];
    if (audioSession.inputAvailable == YES)
        [textVal appendString:@"Audio input device is available\n"];
    ...
}
    ...
}
```

Figure 13-12 shows how the Sensors view controller appears after it discovers all the capabilities on the device.

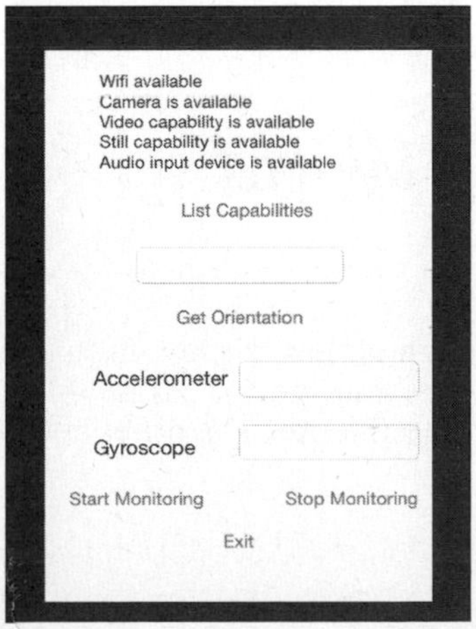

Figure 13-12:
Displaying the capabilities of an iOS device.

Declaring an app's needs in the .plist file

In addition to knowing how to check for capabilities on the device, you need to know how an app declares the capabilities that it needs. You do so in the app's `Info.plist` file. Every app needs such a file. For the Tic-Tac-Toe app, the `.plist` file is `Tic-Tac-Toe-Storyboard-Info.plist`. Take a look at the `.plist` file from Tic-Tac-Toe, and you'll see that Tic-Tac-Toe requires Wi-Fi (see Figure 13-13).

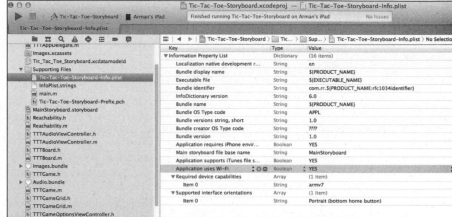

Figure 13-13: Specifying app requirements in the `Info.plist` file.

You can also see that I specified that Tic-Tac-Toe run only in Portrait mode. When this is the only mode set, the app will stay in Portrait mode even when you turn the device sideways or upside down.

For more information on the `Info.plist` file, go to www.dummies.com/go/ iosprogramminglinks and follow the link labeled The Property List (Info. plist) File.

Bringing in the Outside World with Sensors

You've arrived at the penultimate section of this chapter. In this section, I describe one more set of capabilities on your device: its built-in sensors. Just like the GPS senses location (refer to Chapter 12), other sensors on the device are aware of phenomena taking place in the outside world (for example, temperature, the pull of gravity, orientation, magnetic fields, ambient light, and sound). These sensors can feed these sensed values to your app. Your app can then use these values to provide cool functionality. For example, by sensing acceleration as well as twisting, your app can make the phone a device for monitoring your golf swing.

Sensors in the iOS framework operate at two layers of abstraction. At the lowest level of abstraction are the base sensors, such as the acceleration sensor (or accelerometer) and the temperature sensor, that return the actual sensed values. The accelerometer returns the raw values of acceleration in three dimensions. At the next level of abstraction are virtual sensors that interpret raw sensor values returned by the other sensors to provide a higher-order value. An example of such a sensor is the orientation sensor, which interprets the raw values of acceleration in the three dimensions to figure out orientation changes.

Sensing orientation

Because the acceleration sensor interprets the raw values of acceleration in three dimensions to figure out orientation changes, the orientation sensor is considered a *high-order* sensor.

As with all sensors, the orientation sensor must be started from your code before it will return any values. Once it's running, the orientation sensor starts sending changes in orientation to your app. To help you understand how this happens, I start with the ViewDidLoad method of the Sensor view controller (see files named TTTSensorsViewController.h and TTTSensorsViewController.m). Here is the relevant extract from this method:

```
- (void)viewDidLoad{
        ...
    // start listening for orientation changes
    [[NSNotificationCenter defaultCenter]
            addObserver:self
            selector:@selector(orientationChanged:)
            name:@"UIDeviceOrientationDidChangeNotification"
            object:nil];
    [[UIDevice currentDevice] beginGeneratingDeviceOrientationNotifications];
        ...
}
```

In the preceding code, the Sensor view controller adds itself as an observer to the device's notification manager and registers to observe orientation change events. Then the method call to `[[UIDevice currentDevice] beginGeneratingDeviceOrientationNotifications]` starts the process of monitoring the orientation.

Orientation change events are caught and saved by the `orientationChanged` method shown here:

```
- (void) orientationChanged: (NSNotification *) orientationNotification {
    deviceOrientation = [[UIDevice currentDevice] orientation];
}
```

Finally, `getOrientation` can be used to read the saved orientation and display it appropriately. Here's the code for `getOrientation`:

```
- (IBAction) getOrientation:(id)sender{
    NSString *orientationString=nil;
    switch (deviceOrientation){
        case UIDeviceOrientationUnknown:
            orientationString = @"Unknown";
            break;
        case UIDeviceOrientationPortrait:
            orientationString = @"Portrait";
            break;
        case UIDeviceOrientationPortraitUpsideDown:
            orientationString = @"Portrait Upside Down";
            break;
        case UIDeviceOrientationLandscapeLeft:
            orientationString = @"Landscape Left";
            break;
        case UIDeviceOrientationLandscapeRight:
            orientationString = @"Landscape Right";
            break;
        case UIDeviceOrientationFaceUp:
            orientationString = @"Face Up";
            break;
        case UIDeviceOrientationFaceDown:
            orientationString = @"Face Down";
            break;
        default:
            orientationString = @"Unknown";
    }
    [orientationTextView setText:orientationString];

}
```

getOrientation is called when the button labeled Get Orientation is selected. If you set the device on a table and keep it still, bring up the Sensor view controller, and select Get Orientation, the orientation is shown as Unknown. The correct orientation is shown only when you move the device after the Sensor view controller screen appears.

Sensing the accelerometer, gyroscope, and magnetometer

An iOS device has several sensors. However, Apple provides a convenient interface to access only three of them — the accelerometer, the gyroscope, and the magnetometer. The light sensor, for example, has only an internal, undocumented programming interface, which means that (for some reason) Apple discourages apps that use the light sensor.

In any case, in this section, I show you how to use the three with well-documented interfaces — again, the accelerometer, the gyroscope, and the magnetometer.

As with the orientation sensor, the process for these sensors begins by starting and initializing a listener that (you guessed it) listens for sensor events. Here is the code from the ViewDidLoad method of the Sensors view controller:

```
- (void)viewDidLoad{
    ...
    accelerationTextView.enabled = NO;
    gyroscopeTextView.enabled = NO;
    magnetometerTextView.enabled = NO;
    ...
    // Set up the motion manager

    self->motionManager = [[CMMotionManager alloc] init];
    self->motionManager.accelerometerUpdateInterval = 1;
    self->motionManager.gyroUpdateInterval = 1;
    self->motionManager. magnetometerUpdateInterval = 1;
    ...
}
```

The object that gives you access to sensor events is an instance of the CMMotionManager class. You need to create one, and only one, instance of this class (that is, you must treat it like a Singleton, even though it isn't). Then you set properties like the update interval for each of the sensors.

Next, you start the monitoring using the methods `startAccelerometer-UpdatesToQueue`, `startGyroUpdatesToQueue`, and `startMagnetometer-UpdatesToQueue`, as shown in the method `startMonitoringSensors` (which is called when you press the Start Monitoring button):

```
- (IBAction) startMonitoringSensors:(id)sender{
    [self->motionManager
        startAccelerometerUpdatesToQueue:
            [NSOperationQueue currentQueue]
                withHandler:^(CMAccelerometerData *accelerometerData,
                NSError *error) {
                    [self
                       handleAccelerationUpdates:accelerometerData.acceleration];
                }
    ];

    [self->motionManager
        startGyroUpdatesToQueue:
            [NSOperationQueue currentQueue]
                withHandler:^(CMGyroData *gyroscopeData, NSError *error) {
                    [self handleGyroUpdates:gyroscopeData.rotationRate];
                }
    ];
    [self->motionManager
        startMagnetometerUpdatesToQueue:
            [NSOperationQueue currentQueue]
                withHandler:^(CMMagnetometerData *magnetometerData,
                NSError *error) {
                [self handleMagnetometerUpdates:
                        magnetometerData.magneticField];
                }
    ];
}
```

Each of these methods is called with an inline handler block using the `with Handler` construct. These inline handler blocks call the `handle Acceleration Updates`, `handleGyroUpdates`, and `handleMagnetometerUpdates`. These methods are as follows:

```
- (void) handleAccelerationUpdates: (CMAcceleration) accelerationData {
    NSLog(@"Acceleration.x >%f<\n", accelerationData.x);
    NSLog(@"Acceleration.y >%f<\n", accelerationData.y);
    NSLog(@"Acceleration.z >%f<\n", accelerationData.z);
    if (((accelerationData.x > 1.0)||(accelerationData.x < -1.0))||
        ((accelerationData.y > 1.0)||(accelerationData.y < -1.0))||
        ((accelerationData.z > 1.0)||(accelerationData.z < -1.0))){
        [accelerationTextView setText:@"I&#x2019;M GOING FAST"];
    }else{
        [accelerationTextView setText:@"TOO SLOW"];
    }
}
```

```
- (void) handleGyroUpdates: (CMRotationRate) gyroRotationRate {
    NSLog(@"Rotation x >%f<\n", gyroRotationRate.x);
    NSLog(@"Rotation y >%f<\n", gyroRotationRate.y);
    NSLog(@"Rotation z >%f<\n", gyroRotationRate.z);
    if (((gyroRotationRate.x > 0.5)||(gyroRotationRate.x < -0.5))||
        ((gyroRotationRate.y > 0.5)||(gyroRotationRate.y < -0.5))||
        ((gyroRotationRate.z > 0.5)||(gyroRotationRate.z < -0.5))){
        [gyroscopeTextView setText:@"WHEEE!"];
    }else{
        [gyroscopeTextView setText:@"SPIN ME FASTER!"];
    }
}
- (void) handleMagnetometerUpdates: (CMMagneticField) magneticField {
    NSLog(@"Magnetic field x >%f<\n", magneticField.x);
    NSLog(@"Magnetic field y >%f<\n", magneticField.y);
    NSLog(@"Magnetic field z >%f<\n", magneticField.z);
    static float savedX=0.0, savedY=0.0, savedZ=0.0;
    float change = pow((magneticField.x - savedX), 2.0) +
                   pow((magneticField.y - savedY), 2.0) +
                   pow((magneticField.z - savedZ), 2.0);
    NSLog(@"Magnetic field change >%f<\n", change);
    if (change > 3000.0){
        savedX = magneticField.x;
        savedY = magneticField.y;
        savedZ = magneticField.z;
        [magnetometerTextView setText:@"I SENSE SOMETHING!"];
    }else{
        [magnetometerTextView setText:@"ALL CLEAR!"];
    }
}
```

These methods log the raw data (see Figure 13-14).

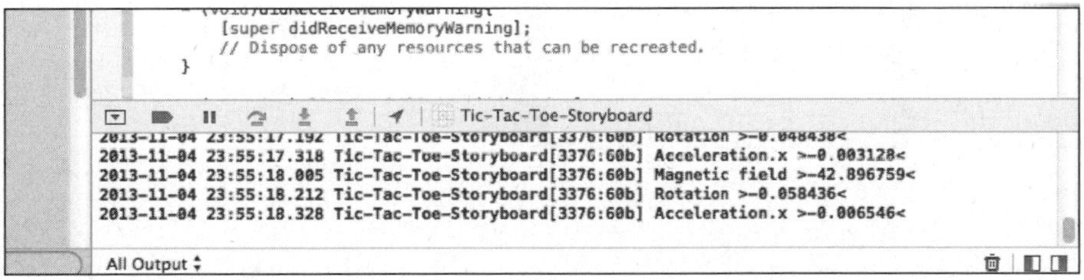

Figure 13-14:
Raw sensor readings displayed by use of NSLog.

The preceding sensor methods also interpret the raw sensor values to generate the view shown in Figure 13-15. That is, the sensors use heuristics to provide meaningful insights:

✔ The accelerometer measures acceleration in g-forces, where 1 g-force is equivalent to the pull of the Earth's gravity.

If the accelerometer senses movement greater than the Earth's gravitational pull in any direction, it excitedly displays the message, I'M GOING FAST! Otherwise, it displays TOO SLOW.

✔ The gyroscope measures rotation of the device's three axes in radians per second (1 radian per second means about a sixth of a rotation every second). Therefore, if it senses most any rotation, it prints WHEE!

✔ In the magnetometer code, I use a *distance* heuristic to sense a large change in the magnetic field.

If such a change occurs, the app shows I SENSE SOMETHING!

If nothing changes for one interval, it goes back to thinking the coast is clear.

Figure 13-15:
The Sensor view controller screen showing interpreted sensor values.

Examining OO and Other Design Principles in this Chapter

This chapter includes several OO techniques and design principles used in the frameworks, as well as related examples. Also some tradeoffs were made in the frameworks and in the Tic-Tac-Toe app. I discuss these techniques, design principles, and tradeoffs in this section.

Seeing uses of loose coupling

Using telephony in the app (see the method `phoneAFriend` in `TTTGameSessionViewController.m`) is a clear example of loose coupling. The only information that must be provided to the telephone application is a URL. This is considered loose-coupling because your app doesn't need to know anything about the telephone application beyond this URL.

Incidentally, loose coupling doesn't apply only to an external component. In the `playVideo` method of the Video view controller (`TTTVideoViewController.m`), you can see a similar loosely coupled use of the media player. You can see similar loose coupling in the use of `UIWebView` in the method `helpWithWebView` in the Help view controller (`TTTHelpViewController.m` — see Chapter 12 for more on this topic).

Using delegation for customized processing

Several of the components previously shown utilize the delegation design technique. In fact, you'd be hard put to find a place where delegation is *not* used. Here are places where you see clear use of delegation:

- In `sendScoresbySMS` and `sendScoresByEmail` (both in `TTTGameSessionViewController.m`), the invoking view controller (Game Session) sets itself as a delegate to the invoked view controller (the e-mail composer or the message composer). When the invoked view controller (the e-mail or message composer) finishes, the callback `didFinishWithResult` is the delegate method called in order to handle any cleanup tasks after the e-mail or SMS is sent or cancelled.

- In both the `play` and `record` methods of the Audio view controller (`TTTAudioViewController.m`), the invoking view controller is set as a delegate to the audio player and the audio recorder. The delegate methods in this case are `audioPlayerDidFinishPlaying` and `audioRecorderDidFinishRecording`.

- In the `takeImage` method of the Image view controller (`TTTImageViewController.m`) and the `recordVideo` method of the Video view controller (`TTTVideoViewController.m`), the invoking view controller is set as a delegate to the `imagePicker` object. The delegate methods for both dealing with still images and video recordings are `imagePickerControllerDidCancel` and `didFinishPickingMediaWithInfo`.

✔ There are several places where delegation is used in the sensor processing examples:

- The `viewDidLoad` method of the Sensor view controller. It registers itself as a delegate to the app's notification center and asks to be notified of changes in orientation.

  The delegate callback method `orientationChanged` deals with these events.

✔ The method `startMonitoringSensors` shows how the base sensors — the accelerometer, gyroscope, and magnetometer — define *inline* delegate functions to handle the events they generate that are registered with `motionManager`, an instance of the `CMMotionManager` class.

Using design patterns

This chapter includes several examples of design patterns being used, mostly in the functionality provided by the iOS framework. Probably the most-used pattern is Singleton. It's often used in conjunction with the Factory Method pattern, as shown in the following examples:

✔ The following line of code is in the `viewDidLoad` method of the Audio view controller (see file `TTTAudioViewController.m`):

```
[[AVAudioSession sharedInstance]
    setCategory:AVAudioSessionCategoryPlayAndRecord error:nil];
```

Here, the method `sharedInstance` is a Factory Method used to return the Singleton instance of the `AVAudioSession`.

✔ In the `viewDidLoad` method of the Sensors view controller (`TTTSensors-ViewController.m`), you see the following:

```
[[UIDevice currentDevice]
    beginGeneratingDeviceOrientationNotifications];
```

Here also, `currentDevice` is a Factory Method that returns the Singleton object that represents the device.

✔ Singletons may also be implicit, in that you're asked to treat certain classes as classes for generating Singleton objects. In the previous `viewDidLoad` method, you saw the instantiation of a `motionManager`. Although it looks like a normal creation of an object from a class, Apple's Developer site asks that you create only one instance of the object to ensure that the program works correctly (refer to the CoreMotion link in the web resources for this chapter at www.dummies.com/go/iosprogramminglinks).

In all these cases, an object that provides an interface to access a set of services is being returned. In some cases (such as with the `motionManager`), the system provides these services. The Singleton class is then acting as a Façade for these services by providing an easy-to-use interface and hiding the gory details underneath.

Finally, you also encounter the Observer pattern in the Sensors view controller. Here are the lines in the `startMonitoringSensors` method:

```
[self->motionManager
  startAccelerometerUpdatesToQueue:
    [NSOperationQueue currentQueue]
    withHandler:^(CMAccelerometerData *accelerometerData, NSError *error){
        [self handleAccelerationUpdates:accelerometerData.acceleration];
    }
];
```

The inline handler attaches a listener for a particular event (the accelerometer change event) to the `motionManager` object.

Design tradeoffs in Tic-Tac-Toe

In this chapter, I made one design tradeoff in Tic-Tac-Toe. I also found a tradeoff in the iOS framework.

I had intended to encapsulate all the UI for the Game Session view controller (see `TTTGameSessionViewController.m`) inside `GameView`. Had I done so, I would have needed to make `GameView` the delegate for the mail, SMS, and video and camera composers and to implement all the callbacks there. This seemed to be too complicated, so, as a design purity versus effort tradeoff, I left the implementations for sending SMS, e-mail, and telephony in the Game Session view controller. I also left this controller as the delegate for the SMS and e-mail composers.

Take a look at a small design tradeoff in the iOS framework. Notice that the `UIImagePickerController` class handles both the video and the still camera. My guess is that because the camera has both video and still capabilities, the iOS framework designers thought that the software interface should be the same.

However, in my opinion, this approach overloads the `UIImagePickerController` class. Although initiating the video and the still image is similar, handling playback of the video after it's taken differs from the way the still image is handled. For the video, playback involves using the media player. The still image, on the other hand, is embedded in a view (a `UIImageView`). Should the iOS framework provide two separate pickers for stills and videos? I think so.

Chapter 14

Publishing to the App Store

*A*fter spending countless hours designing, coding, and debugging, you're finally ready to present your app to the public. You just need to hand over the developer fee and ship it off, right?

Not quite. Publishing your app to Apple's App Store is a fairly complicated process, especially for beginners. You need to create accounts, generate certificates, register devices, recruit beta testers — not to mention forking over your bank information. But don't worry. In this chapter, I walk you through the step-by-step process. After reading this chapter, you'll be confident in your ability to publish a complete, well-tested app that's ready for primetime. After you get an app or two under your belt, you'll see that the process isn't so complicated after all.

Creating Your Developer Account

To publish apps to Apple's App Store, you must be a registered iOS developer.

Don't try to register at the last minute. Allow at least a day for Apple to process your application.

Registration is a two-part process. First, you need to create an Apple Developer account. Doing so is free. Because access to many Apple resources requires an account, you probably already have one.

If you don't have one or if you want to create a new one, go to the iOS Dev Center (you can find the link at www.dummies.com/go/iosprogramminglinks) and click the Register link in the upper-right corner (see Figure 14-1).

As part of the signup process, you either choose an existing Apple ID (for example, the one for your iTunes account) or create a new one.

In the second step, you enroll in the iOS Developer Program. If you live in a country with an online Apple Store, enrollment can be completed in the iOS Dev Center:

1. **Go to the iOS Dev Center (again, using the link at** www.dummies.com/go/iosprogramminglinks**).**

   If you're not already logged in, click the Login link at the top of the page. (If you just finished creating an Apple Developer account, you've already completed this step.)

2. **In the column on the right, click Learn More under the iOS Developer Program section (as shown in Figure 14-2).**

   The iOS Developer Program page appears.

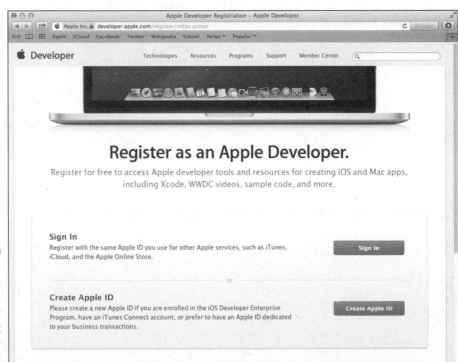

Figure 14-1:
Register for an Apple Developer account at the iOS Dev Center.

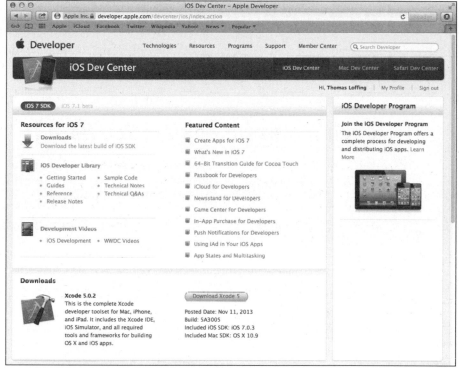

Figure 14-2:
You must
enroll in
the iOS
Developer
Program
to publish
to the App
Store.

3. **Click Enroll Now.**

   An overview of the enrollment process appears.

4. **Click the Continue button and then enter your Apple Developer ID. Choose whether you want to register as an individual or as a company.**

5. **When prompted, indicate that you want to join the iOS Developer Program and continue through the checkout process.**

   To pay the $99 annual fee, you'll need to enter your credit card information.

   Orders (as Apple calls them) generally take one business day to process.

   If you live in a country without an online Apple store, you must fill out a form and fax it to Apple.

   After you submit your order, Apple must approve it. Often Apple completes this process within 24 hours or less, but it may take longer based on the information you provide (or if you faxed your information instead of using the online store).

Distributing Applications

Before your app can be published to the App Store, some basic information is required — for example, the app's name, bundle ID, and version. In addition, you must define all special iOS capabilities that your app uses.

Providing basic application details

To edit the data you use in this section, choose Views➪Navigator➪Show Project Navigator to open the project editor; then pick the target from the Project/Targets menu. Make sure the General tab is selected.

The Identity section, shown in Figure 14-3, contains information about your app's identity and its version.

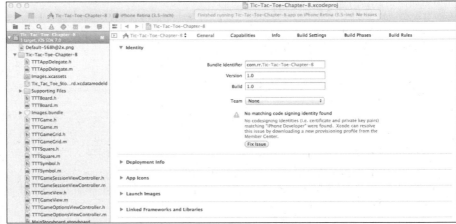

Figure 14-3:
In the Identity section, you define how the app is identified and its version.

The Identity section contains the following fields:

- ✔ **Bundle Identifier:** A bundle ID is a string that uniquely identifies your app. This string should be in reverse-DNS format. So if you're creating an app called "Hello World" and your company's website is mycompany.com, your bundle ID might be com.mycompany.helloworld. Xcode automatically appends your app name, so you provide only the bundle ID prefix here in the editor. When you submit your app, you must specify this bundle ID in iTunes Connect.

- ✔ **Version:** The version consists of three version numbers separated by periods — major version, minor version, and maintenance release (for example, 1.8.5).

This version should match the one you will specify later in iTunes Connect when you submit your app.

✔ **Build:** The build string represents an individual iteration of your app. You must update this string before distributing a new version of your app (for example, for beta testing).

According to Apple, the build string is made up of three non-negative integers that are separated by periods. The first integer must be greater than zero. Note that all leading zeros will be removed, so, for example, 1.2.01 is equal to 1.2.1.

✔ **Team:** The team is either you or your company depending on how you enrolled in the iOS Developer Program. If your team doesn't appear in the list, click Add Account at the bottom of the list to add your Apple ID to Xcode. After selecting the team, you may see a warning about a missing provisioning profile. I explain this warning in the section, "Testing on iOS Devices," later in this chapter. For now, just ignore this warning.

Below the Identity section is the Deployment Info section, shown in Figure 14-4, that defines how your app will run on actual devices. For most of these fields, the value specified after your project is created is acceptable.

Figure 14-4: The Deployment section specifies how your app runs on specific devices.

I want to highlight two of these fields because they require you to make fundamental decisions about your app's audience:

✔ **Deployment Target:** This field indicates the oldest system version that your app will support. In making this decision, you must determine which is more important to you, audience size or feature set.

Weak linking

If you're having trouble deciding what deployment target to choose, you may want to investigate employing a practice known as *weak linking*. This practice allows you to target older OS versions but still use features from newer OS versions. You do so by checking at runtime whether a specific feature is available on the device before actually using it.

Of course, you want to use such features only as supplementary functionality. Using them to implement fundamental elements of your app will render it useless on older devices where the features aren't supported.

By supporting very old OS versions, you can broaden your audience. However, in doing so, you may not be able to use features that are available only in newer OS releases.

✔ **Devices:** This field determines which devices your app supports. The options are

- iPhone (including iPod touch)
- iPad (including iPad mini)
- Universal (all iOS devices)

You specify icons of varying resolutions for use on different devices in the App Icons section of the editor. After expanding this section, click the arrow next to the Source drop-down list, and a screen similar to the one in Figure 14-5 appears. To specify each icon, in the editor, drag the icon file from the Finder and drop it in the appropriate location based on its resolution.

Figure 14-5: Each iOS device has unique requirements for App Icon resolution.

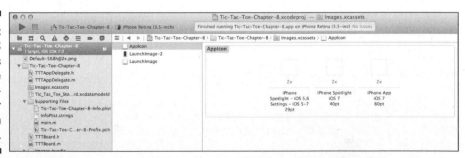

In the Launch Images section, you specify the image users will see while your app is loading. Just as for icons, launch images come in various resolutions based on the devices your app supports. To specify each image, drag a file from the Finder and drop it on the appropriate location (shown in Figure 14-6) based on its size.

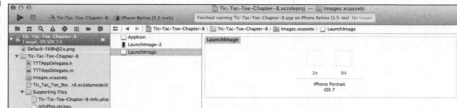

Figure 14-6: Launch images are shown while your app loads.

Consider taking a screenshot of your app on each supported device and using these screenshots as your launch images. To use a screenshot, you can do one of the following:

- ✔ Send the screenshot from your device to the computer on which you're developing your app (for example, by e-mail).
- ✔ Connect your device to your computer and use the New Screenshot button in Xcode's Devices organizer.

Special capabilities

iOS provides capabilities that require special configuration in order to be used. Apple uses a technique known as *code signing* to ensure that apps are granted access to only those capabilities they've been configured to use. When you enable use of a specific capability, a configuration element known as an *entitlement* is added to your app's code signature.

The Capabilities tab of the target editor (shown in Figure 14-7) is where you turn individual capabilities on and off.

Figure 14-7: You must enable certain capabilities before you can use them.

Here are the most frequently used capabilities:

✔ **iCloud:** iCloud is a cloud storage platform that you can use to store app data that you want to make available across multiple devices, whether they're running iOS, OS X, or even Microsoft Windows.

✔ **Game Center:** If you're developing a game, consider using Game Center. Game Center is a social gaming network that developers can use to create leaderboards, auto-match players, and more.

✔ **In-App Purchases:** Apps set up to sell items to users must have In-App Purchases capability.

   Usage examples include Candy Crush Saga, where users can buy additional lives, and Evernote, where users can purchase an upgrade to the premium version of the app.

✔ **Push Notifications:** Apple Push Notifications (APNs) allow apps to display notifications to the user even when the app is not currently in the foreground. For example, Twitter uses this feature to inform users when they have a new follower.

✔ **Maps:** The Maps capability provides routing — for example, to provide driving directions to a specific location.

Some capabilities require you to take additional steps beyond simple enablement. For example, enabling the Maps capability requires specification of a geographic coverage file to indicate the regions that are supported by the app.

Internationalization and localization

If you're targeting users who speak multiple languages or live in different countries, you must prepare your app accordingly, which involves two related concepts — internationalization and localization.

Internationalization is the process of preparing your application to support multiple languages and locales. You'll need to consider issues such as ensuring that text visible to users is defined in properties files rather than in the source code; formatting dates and currency figures based on a user's locale; and writing your app's code so that it accepts user input in all supported languages.

Localization is the process of preparing your app to support a specific language, region, or market. Most of the work in this step involves translating properties files into the desired language.

After you prepare your app for a global audience, don't forget to go to iTunes Connect (described later in the section "Using iTunes Connect") and translate your app's metadata, as well. There's no point in adding Italian language support to your app if your App Store page is available only in English.

For more information about internationalization and localization, see Apple's guide at `https://developer.apple.com/internationalization`.

Testing

The importance of testing cannot be overstated. Nothing will kill your dreams of App Store fame and fortune faster than a buggy app that garners negative customer reviews.

At this point in the book, you're familiar with basic unit testing and running your app on the iOS Simulator, so I don't cover those concepts in this chapter. Instead, this section focuses on two other important facets of testing — testing on actual iOS devices and beta testing.

iOS devices

Before publishing your app, it's critical to test it on actual iOS devices. I suggest testing it on as many supported device-OS combinations as you can. Doing so provides some assurance that your app won't blow up "out in the wild."

Although the iOS Simulator is effective for most testing required during the developmental phase, it has limitations that make it unsuitable for final testing, especially when compared to physical devices. For example, the Simulator has different memory and speed characteristics than physical devices have. It also lacks some hardware (for example, a camera and an accelerometer) and API support (for example, Event Kit) that are on real iOS devices.

Before running your app on an actual device, you need to obtain a signed certificate. Apple requires these certificates for every app that runs on an iOS device for security reasons. When your app is published on the App Store, you'll need to provide a certificate that will be signed by Apple and distributed with your app. However, during development, you'll need to create and sign your own certificate, which you can do two ways. I refer to them as the easy way and the manual way, both of which I discuss next.

The Easy Way: Using Xcode's automatic device provisioning

Xcode tries to make running your app on a device as easy as possible by hiding some of the complex details of the process — things like generating certificates, registering devices, and creating provisioning profiles. This is a good thing when you just need to move along with testing, but it may not be suitable for all your needs. I explain the limitations to this approach in the next section. For now, here are the steps you take to leverage Xcode's automatic device provisioning:

1. **Plug in the device you want to use.**

2. **In Xcode, choose Window⇨Organizer.**

   The organizer window appears.

3. **Click the Devices tab.**

   Your device will be listed.

4. **Click the Use for Development button that's next to your device.**

   A prompt appears asking you to enter your iOS Developer credentials.

5. **Enter your credentials now.**

   Your device is now ready to use, as shown in Figure 14-8.

   After you enter your credentials in the previous step, Xcode does the work necessary to allow your app to run on your device. Specifically, it carries out the following steps:

   • Requests your development certificate.

   • Registers your device.

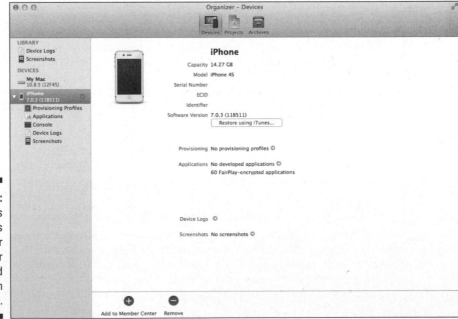

Figure 14-8: Use Xcode's Devices organizer to get your app up and running on iOS devices.

- Creates an app ID using a bundle ID wildcard.

- Creates a provisioning profile using the developer certificate, device, and app ID.

- Updates your project to reflect these actions.

The Manual Way: Using the iOS Provisioning Portal

Sometimes the simple way doesn't work. For example, you may need to use someone else's Apple ID (perhaps one that belongs to your company), or you may want to produce a build for a device that you don't own (perhaps to send to a tester). The simple approach also is unsuitable for testing certain capabilities — like In-App Purchasing — that don't support bundle ID wildcards. Finally, you may just want a better understanding of what it takes to prepare a device for development.

If you find yourself in one of these situations, you need to create your certificates and profiles manually. Begin by creating a certificate signing request (CSR) file as follows:

1. **Open the Keychain Access application (located in Applications⇨ Utilities) and from the drop-down menu, choose Certificate Assistant⇨ Request a Certificate from a Certificate Authority (see Figure 14-9).**

   The Certificate Assistant window appears.

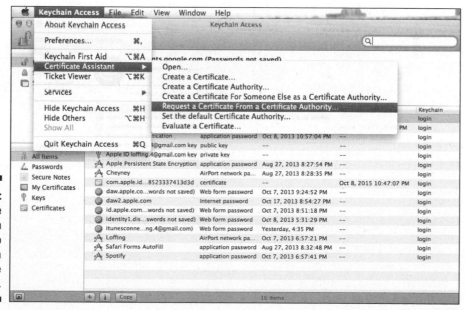

Figure 14-9:
Use
Keychain
Access to
create a
certificate
file.

2. **Enter your name and e-mail address and save the CSR file to disk.**

Next you use this certificate file to create a provisioning profile. To do so, head over to the iOS Provisioning Portal (you can find the link at www. dummies.com/go/iosprogramminglinks), shown in Figure 14-10.

In the Provisioning Portal, complete the following steps:

1. **Click the Certificates link on the left.**

   The iOS Certificates page appears.

2. **Click the Certificate Signing Request link under Request Certificates Manually.**

   If you already have one or more certificates defined, click the + button instead.

3. **Choose iOS App Development and click Continue.**

4. **Click Continue again to skip creating a CSR file (which you did in the previous section).**

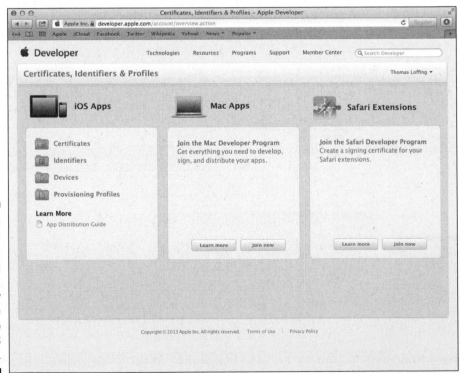

Figure 14-10:
The iOS Provisioning Portal allows you to manually configure your app to run on iOS devices.

5. **Click Choose File.**

   A file browser appears.

6. **Select the certificate file you created in the previous section.**

7. **To generate the certificate, click Generate.**

   After a short wait, your new provisioning profile becomes available for download.

8. **Click the Download button to save the development certificate to disk; then double-click the file to install it in your keychain.**

   Keychain access appears, and the certificate will now appear under the Certificates category.

9. **Back in the iOS Provisioning Portal, click the Devices link on the left.**

   The iOS Devices page appears.

10. **Click the Manually Register Devices link.**

    If you already have one or more devices defined, click the + button instead.

11. **Enter a name for your device and its unique device identifier (UDID).**

12. **Click Continue.**

    The registration page appears.

13. **Click Register.**

    Your device is now registered.

    You can find the UDID by using either of the following:

    - The Devices organizer in Xcode
    - The Devices section in iTunes

14. **Click App IDs under the Identifiers section on the left; then Click the Register Your App ID link.**

    If you already have one or more app IDs defined, click the + button instead.

    An app ID combines a prefix with your app's bundle ID to create a unique identifier for your app.

15. **Provide a description and enter your bundle ID (the one you defined earlier in the "Providing basic application details" section) under Explicit App ID; click Continue and then click Submit.**

    Your app ID is now registered.

16. **Click Development under the Provisioning Profiles section on the left and then click the Manually Generate Profiles link.**

    If you already have one or more development provisioning profiles defined, click the + button instead.

17. **Select iOS App Development and click Continue.**

    The app ID selection page appears.

18. **Select the app ID you created previously and click Continue.**

    The certificate selection page appears.

19. **Select the certificate you created previously and click Continue.**

    The device selection page appears.

20. **Select the device you registered previously and click Continue.**

    The profile generation page appears.

21. **Enter a name for your profile and click Generate.**

    After a short time, your new provisioning profile becomes available for download.

22. **After downloading is complete, double-click the provisioning profile file.**

    The file appears in Xcode's organizer.

Regardless of the method you follow, after you do the prep work, actually running your app on the device is fairly simple:

1. **Open the project editor and select the target (not the project) in the left pane of the editor.**

2. **In the right pane, click the Build Settings tab.**

3. **In the Code Signing section, find the Provisioning Profile property and set its value to that of the provisioning profile created earlier.**

4. **Select your device in the scheme chooser at the top of the Xcode window.**

5. **Connect your device, click the Run button, and enjoy watching your app run on an actual iOS device.**

Beta testing

After you run your app on a few devices and are confident that it's working the way it's supposed to, and before publishing to the App Store, I suggest getting it into the hands of some beta testers. Beta testing allows you to get feedback from actual users and to repair any bugs before the general public sees them. You may be surprised to see the issues that beta testers bring up. Something that may seem obvious to a developer who is intimately familiar with the app may cause major difficulties for someone who is picking your app up for the first time.

Before your beta testers can start their work, though, you need to go back to the iOS Provisioning Portal (you can find the link at www.dummies.com/go/iosprogramminglinks) and build a package that you can send to them to test, which you can do by following these steps:

1. **In the iOS Provisioning Portal, click the Certificates link on the left.**

   The iOS Certificates page appears.

2. **Click the Certificate Signing Request button under Request Certificates Manually.**

   If you already have one or more development provisioning profiles defined, click the + button instead.

3. **Choose App Store and Ad Hoc and click Continue.**

4. **Continue generating and downloading the certificate using the same process and CSR file you used for the development certificate.**

5. **Back in the iOS Provisioning Portal, click the Devices section on the left.**

6. **Register each test device using the same process you used to register your own device.**

7. **Still in the iOS Provisioning Portal, click Distribution under the Provisioning Profiles section on the left.**

8. **Click the Manually Generate Profiles link.**

   If you already have one or more distribution provisioning profiles defined, click the + button instead.

9. **Click Ad Hoc and then click Continue.**

10. **Complete the process of generating and downloading your ad hoc provisioning profile using the same process you used for your development provisioning profile (be sure to select all the test devices you registered).**

11. **In Xcode, update the Build field under the General tab of the target editor.**

    Updating the build string ensures that the package you create gets synced across the test devices.

12. **Select iOS Device (or the test device if it's plugged in) in the scheme drop-down menu at the top of the Xcode window.**

13. **Choose Product⇨Archive.**

    The Archives organizer appears.

14. **Click the Distribute button.**

    The distribution wizard appears.

15. **Select Save for Enterprise of Ad Hoc Deployment and click Next.**

    The profile selection page appears.

16. **Select your ad hoc provisioning profile and click Export.**

    The save dialog box appears.

17. **Save the iOS App Store Package file to disk.**

Now that you have your iOS App Store Package, you can distribute it to your beta testers. Each tester needs to install the package using iTunes:

1. **Connect the device to a Mac running iTunes.**

2. **Double-click the package file.**

    The package file is added to the iTunes library.

3. **Click the Device button in the upper-right corner.**

    The device page appears.

4. **Click the Apps button.**

5. **Locate your app, click Install, and then click Apply.**

    The user is now ready to begin testing your app.

Submitting Your App

Now you're in the home stretch. Your app is polished, tested, and ready to go. After filling out some additional information, you can finally upload your app to the App Store. After it's approved by Apple, your app will be published.

Using iTunes Connect

To upload your app, you use iTunes Connect. This section walks you through the process:

1. **Go to iTunes Connect (see Figure 14-11) at** `https://itunesconnect.apple.com` **and log in.**

    The iTunes Connect home page appears.

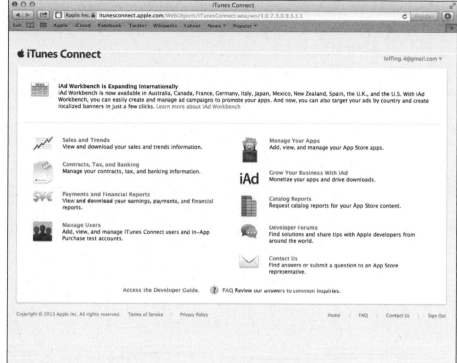

Figure 14-11:
iTunes
Connect lets
you manage
your App
Store
presence.

2. **Decide (if you haven't already) whether you expect your app to generate revenue.**

   You can generate revenue by charging for your app and/or making use of Apple's in-app advertising service known as *iAd*. If you'll be doing either of these, you'll need to request the appropriate contract in the Contracts, Tax, and Banking section. Each contract requires contact information, a bank account, and tax data.

   If your app will be free and you have no plans to use iAd, you can skip filling out these contracts.

With the paperwork out of the way, it's time to specify all the metadata that will be displayed on your app's page in the App Store.

1. **Click the Manage Your Apps link in iTunes Connect.**

   The app management page appears.

2. **Click the Add New App button in the upper-left corner (see Figure 14-12).**

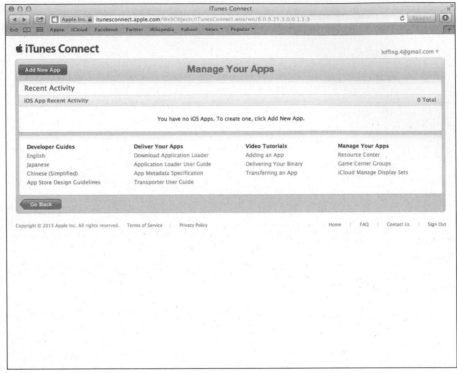

Figure 14-12:
Click
Manage
Your Apps
to begin the
process of
publishing
your app.

Free versus paid

A common question among beginning iOS developers is whether to charge for their apps. Doing so has obvious benefits. Every download of your app will generate revenue, helping to compensate you for the time and energy you invested to bring your app to market. However, there are also major downsides to this approach. Many studies suggest that the majority of smartphone users either never pay for apps or do so only rarely. So a price tag next to your app's name, even if it's only ninety-nine cents, may immediately turn some users off.

But you can make money from your apps even if you offer them for free:

✔ One approach is to use Apple's iAd service to embed advertisements in your app. When users click on these ads, you're compensated.

Don't go too crazy with ads, though, or you'll annoy your users and drive them away.

✔ Another method is to offer a "premium" version of your app for a fee, along with a basic version that's free. Evernote does this, for example. The idea is that if your app is useful or interesting enough, users who initially downloaded the free version will eventually shell out cash for the upgrade.

3. **A wizard walks you through the app submission process and gathers all the data that Apple requires.**

   This includes the following (some uncommon or self-explanatory fields have been omitted):

   - Your app's primary language

   - Your company's name

   - The name of your app

   - Your app's SKU number (an arbitrary string used for tracking purposes)

   - Your app's bundle ID

   - The date you'd like your app to become available in the App Store

   - The price of your app

   - Your app's version (should match what you provided in Xcode)

   - A description of your app

   - Categories and keywords that apply to your app

   - Notes that you'd like reviewers to see during the approval process

   - Rating information

   - Graphic assets (an icon and screenshots)

   After you provide all of this information, your screen should appear similar to the one in Figure 14-13.

4. **Click the View Details button below your app's icon.**

   The app details page appears.

5. **Click the Ready to Upload Binary button in the top-right corner.**

   The export compliance page appears.

6. **Answer the question about whether your app uses cryptography and click Save.**

   Your app is now ready for uploading.

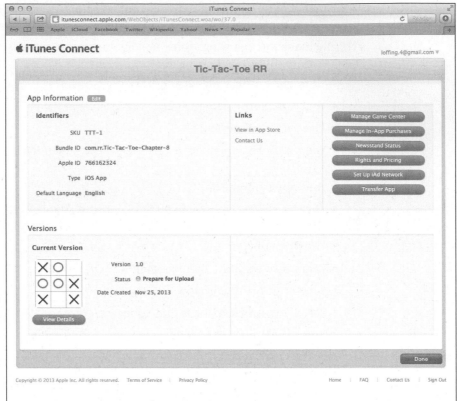

Uploading to the App Store

To begin the app upload process, fire up Xcode and follow these steps:

1. **Create a provisioning profile that will be used to verify your app when it runs on user's devices.**

   The process to create the provisioning profile is the same as the one described in the earlier section "The Manual Way: Using the iOS Provisioning Portal," except that you need to choose App Store as the distribution type instead of iOS App Development.

   After you create, download, and open the App Store provisioning profile, you need to associate it with your project.

2. **Open the project editor and select the target (not the project) in the left pane of the editor.**

3. **In the right pane, go to the Build Settings tab.**

4. **In the Code Signing section, find the Provisioning Profile property and set it to the App Store provisioning profile, as shown in Figure 14-14.**

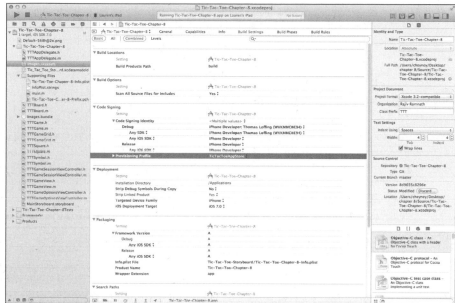

Figure 14-14:
Create and
set your
distribution
provisioning
profile.

You're ready to create and validate an app archive:

1. **Select iOS Device (or your device if it's plugged in) in the scheme chooser at the top of the Xcode window.**

2. **Choose Product➪Archive.**

   The Archives organizer appears.

3. **Click the Distribute button.**

   The distribution wizard appears.

4. **Select Submit to the iOS App Store and click Next.**

5. **Enter your iOS developer username and password and click Next.**

   The application and identity page appears.

6. **Choose the app you want to upload and the App Store provisioning profile you just created; then click Submit.**

   Your app begins uploading.

7. **Assuming no issues occur, click Finish.**

That's it! Your app is now waiting to be reviewed for addition to the App Store. Go back to iTunes Connect to check on the status of your app throughout the process. The waiting period can be several days, but once the review process actually begins, it usually goes fairly quickly. Don't panic if your app is rejected. Apple will send you a detailed e-mail explaining why and what you can do to correct the problem. When your app is approved, it will go up for sale fairly soon.

Supporting Your App

Getting your app published is a huge step, but it's by no means the end of the process. Just because your app is now in the App Store doesn't mean that users will flock to it. You need to do a little marketing to drum up some customers. And once you draw your customers in, you'll need to provide them with good service if you expect your app to stay successful.

Marketing

The marketing process begins in the App Store. You need to design your app's page in a way that will attract attention and prompt users to download it. Here are some ideas:

- ✔ In concise and easy-to-understand language, explain to potential users what your app does and why they should use it.

- ✔ Make sure your screenshots are polished and compelling.

- ✔ Use keywords and categories that are likely to appear in searches relevant to your app. This applies to searches from within the App Store as well as searches from external search engines like Google.

But if you really want to draw a large audience, polishing your app's page might not be enough. You'll need a strategy for reaching your users in other ways, and you'll have to be creative if you want to make your app stand out and attract customers. Here are some thoughts:

- ✔ Make the most of social media.

- ✔ Offer free downloads in exchange for reviews.

- ✔ Run promotions.

- ✔ Mention your app to friends, family members, coworkers — anyone who will listen.

Sales data and customer feedback

So, you've really worked hard to market your app. To figure out just how well this effort has paid off, you need to consult the sales data available in iTunes Connect. From the home page, select the Sales and Trends section. In the window that appears, you can view graphs and tables that explain how many users have downloaded your app and how much money these downloads have generated (unless your app is free). Daily, weekly, monthly, and yearly trends are provided. If you have a well-built, useful app and a good marketing strategy, you'll see your customer base grow over time.

Having customers is great, but not if they're bashing your app. Negative reviews in the App Store are major deterrents to future downloads. Continually monitor your app's customer reviews and respond to all issues your users report. To view your app's customer reviews, go to your app's page in iTunes Connect (under the Manage Your Apps section), click View Details, and then select the Customer Reviews link on the right (shown in Figure 14-15). Use this information to improve user experience.

Fix bugs as quickly as you can. Add detailed descriptions to each new version of your app to explain what defects were fixed and what new features were added.

Figure 14-15:
Monitoring customer reviews is critical to your app's success.

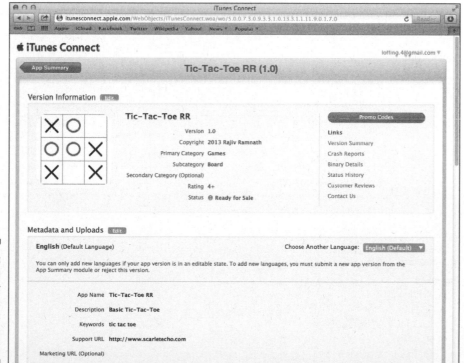

Publishing updates

Publishing periodic updates to your app is a good idea. No matter how thorough your testing process is, end users will always find ways to break things, so you'll need updates to address such issues. Also, even if your app is relatively bug-free, advances in hardware and OS technology make consistent updates a necessity. You don't want your app to appear stale and poorly maintained.

Publishing updates is a simple process, as shown here:

1. **In iTunes Connect, click Manage Your Apps.**

   The app management page appears.

2. **Select the app for which you want to publish an update.**

3. **Click the Add Version button near the lower-right corner (see Figure 14-16).**

The rest of the process is similar to the one you used to publish the original version of your app. Finish supplying the basic information required in iTunes Connect and use Xcode to do the uploading.

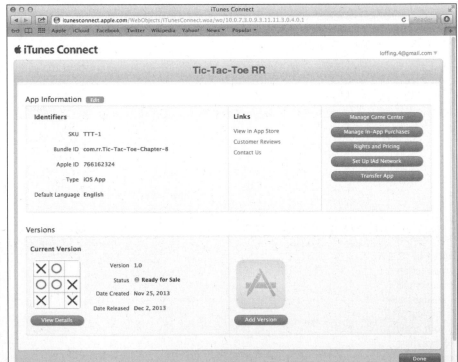

Figure 14-16: Publishing an update to your app is an easy process.

Part V
The Part of Tens

In this part...

- ✔ Object-oriented development resources
- ✔ iOS resources
- ✔ Popular examples
- ✔ Visit `www.dummies.com` for great Dummies content online.

Chapter 15

Ten Resources for Object-Oriented Development

In This Chapter

▶ Familiarizing yourself with seminal books

▶ Learning from industry luminaries

▶ Taking advantage of free online courses

▶ Staying abreast of the latest in OO development

Software engineering, including object-oriented development, isn't a craft you perfect in an undergraduate curriculum and practice, unchanged, for your entire career. True, there are basic concepts that every aspiring software engineer must come to understand, many of which haven't changed in years or even decades. But becoming an effective software developer means making a commitment to continual learning throughout your working life.

Luckily, it's never been easier to acquire the knowledge and skills you need. Just consider the wealth of resources available to you: books, articles, tutorials, sample code, online courses. To help you comb through this (often overwhelming) supply of information, this chapter identifies ten resources you can use to obtain the OO skills you need to be successful.

Design Patterns: Elements of Reusable Object-Oriented Software

In a field as rapidly changing as software development, it's not often that a publication remains relevant over the course of two decades. But *Design Patterns: Elements of Reusable Object-Oriented Software,* first published in 1994, has done just that. At the time of this writing, the book was in its fortieth printing. It's widely considered to be one of the preeminent authorities on object-oriented software development and design. *Design Patterns* was written by a group of authors commonly referred to as the Gang of Four — Erich Gamma, Richard Helm, Ralph Johnson, and John Vlissides.

Design Patterns presents a number of generalized solutions to software development problems that occur frequently. The book isn't a series of concrete solutions that can be plugged into your applications as-is. Instead, think of each pattern as a template that you can tweak and refine to satisfy your specific requirements.

The book begins with introductory material on object-oriented development, including basic OO topics like inheritance, polymorphism, and programming to interfaces. These concepts are illustrated through the case study of a document editor.

The remainder of the book is devoted to twenty-three individual patterns. For each one, the authors describe the problem being solved and why that pattern should be used. Unified Modeling Language (UML) diagrams and sample code are also provided. The patterns are divided into three categories — creational, structural, and behavioral.

Creational patterns are those that create object instances and thereby prevent client code from having to call constructors directly. Examples of creational patterns include the *Factory Method pattern,* which delegates instantiation to subclasses; and the *Prototype pattern,* where new objects are created by cloning existing objects.

Structural patterns deal with how objects are composed to provide various capabilities. Examples in this category include the *Façade pattern,* used to wrap a complex body of code in a simple interface; and the *Decorator pattern,* which is a way to alter the functionality of individual objects rather than every object of a particular class.

Behavioral patterns are concerned with how objects interact with each other. Examples include the *Observer pattern,* useful for notifying dependent objects of state changes; and the *Visitor pattern,* which separates an algorithm from a collection of classes it operates on.

Chapter 4 covers how you can use these patterns in iOS.

martinfowler.com

Martin Fowler is a highly-regarded software engineer known for writing and speaking about various OO topics. Two of his best-known books are *UML Distilled: A Brief Guide to the Standard Object Modeling Language* and *Refactoring: Improving the Design of Existing Code.* He is also coauthor of the "Manifesto for Agile Software Development," written in 2001.

Mr. Fowler's website, http://martinfowler.com (shown in Figure 15-1), is a great resource for all sorts of OO information. It focuses on areas of particular interest to the author — design, refactoring, agile, and others — but anything relevant to software development is liable to appear. In addition to articles from Fowler and some of his colleagues, the site includes talks, descriptions of OO tools, and a newsfeed.

Figure 15-1: Martin Fowler speaks and writes on all things OO.

Object-Oriented Programming with Objective-C

If you're looking for nuts-and-bolts iOS development, the Mac Developer Library presents "Object-Oriented Programming with Objective-C," shown in Figure 15-2. Check www.dummies.com/go/iosprogramminglinks.

This guide defines what OO means from the Object-C perspective. It's not an in-depth examination of the language; instead, it's an explanation of how the language realizes the goals of OO.

The guide begins by explaining why Objective-C was chosen as the language for the Cocoa frameworks. From there, it dives deeply into OO programming and its basic principles — classes, abstraction, inheritance, dynamism, and so on. It then takes a step back and shows how you can employ these concepts to structure an OO application. The guide concludes by providing insight on how to effectively manage OO development projects.

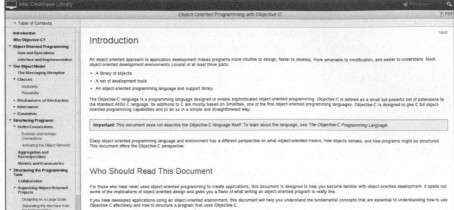

Figure 15-2:
View OO
through
Apple's
perspective.

You can find this guide on Apple's website, both as a series of pages and as a standalone PDF.

The Journal of Object Technology

The "Journal of Object Technology" (JOT) is a free, peer-reviewed journal devoted to, you guessed it, object technology. You can find the journal's website at `http://www.jot.fm` (see also Figure 15-3). JOT was founded in May 2002 by Bertrand Meyer, a well-respected voice in the area of programming languages and creator of the Eiffel programming language.

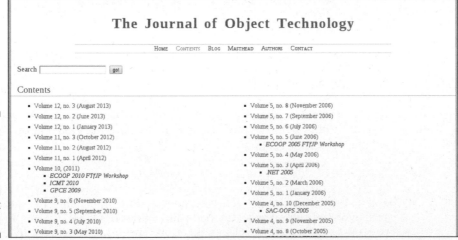

Figure 15-3:
JOT is a
free, peer-
reviewed
journal
about object
technology.

JOT provides previously unpublished articles, surveys, tutorials, and other helpful resources. Although JOT's publication schedule is sometimes sporadic, it remains active and was in its eightieth issue at the time of this writing. Occasionally, JOT produces a special issue, often coinciding with work from a particular conference. All past issues are available for viewing on JOT's website.

The site also features a blog, newsletter, and RSS and Twitter feeds that provide helpful supplementary information.

Massively Open Online Courses (MOOCs)

MOOCs are becoming increasingly popular ways of delivering educational content. The idea is that high-quality courses that were previously available only to students enrolled in a higher learning institution are now provided for free on the web. Anyone can register for an account, enroll in courses of their choosing, and complete them at their own pace. MOOCs often use forums and other means of collaboration to create a mutually beneficial community for its students. The breadth and requirements for completing the courses vary widely among different services.

Many widely popular MOOCs provide courses in computer science and specifically OO development. Figure 15-4 shows three of the most popular MOOCs.

Figure 15-4:
Three popular MOOCs — Udacity, Coursera, and edX.

Udacity is run by a collection of CEOs, professors, and entrepreneurs. Udacity's courses aren't carbon copies of existing university courses; instead, they're created for Udacity by its contributors. Courses of interest to OO developers include general introductory computer science and software design.

Coursera provides a collection of courses from universities around the world. At the time of this writing, this collection included courses in over 500 languages from nearly 100 institutions. Coursera has a good number of computer science courses and a few devoted to OO.

edX was founded jointly by Harvard and the Massachusetts Institute of Technology (MIT) in 2012. edX courses are contributed from its consortium of member universities. At the time of this writing, this consortium contained 29 universities from all over the globe. Among the many computer science courses available on edX, "Paradigms of Computer Programming" provides a thorough look at OO programming and how it relates to other paradigms. This course is provided by the Université catholique de Louvain in Belgium.

Some institutions are providing alternatives to full-blown MOOCs simply by making raw course materials available on the web without the typical structure of an online course. Examples include Stanford Engineering Everywhere (SEE) and MIT OpenCourseWare (OCW). These programs don't offer the sort of guidance and community features that traditional MOOCs do but are still good sources of information. Both SEE and OCW have courses dealing with OO and other software topics.

Ambysoft

Scott Ambler is a software consultant who focuses on agile development practices. Over the years, Mr. Ambler has written hundreds of articles and almost 20 books on all sorts of software engineering topics. Of particular relevance to this book are the resources concerning objects, patterns, reuse, and agile development. You can find the full list of Mr. Ambler's writings at `http://www.ambysoft.com/onlineWritings.html` (see Figure 15-5).

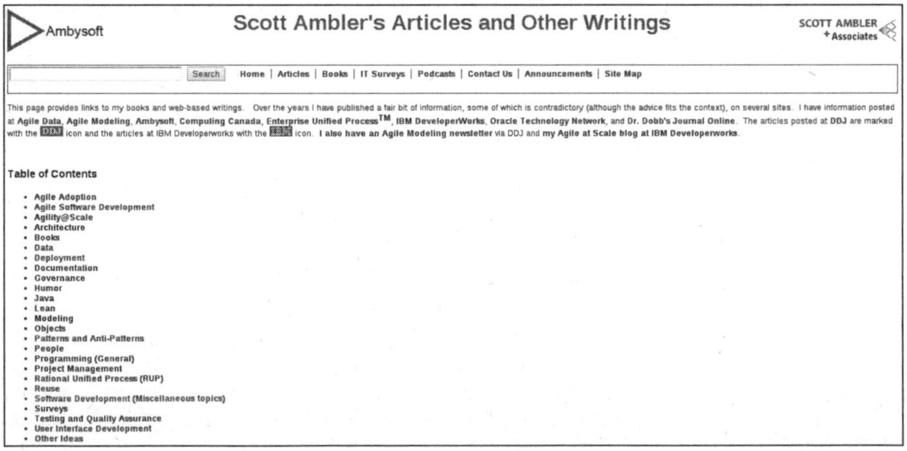

Figure 15-5: Ambysoft provides a vast array of free publications.

Also on Ambysoft's website is a collection of dozens of podcasts and interviews mostly related to agile methods. Mr. Ambler also conducts surveys from time to time about all sorts of topics in IT.

Craig Larman's Use Case Primer

As I discuss in Chapter 2, before beginning development on any iOS application, it's critical to understand the system's requirements. In recent years, especially with the rise of agile development, use cases have become the most widely used mechanisms for capturing requirements. Use cases walk through the steps that the user (or other actor) takes in order to exercise the various capabilities of the application.

Craig Larman's use case primer is a good place to start when you need a thorough understanding of how use cases are structured and used. Larman is a consultant who specializes in applying agile methodologies to large-scale development organizations. He has written several books and articles on agile, as well as others on UML, design patterns, and software architecture.

The use case primer (shown in Figure 15-6) is a chapter from Larman's book *Applying UML and Patterns*. Check www.dummies.com/go/iosprogramminglinks. Although many references are made to the Unified Process (UP), the majority of the information in the chapter can be applied to use cases in general.

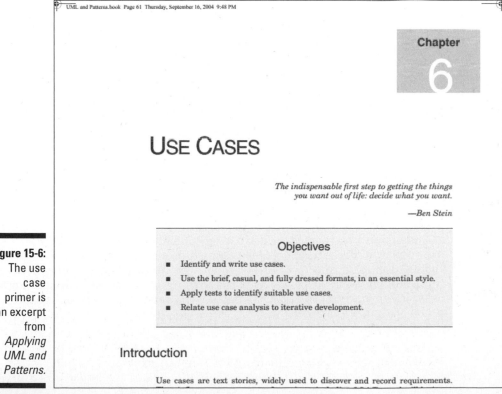

Figure 15-6:
The use case primer is an excerpt from *Applying UML and Patterns.*

The primer begins with an explanation of what a use case is, how it's structured, and why it's useful in capturing requirements. Larman breaks use cases into three categories — brief, casual, and fully dressed — based on size and thoroughness. A fully dressed sample use case is discussed in detail.

Larman then provides a series of guidelines to follow when identifying and drafting use cases. The remainder of the chapter shows how you can use UML to create use case diagrams and how you can utilize use cases within an iterative development process.

uml.org

Although Craig Larman's use case primer makes a good case about why UML is helpful in creating effective use cases, it doesn't go into detail about UML. For that, head on over to `http://uml.org`, shown in Figure 15-7.

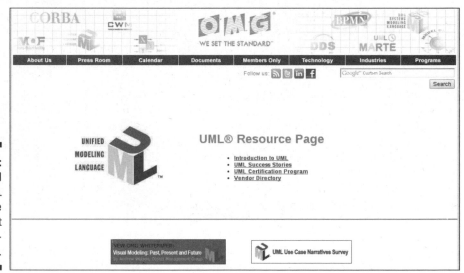

Figure 15-7: Find out all about UML from the Object Management Group.

Grady Booch, Ivar Jacobson, and James Rumbaugh developed UML in the 1990s. In 1997, the Object Management Group (OMG), the standards consortium that runs uml.org adopted it. The website features an extensive introduction to the language and links to third-party tutorials and training classes. If you're feeling really ambitious, you can even download the full

UML specification (warning — it's gigantic). And if you decide to use UML as part of your development process, uml.org also has a list of tools and vendors that will help you get the most out of the language.

For those who have a deep interest in UML, OMG offers a certification program meant to be a "rigorous, comprehensive, and fair test of a person's knowledge of OMG's specifications for unified modeling language." Three levels of certifications are offered — fundamental, intermediate, and advanced.

Agile Alliance

Even the most beautifully conceived object-oriented application can fail if the development process is inadequate. That's why a portion of Chapter 2 is devoted to software development lifecycle (SDLC) processes. As mentioned there, these processes help to ensure quality, traceability, and repeatability (among other characteristics) within your software development project.

Most of the widely used software development processes in the industry today fall into the category of agile. While agile has many manifestations — scrum, extreme programming, and test-driven development to name just a few — all of them share the same underlying philosophy. Development tasks are completed in short iterations that add incremental value to the product. Feedback from stakeholders is frequent and requirements are refined along the way.

The Agile Alliance seeks to promote the use of agile methods to improve the software industry as a whole. The Alliance's website (http://www.agilealliance.org, shown in Figure 15-8) is a great resource regardless of your knowledge about the subject. Beginners will want to start with the What Is Agile? section and then take a look at the Agile Manifesto and the Twelve Principles of agile. More advanced readers can skip over to the Resources section, where you'll find a list of books, articles, guides, and user groups. Note that some resources, such as the research papers made accessible through a collaboration with IEEE, require an Agile Alliance membership. Memberships are available at the individual and corporate levels. Major corporate members include IBM, PayPal, and Lockheed Martin.

The Agile Alliance has been hosting an annual conference since 2002. Resources from each of these conferences is made available on the website.

Figure 15-8:
The Agile
Alliance
promotes
the use of
agile meth-
odologies.

Rajiv's YouTube Video Series

In the spirit of open online learning espoused by the MOOCs previously described, your trusty author along with collaborators Michael Herold, Joe Bolinger, Thomas Bihari, and Jay Ramanathan have developed a curriculum designed to expose students to the end-to-end process of software development as practiced in industry. This curriculum is available as a series of YouTube videos, the first of which is shown in Figure 15-9.

Figure 15-9:
Rajiv's
video series
explains
software
develop-
ment from
beginning to
end.

The video titles and their links are as follows:

- ✔ Enterprise Software Engineering
- ✔ Introduction: www.youtube.com/watch?v=VPbKo7uSOYM
- ✔ Business Context: www.youtube.com/watch?v=nHsU-TpyJZI
- ✔ Software Engineering Process: www.youtube.com/watch?v=jnHXggkb_vM
- ✔ Software Engineering Process Examples and Case Studies: www.youtube.com/watch?v=RU9a2Gd-vMQ
- ✔ Requirements: www.youtube.com/watch?v=Hsr-Npd_YHE
- ✔ UML: www.youtube.com/watch?v=7zUaFyCMg3I
- ✔ Analysis: www.youtube.com/watch?v=Hy169OyrSvA
- ✔ Architecture: www.youtube.com/watch?v=Sztag3aqZr0
- ✔ Project and Risk Management: www.youtube.com/watch?v=ArfaMzcI8Uc

The goal of this curriculum is to give the student a holistic view of how software is conceived, designed, built, and maintained in the real world. It was generated by an awareness that many students coming out of traditional computer science undergraduate programs view software engineering as being too narrow and often limited to constructional aspects learned from textbooks and small-scale projects. Such students struggle to extrapolate abstract concepts to on-the-job situations because they lack an understanding of software development as a whole.

Of course, this curriculum covers object-oriented development and many of the other related topics described in this book, such as UML and agile methodologies.

Chapter 16

Ten Developer Resources for iOS

*E*ver since Google became a verb (and probably even before), people have been increasingly reliant upon search engines to find information, and with good reason. Thanks to the effectiveness of these tools, it's never been easier to wade through the almost unimaginable volume of data on the Internet and find what you're looking for. However, in many cases, it's still useful to have a collection of go-to resources when you need to find out about a new topic, solve a problem, or keep track of the latest news. With that in mind, this chapter provides a list of resources that can save you time and effort on your journey toward iOS mastery.

iOS Dev Center

What better way to get information on iOS than by going directly to the source? Apple's iOS Dev Center (`https://developer.apple.com/devcenter/ios/index.action`) provides all kinds of useful resources for developers wanting to know more about the platform. Figure 16-1 shows what this site has to offer.

You can think of the iOS Dev Center as a gateway to the vast amount of information that Apple makes available. If you're overwhelmed on your first visit, just go to the Getting Started section, which, oddly enough, is a great place to get started. You'll find a series of resources organized into guided learning paths. These paths cover many topics — for example, networking, graphics, data management, and security. Along with these guides, you'll also find an impressive collection of sample code that can help you understand how to implement these abstract concepts on the iOS platform.

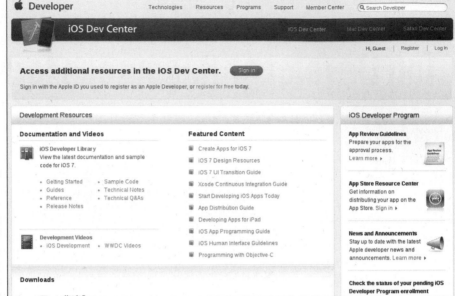

Figure 16-1:
The iOS Dev
Center has
a wealth of
information
for budding
developers.

After you have your fill of the introductory resources, you may want to take a look at some of the detailed guides published by Apple. These guides cover a wide array of topics — everything from UI best practices to performance tuning to preparing to launch in the App Store. Of course, if you want to dive deep into any particular piece of iOS, the API documentation awaits.

Apple Worldwide Developers Conference

If you're more of an in-person type, the Apple Worldwide Developers Conference (WWDC) may be for you. As you can see in Figure 16-2, the 2013 edition of WWDC was held in San Francisco.

If you can manage to get a ticket (WWDC 2013 sold its 5,000 ticket allotment in 71 seconds), you'll be treated to a week of keynote addresses from industry luminaries, new technology showcases, and labs hosted by Apple engineers and designers.

TIP

If you can't make it to the event, you can still benefit from dozens of session videos that Apple posts after the conference. A number of downloads for previously released software is usually made available, as well.

Figure 16-2:
WWDC
is Apple's
annual
developer
conference
held in
California.

Apple Worldwide Developers Conference
June 10–14, San Francisco

iOS Dev Weekly

Rather than searching for iOS information yourself, you can sign up for the iOS Dev Weekly newsletter (http://iosdevweekly.com) and have all sorts of interesting news, tutorials, and resources delivered right to your inbox each week. Figure 16-3 shows the newsletter's website where signing up is as easy as providing your e-mail address.

Dave Verwer, a veteran iOS developer and trainer, maintains the iOS Dev Weekly. Because of its varied content, it's a great way to stay abreast of the latest developments in the iOS community. At the time of this writing, the newsletter had well over 100 issues, all of which you can view on the website's archive.

Figure 16-3:
Sign up for
the iOS Dev
Weekly
newsletter
and view
past issues
online.

raywenderlich

When it comes to iOS tutorials and sample code, raywenderlich (`http://www.raywenderlich.com`) is one of the most popular resources on the web. The home page, shown in Figure 16-4, boasts of the site's extensive tutorial collection, which topped 300 at the time of this writing.

This blog features dozens of contributors from all sorts of backgrounds. It focuses on developing high-quality tutorials that "take the coolest and most challenging topics and make them easy for everyone to learn — so we can all make amazing apps." If you enjoy their free tutorials, you may want to consider purchasing one of their bundles, each of which contains a series of more in-depth tutorials organized around a specific theme or project. In addition to tutorials, the site provides a monthly newsletter and hosts a lively forum.

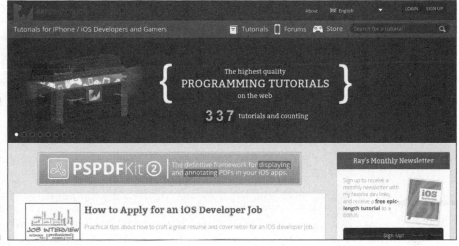

Figure 16-4:
ray-
wenderlich
prides itself
on creat-
ing high-
quality iOS
tutorials.

AppCoda

AppCoda (www.appcoda.com) is another well-known source of iOS tutorials and sample code. Figure 16-5 shows the blog's home page.

Figure 16-5:
AppCoda is
a popular
iOS blog
that fea-
tures great
tutorials.

One thing that makes AppCoda interesting is that it has organized a collection of its tutorials into a complete iOS programming course. The course begins with tutorials about iOS fundamentals and builds up to more advanced topics like video recording and social media integration. The course is organized so that each tutorial builds upon the last. A game starter kit that will include the full source code for a memory game along with an explanatory guide is currently under development. Like raywenderlich, AppCoda also provides a newsletter and forum.

Stack Overflow

Virtually everyone who has done any significant programming (in any language) is familiar with Stack Overflow (www.stackoverflow.com). Stack Overflow is a question and answer site geared specifically toward programmers. The site's home page (shown in Figure 16-6) lists top questions based on a number of different categories.

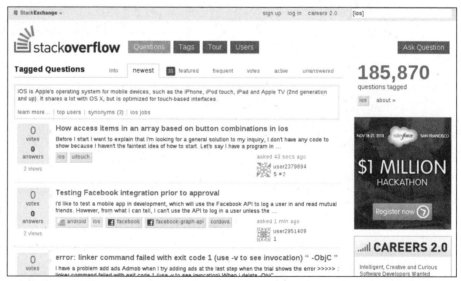

Figure 16-6:
Stack
Overflow.

Each question is tagged with one or more keywords for easy searching. At the time of this writing, Stack Overflow had nearly 200,000 questions tagged with *iOS*. After registering with the site (or using one of your existing OpenIDs), each question, answer, or comment that you provide helps you build your reputation and earn various badges. Not only does this system provide a nice way to demonstrate your technical prowess, it also helps to moderate the quality of the site since certain privileges, like creating new tags and deleting questions, are available only to users with an established reputation. So it pays to be active.

Maybe the reputation you've built will help you land an interview for one of the postings on Stack Overflow's career sites.

iPhoneDevSDK

iphoneDevSDK (`www.iphonedevsdk.com`) is a forum mainly focused on iPhone app development. The site's home page is shown in Figure 16-7.

Figure 16-7: iPhone DevSDK.

This site provides a number of useful resources in addition to the general development forum. There is a forum dedicated to tools and utilities (like Xcode) as well as one dedicated specifically to game development. There's a forum for marketing techniques and one (called, appropriately, Shameless Advertising) where you can promote your apps.

Forums dedicated to tutorials are among the most useful forums. If you don't see the tutorial you're looking for, create a post to request it.

pttrns

If you've ever struggled with laying out screens for your app, pttrns (`http://pttrns.com`) may prove to be a valuable resource. pttrns is a gallery of iOS UI design patterns (over 1,500 at the time of this writing) that are categorized by tasks. A few example designs are shown in Figure 16-8.

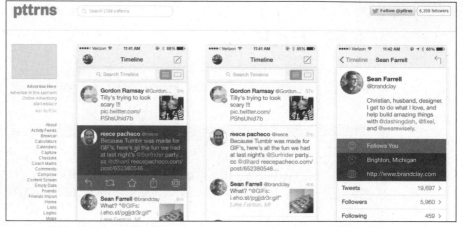

Figure 16-8: pttrns can help when you're not sure how to lay out your app's screens.

pttrns makes it easy to find inspiration for screens that are common across all kinds of apps — login screens, about pages, settings screens, sign up forms, and many more. Use the site for some general inspiration or download a specific design (some free, some not).

Once you're comfortable with UI layout in iOS, you may want to consider contributing some designs of your own.

Cocoa Controls

Sometimes, even if you've nailed down your overall app design, there's still one screen or maybe even an individual widget that's difficult to implement. Whether you need to create a complicated one-off UI element or just tweak an existing one, Cocoa Controls (`https://www.cocoacontrols.com`) may have what you're looking for. Figure 16-9 shows the layout of the site.

Figure 16-9:
Cocoa
Controls
makes it
easy to find
that widget
you've been
looking for.

Cocoa Controls is a collection of open-source and proprietary UI components for iOS and OS X. A quick search through the site to see whether someone has already tackled the problem you're trying to solve could save you a lot of time and effort. Also, because the site provides a filter for specific software licenses, you can be sure that the solution you find will satisfy your app's requirements.

Cocoa Controls also allows you to look at the open-source controls that various apps use. You'll be surprised at the number of high-profile apps that use these open-source widgets, including at the time of this writing YouTube, Google Maps, Evernote, and Flickr.

MacRumors

MacRumors (www.macrumors.com) is in part what it sounds like — a site dedicated to leaked information, insider reporting, and general speculation about everything Apple. The site is shown in Figure 16-10.

However, in addition to rumors (more reliable reporting than crazy speculation), the site also features an iOS-specific blog, roundups of the latest Apple products and iOS versions, buyers' guides, and a forum. Also, if you just can't wait to hear the latest in Apple news (and you have a system that runs OS X 10.9 or later), you can sign up for push notifications so you'll be among the first to hear what's coming around the corner.

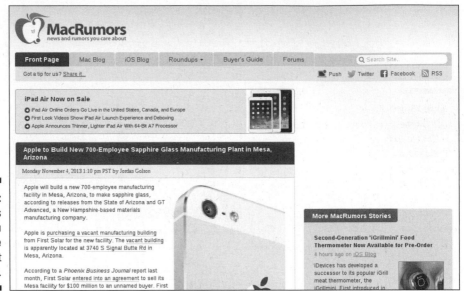

Figure 16-10:
MacRumors
will keep you
up-to-date
on the latest
Apple news.

Index

• B •

• C •

• N •

• O •

• *P* •

• Q •

About the Authors

Dr. Rajiv Ramnath is Director of Practice at the Collaborative for Enterprise Transformation and Innovation (CETI), Associate Director for the Institute of Sensing Systems, and Associate Professor of Practice in the Department of Computer Science and Engineering at The Ohio State University. He was formerly Vice President and Chief Technology Officer at Concentus Technology Corp., in Columbus, Ohio, and led product-development and government-funded R&D – notably through the National Information Infrastructure Integration Protocols program funded by Vice President Gore's ATP initiative. He is now engaged in developing industry-facing programs of applied R&D, classroom and professional education (he has won two teaching awards while at OSU), and technology transfer. His expertise ranges from wireless sensor networking and pervasive computing to business-IT-alignment, enterprise architecture, software engineering, e-Government, collaborative environments and work-management systems. He teaches software engineering at OSU and is heavily involved in industry-relevant and inter-disciplinary curriculum development initiatives. Dr. Ramnath received his Doctorate and Masters' degrees in Computer Science from OSU and his Bachelors' degree in Electrical Engineering from the Indian Institute of Technology, New Delhi. Rajiv is also a member of the Association of Computing Machinery. You can contact him at ramnath@acm.org.

Cheyney Loffing is a software engineer at IBM in Dublin, Ohio. He works in the B2B group and is currently focused on a project that implements the increasingly popular AS4 protocol. Prior to working at IBM he was employed at Flairsoft where he worked as a software engineering contractor on a project for the United States Air Force. Mr. Loffing received his Master's and Bachelor's degrees in Computer Science and Engineering from The Ohio State University. He can be reached at loffing.4@gmail.com.

Dedication

Rajiv Ramnath: This book is dedicated to my wife, Priya, and son, Arman.

Cheyney Loffing: This book is dedicated to my parents, Ken and Debbie.

Authors' Acknowledgments

We would like to sincerely thank our project editor Pat O'Brien and our acquisitions editor Kyle Looper. Your efforts helped keep the book on track and finally published. We'd also like to give a shout out to all the mostly anonymous folks on the Web who ask and answer questions in the iOS forums. We have found so much useful information and tips to solve problems that we would otherwise have to research and discover on our own. We can't thank you enough!

Rajiv Ramnath: My co-author, technical editor, and former graduate student Cheyney Loffing also gets my sincere thanks. It couldn't have been easy "grading" the work of your former professor, and doing such a careful, thoughtful job – while also writing 5 chapters of the book. Could it?

Cheyney Loffing: I'd like to thank Rajiv for giving me the opportunity to edit and co-author my first book. I have a newfound respect for the amount of time and effort that the process requires. I'd also like to thank Lauren for putting up with the long hours and late night.

Publisher's Acknowledgments

Acquisitions Editor: Kyle Looper

Project Editor: Pat O'Brien

Copy Editor: Melba Hopper

Technical Editor: Cheyney Loffing

Editorial Assistant: Anne Sullivan

Sr. Editorial Assistant: Cherie Case

Project Coordinator: Rebekah Brownson

Cover Image: ©iStockphoto.com/adventtr

Apple & Mac

iPad For Dummies,
6th Edition
978-1-118-72306-7

iPhone For Dummies,
7th Edition
978-1-118-69083-3

Macs All-in-One
For Dummies, 4th Edition
978-1-118-82210-4

OS X Mavericks
For Dummies
978-1-118-69188-5

Blogging & Social Media

Facebook For Dummies,
5th Edition
978-1-118-63312-0

Social Media Engagement
For Dummies
978-1-118-53019-1

WordPress For Dummies,
6th Edition
978-1-118-79161-5

Business

Stock Investing
For Dummies, 4th Edition
978-1-118-37678-2

Investing For Dummies,
6th Edition
978-0-470-90545-6

Personal Finance

Personal Finance
For Dummies, 7th Edition
978-1-118-11785-9

QuickBooks 2014
For Dummies
978-1-118-72005-9

Small Business Marketing
Kit For Dummies,
3rd Edition
978-1-118-31183-7

Careers

Job Interviews
For Dummies, 4th Edition
978-1-118-11290-8

Job Searching with Social
Media For Dummies,
2nd Edition
978-1-118-67856-5

Personal Branding
For Dummies
978-1-118-11792-7

Resumes For Dummies,
6th Edition
978-0-470-87361-8

Starting an Etsy Business
For Dummies, 2nd Edition
978-1-118-59024-9

Diet & Nutrition

Belly Fat Diet For Dummies
978-1-118-34585-6

Mediterranean Diet
For Dummies
978-1-118-71525-3

Nutrition For Dummies,
5th Edition
978-0-470-93231-5

Digital Photography

Digital SLR Photography
All-in-One For Dummies,
2nd Edition
978-1-118-59082-9

Digital SLR Video &
Filmmaking For Dummies
978-1-118-36598-4

Photoshop Elements 12
For Dummies
978-1-118-72714-0

Gardening

Herb Gardening
For Dummies, 2nd Edition
978-0-470-61778-6

Gardening with Free-Range
Chickens For Dummies
978-1-118-54754-0

Health

Boosting Your Immunity
For Dummies
978-1-118-40200-9

Diabetes For Dummies,
4th Edition
978-1-118-29447-5

Living Paleo For Dummies
978-1-118-29405-5

Big Data

Big Data For Dummies
978-1-118-50422-2

Data Visualization
For Dummies
978-1-118-50289-1

Hadoop For Dummies
978-1-118-60755-8

Language &
Foreign Language

500 Spanish Verbs
For Dummies
978-1-118-02382-2

English Grammar
For Dummies, 2nd Edition
978-0-470-54664-2

French All-in-One
For Dummies
978-1-118-22815-9

German Essentials
For Dummies
978-1-118-18422-6

Italian For Dummies,
2nd Edition
978-1-118-00465-4

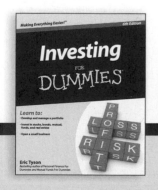 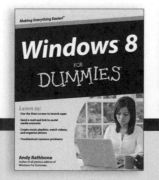  

e **Available in print and e-book formats.**

Available wherever books are sold. **For more information or to order direct visit www.dummies.com**

Math & Science

Algebra I For Dummies,
2nd Edition
978-0-470-55964-2

Anatomy and Physiology
For Dummies, 2nd Edition
978-0-470-92326-9

Astronomy For Dummies,
3rd Edition
978-1-118-37697-3

Biology For Dummies,
2nd Edition
978-0-470-59875-7

Chemistry For Dummies,
2nd Edition
978-1-118-00730-3

1001 Algebra II Practice
Problems For Dummies
978-1-118-44662-1

Microsoft Office

Excel 2013 For Dummies
978-1-118-51012-4

Office 2013 All-in-One
For Dummies
978-1-118-51636-2

PowerPoint 2013
For Dummies
978-1-118-50253-2

Word 2013 For Dummies
978-1-118-49123-2

Music

Blues Harmonica
For Dummies
978-1-118-25269-7

Guitar For Dummies,
3rd Edition
978-1-118-11554-1

iPod & iTunes
For Dummies, 10th Edition
978-1-118-50864-0

Programming

Beginning Programming
with C For Dummies
978-1-118-73763-7

Excel VBA Programming
For Dummies, 3rd Edition
978-1-118-49037-2

Java For Dummies,
6th Edition
978-1-118-40780-6

Religion & Inspiration

The Bible For Dummies
978-0-7645-5296-0

Buddhism For Dummies,
2nd Edition
978-1-118-02379-2

Catholicism For Dummies,
2nd Edition
978-1-118-07778-8

Self-Help & Relationships

Beating Sugar Addiction
For Dummies
978-1-118-54645-1

Meditation For Dummies,
3rd Edition
978-1-118-29144-3

Seniors

Laptops For Seniors
For Dummies, 3rd Edition
978-1-118-71105-7

Computers For Seniors
For Dummies, 3rd Edition
978-1-118-11553-4

iPad For Seniors
For Dummies, 6th Edition
978-1-118-72826-0

Social Security
For Dummies
978-1-118-20573-0

Smartphones & Tablets

Android Phones
For Dummies, 2nd Edition
978-1-118-72030-1

Nexus Tablets
For Dummies
978-1-118-77243-0

Samsung Galaxy S 4
For Dummies
978-1-118-64222-1

Samsung Galaxy Tabs
For Dummies
978-1-118-77294-2

Test Prep

ACT For Dummies,
5th Edition
978-1-118-01259-8

ASVAB For Dummies,
3rd Edition
978-0-470-63760-9

GRE For Dummies,
7th Edition
978-0-470-88921-3

Officer Candidate Tests
For Dummies
978-0-470-59876-4

Physician's Assistant Exam
For Dummies
978-1-118-11556-5

Series 7 Exam For Dummies
978-0-470-09932-2

Windows 8

Windows 8.1 All-in-One
For Dummies
978-1-118-82087-2

Windows 8.1 For Dummies
978-1-118-82121-3

Windows 8.1 For Dummies,
Book + DVD Bundle
978-1-118-82107-7

Available in print and e-book formats.

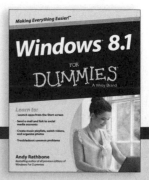

Available wherever books are sold. **For more information or to order direct visit www.dummies.com**